FRAMEWORK AGREEMENTS, SUPPLIER LISTS, AND OTHER PUBLIC PROCUREMENT TOOLS

PURCHASING UNCERTAIN OR INDEFINITE REQUIREMENTS

This book looks at regulation, policy and implementation of framework agreements, supplier lists and other similar public procurement tools, with a strategic and pragmatic perspective.

Whilst procurements of huge volumes and value are performed worldwide through such tools on a daily basis, and despite their complexity and diversity, this topic has rarely been studied in a systematic way. The book fills this major gap. It examines a series of public procurement systems or legal instruments selected to ensure wide coverage – the UNCITRAL Model Law on Public Procurement, the World Bank, the US federal procurement system, EU law, France, Romania, and the UK pre- and post-Brexit.

By deconstructing over 20 'clusters' of tools into their key features along a pattern for analysis, the book reconstructs a conceptual framework for purchasing uncertain or indefinite requirements through a transversal perspective across public procurement systems. In this way, the book provides valuable orientation to law and policy makers for improving or reforming this area, to procurement officers in interpreting existing regulation and identifying innovative practical solutions, and to lawyers and the judiciary for a balanced application of the regulation.

The book delivers essential material for procurement of uncertain or indefinite requirements.

Framework Agreements, Supplier Lists, and Other Public Procurement Tools

Purchasing Uncertain or Indefinite Requirements

Şerban Filipon

•HART•

OXFORD • LONDON • NEW YORK • NEW DELHI • SYDNEY

HART PUBLISHING

Bloomsbury Publishing Plc

Kemp House, Chawley Park, Cumnor Hill, Oxford, OX2 9PH, UK

1385 Broadway, New York, NY 10018, USA

29 Earlsfort Terrace, Dublin 2, Ireland

HART PUBLISHING, the Hart/Stag logo, BLOOMSBURY and the Diana logo are
trademarks of Bloomsbury Publishing Plc

First published in Great Britain 2023

Copyright © Şerban Filipon, 2023

Şerban Filipon has asserted his right under the Copyright, Designs and
Patents Act 1988 to be identified as Author of this work.

While every care has been taken to ensure the accuracy of this work, no responsibility for
loss or damage occasioned to any person acting or refraining from action as a result of any
statement in it can be accepted by the authors, editors or publishers.

All UK Government legislation and other public sector information used in the work is
Crown Copyright ©. All House of Lords and House of Commons information used in
the work is Parliamentary Copyright ©. This information is reused under the terms
of the Open Government Licence v3.0 (http://www.nationalarchives.gov.uk/doc/
open-government-licence/version/3) except where otherwise stated.

All Eur-lex material used in the work is © European Union,
http://eur-lex.europa.eu/, 1998–2023.

A catalogue record for this book is available from the British Library.

A catalogue record for this book is available from the Library of Congress.

Library of Congress Control Number: 2023934012

ISBN: HB: 978-1-50995-990-7
       ePDF: 978-1-50995-992-1
       ePub: 978-1-50995-991-4

Typeset by Compuscript Ltd, Shannon

To find out more about our authors and books visit www.hartpublishing.co.uk.
Here you will find extracts, author information, details of forthcoming events
and the option to sign up for our newsletters.

To Magda

To all friends here; and there

FOREWORD

When we think of public procurement we often think of this taking place through 'one-off' tendering exercises. However, a vast amount of public procurement activity actually occurs through ongoing arrangements for repeat or urgent requirements. These are set up for a period of time, often with more than one supplier, and then called on for specific purchases each time a concrete need arises. Such ongoing arrangements are used for anything from restocking the stationery cupboard and ad hoc consultancy work, to the procurement and repair of major items of infrastructure. These arrangements are recognised in numerous different (often overlapping) forms in different legal systems, with a variety of labels: for example, under the UNCITRAL Model Law the recognised arrangements are all referred to as framework agreements; the EU Directives also refer to framework agreements, but using that concept in a different (narrower) way from the Model Law, as well as to dynamic purchasing systems and qualification systems; while in the US federal system, indefinite delivery contracts and multiple-award schedules are some of the purchasing concepts that fall within this area.

Properly used, these arrangements can have many advantages over traditional one-off transactions, including reduced transaction costs and more rapid procurement – particularly useful in emergencies. As Dr Filipon points out, they have an important role in creating a strategic rather than purely bureaucratic or reactive approach to achieving the goals of public procurement systems. They have increasingly been provided for in international instruments and models on public procurement, as well as in national systems, and many countries contemplating reform programmes are now considering whether and how to incorporate them. Their value has been highlighted recently in the COVID-19 pandemic when many countries found these kind of arrangements – whether existing ones or new ones – to be invaluable in procuring their uncertain medical and other needs relating to the pandemic. On the other hand, however, such arrangements also present numerous risks and challenges, including risks of reduced competition and of collusion by suppliers. Thus they need to be very carefully designed and operated.

How to balance the costs and benefits involved in regulating and using these arrangements is a difficult and complex question. As is well understood, there is no 'one size fits all' solution to regulating public procurement and the question of how to treat such ongoing purchasing arrangements is a stark illustration of that. Given the risks and complexities of these arrangements, the regulatory regime needs to be carefully tailored to the particular environment, not least the commercial skills available in the acquisition workforce and the risks of abuse in the particular procurement system.

Fully understanding how to regulate these arrangements and how to operate them within any given regulatory framework requires answers to many questions. What are the various types of arrangement and how are they similar and how different? What are the advantages of each – and what risks do they pose? How can the risks be mitigated? Taking account of all of this, which arrangements are most suitable for the system in question? What do the regulatory provisions of the specific system actually allow – or not allow? And how should the arrangements be operated in practice within these provisions?

These are questions that I have pondered myself since the early 1990s, both in my publications and in my work on procurement law reform, including as a member of the advisory committees of the European Commission, UNCITRAL, World Bank and, most recently UK Cabinet Office, and I have always found this to be one of the most tricky – and most misunderstood – areas of public procurement. Dr Filipon's book makes an outstanding contribution to unpacking the enormous complexities of this area with a view to providing guidance to stakeholders worldwide on how to treat this topic.

Drawing on a detailed study of seven different systems, both national and international, and drawing from different legal traditions, he develops a rigorous and comprehensive framework for analysing this subject in a general way. Cutting across the – often confusing – terminology and differences in detail of different systems and types of arrangement, he identifies the core elements of the phenomenon in question and assesses the underlying policy considerations of the numerous possible approaches. In this way he has produced an invaluable resource for anyone from any legal system who is involved in regulating the field or in interpreting, operating or critiquing current regulatory provisions. While that is the main objective of the study, the book is also, of course, of inestimable value for those interested in the systems that are the subject of the specific case studies, namely those of the World Bank, UNCITRAL, US federal government, EU, EU Member States of France and Romania and, finally, the UK, where the book considers both the UK's position under its EU membership and the changes to the system proposed after Brexit.

This is a rare work that combines both academic rigour and a detailed understanding of practice, reflecting the author's own background in both the academic study and practice of public procurement. The work originates in a PhD (of which I was the lead supervisor) completed by Dr Filipon at the University of Nottingham several years ago, which has been extensively developed and updated for publication. I personally have benefited enormously from my involvement with this work and consider it to be one of the outstanding works on public procurement in recent decades – a rare gem that adds significant value for the global community. If ongoing purchasing arrangements are going to work well and realise the potential that they hold, both those who design the regulatory system and those who work within it – purchasers, lawyers, suppliers and other stakeholders – need to understand the issues fully, and not shy away from the complexities of what is an inherently complex subject. Anyone who is serious about understanding public procurement should read and study carefully the contents of this book and will find their efforts rewarded with a deep appreciation of a vital topic.

Sue Arrowsmith
Professor Emerita, University of Nottingham

ACKNOWLEDGEMENTS

This monograph is based on my PhD research and thesis titled 'Non-Traditional Regular Purchasing Arrangements in Public Procurement – A Doctrinal and Comparative Analysis of Regulation and Implementation Systems', University of Nottingham, Faculty of Law and Social Sciences, School of Law (2018).

I express my gratitude to my PhD academic supervisors, Professor Emerita Sue Arrowsmith KC (hon) and Professor Annamaria La Chimia.

Similarly, I wish to extend my many thanks to the Public Procurement Research Group, the School of Law, and the Hallward Library at the University of Nottingham.

I am also grateful to the editorial team at Hart Publishing, and in particular to Roberta Bassi, Linda Goss, and Joanne Choulerton, as well as to the typesetters and everyone involved in the production process of this book.

BRIEF CONTENTS

DETAILED CONTENTS

LIST OF ABBREVIATIONS

APA	alternative procurement arrangements (World Bank)
BPA	blanket purchase agreements (US)
CCP or 2019CCP	Code de la Commande Publique (Public Procurement Code, France) (2019)
CCS	Crown Commercial Service (UK)
CICA	Competition in Contracting Act (US) (1984)
CJEU	Court of Justice of the European Union
CMP	Code des Marchés Publics (Public Procurement Code, France) (this instrument is no longer in force; the year preceding the abbreviation refers to the version of the instrument)
CPB	central purchasing body
DD or Defence Directive	Directive 2009/81/EC of the European Parliament and of the Council of 13 July 2009 on the coordination of procedures for the award of certain works contracts, supply contracts and service contracts by contracting authorities or entities in the fields of defence and security, and amending Directives 2004/17/EC and 2004/18/EC [2009] OJ L216/76.
DM	dynamic market(s) (under the UK post-Brexit procurement reform instruments)
DPS	dynamic purchasing system(s) (under the EU procurement directives for the public and utility sectors, and/or, as the context indicates, in relevant EU Member States)
DPS+	new Dynamic Purchasing System, as provided in the UK post-Brexit Green Paper 'Transforming Public Procurement' (2020)

DSL	defence and security procurement law – Government Urgency Ordinance 114/2011 (MO 932/29.12.2011), as amended by Law 195/2012 (MO 753/8.11.2012) (Romania)
DSPCR	Defence and Security Public Contract Regulations (SI 2011/1848) (UK)
DVA	Department of Veteran Affairs (US)
EC	European Community
FA	framework agreement(s) (context will indicate the system/instrument under which the arrangement is referred to)
FAR	Federal Acquisition Regulation (US)
FASA	Federal Acquisition Streamlining Act (US)
FSS	Federal Supply Schedule (US)
GAO	Government Accountability Office (US)
GD	Government Decision (Romania)
GPA	World Trade Organization's Agreement on Government Procurement (2012)
Green Paper	Green Paper called 'Transforming public procurement', December 2020 (CP 253) issued by the Cabinet Office
GSA	General Services Administration (US)
Guidance on Frameworks	'Procurement Guidance: Framework Agreements – An Overview of How to Design, Establish and Operate a Framework Agreement in Investment Project Financing (World Bank, 2018)
Guide or Guide to Enactment	UNCITRAL, 'Guide to Enactment of the UNCITRAL Model Law on Public Procurement' (Vienna, United Nations, 2014)
GWAC	Governmentwide Acquisition Contract(s) (US)
IBRD	International Bank for Reconstruction and Development
IDA	International Development Association (World Bank)

IDC	indefinite delivery contract(s) or price agreement(s) (World Bank)
ID/IQ	indefinite-delivery/indefinite-quantity [contract(s)] (US)
MAS	Multiple Award Schedule [Program] (US)
Model Law or 2011 Model Law	UNCITRAL Model Law on Public Procurement (2011), unless the context refers to another Model Law
OFPP	Office of Federal Procurement Policy (US)
PB or Procurement Bill	Procurement Bill as introduced in the House of Lords on 11 May 2022 [HL Bill 4] (UK; post-Brexit)
PCR	Public Contracts Regulations 2015 (SI 2015/102) (UK)
PIN	implementing norms for the Public Procurement Law (public sector), approved by GD 395/2016 (MO 423/6.6.2016) (Romania)
PPL	Public Procurement Law (Law 98/2016, MO 390/23.5.2016) (Romania)
PR or Procurement Regulations or Regulations	Procurement Regulations for IPF Borrowers: Procurement in Investment Project Financing – Goods, Works, Non-Consulting and Consulting Services (The World Bank, 4th edn, 2020) (unless the context refers to other Regulations or Procurement Regulations)
PRL	Procurement Remedies Law (Law 101/2016, MO 393/23.5.2016) (Romania)
PSD or 2014PSD or Public Sector Directive	Directive 2014/24/EU of the European Parliament and of the Council of 26 February 2014 on public procurement and repealing Directive 2004/18/EC [2014] OJ L94/65
PUIR	purchasing (procurement of) uncertain or indefinite requirements
SOW	statement of work (US)
SPD	standard procurement document(s) (World Bank)
TFEU	Treaty on the Functioning of the European Union

UCR	Utilities Contracts Regulations (SI 2016/274) (UK)
UD or 2014UD or Utilities Directive	Directive 2014/25/EU of the European Parliament and of the Council of 26 February 2014 on procurement by entities operating in the water, energy, transport and postal services sectors and repealing Directive 2004/17/EC [2014] OJ L94/243
UIN	implementing norms for the Utilities Procurement Law, approved by GD 394/2016 (MO 422/6.6.2016) (Romania)
UNCITRAL	United Nations Commission on International Trade Law
UPL	Utilities Procurement Law (Law 99/2016, MO 391/23.5.2016) (Romania)
USAID	United States Agency for International Development
USC	United States Code
WB	The World Bank
WBG	The World Bank Group
2004PSD	Directive 2004/18/EC of the European Parliament and of the Council of 31 March 2004 on the coordination of procedures for the award of public works contracts, public supply contracts and public service contracts [2004] OJ L134/114 (this instrument is no longer in force)
2004UD	Directive 2004/17/EC of the European Parliament and of the Council of 31 March 2004 coordinating the procurement procedures of entities operating in the water, energy, transport and postal services sectors [2004] OJ L134/1 (this instrument is no longer in force)
2011 Procurement Guidelines	The World Bank, 'Guidelines – Procurement of Goods, Works and Non-Consulting Services under IBRD Loans and IDA Credits and Grands by World Bank Borrowers' (2011)

1

Introduction – Purchasing Uncertain or Indefinite Requirements in Public Procurement: Overview and Paradoxes

1.1. Variety of Arrangements, Commonality, and a Substantive Definition

This book analyses the regulation of, and policy towards, tools used in public procurement for the purchase of uncertain or indefinite requirements, as well as practical implications. Such tools include, for example, framework agreements, dynamic purchasing systems and qualification systems in the EU, indefinite delivery contracts and multiple-award schedules in the US federal procurement system, or dynamic markets in the UK post-Brexit procurement reform consultation documents and Procurement Bill, to name just a few. Whilst in many cases such tools are regarded in regulation or practice as instruments for recurrent or ongoing procurements, and they are used in this way, the key to them resides in addressing the uncertain or indefinite nature of the procurement needs they refer to, and this also opens their strategic horizons. Simply repeating reactively similar full procurement processes each time when 'one-off' needs for the same items materialise does not constitute any of the tools which this monograph analyses, and, similarly, combining repeat requirements into a transaction whose elements are all certain and definite does not warrant such a tool: in both cases 'traditional' procurement(s) and 'traditional' procurement contracts are likely to be the outcomes. In contrast, procurement vehicles such as, for example, framework agreements approach recurrent or ongoing needs proactively, more strategically, usually on a longer-term basis, and they involve some element of uncertainty.

It is for these reasons that the tools analysed in this monograph are referred to as arrangements for purchasing uncertain or indefinite requirements (PUIR), and in particular to differentiate these tools from 'traditional', 'one-off' procurements. Many public procurement systems world-wide currently address in some ways and/or use PUIR arrangements, and the varied terminology reflects the even wider variety of the arrangements themselves and of the approaches to regulating them. The various facets of PUIR arrangements are reflected in, inter alia, single or multiple contractor arrangements, single or multiple purchaser arrangements, committing or non-committing arrangements, whether the arrangement establishes terms of future purchases and (if so) how are terms formed, the methods for setting up an arrangement and when can interested parties join it, or the way of selecting a contractor who is a party to or registered onto an arrangement to actually execute specific orders or contracts. The detailed drawing of these main perspectives illustrates specific types or configurations of PUIR arrangements in the regulation of public procurement, within and sometimes across public procurement systems, that further expand the diversity of the phenomenon.

Beyond very significant differences, the underlying feature of these (usually) long-term arrangements is that some elements of the intended purchases – specifications, quantities, delivery times and locations, commitments and/or terms – are uncertain or indefinite at the time when the procurement process is initiated. The arrangements can thus facilitate a strategic approach towards a large portion of an organisation's procurement portfolio. Rather than waiting for procurement requirements to materialise and then reacting, the purchaser takes a pro-active approach and starts building its approach to the market on the basis of an estimation of needs, thus saving precious lead times or gaining security of supply. Rather than repeating a fully-fledged procurement process for the same or somewhat similar recurring needs, the purchaser bundles them or, as applicable, it bundles their *common* elements, thereby potentially facilitating efficiency, savings, better terms, administrative convenience or, again, security of supply. Further, rather than committing to purchase fixed quantities, or to bespoke specifications that are fully detailed upfront, or to specific terms, the purchaser may build into the procurement process the necessary flexibility to accommodate, for example, specific needs of various users (customisation), or the dynamics of the relevant market segment.

In light of the above, the procurement arrangements that form the subject-matter of this monograph are defined as those arrangements designed and/or implemented to meet on-going, recurrent, uncertain or indefinite requirements for a long-term period through purchasing items from the free market, and whereby the parties, at the initiative of the purchaser, seek to go through a number of procedural stages (for example, 'suitability') and/or to establish a number of contractual terms, but not all, in advance of the moment when an actual need for specific items arises; this is followed by placement of subsequent contracts or orders (also referred to as call-offs) whenever the actual needs for items arise, based on the procedural stages conducted in advance, or based on the terms agreed beforehand. It can be easily noticed that this definition covers a wide range of potential arrangements from mere lists of potentially interested suppliers, possibly subject to a very brief 'suitability' assessment, to arrangements where a full 'suitability' assessment is conducted before actual and/or fully specifiable needs arise, and further to arrangements where some or most, but not all, contractual elements and terms for the future purchases are established before the needs above arise.

Within the defined landmarks, the possible arrangements outline the nuances of the phenomenon addressed by this book,[1] and the over 20 'types' of arrangement identified (or inferred) in the seven public procurement systems examined populate this map to various degrees.

Examples include, along the spectrum described, qualification systems in the EU utilities sector, dynamic purchasing systems in the EU public sector, framework agreements in the UNCITRAL, IBRD and EU public procurement systems, indefinite-delivery / indefinite-quantity contracts (ID/IQ) and requirements contracts in the US federal system. It needs mentioning though that this 'list' presents some risk of oversimplification since most 'types' of arrangement, as provided for or implicitly permitted by regulation, comprise a multitude of complex features, sometimes blurring their 'position' within the range. For instance, depending on the configuration used, an (EU) dynamic purchasing system could involve, it is argued, in its first stage of admitting suppliers onto the arrangement, either just a 'suitability' assessment (the 'default' configuration), as well as this assessment and the establishment of certain terms concerning future purchases, as it can be inferred from the provisions concerning the use of electronic catalogues in dynamic purchasing systems, which has important practical consequences.[2]

From this perspective a conceptual distinction should be made from the outset between arrangements that establish terms of future purchases, hereinafter referred to as 'framework arrangements', and arrangements that do not establish terms for such purchases, hereinafter referred to as 'supplier lists'. Some terminological notes of caution are also needed. The use of the same term 'framework *agreement*' in the EU directives, the UNCITRAL Model Law on Public Procurement, and in the IBRD procurement regulations certainly does *not* mean that the same rules apply to framework agreements in those systems, as will become apparent in the following chapters of this book. Whilst some configurations of framework *arrangement* might be accommodated in more than one public procurement system this is not always the case, and variances can also be found, within the EU, in the regulation of framework agreements in various Member States. Also, individual 'types' or 'categories' of PUIR arrangement in a procurement system tend to comprise under their roof a number of 'sub-types'. As shown, EU dynamic purchasing systems may involve two quite distinct configurations, one involving only a 'suitability' assessment during the first stage (ie, a supplier list arrangement) and another one also involving the formation of terms (ie, a framework arrangement). This is not at all a singular case. Under the UNCITRAL system, framework agreements comprise closed

---

[1] S Arrowsmith, 'Framework Purchasing and Qualification Lists under the European Procurement Directives: Part I' (1999) 8 *PPLR* 115, 116. The idea of nuances or shades of a spectrum of arrangements in the PUIR phenomenon was emphasised by Emerita Professor Sue Arrowsmith in our academic discussions.

[2] See Chapter 5, section 5.3.3.1 of this book.

and open frameworks that are different arrangements, whilst EU framework agreements (the relative equivalent of UNCITRAL *closed* framework agreements alone) cover a significant variety of potential sub-types as well: ranging, for instance, from a framework with a single purchaser and a single contractor to, at the other end of this spectrum, a centralised framework agreement potentially involving hundreds of purchasers and multiple contractors where the second stage includes contract awards with or without reopening competition amongst framework contractors; there clearly are significant differences between such sub-types of framework, and many possible configurations of frameworks between the two ends of this spectrum.

Additional to these preliminary considerations, a few matters arise from the definition of arrangements covered by this book. First, as shown, they concern on-going, recurrent, uncertain or indefinite needs of a purchaser for a period of time, and not one-off needs, and thus PUIR arrangements differ from procurement regarding 'one-off' needs. The on-going or recurrent nature of the requirements tends to be central to the arrangements investigated, although *exceptionally*, there can be contemplated, under certain regimes, PUIR arrangements which end up filling, or intentionally target, one-off needs, namely where a single procurement contract or order is being placed.

Second, in PUIR arrangements the procurement (transactional) process is initiated before a specific need becomes actual for the purchaser and/or specifiable in all respects. From this perspective, this book covers urgent procurement, in so far as potentially recurrent but indefinite or uncertain needs can be estimated to some extent on the basis of an assumption that urgent situations, such as disasters or crises, are inevitable and that the type of items needed to deal with such events, or their consequences, can broadly be identified in advance.[3] A relevant angle on urgent procurement in this book is the specific design of (certain) PUIR arrangements in anticipation of potential disasters, namely where a purchaser initiates the procurement transactional process in advance of such events, in contemplation of placing subsequent contracts or orders as and when needs materialise, namely upon the occurrence of a disaster or crisis.[4] In this context, the book takes stock of developments during the coronavirus pandemic in the procurement systems examined, discerning potential lessons for a strategic direction concerning the procurement of uncertain or indefinite requirements.[5]

Third, PUIR arrangements involve aggregation of procurement requirements usually into a *single* procurement exercise, initiated before needs materialise

---

[3] See, eg, JI Schwartz, 'Katrina's lessons for ongoing US procurement reform efforts' (2006) 15 *PPLR* 362.

[4] Such PUIR arrangements might end up with just one call-off or even with no call-offs, but depending on a variety of factors including the geographical area covered, likeliness or frequency of disasters, or the number of agencies using the arrangement in question, many call-offs could be needed.

[5] See especially S Arrowsmith et al (eds), *Public Procurement in (a) Crisis: Global Lessons from the Covid-19 Pandemic* (Oxford, Hart Publishing, 2021).

and resulting in a number of subsequent orders or contracts throughout the life of the arrangement, as and when needs do materialise. From this angle, PUIR arrangements are distinct from 'traditional' procurement by 'lots' concerning one-off actual / fully specifiable procurement needs, but it is possible to conduct PUIR arrangements divided into lots and this occurs in practice quite often.[6] Procurement by lots brings under a single procurement exercise items that may be different in nature or not offered (at best terms) by a single supplier, though the items could be somehow 'linked' or serve the same need of the purchaser.

Fourth, the subject-matter of procurement under PUIR arrangements tends to consist of rather standard items where the arrangement establishes most of the terms and/or specifications for future purchases, and may range to quite complex items where the arrangement only establishes some terms and specifications for future purchases or where it does not establish terms at all. The more complex an item is, the more difficult it could be to establish precise terms and specifications in advance, or to go through a significant part of the procurement process, before the need materialises. However, different considerations may come into play, such as allowing room for product or service customisation, or for accommodating the needs of various users (for example in the case of a centralised arrangement), or for 'capturing' technology developments on rapidly evolving markets, or avoiding remaining stuck with terms that no longer reflect conditions prevailing on the market, and such aspects may point toward an arrangement that does not establish most terms and/or specifications even for fairly standard items. Conversely, recurrent needs for complex items that can be standardised may point toward an arrangement that establishes most terms and specifications in advance.

Lastly, and equally relevant, the book also considers arrangements for procurement of commodities, and whether and how the regulation of PUIR arrangements addresses – or could address – volatile price markets. In these cases, there is a high degree of uncertainty over market conditions, which affects the needed procurement approach.

1.2. Reasons and Objectives, Potential Benefits and Associated Risks

PUIR arrangements may be worth using, despite being rather complex arrangements, with a view to ensuring security and flexibility of supply over a period of time at short notices, particularly where the arrangement provides for a

---

[6] For example, the framework agreements divided into lots under the public procurement system for the EU's external aid programmes, or the frameworks of the European Investment Bank for consultancy services.

commitment by the supplier(s) on the arrangement to supply,[7] or in light of an objective impossibility (or inappropriateness) of establishing all terms of, or best terms for, the requirements well in advance of the actual supply. Sometimes there may be an overlap between reasons and potential benefits from using a PUIR arrangement. Thus, as shown, a purchaser may seek to obtain security or flexibility of supply. But it may also pursue economies of scale that could result from aggregation of demand. Suppliers may be able to offer better terms in light of an expected large volume of sales, and even more so where the purchaser commits to buy certain quantities. On the other hand, an overall reduction of the administrative burden, including transaction costs, can be achieved since the arrangement eliminates the need to repeat a 'full' procurement procedure for every need that materialises during its term.

However, depending on how they are regulated or implemented, PUIR arrangements may present challenges or risks. Because such arrangements are rather complex, usually involving two distinct procedural phases, there will be a need for experienced procurement personnel to understand the arrangement and ensure consistency of approach throughout the entire process. This may not be easily achieved, for example, in the case of multi-purchaser multi-supplier framework arrangements where an institution establishes the arrangement but other institutions place orders under it, completing (or even amending) specifications for the items and establishing the reminder of the terms.[8] Similarly, because PUIR arrangements are longer-term arrangements, their success depends on market dynamics over the relevant period and market awareness is essential. It is important to 'design' arrangements that continue to be relevant for every order during their term, while at the same time avoiding situations where the purchaser remains stuck with terms that no longer reflect the market segment in question. Thus, PUIR arrangements require an increased planning and preparation effort, which is likely to impact their ability to meet specific circumstances and their success in implementation, for example achieving a desired balance between value, flexibility of supply, and administrative convenience (noting that such features may not go hand-in-hand and trade-offs are inherent).

On the other hand, PUIR arrangements may pose a risk to competition.[9] This could affect the arrangement itself, in particular where additional suppliers are

---

[7] See S Arrowsmith and C Nicholas, 'Regulating Framework Agreements under the UNCITRAL Model Law on Procurement' in S Arrowsmith (ed), *Reform of the UNCITRAL Model Law on Procurement: Procurement Regulation for the 21st Century* (Eagan MN, Thomson Reuters/West, 2009) 95, 102–04.

[8] A specific experience is provided in the US federal procurement system. The US Government Accountability Office found that in certain multi-purchaser, multi-supplier framework arrangements (or multi-agency indefinite-delivery / indefinite-quantity contracts) the institution placing orders exceeded significantly the scope of the underlying arrangements. BN Bleicher, WI Dunn, DI Gordon and JL Kang, 'Accountability in Indefinite-Delivery/Indefinite-Quantity Contracting: The Multifaceted Work of the U.S. Government Accountability Office' (2008) 37 *PCLJ* 407.

[9] See, eg, P Trepte, *Public Procurement in the EU: A Practitioner's Guide*, 2nd edn (Oxford, OUP, 2007) 212; P Arden, 'Legal regulation of multi-provider framework agreements and the potential for bid rigging: a perspective from the UK local government construction sector' (2013) 22 *PPLR* 165.

not permitted to join after its establishment[10] or where the second stage of the arrangement is not properly regulated or monitored. The risk could also escalate to affect a relevant market (segment) where the arrangement 'closes' a significant part of that market confining it only to some or just a few of the suppliers usually active on that market. A risk of corruption could also affect large-scale arrangements in view of the potential volume of sales. It is also possible that some PUIR arrangements are not attractive to procurement 'players', for example where procedural requirements are too burdensome, such as those that were provided for the second stage of a dynamic purchasing system under the 2004 EU Public Sector and Utilities Directives.[11] These defeated the efficiency expected of the arrangement.

The above challenges regarding PUIR arrangements illustrate how important a balanced legal regulation of such arrangements is for their success (or otherwise), particularly due to the impact that legal regulation has on behaviours of the persons to whom it applies.[12] Generally, there is consensus that public procurement needs to be regulated.[13] A main question that emerges is how best to regulate public procurement so as to guide procurement activity toward the wider objectives of a specific procurement system[14] and encourage an appropriate use of certain purchasing 'techniques'. At the same time regulation should consider the market rules and influences that are inherent to the underlying 'core' commercial process of purchasing items from a free market. This approach is used in analysing and conceptualising the phenomenon of procuring uncertain or indefinite requirements in the public/regulated sectors (including, for example, utilities or defence and security). Similarly, policy, guidance, and interpretation in implementation can have a strong 'say' in the appropriate and strategic use of PUIR arrangements.

1.3. Amplitude and Complexity of the Phenomenon, but Limited Attention So Far

Some forms of 'PUIR' arrangements can be identified in regulation and practice over the past several decades, such as the US General Service Administration (GSA) Multiple Award Schedule (MAS) Program, or various types of 'framework' contracts in the French public procurement system. During the 1990s and, in

---

[10] Referred to as 'closed arrangement'.

[11] Rules concerning dynamic purchasing systems were changed in the 2014 EU directives. See Chapter 5 of this book.

[12] N Popa, *Teoria generala a dreptului [General Theory of Law]* (All Beck, 2002) 134.

[13] See general literature on public procurement regulation, eg, P Trepte, *Regulating Public Procurement – Understanding the Ends and Means of Public Procurement Legislation* (Oxford, OUP, 2004). Also, Ş Filipon, *A Review of European Union's Public Procurement Procedures in External Environments*, MSc Dissertation, University of Strathclyde, UK, 2006.

[14] For example, efficiency, fairness, value, promotion of international trade, etc, as relevant.

particular, into the new millennium the regulation of what this book refers to as PUIR was introduced or has been developed, with a view to enhancing efficiency and effectiveness in public procurement. This can be seen at the level of the EU, including Member States, UNCITRAL, the World Bank regulations, as well as in US federal procurement. Most recently, after 2020, the UK post-Brexit public procurement policy reform preoccupations, which are ongoing at the time of writing, could bring PUIR policy and regulation to new heights depending on how the reform, and the proposed new legislation, will be completed, as is discussed in Chapters five and six. A significant increase in the use of such arrangements has been recorded in some procurement systems during the same period.

These arrangements are particularly important from both practical and theoretical perspectives. First, huge volumes of purchases are being made through them, including as a share of a public procurement market, or of the procurement portfolio of a contracting agency. For instance, procurements of an aggregated value of over US$30 billion are conducted solely by using US GSA schedules yearly,[15] whereas about 14 per cent of the total EU directives purchase volume was accounted for solely by framework agreements.[16] For a number of US agencies over 30 per cent of their procurement spend goes through GSA schedules,[17] whilst in each of seven EU Member States 'framework agreements covered more than a quarter of all contract notices.'[18] Procurements under a single framework agreement may be worth billions of, say, sterling, and a single order under, say, an ID/IQ contract could be worth multi-million dollars.[19] Second, the practical importance of PUIR arrangements arises from the purposes that these can serve, such as aggregation of demand for recurring or ongoing needs, economies of scale, administrative convenience, security of supply, or dealing with emergency situations, thereby facilitating a strategic approach towards a large portion of an organisation's procurement. Third, as shown, these arrangements may also present elevated risks of being misused or abused, and could significantly affect competition. Fourth, 'PUIR' arrangements are very differently regulated and classified in the various procurement legal systems or instruments, whereas each regulatory system tends to have its own imbalances (potentially unnecessary restrictions, lack of relevant requirements/controls, ambiguities) including in relation to the overall objectives of the system in question.

---

[15] eg, EL Tomey and MT Zomer, 'Government Contracts: GSA Multiple Award Schedule Contracting', Practice Note, *Practical Law* (Thomson Reuters, 2020), referring to Fiscal Year 2019 at www.foley.com/en/files/uploads/News/Government%20Contracts%20GSA%20Multiple%20 Award%20Schedule%20Contracting%20(w-001-6439).pdf. See also Chapter 4 of this book.

[16] European Commission, 'Annual Public Procurement Implementation Review 2012' (Brussels, 9.10.2012, SWD(2012)342 final) 26, referring to year 2010. See also Chapter 5 of this book.

[17] FEDSched, 'Agency Spending through GSA Schedule' (Report 8/6/21), at https://gsa.federalschedules.com/resources/agency-spending-through-gsa-schedules/.

[18] European Commission, 'Annual Public Procurement' (2012) 26, referring to year 2009.

[19] See Chapter 4 of this book.

However, despite their theoretical and practical importance, the regulation of and policy regarding PUIR have received limited attention, including in the literature. Whilst there have been genuine developments in regulation – such as the introduction of explicit provisions concerning framework agreements in the 2004 EC public sector procurement directive, and in the 2011 UNCITRAL Model Law on Public Procurement, the adjustment of provisions concerning dynamic purchasing systems in the 2014 EU public and utilities directives, or the 2016 reform of the World Bank procurement regulations – the 'landscape' still looks like 'work in progress' in various respects, as is explained throughout this book. A breakthrough could be provided by the UK post-Brexit procurement reform, depending on how the procurement bill, in its final version as enacted (as well as any further secondary legislation, and possibly guidance) will address PUIR. Literature in the area of PUIR is rather scarce, in particular when it comes to addressing the internal structure and logic of the regulation of PUIR *across* varied procurement systems and/or legal instruments. With very notable exceptions, pieces on the subject tend to be centred on a single procurement system or instrument (or just a few *related* ones), rather descriptive of the 'current' regulation they discuss, and/or focusing on a single type of arrangement, or some types and/or configurations. Certain areas have not been addressed at all in the literature so far, such as PUIR under the World Bank and Romanian systems, or in the security and defence sectors under the relevant EU directive (and/or under instruments of selected Member States).

This book fills these major gaps. It structures a rather unarticulated area of legal research and practice, and develops a framework for analysis and interpretation of the PUIR phenomenon that can be adjusted and applied to specific contexts, and used by scholars, regulators, policy-makers, and practitioners in the discharge of their functions. It identifies the main elements of the PUIR phenomenon, captures the underlying logic of PUIR regulation, and assesses considerations that tend to promote or detract from achieving objectives of PUIR regulation, always bearing in mind that different objectives (or balances of objectives) and different circumstances are relevant and specific to each individual public procurement system or context. The book thus provides detailed and recent information for all those interested or involved in this field, and helps them learn from the approaches and experiences in other procurement systems.

By deconstructing PUIR arrangements, as currently regulated, into basic elements in relation to the 'core' commercial purchasing process, the book reconstructs a corpus of guidance and a perspective for regulating PUIR taking into consideration system-specific objectives and circumstances, as well as for interpretation by practitioners, particularly from a teleological point of view, in areas where existing regulation in their procurement systems is silent, inconsistent or unclear. In the context of this book, such guidance relates to aspects worth considering in a wide context by policy-makers, legislators or practitioners when introducing or reviewing public procurement regulation concerning PUIR, or when actually implementing PUIR arrangements. This guidance does not refer to (and does not imply) a 'recipe' for PUIR, which is most likely unachievable, but to an 'orientation' within a complex phenomenon by considering experiences of various different systems, and how such experiences may, should, or should not be used/adapted/incorporated in particular circumstances of a given system, or by reference to certain objectives of a certain system.

The book thus articulates what can be regarded as a general discipline concerning the regulation of, and policy towards, PUIR in public procurement. This discipline provides a novel approach that can better facilitate the attainment of the specific objectives pursued by a procurement system through the regulation and (appropriate) use of arrangements for PUIR. It also cascades to the level of individual purchasers by providing considerations regarding procurement portfolio structuring and approach in light of PUIR, as well as practical scenarios concerning the interpretation and application of specific PUIR regulations in practice.

1.4. Brief Diagnosis: Current Trends and Desirable Future Directions

Recent decades have witnessed significant developments in the area of PUIR and expansion in the use of this category of arrangements, and some 'milestones' were shown in the preceding section. However, challenges are faced, in various ways, by all systems analysed in 'calibrating' regulation of PUIR to their intended objectives *and* to the inherent uncertainties or indefinite aspects of such arrangements. Such challenges tend to arise from the potential complexity of PUIR, the regulation of multiple configurations of arrangements under the same 'roof' (eg, the various forms of framework agreements in the EU directives), and/or regulating PUIR as a 'derived' type of traditional, 'one-off' procurement, whereas some types or configurations of PUIR arrangements can indeed be very remote in both complexity and implications from 'one-off' procurement. From this perspective, for example, 'painting' dynamic purchasing systems in the 2014 EU public and utilities procurement directives as an adjusted 'restricted procedure'[20] appears somewhat of a fantasy.

Many types (or configurations) of arrangement are missing from one procurement system or another. Wide ranges of potential arrangements in the PUIR spectrum are repudiated by the current systems, whilst some aspects of

---

[20] Directive 2014/24/EU [2014] OJ L94/65, art 34(2); Directive 2014/25/2014 [2014] OJ L94/243, art 52(2).

the recognised arrangements may benefit from increased attention in the regulation. This seems, to varying degrees, a common feature of the procurement systems examined. It is not suggested that all systems should permit the same types or configurations of PUIR arrangements or that they should be regulated in exactly the same way. Despite increased international harmonisation, much will continue to depend on the objectives of individual systems, institutional and human resource capacity, and legal or administrative culture. But, currently, regulations in the procurement systems (or legal instruments) examined contain both unnecessary limitations on the use of PUIR, as well as insufficient conditions or coverage concerning certain elements of the arrangements they provide for, which could quite easily offer gaps sheltering improper or abusive use of such arrangements. These combined imbalances in regulation potentially preclude procurement officers from using valuable tools for efficient grouping and organising of a wide range of indefinite but predicted purchasing needs in their portfolio, and could detract from achievement of better performance at procurement system level.

A broad trend relates to recent reforms of major public procurement systems or instruments (eg, UNCITRAL, EU public sector, World Bank) that have generally manifested a continued preference for framework arrangements over supplier list type arrangements. However, reservations towards supplier lists do not appear justified if proper regulation of such arrangements is in place, including adequate (permanent) publicity and other relevant transparency measures, objective criteria, procedural controls and requirements safeguarding fairness, and effective review mechanisms. The post-Brexit public procurement reform provides an excellent opportunity to reverse this trend, as well as other types of imbalances discussed above, for example by removing unnecessary limitations that currently (still) apply to dynamic purchasing systems in the EU. The extent to which such new heights are to be achieved will depend on the clarifications and provisions that the new UK procurement bill, and any relevant secondary legislation (and possibly guidance), will include when finalised.

Thus, a significant expansion of the permitted range of PUIR arrangements appears desirable in the future, notably, without limitation, towards supplier list type arrangements, coupled with a more focused, direct and contained approach in regulation and policy towards PUIR, including a recalibration of conditions and controls applicable to PUIR processes. This should provide procurement officers with appropriate tools for a wider variety of procurement needs and market structures, and support the use of those far-reaching possibilities appropriately on a case-by-case basis, releasing potential for increased efficiency and effectiveness in public procurement. Certainly, solutions in regulation and practice will depend on specific circumstances in each public procurement system, and this book analyses in detail seven carefully selected public procurement systems, as well as lessons arising from transversal perspectives across them.

1.5. Direct and Indirect Coverage of the Monograph, Plus Wider Relevance

As shown, this monograph directly covers seven very different public procurement systems that are addressed in detail in Chapters two to five. PUIR in each of these systems is placed in perspective revealing a variety of angles. The selection process carefully considered the size of the public procurement markets in question, their experiences and characteristics and/or their actual or potential influence on other procurement systems, so that the book provides wide coverage and representativeness, as well as global relevance through exploration of and orientation to the main elements of the PUIR phenomenon arising from a structured and articulated analysis across varied public procurement systems.

Thus, the EU public procurement system, regulated by the relevant EU directives,[21] seeks to open national procurement markets to suppliers from other Member States, in line with the economic integration and the development of the European common market envisaged by the EU Treaties, and is less interested in providing for detailed rules or guidance on how purchasers achieve efficiency in procurement.[22] Thorough consideration of this public procurement system is particularly relevant in light of the volume of public procurement conducted within this large market – comprising over 250,000 procuring entities with an aggregate yearly procurement 'spend [of] around 14 per cent of GDP (around €2 trillion per year)'[23] – of its direct influence on its (currently) 27 national public procurement systems of the Member States, and its influence on international instruments and on countries aspiring to become EU members. The availability of primary and secondary literature in the English or French languages facilitated the examination of this procurement system. It is important to point out that before Brexit, the EU also had a direct influence on the UK public procurement system, though some influence is likely to continue even after Brexit, for example in regulating public procurement through 'hard law' instruments, something that had not been specific to the UK prior to its EU accession.[24]

Among the national procurement systems of EU Member States, this book addresses specifically France, Romania and the UK, to provide for a range of experiences and legal traditions. France is a founding member of the European Community, whereas the UK joined in 1973 (and left in 2020), so both these states are experienced in EU public procurement. But their practice and traditions differ, France having a Napoleonic (civil law) legal system, the UK

---

[21] The most recent reform resulted in certain new directives being adopted in 2014.

[22] See, eg, Trepte, *Regulating Public Procurement* (n 13) 42 and 342–67.

[23] European Commission, Internal Market Industry Entrepreneurship and SMEs, Public Procurement, https://single-market-economy.ec.europa.eu/single-market/public-procurement_en.

[24] S Arrowsmith, 'Transforming Public Procurement Law after Brexit: Early Reflections on the Government's Green Paper' (15 December 2020), http://dx.doi.org/10.2139/ssrn.3749359, s 2.

(the Westminster jurisdiction that the book analyses) having a common law system. France has a tradition of issuing detailed legally binding regulations,[25] and a rather prescriptive approach to regulating procurement. As a legal/procurement system, it influenced other civil law states and has a direct impact in France's overseas territories. In the UK the conduct of public procurement has traditionally been, to a high degree, left at the discretion of purchasers and procurement officers,[26] emphasis being placed on their professional expertise and ability to make sound procurement decisions for each individual need they have to meet via purchasing. When transposing the EU procurement directives (while an EU Member State), the UK merely passed on the options provided by the directives to the Member States, further onto purchasers. The UK has a very extensive historical experience with framework arrangements and was one of the main drivers for ensuring they were appropriately addressed in the EU directives. The UK system presents an interesting balance between rigidity and flexibility in the regulation of public procurement. The UK left the EU in January 2021, and a post-Brexit public procurement reform is underway, in line with the new UK objectives outside the EU and no longer subject to EU law and jurisdiction, which makes the UK a very relevant case-study in its evolution. In contrast, Romania is a relatively new Member State of the EU (having joined in 2007) and a former centralised economy until 1989. Therefore, its procurement experience, in the sense of public institutions purchasing from the free market,[27] is more limited. But Romania's perspective is relevant for other former socialist countries in Eastern Europe, whether EU Member States or states aspiring to EU membership. The first piece of coherent public procurement legislation in Romania was dated 2001. Consistent with commitments related to EU integration, new legislation was enacted in the summer of 2006 transposing the relevant EU instruments into domestic law. However, the domestic procurement legislation underwent numerous changes in the following years, until it was completely revised in 2016 in light of the 2014 directives.

On the other hand, the US federal procurement system could not be absent from this book, offering as it does extensive experience with PUIR, particularly in complex multi-purchaser/multi-supplier arrangements. This procurement system focuses on efficiency and speed of supply, at the cost of 'contestability' in some cases, such as the ordering stage of some indefinite delivery contracts. This seems aligned with the US Government's balance of objectives and a tendency towards more business-like procurement. Whilst it is probably impossible to accommodate all desiderata of public procurement like efficiency, value for money, transparency,

---

[25] For example, in the form of Decrees or Ordinances (or Codes).

[26] See, eg, S Arrowsmith, 'Framework Agreements in the EC and UK' in S Arrowsmith (ed), *Reform of the UNCITRAL Model Law on Public Procurement* (n 7) 131, 141–44.

[27] Trepte (n 13) 19.

competition, integrity, etc, and some will have to be traded-off against others,[28] the US appears to have made its choices. Nevertheless, after 2008, there has been some preoccupation for enhanced competition, transparency and wider contestability at ordering stage.[29] The size of the US public procurement market, its influence on certain international instruments, such as the Government Procurement Agreement (GPA) of the World Trade Organization (WTO) or the UNCITRAL Model Law on Public Procurement, and the availability of literature in the English language are further reasons for addressing this system.

The World Bank procurement system is an international procurement system employed by an international development loan provider, mainly applicable for borrowing institutions in borrowing countries. It is of particular relevance since: it is applied in, and has influenced the procurement systems of a large number of various countries; it is used as an example for other development banks; it provides the perspective of an international loan organisation. The procurement regulations[30] are intended to ensure the success of the projects financed through such loans, unless the Bank agrees that an alternative procurement regime can be applied to a project.

Finally, the preparatory works for revision of the UNCITRAL Model Law on Public Procurement, and the resulting revised (2011) Model Law with its attending guidance are of particular interest. The purpose of the UNCITRAL is to promote international trade through harmonisation of international trade law, and the Model Law seeks to provide guidance to states in drafting or updating their own national public procurement legal systems. These international instruments are based on wide input from many states, in most cases involving consensual decisions, and are intended to provide guidance for legislators in varied contexts. One of the novelties of the 2011 Model Law was the introduction of certain types of PUIR arrangement and it provides a particular perspective on the legal technique employed for expressing the agreed norms in a 'legal language' of a very general level, as required by such an international model law. The influence and further potential influence of the UNCITRAL Model Law on a large number of systems makes this system particularly relevant.

1.6. Approach and Organisation of the Monograph

Certain methodological approaches make this book unique in analysing PUIR systematically and comprehensively in and across very different public procurement

---

[28] SL Schooner, 'Desiderata: Objectives for a System of Government Contract Law' (2002) 11 *PPLR* 103.

[29] See, eg, DI Gordon and GM Racca, 'Integrity challenges in the EU and U.S. procurement systems' in GM Racca and CR Yukins (eds), *Integrity and Efficiency in Sustainable Public Contracts: Balancing Corruption Concerns in Public Procurement Internationally* (Brussels, Bruylant, 2014) 117, 138.

[30] Since July 2016: 'The World Bank Procurement Regulations for IPF Borrowers'.

systems. The same structure for the analysis of each arrangement in every system examined was developed and used enabling substantive and meaningful legal doctrinal analysis in context and comparative perspectives. This structure includes two main parts. A general one refers to the relevant 'procurement environment',[31] discussing briefly the legal and institutional background, history, traditions and other features of the procurement system or instrument in question that point to the logic and objectives of regulating PUIR in that system. The specific part of the structure relates directly to the 'core' components of PUIR arrangements in their legal, policy, as well as commercial 'directions', namely to the legal definition/ description, classification, conditions for use, controls (measures aiming at securing an appropriate use during implementation), first and second stage procedures, and review mechanisms. Within this compass, there certainly are some variations of detail relevant to individual procurement systems, instruments, or specific arrangements, arising from the differences amongst various systems, since not all elements are present in all systems or arrangements. Examples of such elements include an intermediary or third stage under certain framework agreements in France, or in the case of blanket purchase agreements placed against schedule contracts in the US federal procurement systems.

This structure secures a valid application of '*tertius comparationis*' or the comparability rule, which is the essence of comparative analysis. In other words, 'only comparable things can be compared but only the comparison itself will in the end indicate whether the things were comparable'.[32] Despite the wide range and variety of PUIR arrangements, the comparative element in our case concerns the fashion in which regulation in different systems relates to the commercial process of dealing with uncertain or indefinite procurement needs for a longer-term period. The structured approach has also made it possible to eliminate the risk for the outcomes of comparative perspectives to remain somehow: (i) superficial, simply describing in parallel the various case studies and outlining randomly some connections between their various elements; and/or (ii) irrelevant, ie operating 'micro-comparisons'[33] between various elements of the case studies taken in isolation, likely to result in accurate but fragmented data that is unable to offer the insights and the depth of knowledge required to draw guidance for legislators and practitioners.

The structure for analysis, which can be recognised in each of Chapters two to six, enables three types of comparative perspectives. First, there are intra-system (vertical) comparisons amongst various issues of different PUIR arrangements within the same procurement system. They help in understanding and contrasting

---

[31] S Arrowsmith, J Linarelli and D Wallace Jr, *Regulating Public Procurement: National and International Perspectives* (Kluwer Law International, 2000) 18–22.

[32] L-J Constantinesco, *Tratat de Drept Comparat [Comparative Law Treatise]* Volume 1 (Bucharest, ALL, 1997) Foreword p XII.

[33] ibid, 228.

each individual type of arrangement, in particular as regards 'bordering' configurations that present nuances and shades on the spectrum of potential arrangements. Second, there are cross-system comparison exercises. These can be amongst various issues concerning two or more PUIR arrangements in two or more different procurement systems. They mainly help in identifying potential solutions or inferring potential consequences of regulation, policy or interpretation within individual procurement systems.

The two types of comparative perspectives referred to above are numerous and can be found throughout Chapters two to five, on individual public procurement systems. Thirdly, transversal/horizontal comparative perspectives transgress all procurement systems and all PUIR arrangements investigated, as relevant, in relation to each element of the template developed and used for the examination of individual PUIR arrangements. This is how Chapter six is constructed, thereby providing substantive orientation to regulators and policy-makers when considering PUIR regulation and policy, to practitioners in connection with planning the procurement portfolio of a buyer and carrying out procurement operations, as well as stimulating academic debate and further research.

These intertwining perspectives of the monograph shed light on how PUIR arrangements are regulated in the selected procurement systems, why they are regulated as they are, and provide a conceptual framework for assessing important considerations regarding the manner in which regulation responds to objectives of those systems, or how regulation could be made significantly more responsive, including in procurement systems not directly covered by this book.

Finally, it is relevant to point out that references in this book to legal instruments in force as at May 2022 refer to the instruments as amended by that time (if applicable).

PART I

Purchasing Uncertain or Indefinite Requirements in Selected Public Procurement Systems or Instruments

2

The UNCITRAL Model Law
on Public Procurement

2.1. Procurement Context

2.1.1. UNCITRAL: Institutional Considerations and its Work

The United Nations Commission for International Trade Law (UNCITRAL) is described as 'the core legal body of the United Nations system in the field of international trade law'.[1] UNCITRAL was set up in 1966 via Resolution No 2205 of the UN General Assembly, providing that UNCITRAL's mandate is to promote a 'progressive harmonization and unification' of international trade law in a structured, coherent and organised fashion, as well as to coordinate the activity of other organisations acting in the area of international trade law by promoting cooperation among them. It notes that harmonisation plays an important role in the development of international trade. UNCITRAL's methods and work are highly participative and consensual,[2] enabling UNCITRAL's instruments to be based on a broad range of experiences and to present a high degree of acceptability and implementation among member states.[3] Seventy states are part of UNCITRAL (as of 2022), which are elected by the General Assembly for six years according to an algorithm aiming to ensure a wide representation of geographical areas, trade and legal traditions. There are three levels of UNCITRAL's work: UNCITRAL (also referred to as the Commission), working groups, and secretariat.[4] The Commission convenes at annual sessions covering a number of

---

[1] https://uncitral.un.org.

[2] S Arrowsmith and C Nicholas, 'The UNCITRAL Model Law on Procurement: Past, Present, and Future' in S Arrowsmith (ed), *Reform of the UNCITRAL Model Law on Procurement: Procurement Regulation for the 21st Century* (Eagan MN, Thomson Reuters/West, 2009) 1, 5–6. See also C Nicholas, 'UNCITRAL and the Internationalization of Government Procurement Regulation' in AC Georgopulos, B Hoekman and PC Mavroidis (eds), *The Internationalization of Government Procurement Regulation* (Oxford, OUP, 2017) (electronic book).

[3] Arrowsmith and Nicholas, 'The UNCITRAL Model Law' (n 2) 5–6.

[4] See UNCITRAL, 'A Guide to UNCITRAL: Basic Facts about the United Nations Commission on International Trade Law' (Vienna, United Nations, 2013) 5–10, via https://uncitral.un.org/en/library/publications ('Guide to UNCITRAL').

subjects, such as: finalisation and adoption of draft texts prepared by working groups, selection of topics for future work, and monitoring developments of the case law concerning UNCITRAL text systems.[5] Decisions are taken (by member states of the Commission) by consensus rather than vote,[6] in order to facilitate general acceptance, to the extent possible, of a final text.[7] Only where consensus is not achieved are 'decisions ... to be taken by voting'.[8]

Usually Working Groups meet in sessions once or twice annually, and report on their progress to the Commission. Working Groups include all member states of UNCITRAL, and delegations of states normally include Government officials, academics, experts, and lawyers specialising in the subject-matter of that Working Group.[9] Working Groups are assigned substantive preparatory work by the Commission on subjects considered of particular importance for the development of international trade through harmonisation or unification of international trade law. Between 2004 and 2012 a Working Group dealt with the revision of the Model Law on Public Procurement. 'A model law is a legislative text that is recommended to States for enactment as part of their national law'.[10] The main advantage it provides for is flexibility while simultaneously creating premises for a good level of legal harmonisation. Enacting States have the option to make adjustments to the text of a model law, or to take over only certain provisions. However, states are generally encouraged by UNCITRAL to make as few changes as practicable when transposing model laws into their national law. More recently, model laws are usually accompanied by guides to enactment explaining the background of the model law. Guides to enactment also address the potential consequences of using various options provided for by a model law, or deviations from the provisions of a model law.

2.1.2. The UNCITRAL Model Law on Public Procurement: Approach, Evolution, Relevance

The fact that UNCITRAL addresses international harmonisation of public procurement legislation via a model law technique gives a clear indication of its approach to the subject. The main reason for this is that, as observed in the relevant literature,[11] there can be no universal 'recipe' for public procurement,

---

[5] See CLOUT via https://uncitral.un.org; however, it does not appear to include case law relating to the Model Law on Public Procurement.

[6] Guide to UNCITRAL (n 4) 6.

[7] Such acceptance was described in literature as meaning that a final text 'is relevant to States with different legal systems and levels of economic and social development'; Arrowsmith and Nicholas (n 2) 6.

[8] n 6.

[9] Guide to UNCITRAL (n 4) 8.

[10] ibid, 14. Further on model laws, 14–16.

[11] See P Trepte, *Regulating Public Procurement: Understanding the Ends and Means of Public Procurement Legislation* (Oxford, OUP, 2004) 7.

as solutions will depend on many factors, such as policy objectives, legal and administrative traditions, the structure of the market, the capacity of public institutions and procurement staff, the corruption and anti-corruption 'culture'. Certainly, flexibility is needed in approaching public procurement at an international level if states are to harmonise further their procurement rules, by allowing them to adjust their public procurement 'solutions' to the local circumstances, traditions, and policy. Even with flexibility in place, as catered for by a model law that provides options and allows for adjustments – the 'universality' claimed in the Guide to Enactment[12] appears to be an over-statement to some extent. In particular, addressing both developing and developed procurement systems appears problematic in some respects. An example concerns the decision not to recognise and regulate supplier lists in light of potential discrimination and despite potential advantages.[13] Nevertheless, there appears to be sufficient coherence of public procurement issues at an international level enabling legislation harmonisation in this area to be conducted, to a significant degree, through the rather structured method of a model law (in comparison with other UNCITRAL techniques). That coherence relates to objectives and principles that are shared by most procurement systems,[14] though the balance of objectives is likely to vary amongst individual procurement systems. The 2011 UNCITRAL Model Law on Public Procurement provides the 'essential principles and procedures'[15] needed to pursue shared objectives, whilst considering the core commercial process of buying items from the free market, and allowing accommodation of local circumstances.[16]

In a way, mutatis mutandis, and noting that different contexts and objectives apply to UNCITRAL's work on the one hand, and to the EU, or WTO's GPA work in the area of public procurement, on the other hand, a certain degree of similarity in approach has been taken by the three (international) organisations. The EU's main concern is to remove barriers to intra-EU trade, and the WTO's GPA concern is, similarly to some extent, to remove barriers in international trade. In contrast, UNCITRAL's main concern is to facilitate harmonisation of public procurement law internationally, together with the promotion of a core and thorough public procurement regulatory framework in general. This last element of UNCITRAL's work in the sector was regarded in literature as 'strikingly different' from the other two instruments, possibly driven by 'a desire to assist procurement reform independently of trade issues'.[17] But irrespective of the angles from which

---

[12] UNCITRAL, 'Guide to Enactment of the UNCITRAL Model Law on Public Procurement' (Vienna, United Nations, 2014) Preface, iii, via https://uncitral.un.org/en/library/publications ('Guide to Enactment' or 'Guide').

[13] For potential use of flexibility for achieving a wider influence of the Model Law, see S Arrowsmith, 'Public Procurement: An Appraisal of the UNCITRAL Model Law as a Global Standard' (2004) 53 *ICLQ* 17. See also section 2.2.5 below.

[14] Arrowsmith, 'Public Procurement: an Appraisal' (n 13) 18–19.

[15] Guide to Enactment (n 12), Preface, iii.

[16] Trepte, *Regulating Public Procurement* (n 11) 8.

[17] Arrowsmith (n 13) 19.

the three international organisations approach the subject of public procurement, it is worth noting that all of them provide (member) states with some degree of flexibility in harmonising national public procurement legislation. For instance, on the spectrum of harmonisation methods, a UNCITRAL model law lies between conventions and other more 'informal' and less systemic approaches, such as guidance or model provisions.[18] Comparably (in a wide perspective), the EU regulates public procurement mostly through directives, rather than regulations.[19]

The preoccupation with public procurement in the context of international trade development is not surprising given the sheer volume of public procurement markets. According to reports, they account for around 14 per cent of GDP on average, or up to 50 per cent of the total government spending in some countries,[20] including large projects of public interest. The first UNCITRAL Model Law on the subject dates since 1993 when the Commission adopted a Model Law for Goods and Construction. The 1993 Model Law did not cover procurement of services, but it was supplemented by the adoption in 1994 of a Model Law for Goods, Construction and Services, also accompanied by a guide to enactment. The influence of that Model Law was 'considerable' in developing countries, though apparently this was not the case in 'developed countries with established systems'.[21] Thirty countries are reported to have included in their national legislation procurement laws or regulations based on the 1994 UNCITRAL Model Law,[22] but the impact has likely been larger since states are not required to notify their implementation of Model Law provisions.[23] A revision of the 1994 Model Law was initiated in 2004; the new Model Law was adopted at the 44th UNCITRAL session in July 2011, and the Guide to Enactment one year later, in June 2012. Further guidance provided for enacting states concerns 'procurement regulations',[24] namely legal instruments used to detail and support implementation of a main 'procurement law'.

The main additions introduced by the 2011 Model Law, versus 1994 Model Law, besides 'introduction of a "toolbox approach" to the choice and use of procurement methods',[25] relate to three areas: use of electronic means in public

---

[18] Guide to UNCITRAL (n 4) 13–17.

[19] See Chapter 5, section 5.2.1 of this book.

[20] eg, World Bank, *Benchmarking Public Procurement: Assessing Public Procurement Regulatory Systems in 180 Economies*, 2017 edn, 13, via https://openknowledge.worldbank.org. See also the presentation of the UNCITRAL Model Law on Public Procurement (2011) at https://uncitral.un.org/en/texts/procurement/modellaw/public_procurement. The text of the UNCITRAL Model Law on Public Procurement (2011) can be accessed via the same link, this legal instrument being referred to further on in this book as 'Model Law' or '2011 Model Law'.

[21] Arrowsmith (n 13) 20–21.

[22] https://uncitral.un.org/en/texts/procurement/modellaw/procurement_of_goods_construction_and_services/status.

[23] C Nicholas, 'Reform of the UNCITRAL Model Law on Procurement' (2010), EBRD Law in Transition, www.ebrd.com/downloads/research/news/lit102.pdf.

[24] Via https://uncitral.un.org/en/texts/procurement.

[25] C Nicholas, 'The 2011 UNCIRAL Model Law on Public Procurement' (2012) 21 *PPLR* NA111.

procurement, electronic reverse auctions, and framework agreements. Regarding frameworks, it was decided that the introduction of rules was necessary in light of the potential benefits of such arrangements, to encourage and control their appropriate use.[26] Alongside the three 'new' subjects, many other changes were made to strengthen, improve and streamline the Model Law. Thus, an area that received particular attention concerned remedies and enforcement, which was significantly invigorated in light of the United Nations Conventions against Corruption.[27] The 2011 Model Law maintains or even extends flexibility in some respects. The fact that the provisions on 'challenge proceedings' are not contemplated as optional does not contradict this statement since flexibility needs to be balanced with principles of sound procurement. If flexibility in approach meant, for example, that value for money could be compromised or transparency or competition requirements eluded without proper and objective justification, then the whole construction of a model law, and any national system based on it, would basically be invalidated.

The Guide to Enactment clearly advises that the main principles of the Model Law, and their procedural safeguards, should not be weakened in the national legislation transposing the 2011 Model Law.[28] It is this fine line between flexibility in approach and clear procedural safeguards for the main procurement principles and processes that ensures success of model laws. A measure of success of UNCITRAL's Model Law(s) on Public Procurement is that leading international or regional organisations use it 'as a benchmark for public procurement law in countries of their operation',[29] and over 20 states are reported to have used the 2011 Model Law in reforming their procurement systems.[30] While these states tend to be transition economies, an important aspect, though difficult to appreciate, relates to the influence the Model Law has on interpretation and implementation of legal instruments in systems outside the traditional 'remit' of the UNCITRAL, such as the EU Member States. As shown later on in this book, elements of 'good practice' from the Model Law, for example concerning framework agreements, could be implemented voluntarily mutatis mutandis under systems not requiring them but permitting them implicitly.

---

[26] Arrowsmith and Nicholas (n 2) 54–60.

[27] ibid, 70–79; Nicholas, 'Reform of the UNCITRAL Model Law' (n 23). Still, post-award review and remedies (concerning concluded contracts) would benefit from additional guidance: C Nicholas and S Arrowsmith, 'The Challenges of Contructing a Supplier Review Mechanism for Urgent Procurement: An Analysis in the Context of the UNCITRAL Framework' in S Arrowsmith et al (eds), *Public Procurement in (a) Crisis: Global Lessons from the Covid-19 Pandemic* (Oxford, Hart Publishing, 2021) 156, 162–65.

[28] Guide to Enactment (n 12) 14–15 (mainly point 51).

[29] For example, the World Bank, EBRD, OECD. See https://uncitral.un.org/en/texts/procurement/modellaw/public_procurement/status.

[30] https://uncitral.un.org/sites/uncitral.un.org/files/media-documents/uncitral/en/overview-status-table.pdf.

2.2. Relevant Arrangements

2.2.1. Common Issues

2.2.1.1. Structure of Provisions, Main Definitions and Approaches

The 2011 UNCITRAL Model Law on Public Procurement (the Model Law) introduced express provisions concerning various forms of purchasing uncertain or indefinite requirements (PUIR), which it calls 'framework agreements'. While this terminology is similar to that used, for instance, under the EU directives to describe some of the EU arrangements, references to 'framework agreements' in this chapter of the book relate specifically to arrangements contemplated by the UNCITRAL Model Law (unless otherwise expressly indicated). The structure of the provisions and additional guidance concerning framework agreements is straight-forward. Thus, relevant definitions are provided at article 2(e) of the Model Law; conditions for use are set out at article 32, under Chapter II, Section 1 (Methods of procurement and their conditions for use); and the main 'package' of provisions concerning the procedures for framework agreements is provided for in Chapter VII (articles 58–63). Some other provisions throughout the Model Law refer explicitly to framework agreements. The regulation of the two stages of the various types of frameworks provides for a mix of 'general procurement' provisions, and 'framework-specific' provisions. For example, the first stage of *closed* framework agreements[31] is generally carried out via the 'general'/'standard' procurement methods envisaged by the Model Law in Chapters III–V (such as the open-tendering method), but these are supplemented by certain 'framework-specific' provisions in Chapter VII of the Model Law. The second stage of closed frameworks is mainly regulated by the 'framework-specific' provisions in Chapter VII. In contrast, both the first stage and second stage of *open* frameworks[32] are mainly regulated under Chapter VII of the Model Law, given the specific features of these arrangements.

A 'framework agreement procedure' is defined in the Model Law as a

> procedure conducted in two stages: a first stage to select a supplier (or suppliers) or a contractor (or contractors) to be a party (or parties) to a framework agreement with a procuring entity, and a second stage to award a procurement contract under the framework agreement to a supplier or contractor party to the framework agreement.[33]

---

[31] See below and sections 2.2.2 and 2.2.3.
[32] As to which see below and section 2.2.4.
[33] Art 2(e).

This is a descriptive definition, and the provisions of the Model Law cover both stages of the award procedure. In turn, a 'framework agreement' is defined as

> an agreement between the procuring entity and the selected supplier (or suppliers) or contractor (or contractors) concluded upon completion of the first stage of the framework agreement procedure.[34]

It is only the second stage that ends with the award of a 'procurement contract' (as defined further in article 2(k)), with the implication that all procedural safeguards provided by the Model Law also apply to the second stage of a framework agreement procedure, unless specifically provided otherwise. These include conditions applying to communication with suppliers, maintaining a record of the procurement, obligations relating to standstill periods as referred to in article 22, and subjecting the decisions taken in the second stage of the framework procedure to the challenge (review) proceedings in Chapter VIII of the Model Law.[35] This approach is particularly important since, as discussed in Chapter four of this book, the experience of the US federal procurement system shows that lack of oversight and control mechanisms during the second stage of ID/IQ contracts led in many cases to misuse or abuse of such closed 'framework' arrangements (protests being barred for many ID/IQ orders).

Three main types of framework agreements are envisaged under the Model Law: closed frameworks without second-stage competition, closed frameworks with second-stage competition, and open frameworks. In a closed framework, suppliers can only become a party thereto at the ('initial') time when the framework is set-up;[36] whereas in an open framework suppliers may also join later, 'in addition to the initial parties' to the framework.[37] In closed frameworks in which 'all terms and conditions of the procurement are established when the framework agreement is concluded' awarding contracts is contemplated without second-stage competition.[38] But in open frameworks and in multiple-supplier closed frameworks where 'certain terms and conditions of the procurement … cannot be established with sufficient precision when the framework agreement is concluded' such terms 'are to be established or refined through a second-stage competition'.[39] These main types of framework cover a wide range of possible arrangements as may be needed to deal with various procurement needs, contexts and markets.

Recognising that frameworks could be 'over-used or inappropriately used', affecting value for money, competition, transparency and integrity, the Model

---

[34] Art 2(e)(i).
[35] S Arrowsmith and C Nicholas, 'Regulating Framework Agreements under the UNCITRAL Model Law on Procurement' in S Arrowsmith (ed), *Reform of the UNCITRAL Model Law on Procurement: Procurement Regulation for the 21st Century* (Thomson Reuters/West, 2009) 95, 117–18.
[36] Art 2(e)(ii).
[37] Art 2(e)(iii).
[38] Art 2(e)(v).
[39] Art 2(e)(iv).

Law provisions were 'designed to facilitate only the appropriate and beneficial use of frameworks, discouraging their use when they are not appropriate'; they thus sought to avoid excessive constraints on use and/or undue inflexibility in procedures,[40] whilst comprehensive guidance on potential risks and ways to tackle them is provided in the Guide to Enactment. For instance, the 2011 Model Law provides that there should be a specific limitation in time of closed framework agreements (maximum duration),[41] to avoid a potential negative effect on competition, or complacency of suppliers within the framework. However, the Model Law does not provide for a specific maximum duration, this aspect being left for the states to consider and include in national legislation. But the Guide to Enactment elaborates on practical experience to date in various jurisdictions concerning the maximum duration of frameworks that usually is considered to allow for the benefits of frameworks to be achieved without improperly affecting competition.[42] Similarly, the Model Law does not require states to include provisions concerning guaranteed minimum and/or maximum quantities to be ordered under a framework agreement, or that the subject-matter of a framework agreement should be procured under that framework only, as ID/IQ contracts, or respectively, requirements contracts in the US federal procurement system do.[43] Nonetheless, the Guide to Enactment points out that where suppliers are aware of the commitments, better value for money is likely to be obtained, trading off for the increased inflexibility that such arrangements involve for the purchaser.[44]

Besides detailed rules concerning each type of framework, the Model Law provides for certain main controls that apply to *any* framework. It is thus provided that procurement contracts can be awarded during the second stage of a framework agreement only to suppliers who are party to the framework agreement, and that such awards will be made according to the terms and conditions of the framework.[45] Changing the description of the subject-matter of the procurement is prohibited throughout the duration of a framework, while other changes are possible but only to the extent expressly permitted under the framework agreement.[46] Detailed information concerning the operation of the framework agreement, including the manner in which contracts are to be awarded at second stage, must be pre-disclosed in the framework solicitation (at first stage), then carried forward into the framework agreement itself, and then (as applicable) into the second-stage invitation to present submissions.[47] This provides an essential

---

[40] ibid, 116.
[41] Art 59(1)(a).
[42] pp 264–65 (points 28–32).
[43] Chapter 4, sections 4.2.3–4.2.4 of this book.
[44] p 266 (point 35).
[45] Art 62(1)&(2).
[46] Art 63.
[47] Arts 58(d), 59(1)(d)(e)(f), and 62(4)(b) for closed frameworks; and arts 60(3)(e), 61(e)(f), and 62(4)(b) for open frameworks.

means for ensuring consistency throughout the duration of a framework across its two stages. Similar controls apply to the subject-matter of the procurement and other elements, such as terms of purchasing that can be refined at second stage, and the duration of the framework (where applicable).

2.2.1.2. *Conditions for Use of Framework Agreements under the Model Law*

Conditions for use of the three types of frameworks are jointly presented in the Model Law, in article 32(1). Thus, the basis for use will be the purchaser's determination that:

(a) The need ... is expected to arise on an indefinite *or* repeated basis during a given period of time; *or*

(b) By virtue of the nature of the subject matter of the procurement, the need ... may arise on an urgent basis during a given period of time (emphasis added).

Under article 32(2) the purchaser is required to record in the procurement file the reasons and circumstances justifying the use of a framework agreement procedure, *as well as* to justify the type of framework agreement selected. The Model Law does not provide specific conditions for use of particular types of frameworks but the Guide to Enactment provides some guidance in this respect. These determinations and decisions require a proper understanding of the purchaser's estimated requirement(s), of the potential response from the market, and its likely evolution over the duration envisaged for the framework. Regarding conditions for use of a framework agreement in general (as opposed to using 'traditional procurement'), neither the Model Law nor the Guide to Enactment, elaborate as to what 'is expected' in article 32(1)(a) of the Model Law means. Namely, the type of assessment required to substantiate the 'expectation' that the needs are to arise on an indefinite or regular basis is not clarified. The Guide to Enactment simply states that the term should be 'addressed' at the level of individual procurement systems through 'rules or guidance', and that the same should apply to 'how to assess in an *objective* manner ... the anticipated need' (emphasis added).[48]

A separate matter related to conditions in article 32(1)(a) of the Model Law concerns the 'indefinite *or* repeated' (emphasis added) nature of expected needs. This suggests that a framework agreement could be used both to address recurrent (and indefinite) needs, and also 'in view of a need that is expected to arise on an indefinite basis, but not necessarily on a repeated basis'.[49] In effect, the circumstance

---

[48] Guide to Enactment (n 12) p 260 (point 18). Objectivity is contemplated despite flexibility of conditions (point 3, 268–69).

[49] Ş Filipon, 'The Winding Road from Policy Objectives and Procedural Rules to Practical Reality – An Overview of Framework Agreements and Electronic Procurement under the New UNCITRAL Model Law', Section 2.3 (Paper prepared for the PPGR VI Conference, June 2013, Nottingham, UK).

could result in, or even be intended for, a framework agreement involving a single call-off. An 'indefinite' nature of anticipated needs, not attached to a 'recurrent' nature, goes beyond the 'classic' view on the 'remit' of framework agreements. This is considered a positive development to the extent that an appropriate decision-making process is in place at the level of the purchaser ensuring that the additional costs and complexity of the arrangement, compared to a 'traditional' purchasing method, are outweighed by the benefits of establishing some terms (and possibly commitment) in advance of materialisation of the need.[50] On the other hand, article 32(1)(b) of the Model Law refers to the use of frameworks for urgent procurement. The situation envisaged here is not that of establishing a framework when an emergency arises; it is that of pre-establishing a framework for items usually needed in urgent or crisis situations, enabling purchasers to make quick orders and supply arrangements when emergencies occur.[51] Using framework arrangements for urgent procurement inevitably involves anticipated needs of an indefinite and/or recurrent nature, and objectivity is thus requested for the assessment of the 'urgency' ground as well,[52] concerning at least the type and likelihood of emergencies to be addressed, and the selection of items needed to deal with that type of emergency.

The Guide to Enactment provides for an instrument to support decisions to embark on a 'framework agreement', rather than on 'traditional' procurement, from the perspective of costs involved in a framework arrangement procedure that are likely to be 'higher than those for one single-stage procurement'.[53] Thus, a cost-benefit analysis should be undertaken by the purchaser to assess whether the higher administrative costs of establishing and operating a framework agreement would be amortised or exceeded by the savings obtained through repeat purchases. When indefinite or urgent needs are contemplated, this type of cost-benefit analysis may be more difficult to undertake in a way that would ensure meaningful results, since it basically seeks to compare the additional administrative costs of a two-stage procedure, with benefits that might not be directly convertible into monetary/cost terms. In any event, the Guide to Enactment concludes that the purchaser 'will need to conduct a cost-benefit analysis based on probabilities before engaging in a framework agreement procedure'.[54] It might, however, be

---

[50] See also Guide to Enactment (n 12) 260–61 (point 18).

[51] Filipon, 'The Winding Road'. The subject of emergency procurement, including through 'advance mechanisms' such as framework agreements, in terms of both planning strategically for eventual crises and reacting to crises, in the context of the Model Law is addressed in detail in S Arrowsmith, 'The Approach to Emergency Procurement in the UNCITRAL Model Law: A Critical Appraisal in Light of the COVID-19 Pandemic' in S Arrowsmith et al (eds), *Public Procurement in (a) Crisis: Global Lessons from the Covid-19 Pandemic* (Oxford, Hart Publishing, 2021) 21.

[52] Guide to Enactment (n 12) notes that similar considerations should apply as for 'indefinite purchases', p 261 (point 19).

[53] ibid, p 269 (point 4).

[54] ibid.

over-optimistic to contemplate that any decision to proceed with a framework agreement rather than 'traditional' procurement, taken by any purchaser in any enacting state will be substantiated objectively with a proper cost-benefit analysis. If inclusion of such an analysis in the procurement record was intended,[55] it is unclear why the requirement is not provided for in the Model Law itself. Nevertheless, the mere fact that this tool is referred to in the Guide to Enactment suggests that the actual methodology for carrying out a cost-benefit analysis is left for enacting states to consider.

Another matter addressed to some extent in the Guide to Enactment concerns issues to consider when choosing among various types of framework agreements.[56] It is to be remembered that the Model Law itself does not include provisions in this connection. However, the Guide to Enactment specifies that 'the link between the type of framework … available and the type of framework … to be selected by a procuring entity should be explained in the rules or guidance' issued by an enacting state.[57] The Guide itself provides some background by stating that the 'circumstances of the procurement will determine whether the use of a framework … is appropriate and, if so, its structure, such as the type of framework agreement, the scope …, the number of supplier or contractor parties'.[58] It then concludes that:

> effective use of framework agreements procedures will require the procuring entity … to consider the type of framework agreement that is appropriate by reference to the complexity of the subject matter to be procured, its homogeneity or otherwise, and the manner in which competition is to be ensured.[59]

More specifically, the Guide starts from 'How narrowly the procurement can or should be determined at the first stage' which 'will dictate the extent of competition that is possible and appropriate at that stage', which then determines the extent of competition that will be appropriate at the second stage (if any).[60] The Guide also touches options between single- and multiple-supplier frameworks,[61] as well as the (conflicting) relationship between second-stage flexibility, administrative convenience and efficiency, security of supply, facilitating SMEs' participation in procurement, and/or obtaining better terms from aggregation of demand.[62]

---

[55] Guide to Enactment (n 12), p 270 (point 8).
[56] ibid, particularly pp 261–63 (points 21–24).
[57] ibid, p 261 (point 21).
[58] ibid, p 259 (point 15).
[59] ibid.
[60] p 261 (point 22).
[61] For a relevant perspective on this option, see also Chapter 4 of this book.
[62] The rationale for, and policy issues concerning, the use of different types of frameworks in general are extensively covered in S Arrowsmith, 'Framework Purchasing and Qualification Lists under the European Procurement Directives: Part I' (1999) 8 *PPLR* 115, 117–26.

On the other hand, no provision or recommendation in UNCITRAL instruments suggests that where the conditions for use are met a framework agreement must or should be pursued. However, some enacting states might consider such a step, should they trust their institutional capacity to a degree that would permit such an approach. Indeed, sound 'framework' decisions may require significant levels of professional and institutional capacity and, thus, capacity-building should be in place when introducing or updating rules on frameworks, as the Guide recommends.[63] Specific advisory/consulting services should also be used to 'tailor' the approach to a specific state and market. Consideration may be given by states with a more limited experience in procurement to a gradual introduction of the various forms of frameworks, for example, the introduction, at an initial stage, of open frameworks for purchasing commonly used items only, a possibility which the Guide to Enactment provides for expressly.[64] Once additional experience is gained, the state in question may consider introducing more novel techniques such as frameworks for indefinite or urgent procurements.

The justification for embarking on a framework agreement, as well as the justification of the selected type of framework, are to be made available to any person, on request, 'after the successful submission has been accepted or the procurement has been cancelled', under article 25(2) of the Model Law. Those justifications could be challenged under article 64, like any decision or action of a purchaser, although it is not entirely clear when and how this could be done, since articles 66 and 67 require acts/decisions to be challenged – in most cases – before or within standstill periods, ie *before* the successful submission has been accepted.[65] Nonetheless, the intention of the Model Law is that any decision or action of a purchaser should, at least in theory, be challengeable. The possibility to challenge, and for an independent body to review such a decision is likely to generate two main beneficial effects. First, the purchaser is encouraged to consider seriously the justifications it prepares before engaging in a framework procedure (a preventive effect). Second, the local independent review body (or relevant court) is to nuance and detail, via its case law, what is considered to be an acceptable justification.

2.2.1.3. *Challenge Proceedings*

2.2.1.3.1. General

As shown, by comparison to the 1994 Model Law, the 2011 Model Law has strengthened challenge proceedings in general and this also has specific effects concerning the control and review of both stages of framework agreements. Under the 2011 Model Law and the attending Guide to Enactment, an effective challenge

---

[63] Guide to Enactment (n 12) p 259 (point 15).
[64] ibid, p 257 (point 9).
[65] See further section 2.2.1.3.2 below.

proceedings system is viewed as an indispensable part of a functioning public procurement system, and it is not regarded as optional any longer. Its purpose is to avoid discretionary or abusive behaviour on the part of purchasers, in particular by: (i) enabling participants in a procurement process (in particular bidders), who have a direct interest in connection with the procurement proceedings, to challenge decisions or actions of the purchaser that are non-compliant with the applicable regulations and of nature to cause loss or injury; (ii) having the challenge reviewed by an independent body; (iii) having the possibility to appeal a first instance decision; and (iv) securing the possibility to have a final decision in a challenge proceeding enforced.

The main 'package' concerning challenge proceedings and remedies that may be sought or obtained by aggrieved bidders, is provided for in Chapter VIII of the 2011 Model Law (articles 64–69). Other provisions are also relevant for the challenge system, such as articles 22 and 23 concerning acceptance of successful submissions, notification of these decisions, standstill periods, entry into force of procurement contracts and contract award notices. In order to enable bidders to challenge purchaser's acts or decisions that are deemed non-compliant by the former, special attention has been given in the Model law to transparency issues, since bidders or potential bidders can only challenge procurement acts or decisions if they are aware of them in due time. A significant strengthening of 'contestability' has been brought by the 2011 Model Law through broadening the range of acts or decisions that can be challenged, basically to any act or decision of the procuring entity.[66] This approach has important implications for framework agreements (as is discussed later in this chapter).

In general, the improvements brought by the 2011 Model Law as regards challenge procedures can be summarised to three main issues. First, an application for 'reconsideration' by the purchaser of a decision or action of that purchaser is currently optional, and the decision arising from such reconsideration is appealable.[67] Secondly, any aggrieved bidder can have recourse to a review body that is independent from the purchaser,[68] thus ensuring an objective review of a challenge. Thirdly, any first instance resolution is to be appealable before a Court.[69] An important issue is that of standstill periods, or the compulsory delays between the notification to all bidders of the acceptance of a successful submission, and the actual conclusion of the procurement contract. This delay is aimed particularly at allowing for challenges to be lodged by unsuccessful bidders before a procurement contract is concluded, in case they consider the acceptance decision to be non-compliant with the applicable regulations, since the conclusion of a procurement contract might make potential remedial measures less effective or meaningful.

---

[66] Art 64(1).
[67] Arts 64, 66 and 67, and Guide to Enactment.
[68] Art 67.
[69] Art 64(2) and (3).

A certain degree of discretion is allowed to the purchaser to proceed to contract-ing without a standstill period where it determines that 'urgent public interest considerations' so require.[70] The actual duration of standstill periods is left for purchasers to establish on a 'procurement-by-procurement basis', observing however the minimum durations established by enacting states in their own legislation.[71] The 2011 Model Law also provides a wide range of pre-award remedial and interim measures, such as suspension, set-aside, damages, and other measures for an effective remedial system. However, as shown, post-award measures are more limited and provided in the Model Law as options.

2.2.1.3.2. Applicability to Frameworks

Under the 2011 Model Law the full system of challenge proceedings *does* apply to both stages of a framework agreement procedure, with very limited exceptions. Of particular relevance is the application of challenge proceedings and safeguards to the second stage of framework agreement procedures, mainly where competi-tion is involved. In other public procurement systems this approach is either not thoroughly articulated,[72] or explicitly repudiated by a legal 'ban' on 'delivery or task order protests'.[73] Traditionally, the second stage of a framework arrangement may in many cases be characterised by lack of transparency (eg, award criteria for call-offs not included in the 'umbrella' arrangement, lack of notifications on successful submissions or awards, etc). This limits to a significant degree poten-tial challenges, and might thus encourage non-competitive, abusive or corrupt behaviour. In this context, while acknowledging that balancing procurement efficiency with transparency and contestability is undoubtedly a complex task, it is submitted that the application of full transparency and challenge proceed-ings to the second stage of a framework agreement, with relevant safeguards and some potential adaptations to specific circumstances, is a major step ahead. It encourages a beneficial use of frameworks, that promotes the advantages and that avoids, to the extent possible, the potential risks of improperly using this method of procurement.

In this direction, the legal 'construction' of the Model Law provisions is articulated in a number of general provisions and specific reconfirmations. As shown, article 2(k) of the Model Law defines a procurement contract as 'a contract concluded between the procuring entity and a supplier ... at the end of the procurement proceedings'. Specifically, article 2(e) states that the purpose of the *second* stage of a framework agreement is 'to award a procurement contract'.

---

[70] Art 22(3)(c). In this case, challenges could still be lodged, including against the decision to proceed without a standstill period, under art 67(2)(ii), but remedial action will be considered or taken in the circumstances of an existing procurement contract.
[71] Guide to Enactment (n 12), p 115 (points 11 and 12).
[72] eg EU system (Chapter 5 of this book).
[73] See US chapter, ID/IQ contracts (Chapter 4, section 4.2.4 of this book).

A framework agreement procedure is classified as a method of procurement under article 27(2), whereas article 62 regulates in detail the 'second stage of a framework agreement procedure'. These provisions clearly emphasise that under the Model Law, framework agreements are deemed to be *methods of procurement* (specific procurement procedures) and not forms of procurement contracts.[74] Under article 64(1) any decision or action of the purchaser may be challenged, which, by implication, means decisions or actions during the first or second stage of a framework agreement procedure.

Other provisions refer specifically to how challenge proceedings apply to either or both stages of a framework agreement. Thus, article 65(1) provides that 'The procuring entity shall not take any step that would bring into force a procurement contract or a framework agreement' where it is informed that a challenge has been lodged. This reconfirms that the prohibition on entering a framework agreement or contract applies to both stages of a framework agreement procedure. Further, articles 58(3) and 62(3) make it clear that notification concerning successful submissions and standstill periods apply in principle to both the first and the second stage of a framework agreement procedure. However, article 22(3) provides that such notification and standstill periods shall not apply, among other limited situations, to the award of procurement contracts 'under a framework agreement procedure without second stage competition'. *Per a contrario* this means that standstill periods *shall* apply to the award of procurement contracts (exceeding the relevant threshold amount) under framework agreement procedures that *do* involve second-stage competition, which is actually explicitly confirmed in article 62(4)(d). Still, exempting all awards without second-stage competition (above the threshold) from such requirements may not be justified in multiple-supplier frameworks[75] (as allocation of work amongst framework suppliers occurs upon such awards) and could weaken oversight and enforcement, in particular where post-award remedies are unsubstantial, since framework contractors are likely to learn about an award after the entry into force of that contract.[76] On the other hand, the exemption from standstill periods in light of 'urgent public interest considerations'[77] that may apply to awards under frameworks with second-stage competition certainly provides some needed flexibility, for instance in case of unfolding of crises or catastrophes or dealing with their aftermath.[78] A more nuanced approach could provide an option

---

[74] As some states consider(ed), for example France and the US. By taking this approach the second stage of awarding tasks based on the framework arrangement could fall into the contract management area, and thus would not be subject to the transparency and challenge proceedings inherent to procurement procedures.

[75] eg Nicholas and Arrowsmith, 'The Challenges of Contructing a Supplier Review Mechanism' (n 27), p 171.

[76] From the notice under art 22(10) or award notice under art 23.

[77] Art 22(3)(c).

[78] Further on interaction between speed of supply and contestability in urgent procurement, see Nicholas and Arrowsmith (n 27).

to states (or purchasers) between observing standstill and the potential setting aside of the contract (if there have been breaches in its award), irrespective of urgency, as in the EU directives and in the UK,[79] but this would require a thorough and nuanced post-award remedies system, as well as (significant) capacity of contracting teams and review fora.

Another aspect of interaction between 'transparency' over certain decisions and contestability, as pointed out at section 2.2.1.2 above, relates to challenges against decisions to proceed to a framework agreement and/or against the type of framework chosen. Under article 25(2) the purchaser's justification concerning these decisions 'shall, on request, be made available to any person after the successful submission has been accepted or the procurement has been cancelled.'

This is all too late, since the information in the justification is essential for such a challenge and the time-limits provided for lodging a complaint expire in most cases *before* acceptance of the successful submission.[80] The delay in permitting access to justifications limits drastically the ability to challenge 'framework decisions', which appears to be against the intention of the Model Law. In reality, the appropriate time to challenge 'framework decisions' is as early as possible during the process, so that as little time and effort as possible is spent on an award procedure that might in the end be cancelled (if the decision is found as unjustified by the review body). This could be easily achieved, for example by requiring explicitly that the justification be included in the solicitation and/or solicitation document, thus permitting challenges, as generally intended under the Model Law, 'before the deadline for presenting submissions' under articles 66(2) and 67(2)(a). Alternatively, access to certain aspects of the procurement record under article 25, such as 'framework justifications', could be allowed at any time. In any event, a solution should be sought, since the issue seems wider, affecting in a similar way justifications for using procurement procedures other than open tender, and not just 'framework decisions'.

2.2.2. Closed Framework Agreements without Second-Stage Competition

2.2.2.1. *Definition and Sub-Types*

The 2011 Model Law defines a 'Closed framework agreement' as a 'framework agreement to which no supplier or contractor that is not initially a party to the framework agreement may subsequently become a party'.[81] It further defines the

---

[79] Chapter 5, sections 5.3.2.5 and 5.3.3.4 of this book.
[80] Arts 66(2) and 67(2) in conjunction with art 22(4).
[81] Art 2(e)(ii).

'Framework agreement procedure without second-stage competition' as a 'procedure under a closed framework agreement in which all terms and conditions of
the procurement are established when the framework agreement is concluded'.[82]
By aggregating the two texts of the Model Law, a comprehensive definition of
closed framework agreement without second-stage competition arises. A distinction should be made, though, between setting terms and conditions at the first
stage of a framework and concretising obligations that arise at second stage. If
'all terms and conditions' in the definition above were to be interpreted under
a narrow and literal vision to include for example firm quantities and deliveries
being established when the arrangement is concluded, then a second stage of the
arrangement would be neither required nor justified. Whilst frameworks establishing all terms lean closest to 'traditional' procurement,[83] they tend to involve
some 'non-core' aspect of uncertainty. They can be concluded with one, or more
suppliers. It is the only type of framework under the 2011 Model Law that can be
concluded with a single supplier. This means that single-supplier frameworks must
always establish all terms, which provides less flexibility but possibly additional
control against misuse. The Model Law does not limit sub-types of frameworks.[84]
Thus, a framework without second-stage competition could involve a minimum
quantity guaranteed, a minimum or a maximum, or neither of these, and could
commit, or otherwise, either or both parties. The guidance addresses briefly when
such features could be useful.

2.2.2.2. Selecting This Type

Justifying this type of arrangement could be challenging, irrespective of whether it
involves a single- or multi-supplier arrangement. Where almost all characteristics
of a procurement requirement are known and fully specifiable at the time when
the procurement procedure is started – except for a few non-core ones that may be
established in detail/concretised after the framework agreement is in place (such
as the precise timing, location, or quantities for deliveries)[85] – then a purchaser
may have good reasons to consider using a closed framework agreement without
second-stage competition. In this connection, the Guide to Enactment states:

> If precise specification of the procurement needs is possible and if they will not vary
> during the life of the framework agreement, a framework agreement without second
> stage competition … will maximize competition at first stage and should produce best
> offers.[86]

---

[82] Art 2(e)(v).

[83] Or could even overlap to some extent.

[84] Other than what may result from the rules concerning their establishment/operation.

[85] Within certain limits or ranges provided for in the solicitation (and the framework). Where no
(rather tight) limits or ranges can be established in the solicitation for such 'non-core terms', a framework agreement with second-stage competition may be preferable.

[86] Guide to Enactment (n 12) p 261 (point 22).

Because there is no reopening of competition at the second stage and all terms have been established when the framework was concluded, this type of arrangement offers most administrative convenience at that stage, namely less complex ordering procedures and shortest lead-times, which also make it desirable (from this perspective) in urgent or emergency situations.

However, frameworks without second-stage competition present some disadvantages in certain circumstances. The Guide to Enactment explains that

> this approach is inflexible and requires precise planning: rigid standardization may be difficult or inappropriate, especially in the context of centralized purchasing where the needs of individual purchasing entities may vary, where refinement of requirements may be appropriate so needs are expressed with lesser precision at first stage, and in uncertain markets (such as future emergency procurement).[87]

Further, where 'the procuring entity's needs may not vary, but the market is dynamic or volatile, second-stage competition will be appropriate unless the volatility is addressed in the framework agreement (such as through a price adjustment mechanism)'.[88] The risk of the purchaser remaining stuck with terms that no longer reflect the market and/or even its own needs could be higher for this type of framework, in comparison to frameworks that involve reopening of competition at the second stage. Similarly, while a purchaser's commitment to buy all of his relevant requirements, or part thereof, or a certain quantity, under the arrangement, is likely to result in better terms (aggregate discounts), such commitment could also exacerbate negative consequences for the purchaser, where it exceeds actual needs or does not reflect evolving needs.[89]

Another decision that needs to be made by a purchaser and justified under article 32(2) of the Model Law is whether the framework will be with one or with more suppliers. Where individual suppliers present in the market are likely to be able to meet each individual delivery (order), as well as all deliveries (orders) expected under the framework agreement, then consideration should be given to a single-supplier framework for the reasons of savings from aggregation of demand, as well as for administrative convenience in, and potentially reduced costs of, managing the framework. If there is doubt as to whether potential suppliers would have such capacity or interest (ie, each to provide on its own all requirements under the framework), then the purchaser may like to consider a multi-supplier arrangement for increased security of supply. The decision to proceed with a multi-supplier arrangement may also be determined by other considerations. The main reasons are discussed by Arrowsmith[90] and some of them could be particularly relevant for frameworks establishing all terms. Thus, 'Where the nature of

---

[87] ibid, pp 261–62 (point 22).

[88] ibid, p 262 (point 22).

[89] ie, having to procure things that are not needed, or suffer contractual consequences (such as paying damages) for failing to order committed quantities.

[90] Arrowsmith, 'Framework Purchasing and Qualification Lists' (Part I) (n 62) 122–26.

the order varies on each occasion, which bid offers the best value for money for a particular order may also vary, according to the precise nature of the order.[91] This could be the case, for example, where the specifications and needed terms applicable to the various items to be procured under the framework are known at the time of its conclusion, but the quantities that will be needed of each item (for each delivery) are not known in advance. Since the unitary prices offered by various suppliers for each item could vary, the framework contractor offering best value for individual orders could also vary. A similar situation could be where delivery locations are not known in advance with precision for various quantities of items to be ordered and delivery to each individual location is costed separately by suppliers when establishing the framework. Socio-economic considerations, such as promoting SMEs, if applicable under the relevant national regulations, could be another reason for choosing a multiple-supplier framework. SMEs might be able to compete for and deliver smaller orders under a framework agreement. These considerations are also referred to in the Guide to Enactment, in the context of 'bundling'.[92] As is discussed in Chapter four, decisions between single- and multiple-supplier framework 'arrangements' receive a thorough but specific approach under the US federal regulations.[93] Thus, inspiration for other potentially relevant aspects in the use of either type could be identified there, though any such aspect would need to be analysed in the specific US federal context and only then considered, mutatis mutandis, if appropriate, in other contexts.

On the other hand, because in closed framework agreements suppliers that are not a party to such an arrangement may not bid (or be considered) for requirements procured under it during its duration, the issue of a limitation of competition may arise. This is particularly the case if too large a share of the relevant market is reserved under a closed framework for too long a period. The issue could appear prima facie less problematic for closed frameworks without second-stage competition. It might be argued that, since this type of arrangement involves full competition at the first stage, there is not much difference from 'traditional' procurement, particularly as regards single-supplier frameworks. But caution should be exercised in light of the natural tendency toward aggregation of requirements for longer periods of time under frameworks, stemming from the recurrent or indefinite nature of requirements. Market research and the review of expected needs conducted prior to starting a framework procedure should inform a wide range of decisions concerning the procurement(s) in question, such as the duration of the framework, or the number of framework suppliers.[94] The potential anti-competitive effect should be borne in mind when making these decisions,

---

[91] ibid, 123–25.
[92] Guide to Enactment (n 12) p 262 (point 23).
[93] Chapter 4, sections 4.2.3 and 4.2.4 of this book.
[94] See Guide to Enactment (n 12), p 259 (point 15), p 273 (point 11), and p 274 (point 12).

whether or not under a particular procurement system justification for them is required.[95]

2.2.2.3. Procedures

2.2.2.3.1. First-Stage Procedures

Article 58 of the Model Law provides that closed framework agreements, with or without second-stage competition, must be established via the open tendering method or, exceptionally and where justified, via the other procurement methods referred to in Chapters II, IV, and V of the Model Law. Nicholas[96] makes an analysis of procurement methods, other than open tendering, that might be employed for establishing a closed framework agreement, concluding that in most cases procurement methods other than open tendering are likely to be inappropriate, particularly as regards closed frameworks with second-stage competition. For instance, a dialogue-based method to establish a framework could be difficult to conceive since highly complex items 'are unlikely to be repeated purchases'; while single-source or competitive negotiations on the basis of *urgency* may be at odds with the idea of a two-stage procedure such as that involved in frameworks.[97] Nicholas acknowledges though that using some of the procurement methods other than open tendering during the first stage of a framework agreement is more likely to be justified, depending on circumstances, in the case of some closed frameworks without second-stage competition, since such arrangements would be more similar to 'traditional' or 'classic' procurement. Thus, the procurement method to be employed during the first stage of a (closed) framework exercise would usually be open tendering, whereas other procurement methods under the Model Law may only be used as an exception justified by specific circumstances, if the conditions provided for under the Model Law are met. The use of such other procurement methods will need to be justified under article 25(e) of the Model Law, separately from, and additionally to, the justification of the use of a framework agreement, and of the type of framework agreement selected, as required by articles 32(2) and 25(g) of the Model Law.

The provisions of the Model Law concerning the 'general' procurement methods, including the contents of the solicitation, shall apply mutatis mutandis to the first stage of a closed framework agreement, and these shall be supplemented by the specific provisions in articles 58(2) and 59. Thus, the solicitation will have

---

[95] eg even where the duration contemplated does not exceed the general maximum provided by an applicable regulation.

[96] C Nicolas, 'A Critical Evaluation of the Revised UNCITRAL Model Law Provisions on Regulating Framework Agreements' (2012) 21 *PPLR* 19, 39–40. See also GL Albano and C Nicholas, *The Law and Economics of Framework Agreements: Designing Flexible Soluctions for Public Procurement* (Cambridge, CUP, 2016) 118.

[97] Though such configurations might be conceived when dealing with the aftermath of a crisis (see Arrowsmith, 'The Approach to Emergency Procurement' (n 51) 29).

to specify: (i) that a framework agreement procedure is involved, leading to the award of a closed framework agreement without second-stage competition; (ii) whether the framework will be concluded with one or more suppliers, and any minimum or maximum number of suppliers that will become parties to the framework;[98] (iii) the duration of the framework agreement;[99] (iv) the description of the subject-matter of the framework, and of all other terms and conditions established when the framework is concluded; (v) whether the award of orders at the second stage will be to the lowest-priced or most advantageous submission and the manner in which the procurement contract(s) will be awarded;[100] and (vi) all further information necessary for the effective operation of the framework agreement in question, as applicable. The specific information required to be included is aimed, on the one hand, at enabling bidders to make substantive decisions as to their interest and/or capacity to participate in the procurement as well as to prepare meaningful offers and, on the other hand, at providing controls and safeguards against potential misuse or abuse of the framework by the purchaser. All information that is relevant to the implementation of the framework, resulting from conducting the first stage, is to be carried forward and recorded in writing into the actual framework. This contributes significantly to ensuring consistency between the two stages, ie, so that what is achieved at first stage is not defeated at the second.

For avoidance of doubt, article 58(3) clarifies that article 22, concerning the notification of the successful bidders and standstill periods, does apply mutatis mutandis to the award of a closed framework agreement. This provision was necessary since article 22 mainly refers to procurement contracts, whilst a framework agreement is not considered to be a procurement contract under the Model Law.

2.2.2.3.2. Second-Stage Procedures

Choosing a Framework Supplier to Perform an Order
A clear rule deriving from the definition of a framework agreement procedure and applicable to all types of framework is that:

> A procurement contract under a framework agreement may be awarded only to a supplier or contractor that is a party to the framework agreement.[101]

---

[98] Setting a low maximum number of suppliers to be admitted on a framework is likely to stimulate competition at first stage and encourage better value offers. Also, specifying the expected number of suppliers may discourage uncompetitive firms from submitting offers. For example, my practical experience includes involvement as a member of an evaluation committee, where the solicitation did not state the number of firms that were to be allowed onto the framework. Over 20 submissions were received, but less than five were actually considered technically responsive such as to enter the framework.

[99] That must not exceed the maximum duration provided for the national legislation of the enacting state.

[100] See section 2.2.2.3.2.

[101] Art 62(2) of the Model Law.

However, the provisions of the Model Law and guidance concerning allocation of orders among framework contractors under closed multiple-supplier frameworks without second-stage competition – ie choosing a framework supplier for each individual order – are very limited. This is a weakness. Enacting states might like or should be encouraged to clarify and detail the matter if they choose to recognise and permit this type of framework. In my view, whilst objective conditions for allocating 'work' among framework contractors *are* required by the Model Law, they ought to be turned into much more visible requirements and clearly detailed options. These should be in direct relation to the circumstances that determined selection of this type of framework in the first place.[102]

Article 58(2) in conjunction with article 59(1)(e) and (f) require that 'the manner in which the procurement contract will be awarded' and whether that award 'will be to the lowest-priced or the most advantageous submission' must be predetermined from the first stage and 'provided to suppliers when first soliciting their participation … at that stage'. These provisions have a number of implications. First, rightly, purchasers are denied full discretion to allocate orders once a framework is concluded, which could easily result in favouritism, and affect 'fair, equal and equitable treatment'[103] or value. Second, a 'rotation' system, where each individual supplier within the framework is in turn awarded orders, consecutively, as individual needs arise (for example in the alphabetical order of the name of suppliers), also *seems* to be denied by the Model Law. Indeed, such an allocation manner seems unlikely to take account of 'the lowest-priced or the most advantageous submission'. It could also be easily abused by placing larger orders with favoured suppliers, or larger orders could just happen to go to suppliers that did not offer the best terms for that call-off. But a configuration where each of the framework suppliers is guaranteed individually a certain quantity of items to be procured under the framework, along with the supplier's commitment to supply such quantities, could be less problematic, facilitating security of supply at agreed prices without affecting overall value under the framework. It would, however, be essential under such configuration that, where quantities guaranteed individually take the form of a minimum rather than fixed quantity, any orders after satisfying those minima be placed using methods taking account of the best terms offered, in lieu of 'aleatory' methods. Anyhow, the position concerning 'rotation' is not fully clear in the UNCITRAL instruments,[104] and if contemplated by enacting states it should be carefully considered and detailed.

---

[102] See section 2.2.2.2 above.

[103] See Preamble to the Model Law, letter (d).

[104] See for instance Guide to Enactment (n 12), p 280 (point 14), p 284 (point 7). Also, it is worth pointing out that, while permitting 'criteria and rules … not limited solely to those that normally apply to choosing between tenders' (like rotation) might have been contemplated at some point, this option does not appear to have made its way properly into the Model Law (quoted text is from Arrowsmith and Nicholas 'Regulating Framework Agreements' (n 35), p 127). On the other hand, rotation seems to be ruled out by Albano and Nicholas, *The Law and Economics of Framework Agreements* (n 96) p 118 and fn 149.

The economy of the published text of the Model Law suggests that the main method contemplated for allocating orders under frameworks without second-stage competition is by taking account of the best terms offered. One option may be for each call-off to be allocated in the order of the ranking of the submissions, as resulting from their assessment at the first stage of the framework procedure, subject to the availability of the supplier. When an order is to be placed, availability is checked with the bidder whose submission was ranked first. If this supplier is available to supply then the order goes to him. If this bidder is not available, the availability of the bidder that submitted the second ranked submission is checked and, if available, the order will be placed with this bidder, and so on ('cascading' in the order of ranking). This system could be appropriate where there is a significant level of homogeneity and consistency of requirements among orders, security of supply is sought, and a single supplier might not be able to fulfil any and all orders. This method might in the end mean that all orders under a framework agreement will be awarded to the same supplier, if the highest ranked bidder is capable and available to supply them. But the approach allows a bidder to participate in the framework agreement even if he may not able to meet certain orders. At the same time, it can offer the purchaser an optimal combination of security of supply *and* value for money.

However, this approach presents the risk that orders would be placed in the order of priority of the best terms offered by suppliers in light of requirements *estimated* overall for the framework at the first stage. In many cases these may not coincide with best terms for the *actual* orders placed, in particular where 'the nature of the order varies on each occasion',[105] such as where the combinations of items and the quantities for orders are not known at the first stage and unit prices offered by various suppliers vary. In this case it is thus preferable, or even strongly advised, for orders to be placed by applying the terms offered by suppliers at the first stage to the *specific* requirements of each order. It is submitted that this is the main allocation method contemplated by the Model Law. It is not trouble-free though, and enacting states need to circumstantiate it. The main issue it raises is the *criteria* that are to be used when applying the terms offered at the first stage to the specific requirements of an order. In this connection the Guide to Enactment states: 'The basis of the award will normally, but need not necessarily, be the same as for the first stage'.[106] The example it then gives concerning the use of a different basis for award seems to relate to frameworks involving second-stage competition, but this should not exclude those without such competition.

The application of the same criterion/a as for the first stage is likely to be uncontentious, whether it involves award to the lowest-priced or the most advantageous submission (ie price and other award criteria, as provided for the evaluation of 'tenders' under articles 10 and 11 of the Model Law). This approach is likely to be

---

[105] Arrowsmith (n 62) 123–25 (see section 2.2.2.2 above).
[106] Guide to Enactment (n 12) p 280 (point 14).

appropriate for straight-forward frameworks with significant levels of consistency among orders (and between the original estimation and actual orders). Similarly, it is likely to make sense in many cases to select framework contractors on the basis of most advantageous submissions (cost and quality), and to then place orders at the second stage, among framework suppliers, on the basis of the lowest-price submission as applied to the specific requirements of the order in question. This approach could provide appropriate value where 'the nature of the order varies on each occasion'[107] (within the 'parameters' originally set). Potentially more problematic seem to be the situations where the criterion at the first stage would have been the lowest price, whereas orders would be placed (at the second stage) by using a combination of factors, since the lowest-price criterion at first stage might have rejected submission(s) that could then best meet the other criteria to be used at the second stage. Some situations can also be problematic where a certain set of criteria is used to determine the most advantageous submissions at the first stage, and a different set and/or different weightings are employed to determine the most advantageous submissions at call-off stage, for similar reasons as above. It might also be possible to use different criteria and/or weightings for different orders under the same framework, if objective conditions for determining which criteria/weightings apply to each order (eg the quantity or value of an order) are pre-disclosed from the initiation of the first stage.[108] In all such cases sound commercial judgement needs to be exercised at the level of the purchaser since incongruent or conflicting criteria between the two stages of a framework procedure could defeat the very objectives of a framework.[109]

In any event, the requirement in article 59(1)(e) – that the framework (and the solicitation for it) must specify whether the award of contracts at the second stage 'will be to the lowest-priced or to the most advantageous submission' – cannot suffice. The criteria and weightings should also be pre-disclosed, as is currently required (only) for frameworks with second-stage competition in article 59(1)(d)(iii) of the Model Law. In light of potential complexities, enacting states should consider whether to limit the use of certain 'configurations' of framework without second-stage competition, as well as supplement the rules with additional safeguards as discussed here.[110]

---

[107] See text to n 105.

[108] It should, however, be noted that some room for 'maneuvering' orders may occur and thus specific monitoring/oversight may be needed.

[109] See relevant discussion in an EU context in S Arrowsmith, 'Methods for Purchasing On-Going Requirements: The System of Framework Agreements and Dynamic Purchasing Systems under the EC Directives and UK Public Procurement Regulations' in S Arrowsmith (ed), *Reform of the UNCITRAL Model Law on Procurement: Procurement Regulation for the 21st Century* (Thomson Reuters/West, 2009) 131, 171.

[110] Variation of weightings among specified ranges should probably be precluded in all cases in frameworks without second-stage competition, since this seems inconsistent with the idea of a framework that 'establishes all terms and conditions'.

Transparency

Under frameworks without reopening of competition, there is no requirement for the purchaser to notify framework suppliers of its intention to award an upcoming order, for example prior to initiating assessment of first-stage submissions with regard to that order. Article 62 of the Model Law regulates the 'Second stage of a framework agreement procedure' jointly for all types of frameworks. It comprises just one specific provision concerning frameworks without second-stage competition. This is found in paragraph (3) providing that the acceptance of a successful submission will follow the process and notification described in article 22, but that paragraph (2) thereto will not apply. Thus, no standstill periods apply to the award of procurement contracts under framework agreements without second-stage competition. Also, once a 'successful submission' is established by the purchaser for an order, the purchaser need not notify the other framework suppliers about its determination or the reasons therefor. Instead, the purchaser simply proceeds to 'dispatch the notice of acceptance of the successful submission to the supplier ... that presented that submission' under article 22(4). Then, once contract conclusion formalities are complete, the purchaser gives notice of the contract 'to other suppliers' under article 22(10). In addition, under article 23 of the Model Law, the publication of award notices is compulsory for all procurement contracts, including those awarded under frameworks without second-stage competition. For under the threshold contracts, award notices are to be published cumulatively from time to time, at least annually.[111]

2.2.2.4. Challenges

It follows from the section above that the ordering process under a framework without second-stage competition remains internal to the purchaser up to the time of informing the successful supplier, and unknown to 'fellow' framework suppliers until the awarded contract is concluded and in force. This means that challenges concerning second-stage awards can only be lodged after the conclusion of the contract, since aggrieved parties would have been unaware that an award was intended prior to that point.

Thus, only post-award remedies may be available, such as cancellation of the contract or damages, and remedial action could be more difficult and less efficient, in particular where, by the time the challenge is settled, the contract has already been executed; or, as shown, where the post-award remedial system is unsubstantial.[112] Enacting states should consider strengthening the challenge system, for instance by providing for standstill periods for order award decisions (including under frameworks without second-stage competition), with an option

---

[111] Art 23(2).
[112] Section 2.2.1.3.2 above.

for exemption from standstill where setting aside of the resulting contract is avail-able under post-award remedies.[113] However, even as it currently stands, namely without potential strengthening discussed above, the UNCITRAL provision offers better transparency than, for instance, the EU directives.[114] In the case of more complex configurations of framework, or based on risk assessment, enacting states may like to consider supplementing their legal review system with ex-ante or ex-post verifications or audits, in particular where breaches of law may more easily pass unnoticed by framework suppliers,[115] or there could be little interest in challenging.

2.2.3. Closed Framework Agreements with Second-Stage Competition

2.2.3.1. Definition and Sub-Types

A closed framework agreement is defined in the Model Law as 'a framework agreement to which no supplier … that is not initially a party to the framework agreement may subsequently become a party'.[116] Article 2(e)(iv) of the Model Law defines a framework agreement procedure without second-stage competition as

> a procedure under an open framework agreement or a closed framework agreement with more than one supplier … in which certain terms and conditions of the procurement that cannot be established with sufficient precision when the framework agreement is concluded are to be established or refined through a second-stage competition.

By aggregating the two definitions, a comprehensive definition of closed frame-work agreements with second-stage competition arises. As for frameworks without second-stage competition, the Model Law does not limit sub-types of frameworks.[117] However, enforcing framework suppliers' commitments to supply (where applicable) could be more difficult since framework suppliers may either not attend second-stage competition, or may present unattractive submissions.

On the other hand, the definition itself outlines two 'sub-types' of frameworks with second-stage competition: one in which at the first stage some terms are not established with precision, but are established within certain limits or param-eters, and are to be established with precision at the second stage; and another one in which some terms are not established *at all* at first stage, and are to be (fully) established at second stage only. The latter sub-type may present additional

---

[113] See eg wider discussion in Nicholas and Arrowsmith (n 27) 164–65, 169–71. I suggest considera-tion might also be given to including reduced standstill periods for awards under frameworks without second-stage competition (ie, shorter than those applicable to the other types of awards), since in this case challenges should be straight-forward.

[114] See Chapter 5, sections 5.3.2.4–5.3.2.5 of this book.

[115] See eg text to n 108.

[116] Art 2(e)(ii).

[117] See section 2.2.2.1 and n 84 above.

flexibility, but also higher risks, since there would be no pre-established limits for the terms not established at first stage, whereas competition is limited to the framework suppliers at second stage. Thus, additional caution is advised for this sub-type.[118]

2.2.3.2. *Selecting This Type, and Level of Competition at Each Stage*

The definitions in article 2(e) of the Model Law might suggest that reopening of competition at the second stage is not possible under frameworks that establish all terms with precision. It is submitted that this would be an unnecessary limitation.[119] Even where all terms are established at the first stage, a purchaser may for example contemplate that even better terms could be obtained for (very) large orders though there might be no guarantee that such large 'one-off' needs would actually materialise. In this case the purchaser may like to reserve the right to reopen competition for orders above a certain volume/value.

Closed framework agreements with second-stage competition represent one more step further away from 'traditional' procurement. First, the subject-matter of the procurement need not be fully specified when initiating the award procedure for the framework. Second, not all terms and conditions are to be fully established during the first stage of the procedure, some of them being refined or established during the second stage. Submissions presented during the first stage of the procedure are not final[120] by reference to the actual procurement contract(s) that will be concluded during the second stage. Thus, first-stage submissions and their evaluation is used for selecting the framework suppliers and for establishing certain terms and conditions for the actual contract(s) but not all and/or not all with precision. Third, the second-stage competition is reopened among framework suppliers, in order to establish the 'best value' offer for each individual order, and to refine or establish terms that were not 'finalised' during the first stage. It can be noticed that closed framework agreements with second-stage competition provide increased flexibility for the purchaser and better chances of meeting specific needs that cannot be fully anticipated in every detail at the time when the framework is initiated. The potential for 'late customisation' of requirements makes this type of framework more amenable to be used as 'multi-agency' or multiple-user arrangements. On the other hand, closed framework agreements with second-stage competition offer a means for some adaptation of terms to dynamic or volatile markets.[121] Thus, they could be useful where 'It may not be possible when the

---

[118] See collusion risks at section 2.2.3.3.2 below.

[119] The EU 2014 Public Sector Directive explicitly provides for the possibility to reopen competition where all terms are established at the first stage, subject to pre-disclosing this together with the objective criteria determining whether or not competition reopens for an order.

[120] And could be partial where some terms are not established at all at the first stage.

[121] Guide to Enactment (n 12) 262 (point 22).

basic terms and conditions are agreed, to know who will be able to make the most advantageous bid at the precise time the order is placed'.[122] Specific examples could include 'information technology products', where 'regular changes occur not just in relation to price but also … to quality', some 'professional services' and 'business consulting services'.[123]

However, the additional flexibility brought by this type of framework comes at the 'cost' of second-stage convenience. Reopening competition means that ordering is a more complex process and requires more time than in the case of frameworks without second-stage competition. The higher the number of terms being left to be refined or established at the second stage, and the higher the number of suppliers admitted onto the framework, the 'heavier' the second-stage process is likely to be.[124] Where requirements (and terms) can be defined from the beginning in quite some detail, increasing the competition at the first stage by allowing a rather limited (small) number of framework suppliers may encourage the receipt of good value and meaningful submissions, since suppliers will see more opportunities of business at the second stage as there will not be many competitors at that stage. If, during the second stage, suppliers are required to present enhanced offers for the specific features of each individual order, in a further competitive exercise among framework suppliers, then good value and terms that are in accordance with prevailing market conditions are likely to be obtained. Nonetheless, the number of framework suppliers should not be too low, either, in order to allow for a meaningful competition at the second stage.[125]

When (only) a less detailed description of future procurement requirements and applicable terms is possible at the first stage, it appears more sensible to enhance competition at the second stage by allowing higher numbers of framework suppliers to join the framework. Insufficient details available during the first stage could mean that first-stage submissions may not be fully relevant to the actual orders. Care needs to be exercised since very loose terms and very broad descriptions of requirements at the first stage may well result in an irrelevant selection of framework suppliers.

2.2.3.3. *Procedures*

2.2.3.3.1. First-Stage Procedures

The first stage of a closed framework agreement procedure with second-stage competition is to some extent similar to that of a closed framework agreement without second-stage competition. It will usually be required to follow the open tendering procedure, whilst the use of the other award procedures (provided by

---

[122] Arrowsmith (n 62) 122–23.
[123] ibid.
[124] n 121.
[125] See also collusion risks at section 2.2.3.3.2 below.

the Model Law) is only permitted exceptionally if the conditions for the use of those procedures are met. In comparison to 'traditional' purchasing, additional information will need to be included in the solicitation and in the framework agreement itself (articles 58 and 59 of the Model Law). Such information is similar to that required for frameworks without second-stage competition,[126] except for stating that the procurement will be conducted as a closed framework agreement with second-stage competition, *and* subject to including supplementary information provided for specifically for this type of framework under article 59(1)(d).

Thus, the following shall be specified: '[a] statement of the terms and conditions of the procurement that are to be established or refined through second-stage competition';[127] the procedures for and anticipated frequency of 'any second-stage competition, and envisaged time-limits for presenting second-stage submissions';[128] '[t]he procedures and criteria to be applied during the second-stage competition, including the relative weight of such criteria and the manner in which they will be applied', which *must* be compliant with articles 10 and 11 of the Model Law;[129] and the 'permissible range' for varying the relative weights of evaluation criteria during the second stage (if applicable).[130] The compulsory content of a solicitation for a closed framework agreement with second-stage competition, that is also to be carried forward in the actual framework agreement, aims to ensure coherence throughout the two stages and 'motivate' proper procurement planning.

2.2.3.3.2. Second-Stage Procedures

The second stage of a framework agreement is regulated by article 62 of the Model Law, and most of its provisions concern the type of framework agreements that involve second-stage competition.[131] These are included in article 62(4), and their main purpose is to ensure full transparency, competition and contestability for all framework suppliers in connection with all orders that are to be issued. As for any type of framework, second-stage procedures may only be conducted with suppliers that are parties to the framework and contracts may only be awarded to such parties.[132]

Thus, for frameworks with second-stage competition, the first requirement is for the purchaser to simultaneously invite all framework suppliers to present submissions, or only those capable of meeting the order in question,

---

[126] See section 2.2.2.3.1 above.
[127] Art 59(1)(d)(i).
[128] Art 59(1)(d)(ii).
[129] Art 59(1)(d)(iii).
[130] ibid.
[131] Closed framework agreements with second-stage competition and open framework agreements.
[132] Art 62(2).

provided, though, that *all* framework suppliers be given notice of the second-stage competition.[133] This allows framework suppliers to participate if they wish, precluding a purchaser from discretionarily inviting only some framework suppliers that are deemed 'capable' of meeting a specific order. It is an excellent safeguard against unjustified use of limitations to (or exemptions from) second-stage competition. Whilst the Model Law is silent on what could be valid reasons for such limitation, these might include situations where a supplier does not offer delivery to some place(s), or a certain combination of items, or where its capacity is busy with a previous order. The invitation shall provide full information concerning the order in question, including a 'restatement of terms and conditions of the framework agreement' that are to be carried forward into the actual procurement contract, a restatement of the award procedures, award criteria and relative weights, a statement concerning the terms and conditions that are to be refined or established through the second-stage competition, as well as full details concerning the procedures for presenting submissions.[134] The purchaser must evaluate the submissions that are received by the deadline for their receipt[135] in accordance with the award criteria stated in the invitation to second-stage competition. The acceptance of the successful submission will have to observe all procedural requirements under article 22 of the Model Law, including the application of standstill periods.[136]

An important issue here is requiring, whenever possible, that second-stage submissions present enhancements compared to the first-stage submissions (in addition to being compliant with the specification and terms of the solicitation for the framework and with those established at the first stage). In many cases, for example, it would not make sense to allow a certain supplier to enter a framework on the basis of its price as submitted during the first stage, if during the second stage he would be allowed to present much higher a price. Prima facie, it may be considered that the further competition at the second stage could, in itself, prevent the submission of higher offers, but there is a risk of collusion between framework suppliers (in particular if they are few in number), as they will know each other's identities. They could thus make an 'under the table' agreement where they 'slice the pie' (the total requirements to be procured under the framework) among themselves and raise their financial offers artificially for each order, such that each is allowed to 'win' certain orders at higher prices. If that happens, opportunities provided by this type of framework would be lost, best value would not be obtained, and effective competition could be seriously damaged. The risk of collusion could be exacerbated in connection with terms that are not established

---

[133] Art 62(4)(a).

[134] Additional information required to be included in a second-stage invitation is provided in art 62(4)(b).

[135] As stipulated in invitations to second-stage competition (art 62(4)(b)(iv)).

[136] Art 62(4)(d). However, standstill will not apply for 'under the threshold orders' or where the purchaser determines that urgent public interest require the procurement to proceed without a standstill period (art 22(3)(b) and (c)).

at all during the first stage. However, there may be practical situations when 'capping' the prices or terms offered at the second stage – eg so that only improvements (lower prices and/or better terms and specification) be accepted – may not be feasible. One such situation could refer to dealing with emergencies (rather than having planned for them),[137] whereas others could relate to dynamic markets or changes in relevant supply chains. In such cases, clear conditions, such as the application of objective price (or terms) revision clauses, should be included in the solicitation and the framework agreement relating to potential offers during the second stage that would/could be more onerous than those made initially. But price (or terms) adjustment clauses can also be useful where market evolutions are likely to result in better (lower) prices (or better) terms prevailing on the general market, so that any second-stage offers under the framework would not become 'detached' from the relevant market, and the purchasers thus secure envisaged value through the framework.

In regard to criteria to be used at second-stage competition, there is an explicit requirement that they must be among those that are applicable to the evaluation of tenders, and must be pre-disclosed at the solicitation of the initial stage of the framework procedure.[138] From the relevant provisions, as discussed in the context of frameworks without reopening of competition,[139] it can be inferred that second-stage criteria may or may not be the same as those used at the first stage. It might also be possible to use different criteria and/or weightings for different orders under the same framework, if objective conditions for determining which criteria apply to each order are pre-disclosed from the initiation of the first stage.[140] As regards the weightings for criteria, the Model law expressly provides that these 'may be varied during the second-stage competition' provided that 'the permissible range' is specified in the solicitation for the framework and carried forward into the actual framework.[141] Finally, commercial judgement needs to be exercised to ensure that the (sets of) criteria and, as applicable, weightings used at the two stages are consistent and converge towards achieving the intended objectives of the framework. At the same time, enacting states may like to limit possibilities to amend second-stage criteria during the implementation of the framework (under article 63).

2.2.3.4. Challenges

All actions or decisions taken by a purchaser during the second-stage competition are challengeable, as expressly stipulated under article 62(4)(b)(ix) of the

---

[137] See Arrowsmith (n 51) 32–33.
[138] Art 59(d)(iii), referring to arts 10 and 11; art 58(2)(d).
[139] See section 2.2.2.3.2 above.
[140] For example, most advantageous submission for orders larger than a certain value, and lowest price for those below that value.
[141] Art 59(d)(iii).

Model Law. All relevant information in this connection, including the applicable standstill periods,[142] must be included in the invitation to the second-stage competition. Notices concerning the second-stage competition addressed to framework suppliers not invited to take part (issued at the same time as invitations to framework suppliers deemed 'then capable' of meeting the needs of the order)[143] may also be challenged where deemed 'non-compliant'.

On the other hand, article 22 concerning acceptance of the successful submission is fully applicable to second-stage competitions. Thus, once the evaluation of second-stage submissions is complete, the purchaser must 'promptly notify each supplier ... that presented submissions of its decision to accept the successful submission at the end of the standstill period.' Since standstill applies (save for 'urgent public interest consideration' or under-the-threshold orders)[144] there is opportunity to challenge an intended award decision before entry into force of a contract, and thus pre-award remedies are available in respect of the second-stage competition. All other transparency requirements concerning any awards are also applicable. These include notices of concluded procurement contracts (article 22(10)) and publication of public notices of award under article 23.

The features above make the challenge system under UNCITRAL frameworks with second-stage competition a particularly advanced one among the procurement systems investigated. Still, procurement efficiency in such frameworks could be improved without significant damage to oversight by maintaining the same level of transparency but providing an option to enacting states (or purchasers) between either observing standstill or risking the setting aside of the contract (where awarded in breach of law).[145]

2.2.4. Open Framework Agreements

An open framework agreement is defined in the Model Law as a 'framework agreement to which a supplier (or suppliers) ... in addition to the initial parties may subsequently become a party or parties'.[146] This type of framework must be established and maintained online[147] and shall provide for second-stage competition.[148] Thus, the potentially negative implications of closed frameworks that limit second-stage competition to the suppliers that joined the arrangement originally can be avoided in open framework agreements, since other suppliers can also participate in second-stage competitions, whilst increased competition

---

[142] Or reasons why standstill does not apply.
[143] Art 62(4)(a)(ii).
[144] Art 22(3)(b)–(c).
[145] See section 2.2.1.2.3 above and Chapter 6, section 6.7.2 of this book.
[146] Art 2(e)(iii).
[147] Art 60(1).
[148] Art 61(1) (also art 2(e)(iv)).

could in turn result in better value offers. However, this is not to say that suppliers that are not a party to an open framework can participate directly in second-stage competitions. They will have to become a party to the framework agreement first,[149] by applying to become such a party at any time during the duration of the framework agreement.[150]

A decision concerning an application to become a party to an open framework agreement should not be deliberately delayed in order to prevent the applicant from participating in a specific order call. On the other hand, article 60(5) of the Model Law provides for a maximum time-limit for the examination of applications to become a party to an open framework agreement, the length of such time-limit following to be established by enacting states.[151] This time-limit 'should be short', since only qualifications and responsiveness are examined during the first stage of an open framework agreement.[152] Because suppliers are to be allowed to apply at any time during the life of an open framework agreement, the 'traditional' methods of procurement (such as the open tendering)[153] cannot be used for the first stage of this type of framework. It is of the essence of those 'traditional' procedures that only submissions received by the purchaser within a clearly defined time-limit (that is *common* for any and all tenderers) are to be examined, whilst submissions received after that deadline are to be rejected. Thus, a specific first-stage procedure is devised in the Model Law for open frameworks, which is a fully open one providing for an on-going application process for entering the arrangement throughout its duration.[154] It can be noticed that in open frameworks the two stages are not necessarily consecutive, as they both run throughout the duration of the arrangement.

The Model Law specifies that the purchaser 'shall solicit participation in the open framework agreement by causing an invitation' to be published in accordance with the requirements for open tendering,[155] and then describes the required content for the invitation.[156] This includes the full data of the purchaser and of any other institutions that are entitled to award procurement contracts under the arrangement.[157] Whilst this provision makes direct reference to the fact that open frameworks can be used for multiple-agency or centralised purchasing, other types of frameworks too can be used in this way.[158] However, plurality of purchasers under the same framework would need adequate consideration and

---

[149] Art 62(2) states that procurement contracts under a framework agreement can only be awarded to a supplier that is a party to the framework agreement.

[150] Arts 60(4) and 60(3)(d)(iv).

[151] The time-limit should be expressed in working-days and appears to flow from the date an indicative submission has been presented to the purchaser.

[152] Guide to Enactment (n 12) p 285 (point 12).

[153] Or others referred to under Chapters II, III, and IV of the Model Law.

[154] Arts 60–61 of the Model Law.

[155] Art 60(2) referring to art 33.

[156] In art 60(3).

[157] Art 60(3)(a).

[158] Guide to Enactment (n 12), eg 10–11, 255, 259.

further detailing in instruments of enacting states contemplating such options, in particular (without limitation) as regards closed frameworks, since there could be complex implications and consequences in some configurations.[159] Returning to open frameworks under the Model Law, the first-stage invitation must also indicate that this specific type of framework is involved, give information about how the framework agreement will operate, including notifications for future procurement contracts under it, and state the 'terms and conditions' for suppliers to be included in the framework. Further, the solicitation shall state all information required to be provided in the framework agreement. This is specified in article 61(1) and it is basically very similar to that provided for closed frameworks with second-stage competition,[160] subject to some variation as regards the establishment of terms for future purchases. Under article 61(2), the purchaser is required to 'republish at least annually the invitation' during the entire duration of the open framework, and also to 'ensure unrestricted, direct and full access to the terms and conditions' of the agreement and to all other information concerning its operation.

The first stage in open frameworks is not a 'competitive' one (as in closed framework agreements), and full competition is employed during the second stage of an open framework procedure. This is natural since the intention is to keep the framework open to suppliers that meet 'suitability' requirements. Therefore, the indicative submissions presented during the first stage are not evaluated competitively by making comparison among themselves (or ranking them on the basis of technical and financial merit), but they are only examined in terms of meeting the qualifications requirements and responsiveness. So, the submission examination exercise at the first stage is not intended to limit the number of framework suppliers by comparing their submissions.[161] Actually a meaningful comparison could not even be made, given that suppliers may apply at any time. These features raise the question of the manner in which the terms of future purchases are set at the first stage, an aspect that receives limited attention in the Model Law and the guidance. The 'indicative' nature of first-stage submissions, the requirement for them not to be evaluated (competitively), but only examined for 'responsiveness' at the first stage,[162] and the fact that they are to be regarded as 'not binding' in relation to second-stage competition,[163] all seem to indicate that – at the first stage – the

---

[159] See, in this connection, discussion in the EU and UK context (Chapter 5, section 5.3.2.3.3 on 'generic frameworks' and section 5.4 of this book), and in a wider perspective Chapter 6, section 6.3.3 of this book.

[160] As regards the duration of the framework, it must be stated in the solicitation and the framework, but enacting states are not required to impose a maximum legal duration since open frameworks do not limit (second-stage) competition in the way closed ones do.

[161] Limiting the number of suppliers is only allowed exceptionally (as an option for enacting states) where required by the 'capacity limitations' of the 'communications system' of the purchaser, under art 60(7) (see also art 60(3)(d)(ii)).

[162] eg, Guide to Enactment (n 12), p 286 (point 15).

[163] Guide to Enactment (n 12), p 257.

terms of future purchases are set by the purchaser as conditions for admittance onto the framework. Basically, an indicative submission from a supplier only confirms that he understands what the requirements (or minimum requirements) of the purchaser are likely to be at the second stage, but they do not affect the terms set at the first stage.[164]

On the other hand, it can be observed that there is a difference in the scope of the second-stage competition by comparison to closed frameworks involving reopening of competition. Thus, under open frameworks, terms and conditions may only be *refined* at the second stage, whilst establishing terms at second stage is not envisaged.[165] This suggests that *all* terms of future purchases should have been set at the first stage, though some of them (possibly many) not with precision. It seems peculiar that under closed frameworks it is permitted to establish terms through second-stage competition (though that type involves some limitation of competition at that stage) and not in open frameworks that do not limit competition. Even if the reason for this is that open frameworks are intended for 'simple standardized items',[166] it has to be recognised that – in light of the manner in which terms are set at the first stage (ie by the purchaser, as discussed above) – the price is actually to be *established* (rather than refined) through second-stage competition. Given potential ambiguity, implementation of the Model Law in enacting states should streamline these aspects in the interests of clarity and legal certainty.

Once a decision has been reached concerning indicative submissions presented, the suppliers shall be promptly notified whether they have become parties to the framework and, if not, about the reasons for the rejection.[167] With this, the first stage of an open framework agreement is complete for the supplier(s) in question, certainly subject to any challenge lodged by an applicant against the purchaser's decision. Because applications to become a party to an open framework can be made at any time within its duration (and the possible overlap of stages) contestability by potentially interested third parties and the application of certain related measures create specific features. Thus, standstill periods will not apply since article 60(8) does not refer to article 22.[168] In other words, a supplier already on an open framework will not have a chance to challenge first-stage admittance decisions concerning new-coming applicants before such decisions are effective. This is sensible since suppliers already on a framework will always want to preclude additional ones from joining, or at least delay additional competition

---

[164] It might, however, be useful for a purchaser to have the option of taking the view (if appropriate in specific cases) that, to the extent a first-stage submission exceeds the minimum requirements of the purchaser, that submission becomes binding for the supplier in question as to the minimum terms that he is to offer in future second-stage competitions. See dynamic purchasing systems in the EU (Chapter 5, section 5.3.3.3.1 of this book).

[165] Art 61(1)(c). Also, Guide to Enactment (n 12), p 288 (point 4).

[166] Guide to Enactment (n 12), p 287 (point 2).

[167] Art 60(8).

[168] Where the law intended art 22 to apply, eg, for the award of closed frameworks, clear references were included, such as in art 58(3) or, for second-stage competition, in art 62(3).

for upcoming orders. Allowing such consequence would defeat the concept of an open framework, whose purpose is to allow for an increased competition during the second stage, and not to limit that competition. Post-admission challenges by fellow framework suppliers should not be affected though.

Conversely, new applicants will not have the procedural safeguard of the purchaser's prohibition on bringing into force the framework agreement where a new applicant challenges the decision to reject him joining the framework. This is because the framework is already in force with other suppliers, and the aggrieved applicant 'will be able to be admitted to the framework agreement for future purchases if a challenge is resolved in its favour'.[169] However, there may be the possibility for suspending the operation of the framework, under article 67(3), which is to be decided by a relevant review body, depending on the circumstances of the case.

The second stage of an open framework agreement will always involve competition, as specified under article 61(1). The provisions concerning such competition, as well as challenges relating to the second stage, are the same as for closed framework agreements with second-stage competition.[170] An electronic reverse auction could also be used during the second stage of a (closed or open) framework involving reopening of competition.[171]

Open framework agreements have sought to achieve some benefits of both 'supplier lists' and the more classic forms of framework agreements, in particular by avoiding the closure of competition that closed frameworks involve, and concentrating competition at the second stage, when a procurement need has materialised and terms offered are likely to reflect actual market conditions. Whilst the recognition and regulation of open frameworks has been a very positive development, it is submitted that this should not have precluded the introduction in the Model Law of provisions concerning 'supplier list' arrangements.[172]

2.2.5. Supplier Lists

Chapter one showed that two major types of PUIR arise from their definition: 'framework arrangements', which at the first stage involve the assessment of 'suitability' of interested suppliers *as well as* the establishment of some terms of future purchases; and 'supplier lists' which at the first stage *do not* involve the establishment of terms for future purchases. It follows that 'supplier lists' may range from a list of registered suppliers potentially interested in supplying

---

[169] Guide to Enactment (n 12), p 287 (point 16). Consideration may be given to damages or other alternative remedies where an aggrieved applicant who is successful in his challenge lost the chance to participate in certain orders under the framework.

[170] See sections 2.2.3.3.2 and 2.2.3.4 above.

[171] eg art 31(2) of the Model Law.

[172] Despite the view expressed in the published Guide to Enactment (n 12), p 254 (point 3).

certain categories of items, to a list of registered suppliers whose 'suitability'[173] to supply specific items has been fully assessed at the first stage.[174] On the other hand, the arrangements explicitly recognised by the Model Law (discussed at sections 2.2.2–2.2.4 above) *do* involve the establishment of terms[175] at the first stage.

It needs mentioning that, at some points during the revision of the (1994) Model Law on Public Procurement, the Working Team considered the idea of introducing the concept of 'supplier list' into the new Model Law.[176] However, in the end this was rejected. The reasoning for it – mainly relating to 'elevated risks to transparency and competition that suppliers' lists are considered to raise'[177] and an inherent lower degree of second-stage efficiency and convenience in comparison to frameworks[178] – is unconvincing. In a number of pieces published over time, Arrowsmith analysed 'supplier list' arrangements, addressing main typologies, as well as potential benefits, risks and legal means to control those risks.[179] In some circumstances, it may be possible to conduct a 'suitability' assessment (or part of it) jointly for a number of subsequent purchases, even though the 'coherence' of envisaged future requirements does not permit the establishment of terms in advance, as would be required under a framework arrangement. Similarly, the subject-matter of procurement can also range to complex future requirements in the case of lists, whereas this is unlikely for frameworks[180] (or even 'precluded' from the open framework concept in the Guide to Enactment). Lists enable a certain degree of administrative efficiency at both the first and second stages, by avoiding the need to repeat a 'suitability' assessment for each individual future requirement, and such assessment can be complex and lengthy for some items, for instance, critical railway safety equipment. Thus, lists can facilitate proper planning of future requirements by grouping estimated future requirements and approaching them strategically in advance, rather than reactively as a series of individual 'one-off' full-cycle procurement processes (when each requirement materialises).

The main perceived risk in relation to lists seems to be that of the arrangement getting 'closed' to new-comers, thereby significantly restricting competition. However, this could be addressed by including legal requirements that the

---

[173] ie qualifications and other applicable conditions.

[174] Arrowsmith and Nicholas (n 2) 60.

[175] Even though the 'degree' and 'method' of establishing them differs among the three (main) types of frameworks, as discussed.

[176] Arrowsmith and Nicholas (n 2) 65–70.

[177] Guide to Enactment (n 12), p 254 (point 3).

[178] ibid, p 288 (point 4).

[179] eg, Arrowsmith (n 62) 115–17, and 'Framework Purchasing and Qualification Lists under the European Procurement Directives: Part II' (1999) 4 *PPLR* 161, 171–73; Arrowsmith (n 13) 33–36; also, Arrowsmith and Nicholas (n 2) 60–70. Note the last two titles related specifically to UNCITRAL instruments.

[180] Arrowsmith and Nicolas (n 2) 61.

arrangement be maintained open and operated fairly, in the same way that an open framework is, ie by requiring regular or permanent advertising (which is nowadays facilitated by electronic means of communication), providing for transparent and objective admittance criteria and conditions, allowing suppliers to apply for registration at any time, providing for a short time-limit for the assessment of applications that is commensurate to the complexity of the assessment involved, and appropriate oversight and challenge mechanisms over the admittance process. Additionally, conditions for establishing a supplier list arrangement could be provided for, together with appropriate justification, for example where the establishment of a framework arrangement is not possible or appropriate for jointly approaching a 'group' of contemplated future requirements that are somehow related, mainly in terms of the qualifications required from suppliers capable of performing them.

Arrowsmith distinguishes between 'mandatory' supplier lists, where registration on the list is a condition of participating in any procurements under it, and 'optional' lists where registration is not compulsory for participating in procurements.[181] In other words, in the latter type, suppliers may request that their qualifications be assessed specifically for an individual purchase, on the occasion of that specific procurement exercise, and need not pre-register on the list in order to be permitted to participate in that specific procurement. This is a very important distinction, since both benefits and risks are likely to be higher with mandatory lists. Whilst the 2011 Model Law does not include any explicit provisions on supplier lists, mandatory lists are (implicitly) prohibited, since article 9(4) provides that 'A procuring entity shall impose no criterion, requirement or procedure with respect to the qualification of suppliers ... other than those provided for in this Law.'

Registration on a list could not be identified in the Model Law.[182] Still, optional lists do not appear to be precluded by the Model Law, given that they are, in principle, an option rather than a requirement for suppliers. However, the lack of explicit recognition is unlikely to encourage the use of optional lists and in particular an appropriate and transparent use.

2.3. Conclusions

While the 1994 UNCITRAL Model Law on public procurement did not regulate 'framework' purchasing at all, the 2011 Model Law has introduced specific and

---

[181] eg, Arrowsmith and Nicholas (n 2) 61. Also, S Arrowsmith, *The Law of Public and Utilities Procurement: Regulation in the EU and UK*, 3rd edn, vol 1 (London, Sweet & Maxwell, 2014) 1311–12.
[182] See Arrowsmith and Nicholas (n 2) 66. For a similar approach, refer to the 2004 and 2014 EU public sector directives, and the 2009 EU Defence and Security Directive (eg Chapter 5, section 5.2.1.3 of this book).

detailed regulations concerning framework agreements, and significant guidance for enacting states. These cover a wide range of 'configurations', capable of meeting a wide range of estimated future procurement needs (for a longer term) involving some indefinite or uncertain aspects. The various types of framework will require different levels of procurement capacity to organise and operate. Thus, enacting states may choose to proceed to a gradual introduction of framework configurations, starting with simpler types and moving onto more complex ones as their purchasers gain additional experience.

The Model Law clearly represents a very advanced and multi-dimensional standard for framework agreements in public procurement. As discussed, some provisions of the Model Law, or the attending guidance, might be improved further (which is natural given the intended generality of the instruments and the consensual work involved in drafting), and this book provides a conceptual framework for further considering such issues in various contexts.[183] These issues include providing access to the procurement record from the initiation of a framework procedure; elaborating on criteria and method for awarding contracts under frameworks without second-stage competition; adjusting the approach on standstill across awards under frameworks with and without competition, together with facilitating further procurement efficiency where appropriate by providing an option between application of standstill periods and strengthened potential for the setting aside of the order contract; elaborating on multiple-agency frameworks, and potential further flexibilities needed in open frameworks, such as permitting new purchasers to join after the initiation of the arrangement, and explicitly permitting the establishment (rather than just refining) of terms at the second stage, as in the case of closed frameworks with second-stage competition.

However, the opportunity to recognise and regulate open supplier lists in the Model Law has been missed. It is suggested that this aspect should be reconsidered in the not too distant future.

---

[183] See in particular Chapter 6 of this book. For experiences in specific systems or instruments that might be considered mutatis mutandis, see the other chapters in this Part I.

3

Procurement in World Bank Financed Projects

3.1. Procurement Context

3.1.1. Institutional Perspective

The World Bank Group (WBG) is described as a 'premier development institution with global membership', whose purpose is to help developing countries 'adapt to this new landscape and take advantage of emerging opportunities', and to 'assist developing countries and their people to overcome poverty and establish a sustainable path for development'.[1] In order to pursue these generous and wide objectives, the WBG provides a variety of products and services, through the five institutions of the Group. However, only two of these institutions, jointly referred as the World Bank (WB),[2] are relevant to our case study: the International Bank for Reconstruction and Development (IBRD) and the International Development Association (IDA). They provide financial assistance to Governments as low-interest or interest-free lending for middle-income or low-income countries (some of whom can also benefit from grants).[3]

The WB falls within a 'classic' definition of an international development bank, ie an institution that funds projects that do not otherwise meet standard commercial criteria.[4] Where beneficiaries of internationally financed projects are Governments, then public procurement considerations become particularly relevant, since the implementation of relevant public procurement rules and policies actually constitutes a main disbursement method for funds provided to borrowing countries.[5] The term World Bank was initially used to refer only to the IBRD, and it first appeared in *The Economist* magazine in July 1944.[6]

---

[1] *A Guide to the World Bank*, 3rd edn (World Bank, 2011) xi–xii.
[2] S Williams-Elegbe, *Public Procurement and Multilateral Development Banks: Law, Practice and Problems* (Oxford, Hart Publishing, 2017) 10.
[3] ibid.
[4] S Arrowsmith, J Linarelli, and D Wallace Jr, *Regulating Public Procurement: National and International Perspectives* (Alphen aan den Rijn, Kluwer Law International, 2000) 99.
[5] ibid.
[6] World Bank, A *Guide to the World Bank* (n 1) 11.

The foundational moment of the IBRD is considered to be the United Nations (UN) Monetary and Financial Conference, which took place in Bretton Woods, New Hampshire, in 1944. The IDA was then established in 1960 as part of the World Bank, and since 1975 the World Bank became the official name of both the IBRD and the IDA. The first mission of the WB was to help Europe reconstruct itself after the Second World War, but after 1968 it focused on developing countries. The original focus on infrastructure projects has shifted in time to 'financial and private sector development'.[7]

The WB is a specialised agency of the United Nations (UN). The members of the World Bank – 189[8] (of which over 150 are borrowing member countries)[9] – have to be members of the UN and of the International Monetary Fund. As a multilateral institution with worldwide activity, the WB maintains close relations and cooperates with other international organisations. It has to follow the UN Charter,[10] collaborates with other UN bodies and agencies and enters many partnerships with multilateral financial institutions, such as the four regional development banks.[11]

3.1.2. Procurement Operational Environment: World Bank Financed Projects

The operational environment for WB procurement is formed by the WB financed projects, whose main and very wide objectives are to reduce poverty and improve standards of living in all countries of the world. A few specific features characterise procurement in this context. WB financed projects are governed by Legal Agreements[12] concluded between the Bank and a Borrowing Country, and are implemented by the Borrowing Country.

Unlike in national procurement systems, the issuer of the public procurement regulation or guidance (ie, the Bank) is not actually the party who is to ensure the direct application in real life of such instruments. Also, the party applying them (ie a relevant agency of the Borrower) is not a party that is subject to the jurisdiction of the issuer of the procurement regulation,[13] such as would be, for example,

---

[7] Williams-Elegbe, *Public Procurement and Multilateral Development Banks* (n 2) 11.

[8] In 2022, see www.worldbank.org/en/about/leadership/members.

[9] S Moss, 'Procurement and Distribution of Critical COVID-19 Supplies by International Organizations: The World Bank' in S Arrowsmith et al (eds), *Public Procurement in (a) Crisis: Global Lessons from the Covid-19 Pandemic* (Oxford, Hart Publishing, 2021) 271.

[10] GA Sarfaty, *Values in Translation: Human Rights and the Culture of the World Bank* (Stanford University Press, 2012) 54.

[11] World Bank (n 1) 99; Williams-Elegbe (n 2) 11–16.

[12] Previously 'Loan Agreements'.

[13] An exemption could apply under alternative procurement arrangements (APA); see The World Bank, *Procurement Regulations for IPF Borrowers: Procurement in Investment Project Financing – Goods, Works, Non-Consulting and Consulting Services* (4th edn, 2020) ('PR') https://thedocs.worldbank.org/en/doc/178331533065871195-0290022020/original/ProcurementRegulations.pdf, para 2.4.

a governmental department or agency in a national procurement system. This apparent disparity has to some extent been resolved through a legal 'construction'. The WB procurement regulations become binding by their 'inclusion' (through express reference) in the Legal Agreement that also commits the Borrowing State to ensure that the Agreement has priority over its national law. Additional project-specific details are included in the Procurement Plan that also becomes a part of the Legal Agreement.[14] This plan comprises, amongst other aspects, the selection methods to be applied for each procurement under the project, cost estimates, time-limits and review methods.[15] The Borrower is also required to justify its approach to each procurement, as stated in the Procurement Plan, in a Project Procurement Strategy for Development.[16]

Whilst the Bank is not directly involved in the actual application of the procurement regulations, it maintains a 'supervisory role'.[17] Such role arises from the IBRD's Articles of Agreement, requiring that any funds loaned be used only for the intended 'purposes' of the loan with appropriate consideration given to 'economy and efficiency and without regard to political or other non-economic influences',[18] and Trepte observes that this is the 'source' of 'the Bank's procurement policy'.[19] However, the Bank remains a third party in relation to any bidder or contractor in procurement conducted by the Borrower.[20]

3.1.3. The 2016 Reform and Procurement Regulations

Between 2012 and 2016 a reform of the WB procurement instruments was conducted with a view to modernising the procurement rules applicable to WB financed projects. Trepte groups the main reasons for the reform into three categories: the change in the type of the Bank's projects, which required a more prominent adaptation of the procurement methods to actions other than large infrastructure projects; the 'increasing wealth of middle-income countries' resulting in their capability to contract other loans, possibly with less 'onerous' procurement conditions; and the emergence of 'New international instruments and arrangements ... which impose new obligations in respect of public procurement', or establish new international standards.[21]

The reform was informed by wide consultations.[22] As a result of the reform, in July 2016 'The Bank Policy: Procurement in IPF and Other Procurement

---

[14] Para 4.2PR.

[15] Para 4.4PR.

[16] Paras 4.1–4.3PR and Annex V PR.

[17] Williams-Elegbe (n 2) 3. This role is also preserved in case of APA (eg PR Annex II, s 2.2).

[18] Art III s 5(b) (via www.worldbank.org/en/about/articles-of-agreement/ibrd-articles-of-agreement).

[19] P Trepte, 'All change at the World Bank? The new procurement framework' (2016) 25 *PPLR* 121, 122. See also para 1.2PR.

[20] Para 2.1PR.

[21] Tepte, 'All change' (n 19) 122–26.

[22] https://consultations.worldbank.org/consultation/procurement-policy-review-consultations.

Operational Matters'[23] (Procurement Policy) and 'The World Bank Procurement Regulations for IPF Borrowers' (PR)[24] became effective. The procurement framework further includes Bank Procedure, Bank Directive, and Guidance (also covering framework agreements).[25] Procurement Regulations are 'complemented' with standard procurement documents (SPD) (some also covering framework agreements). The new procurement 'framework' is based on seven principles, which are enshrined in the Procurement Policy: value for money, economy, integrity, fitness for purpose, efficiency, transparency, and fairness. The Policy articulates a vision whereby 'procurement … supports Borrowers to achieve value for money with integrity in delivering sustainable development'.[26] According to Moss, this vision facilitated a significant change of the Bank's 'posture on procurement' to a 'more proactive stance', providing support to procurement conducted by Borrowers, including in the response to the Coronavirus pandemic.[27]

Consistently with the policy, 'the Regulations provide many choices for Borrowers to design the right approach to market' and 'specify the rules that must be followed'.[28] The Regulations (PR) replaced the previous (2011) Guidelines for Procurement of Goods, Works, and Non-consulting Services, as well as the (2011) Guidelines for Selection and Employment of Consultants. Whilst PR consolidate rules for all types of requirements into a single instrument, selection methods for consulting services are dealt with distinctly,[29] given the specific features and importance of such services in international development aid. New procurement methods have been included such as the request for proposals or the competitive dialogue (for goods, works and non-consulting services).[30] Also, a specific mechanism for dealing with procurement complaints was introduced in the Regulations in relation to procurement for which the WB standard procurement documents are used,[31] whereas complaints concerning other procurement are to be handled 'as agreed by the Bank'.[32] All complaints continue to be addressed by the Borrower,[33] but failing to do this 'in accordance with the applicable requirements' may result in the Bank 'exercising legal remedies' or 'declaring misprocurement'.[34] Notably, standstill periods have been

---

[23] Applicable to the IBRD and IDA, and revised in November 2017.

[24] References in this book are to the 2020 edition (n 13).

[25] www.worldbank.org/en/projects-operations/products-and-services/brief/procurement-new-framework.

[26] See further, CR Yukins and S Williams-Elegbe, 'The World Bank's Procurement Framework: An Assessment of Aid Effectiveness' in A La Chimia and P Trepte (eds), *Public Procurement and Aid Effectiveness: A Roadmap under Construction* (Oxford, Hart Publishing, 2019) 277.

[27] Moss, 'Procurement and Distribution' (n 9) 279.

[28] Introduction to PR (n 13).

[29] In Section VII of the Regulations (PR).

[30] Trepte (n 19) 134–36.

[31] Paras 3.27–3.32 and Annex III PR.

[32] Para 3.31PR.

[33] Consistent with the approach that the WB is a third party to such procurement.

[34] Para 3.25PR.

introduced, subject to some exceptions which include call-offs under framework agreements.[35]

Under certain conditions, alternative procurement arrangements (APA)[36] may be used for a project, meaning the procurement rules of either an international or bilateral organisation or those of the Borrower's agency, subject to appropriate assessment of such rules and approval from the Bank. But unlike the earlier feeble 'use of country systems' trial approach which involved a stiff appraisal of equivalence with the Bank's Guidelines, in APA the Bank assesses 'consistency with its Core Procurement Principles'.[37] Where, for instance, a country has enacted legislation based on the UNCITRAL Model Law on Public Procurement, 'the Bank will engage with UNCITRAL to determine' the scope of assessment if any needed.[38] A separate course of action, in emergencies, could involve the use by a Borrower of a framework agreement established by the Bank with a UN Agency, if available (and if agreed by the Bank).[39]

Certainly, the focus of this chapter is on substantive provisions concerning purchasing uncertain or indefinite requirements (PUIR) in the WB procurement regulations (and less on procurement 'vehicles' as could emerge within APA or through cooperation with UN Agencies). From this perspective, it is noted that the PR maintain and develop the provision on framework agreements, slightly adjust the provision for procurement of commodities, but unlike the previous Guidelines, are silent on pre-qualification for a number of subsequent contracts.[40]

3.2. Framework Agreements

3.2.1. Description, Types, and Potential Uses

The main provisions concerning framework agreements (FA) are located in paragraphs 6.57–6.59PR and 7.33PR, and in Annex XV thereto. Other provisions throughout the document apply to FA explicitly, by express reference or implicitly. A framework agreement is described as 'an agreement with one or more firms that establishes the terms and conditions that will govern any contract

---

[35] Paras 3.30 and 5.78–80. A standstill period is not required for call-offs under framework agreements, as is discussed later (in section 3.2.2.2).

[36] Procurement Policy and para 2.4PR.

[37] Moss (n 9) 279.

[38] Trepte (n 19) 142.

[39] Paras 6.48 and 7.28PR.

[40] Whereas 'Procurement Guidance: Framework Agreements – An Overview of How to Design, Establish and Operate a Framework Agreement in Investment Project Financing (World Bank, 2018) ('Guidance on Frameworks') provides certain examples of 'supplier lists' that 'are not considered to be Bank compliant FAs' (pp 6–7) https://thedocs.worldbank.org/en/doc/965231529950446871-0290022018/original/GuidanceFrameworkAgreementsJune252018.pdf.

awarded during the term of the FA (call-off contract)'.[41] A specific feature of FAs is that they are 'established for the anticipated procurement' of items 'as and when required, over a specified period of time'.[42] They are thus intended for anticipated needs for a given period of time,[43] where those needs include some aspect(s) of uncertainty. FAs are classified in PR as a 'particular type of contractual arrangement',[44] whereas the Guidance on Frameworks states that an 'FA does not establish a legally binding contract between the parties'.[45] Unlike the UNCITRAL Model Law,[46] the PR do not distinguish a 'framework agreement procedure'. This (combined) view may have implications concerning review mechanisms at the call-off stage and types of frameworks that can be accommodated under the PR, as is discussed later.

Irrespective of the description, 'framework' purchasing involves a two-stage procurement process (or method), whereas the 'framework agreement' is an interim outcome thereof, and each transaction is completed by awarding a contract under it. As regards terms and conditions established when a framework agreement is concluded, the PR are nearly silent. The overall provision may suggest that most or even all terms could be established at the first stage, and that some of the terms are to be adjusted or refined, or even established at the call-off stage. It seems to encompass a rather wide range of possibilities from this perspective, as may be appropriate depending on circumstances, and this is confirmed to some extent by the variety of standard procurement documents for FAs (for different types of requirements) which have become available after 2020.[47]

It is nevertheless stated that terms established by FA 'will usually include the fee rate, charge rate or pricing mechanism'.[48] This indicates that in most cases a framework agreement must include terms or conditions concerning the 'price' element of future call-offs, eg a set price, adjustable price, and/or price subject to further competition. Indeed, most of the SPDs concerning framework agreements involve the price element at the first stage: ie for goods, non-consulting services, some consulting services ('with financial proposals (rates) invited at the Primary Procurement stage'), and goods within the 'COVID-19 Emergency Response'.[49] However, in certain circumstances the establishment of price (or the pricing

---

[41] Para 6.57PR.

[42] Para 6.57PR.

[43] As to the actual limitation of the duration, see section 3.2.2 following.

[44] In contrast, under the previous (2011) guidelines, The World Bank, 'Guidelines – Procurement of Goods, Works and Non-Consulting Services under IBRD Loans and IDA Credits and Grands by World Bank Borrowers' (2011) ('2011 Procurement Guidelines'), the provisions on FAs were included in Chapter III 'Other Methods of Procurement'; https://thedocs.worldbank.org/en/doc/492221459454433323-0290022014/original/ProcurementGuidelinesEnglishJuly12014.pdf.

[45] See n 40, p 1.

[46] See Chapter 2, section 2.2.1.1 of this book.

[47] www.worldbank.org/en/projects-operations/products-and-services/brief/procurement-new-framework.

[48] Para 6.57PR and points 2.1 and 4.2.(d).(i) Annex XV PR.

[49] See n 47.

mechanism) might not be possible, relevant or appropriate at the first stage.[50] Such situations include the procurement of commodities, for which an 'adjusted' form of framework agreement is provided for separately;[51] some frameworks concerning consulting services 'where financial proposal is invited only at the Second Procurement stage', for which a specific SPD is provided;[52] and some open framework arrangements.

In the literature it has been emphasised that, pursuant to the 2016 review of the WB procurement regulatory framework, the applicability of FAs has been extended, both in terms of 'volume' and coverage.[53] This development is in line with interim outcomes of the consultation process during the reform. Indeed, FAs can be very useful tools in WB project work for a number of reasons. First, they can provide efficient and flexible purchasing vehicles, adaptable to tight time-limits and the possible changes that tend to characterise project contexts. My practical experience in development projects clearly indicates that vital project time and resources may be wasted on rather trivial and repetitive purchases where PUIR arrangements are not available. Economies of scale may also be achieved by aggregating demand. Second, because of the geographically very remote areas where some of the WB projects are implemented, in the absence of aggregation of demand, there may be limited or no interest from the market to supply to those areas (or the costs involved could be extremely high). Similarly, also because of the locations of some of the WB projects (or Borrowers) that are exposed to emergency situations, such as earthquakes or hurricanes or epidemics, pre-established FAs could be usefully employed for procuring, on an urgent basis and on pre-agreed terms, the items needed when such catastrophes arise, to deal with or limit their consequences, secure evacuation, etc.[54] Finally, particularly in a donor aid or investment loan environment, FAs could be used for procurement of consulting services, for which there tends to be a regular need in this sector. Despite the potential beneficial uses, anecdotal evidence suggests that, whilst provision for FAs had been included in the previous 2011 Guidelines for supplies, works and non-consulting services, this type of arrangement was rather rarely employed in practice under those Guidelines.

To deal with such needs the PR state by way of example that 'FAs may be appropriate' for items other than consulting services under four types of circumstances.[55] First, the Regulations refer to 'frequent reordering based

---

[50] On this point see also the discussion in the context of the EU in Chapter 5, section 5.3.2.3.3 of this book.

[51] Para 6.51PR and points 6.7 and 6.8 Annex XII PR. See below.

[52] See n 47.

[53] Trepte (n 19) 137; also, J Górski, 'The World Bank's New Procurement Regulations' (2016) 11 *EPPPL* 301, 309.

[54] A related situation concerns the urgent setting-up of a framework to deal with the aftermath of a crisis, though speed of supply, terms, and security of supply are likely to be superior in cases of pre-existing frameworks purportedly designed for emergencies, where available.

[55] Para 6.58PR.

on the same, or similar requirements, or set of specifications', which basically involves recurrent purchases. The second type of circumstance envisaged is 'where different entities of the Borrower procure the same' items 'and aggregating demand could lead to volume discounts'. It can be assumed that 'similar requirements' are also implied here, and that additional considerations might be accepted to justify a multiple-agency arrangement, even though not explicitly stated in the PR. These could include attracting the market in light of aggregated demand, administrative convenience at the call-off stage, insufficient capacity of some agencies (on behalf of which a framework is carried out by another agency), or overall reduced transaction costs for the agencies.[56] The third type of circumstances provided for refers to 'planning for Emergency Situations'. In other words, this involves setting FAs in advance of an emergency situation, based on some estimation of what may be needed to respond to it, followed by making call-offs as and when such an event arises, as needed. Finally, an appropriate use of FAs could be, under the PR, when 'no single firm is considered to have sufficient capacity', which suggests that ensuring security of supply might be envisaged here. As regards consulting services, appropriate situations for the use of FAs under the PR include 'recurring' needs for such services and consolidating 'requirements' for similar consulting services amongst 'different entities of the Borrower'.[57] In the latter case, it can be assumed that indefinite requirements might also be accommodated, even where not necessarily 'recurrent' for each individual purchaser.

It should, however, be noted that the 'expansion' in the applicability of FAs under the PR (as compared to the 2011 Guidelines) reported in the literature[58] is nuanced. On the positive side, the limitation of maximum aggregated amounts for the use of FAs to those applicable to national competitive bidding under the 2011 Guidelines[59] has now been removed. Some limitation is certainly appropriate, notably in connection with closed frameworks, so as to permit periodic re-advertising and avoid long-term 'market closure' to the requirements procured under the framework, but this can be achieved by limiting the duration of a framework, and/or by assessing a maximum volume (where needed) on a case-by-case basis, depending on individual circumstances of each arrangement, rather than pre-setting it *in abstracto*. That restriction in terms of maximum aggregated value of FA under the 2011 Guidelines could have affected economies of scale (that are in many cases expected to arise from repeat purchases of some volume). It was also not very clear why under those Guidelines a one-off (traditional) contract could have had a higher (or even much higher) value[60]

---

[56] Some of these matters and considerations regarding multiple-agency frameworks are suggested in the Guidance on Frameworks.

[57] Para 7.33PR.

[58] See Trepte (n 19) and Górski (n 53).

[59] Section 3.6 of 2011 Guidelines (n 44).

[60] Where procured under international competitive bidding (ICB).

than a 'group' of contracts to be awarded under an FA. The maximum duration of FAs has also been extended under the Regulations. Whilst the 'basic' maximum period has remained unchanged (at three years), an option for extension 'by up to a further two (2) years' is explicitly provided 'if the initial engagement has been satisfactory'.[61] Increased flexibility is also now catered for under the PR by eliminating conditions concerning the subject-matter of FA, as were previously provided in the 2011 Guidelines, such as 'off-the-shelf' goods (or those of 'common use') or non-consulting services of a 'simple and non-complex nature'. Some level of standardisation and consistency among requirements across call-offs is inherent in FAs. But requirements with a certain degree of complexity might also be procured through some configurations of frameworks, notably those that lean closer to 'traditional' contracts.[62]

Similarly, potential use of multiple-agency frameworks has been generalised under the PR, whereas under the 2011 Guidelines it was only mentioned in the context of non-consulting services. Provision is now also included (in the 2016 instrument) for the potential use of an FA 'pre-existing' to a project, subject to the Bank's satisfaction that such FA 'is consistent with the Bank's Core Procurement Principles'.[63] Presumably, this could include a framework established by the same agency of the Borrower, under a WB financed project, or outside such project, as well as a framework established by another agency of the Borrower to the extent that the agency in question is entitled to use the framework. Such options, where acceptable pre-existing FAs are available, can save valuable project resources and time. The previous 2011 instrument lacked such provision. As regards consulting services, the apparent 'expansion' of FAs to cover such requirements may not be substantive. It is true that the previous 2011 Guidelines only provided for FAs for supplies, services and non-consulting services. However, the separate set of 2011 Guidelines for Consulting Services did provide for an arrangement called 'Indefinite Delivery Contracts or Price Agreements' (IDC), and I submit that IDC were in fact a specific form of FA for consulting and advisory services. Still, the current provision for FAs for consulting services, similarly to the previous provision on IDC, may not fully clarify some practical and procedural matters.[64]

On the other hand, the current Procurement Regulations introduce a number of limitations concerning the types or configurations of FAs that are permitted (for all categories of requirements), not present in the previous Guidelines. It is thus stated that 'An FA does not commit either party to procure or supply'.[65] The limitation is then detailed by specifying that framework contractors 'have

---

[61] Point 4.2(g) Annex XV PR.
[62] See eg Chapter 2, section 2.2.2.3.1 of this book.
[63] Point 2.2 Annex XV PR.
[64] See section 3.2.2.1 below.
[65] Para 6.57PR.

no guarantee of any call-off contracts'[66] and that 'no commitment will be made with regard to possible volumes of Goods, Works, Non-consulting Services, or Consulting Services'.[67] In the same vein, it is also specified that an 'FA is not an exclusive agreement and … the Borrower reserves the right to procure the same or similar' items outside that FA.[68] In other words, only FAs that are (entirely) non-committing and non-exclusive for both parties are permitted. It appears that it is not possible to guarantee the purchase of any quantities (or minimum quantities) under an FA, defined either overall for the arrangement or by reference to each individual framework supplier. Additionally to the impossibility of committing to specific volumes of purchases under the FA, it is also not possible for the purchaser to commit to buy the items covered by that FA from the FA suppliers only.

This type of FA offers flexibility (where quantities cannot be estimated with some degree of precision in advance), and may reduce risks of collusion at the call-off stage in that framework since contractors are uncertain over the 'pie' to be shared,[69] whilst the purchaser is not stuck with the terms of the FA and may use alternative purchasing vehicles for the same items.[70] From this perspective, in light of the fact that WB project procurement is conducted by Borrowers, with possibly more limited means to prevent or address collusion, a preference for non-committing and non-exclusive FAs appears justified to some extent. It should be noted, however, that suppliers are unlikely to be able (or incentivised) to offer prices/terms reflecting volume discounts given the lack of certainty, or confidence, over volumes to be purchased.[71] From this angle, committing and/or exclusive arrangements are much more likely to result in economies of scale, particularly where adequate controls against collusion are included, such as objective call-off price/terms adjustment mechanisms clearly related to the price/terms proposed for admittance to the FA. I submit that the (absolute) prohibition of committing FAs and/or exclusive FAs, as contemplated by the PR, may affect in some cases the ability of this arrangement to adequately meet its stated purposes. This could in particular be the case when 'volume discounts' are sought, for example where 'frequent reordering' or the aggregation of demand from a number of purchasers, or both, are envisaged.[72]

As shown, in the concept of the PR, frameworks are not to be committing for suppliers as well. This may be problematic in case of seeking to use an

---

[66] Point 2.3 Annex XV PR. Similar text is under point 4.2(d)(iv) thereof.

[67] Point 4.2(d)(iv) Annex XV PR.

[68] Point 4.2(d)(v) Annex XV PR.

[69] See eg (in wider context) GL Albano and C Nicholas, *The Law and Economics of Framework Agreements: Designing Flexible Soluctions for Public Procurement* (Cambridge, CUP, 2016), chs 8–11.

[70] For an 'exclusive' configuration of framework that could place the purchaser in a weak position (in Romania) see Chapter 5, section 5.3.2.2.1 of this book.

[71] eg Trepte (n 19) 137.

[72] Para 6.58(a) and (b) PR.

FA for 'planning for Emergency Situations',[73] where an arrangement that obliges framework supplier(s) to supply if and when required by the purchaser is clearly preferable. It does not really help in dealing with an emergency situation if framework suppliers choose not to supply as and when needed. Certainly a correlative commitment to buy certain volumes need not be undertaken by the purchaser, though a commitment to buy exclusively under the framework in case of an emergency may attract more interest and result in better terms being offered for admittance to the framework. Further, in (possibly distinct) situations where security of supply is sought,[74] a lack of commitment from framework suppliers could negatively affect security of supply, even in multiple-supplier frameworks.

Finally, a type of arrangement that has not received increased attention in PR compared to the previous 2011 Guidelines is open frameworks. Indeed, Annex XV to PR states that an FA 'should normally be' a 'closed panel', that is to say that 'the constitution of the panel shall remain unchanged' throughout the duration of the framework.[75] In other words 'additional or replacement firms' must not be 'added'[76] once the framework is concluded, though removal of a firm from the FA is permitted under certain circumstances.[77] Whilst open panels – namely FAs to which suppliers can apply for admittance at any time during their duration – are mentioned as a possibility,[78] no specific procedure is provided for establishing them under the PR. Clearly the references to standstill periods prior to concluding an FA and to a public notice 'of the conclusion of the FA' listing 'the names of all firms that have been included in the FA'[79] are not intended (or appropriate) for open FAs. More generally, the requirement of establishing an FA by using 'open competitive procurement'[80] involves submission of bids or proposals against a set time-limit applicable to any interested party, and a competitive evaluation of the submissions received by that time-limit.[81] These features are incompatible with permitting interested suppliers to apply for admission at any time, which is of the essence in open FAs. From this perspective, regarding FAs as a specific form of contractual arrangement, as the PR do, rather than as a procurement method (or procedure) inherently confines FAs to closed configurations. Whilst the Guidance on Frameworks refers to options such as providing 'the opportunity' to new suppliers to join at predetermined points during the 'framework',[82] it must be recognised

---

[73] Para 6.58(c)PR.
[74] Para 6.58(d)PR.
[75] Point 4.2(d)(iii) Annex XV PR.
[76] ibid.
[77] Point 4.2(d)(vi) Annex XV PR.
[78] Point 4.2(d)(iii) Annex XV PR.
[79] Point 4.3 Annex XV PR.
[80] Point 4.1 Annex XV PR.
[81] eg paras 5.31–32, 5.36–37, 5.40–48PR.
[82] See n 40, at 18.

that such an arrangement is substantively similar to a series of (subsequent) 'closed' frameworks, as is also discussed in the context of 'open frameworks' under the post-Brexit procurement bill.[83] On the other hand, the option where new suppliers 'have the opportunity' to join the arrangement 'continuously' during its duration (ie the genuinely open framework), though recognised explicitly by the Guidance,[84] seems unlikely to be pursued in the absence of express provisions concerning its establishment and operation, such as: specific continuous advertising requirements; no limitation on numbers of framework suppliers that may be admitted (ie, admitting all compliant and responsive submissions); a secondary procurement process; and how terms proposed at the first stage are to be used at the call-off stage.

The above is not to say that open frameworks, or committing, or exclusive arrangements are entirely excluded from WB projects. They might be used where the application of the domestic procurement system of the Borrower (instead of the PR) is permitted under alternative procurement arrangements (APA)[85] and where the domestic system in question caters for such type of framework.[86] The limitations applicable to types of FAs envisaged under the PR simplify decisions concerning their use to some extent. However, choosing between a 'traditional' procurement contract and a framework, or setting the number of framework contractors could remain challenging for Borrowers, as could similarly be the substantiation of the options proposed[87] to the satisfaction of the Bank. As regards the strategy concerning the number of framework suppliers, Annex XV to the PR states that this number 'should be proportionate to the anticipated demand' which 'allows all FA firms an opportunity to be awarded a call-off contract'.[88] From this perspective, delivery locations may also have an impact.[89] It is also provided that a decision as to whether an FA with a single supplier or 'with several' suppliers is to be 'based on the market conditions' and the estimated requirements.[90] Additional 'inspiration' on such matters can be found in Chapter six, section 6.4 of this book, and in the Guide to Enactment attending the UNCITRAL Model Law.[91] For example, where an FA is envisaged for repeat procurement, a cost-benefit analysis indicating that volume discounts would exceed the additional costs of establishing a framework could be helpful, though other aspects are likely to need factoring in.

---

[83] Chapter 5, section 5.4.2 of this book.

[84] See n 40, at 18.

[85] Section 3.1.3 above.

[86] As shown in Chapter 2 of this book, for instance, the UNCITRAL Model Law does not impose on enacting states whether a framework should be committing or non-committing.

[87] In Procurement Plan or Project Procurement Strategy for Development.

[88] Point 2.3 of Annex XV PR.

[89] As pointed out in the Guidance on Frameworks (n 40), at 15.

[90] Point 3.1 of Annex XV PR.

[91] See Chapter 2 of this book.

3.2.2. Procedures and Requirements

3.2.2.1. Establishing a Framework Agreement

As briefly pointed out above, Annex XV (point 4.1) requires the use of 'open competitive procurement with appropriate request for bids/request for proposal documents'. These methods and approach to market offer the widest publicity and, in effect, potentially maximise competition at this stage. The open competitive approach to market 'provides all eligible prospective Bidders/Proposers with timely and adequate advertisement … and an equal opportunity to bid/propose'.[92] Since no distinction is made in Annex XV, a decision on approaching the international or the national market follows the general rules in paragraphs 6.13–6.18PR for goods, services and non-consulting services, and paragraphs 7.24–7.25PR for consulting services. In light of aggregation of requirements, FAs could exceed the relevant country thresholds and thus be required to approach the international market. No other methods or approaches to market are envisaged for the establishment of FAs, which seems appropriate. Because closed FAs potentially restrict for a long time the access of suppliers not originally admitted to the FA to the procurement of items covered by the FA, it is important that the admittance process is as open and competitive as possible. Also, particularly complex items, requiring very specific procurement approaches are less likely to be of a repetitive nature, which is inherent in most frameworks.

The request for proposals and the request for bids, as selection methods (RFP/RFB), are mainly designed for 'traditional' (one-off) procurement. As explained, this makes them incompatible with open frameworks. To be used for establishing (closed) FA the RFP/RFB provisions of the Regulations are supplemented with some additional rules in Annex XV. But these do not appear to provide a full 'adjustment' of 'traditional' mechanisms even for closed FAs, in particular as regards consulting services. Thus, all open competitive selection methods for consulting services involve an initial short-listing process, based on qualifications. The resulting shortlist must include between five and eight firms[93] that are then invited to submit proposals in order to select the successful bidder(s) for being awarded a contract or being admitted to the framework. This may provide an adequate number of proposers where a framework with a single supplier, or with just very few suppliers, is contemplated. However, it could be problematic where a framework for consulting services with a larger number of contractors is appropriate. It appears that a framework with more than eight firms cannot be established under the PR, since the short-listing process (required to start with)[94]

---

[92] Para 6.11PR referring to goods, works and non-consulting services; similar provision in para 7.22PR refers to consulting services.
[93] Para 7.17PR.
[94] Para 7.16PR.

can only result in a short-list comprising a maximum of eight firms. But even for frameworks with eight or slightly fewer than eight firms, the competitive element at the first stage could be insubstantial where, for example, eight shortlisted firms are invited to make proposals and the framework is to be concluded with all of them (or even with slightly fewer). This, in turn, could affect the terms being established through 'competition' at the first stage. On the other hand, an assessment of only qualifications for establishment of a framework agreement is not envisaged by the PR (and this could have turned the arrangement into a 'supplier list' type of arrangement). In regard to consulting services, for short-listing purposes, the criteria to be used 'normally include: core business and years in business, relevant experience, technical and managerial capability of the firm'.[95] However, 'Key personnel are not evaluated at this stage'.[96] As applied to FAs this position differs from that under the previous IDC, where the initial solicitation set 'selection criteria focusing on the relevant qualification and expertise of the required experts'[97] – which tend to be essential in many consulting services – and the result of the process was a 'long list of qualified experts'. Still, the PR might compensate by envisaging FAs for individual consultants as well,[98] whereas in FAs involving consulting firms, key personnel are to be evaluated as part of the assessment of technical proposals.[99]

Returning to Annex XV, it is provided, irrespective of the requirements to be covered, that in case of a multiple-agency FA, 'a lead entity is appointed to act on behalf of the group of entities' and that 'Each entity in the group is identified in the request for bids/request for proposals documents at the time of going to market'.[100] Additionally, the Guidance on Frameworks[101] and SPDs introduce the term 'responsible Agency', basically referring to situations of centralised frameworks (where the responsible Agency manages the framework but it is not a purchaser 'in its own right', unlike a 'lead agency' who manages the framework *and* is a purchaser 'in its own right' thus essentially referring to a 'joint procurement' configuration). The Guidance offers some useful hints into designing multiple-agency frameworks, and also states that agencies entitled to use such frameworks 'must either be named in the Request for Bids … or identified as a specific class of public sector entities'.[102] This latter option might offer useful

---

[95] Point 7.1(f) Annex XII PR.

[96] ibid.

[97] World Bank, 'Guidelines for Selection and Employment of Consultants under IBRD Loans and IDA Credits and Grants by World Bank Borrowers' (2011) s 4.5, https://thedocs.worldbank.org/en/doc/894361459190142673-0290022014/original/ProcurementConsultantHiringGuidelines EngJuly2014.pdf.

[98] Para 7.33PR. However, no specific rules concerning such FAs are provided.

[99] Point 4.1(b) Annex X PR.

[100] Point 3.2 Annex XV PR. However, good practice would probably suggest stating that an FA is involved and identifying each purchaser from the very initial documents for approaching the market such as the Specific Procurement Notice or Request for Expressions of Interest.

[101] See n 40, at iii–iv, 4–5.

[102] See n 40, at 5.

flexibility in some cases, in particular as frameworks under PR are envisaged as non-committing and non-exclusive.[103]

Some aspects concerning the establishment and operation of FAs are required (at a minimum) to be included in RFP (request for proposals) /RFB (request for bids) documents.[104] These include 'a description' of the items to be covered, 'an estimate of the total volume/scope ... and, as far as possible, the volume/scope and frequency of the call-off contracts', 'qualification and evaluation criteria, and evaluation methodology' for establishing the FA, and the duration of the framework. The RFP/RFB must, additionally, include 'terms and conditions of contract that will apply to call-offs', such as statements to the effect that the price (or price mechanism) 'shall be agreed with each firm, and be valid for the term of the FA', that contracts will be placed 'as required', that the FA is 'a closed panel',[105] and that the FA is a non-committing and non-exclusive arrangement, as discussed above. Circumstances that could result in removing a firm from the FA, and the process for it must also be stated. Importantly, the 'secondary procurement method or methods' for the call-off processes must be specified in the first-stage documents for establishing the FA. These express requirements are very welcome. They support controlling an appropriate use of FAs, including stage consistency to some extent, though certainly they are to be further detailed and supplemented on a case-by-case basis. Other elements are clarified in SPDs, for instance dealing in an objective way with the number of suppliers to be admitted to multiple-supplier frameworks during the evaluation/ranking of bids/proposals at the first stage;[106] and the type of criteria (and evaluation method) to be used for various types of requirements (goods, non-consulting services or consulting services). As shown, requirements for informing bidders on the decisions reached during the evaluation of bids, standstill periods, and public notice of conclusion of the framework agreement are explicitly provided to apply for the conclusion of FAs,[107] thus allowing bidders an opportunity for debriefing, as well as to challenge the process where appropriate.

A modified form of 'framework' appears to be envisaged for the procurement of commodities, namely 'items such as: grain, animal feed, cooking oil, fertilizer, or metals' which 'often involves multiple awards for partial quantities to assure security of supply, and multiple purchases over a period of time to take advantage of favourable market conditions and to keep inventories low'.[108] Commodities are thus goods whose price fluctuates depending upon the demand and supply

---

[103] But see also, in the EU/UK context, the discussion on 'generic frameworks' in Chapter 5, section 5.3.2.3.3 of this book.
[104] Point 4.2 Annex XV PR.
[105] Or, possibly (but not 'normally') an open panel.
[106] Provisions in SPDs are clearly preferable than the 'scenario' described in 'example 10' (p 20) of the Guidance on Frameworks (n 40) (the latter could more easily foster favouritism).
[107] Point 4.3 Annex XV PR.
[108] Para 6.51PR (and point 6.7 Annex XII PR).

at any particular time (volatile price markets). Commodity framework suppliers 'may be invited to quote prices linked to the market place at the time of, or prior to, the shipments'.[109] Also, standard contract conditions and forms prevalent on the market, and bid validities 'as short as possible' are to be used.[110] Because of the specific nature and features of commodity markets, the establishment of price, even in the form of an adjustable price or pricing mechanism, for a longer period, such as for the term of an FA is usually not possible. Thus, the price 'element' is likely to be missing from commodity FAs, which also has implications for the process of establishing such an FA. However, the PR do not elaborate on the envisaged adjustments for such processes. The previous 2011 Procurement Guidelines regarded the arrangement as a list of pre-qualified suppliers (rather than an FA) for future multiple awards, to whom requests for quotations were issued when needed.[111]

It could be that only an assessment of qualifications is still permissible for admission to a 'commodity framework' since the PR continue to refer to a 'list of bidders'[112] in this context. Additionally, when e-reverse auctions are used for procuring commodities, this could be done from 'pre-qualified/registered' firms[113] (and it is unclear whether this 'configuration' is regarded as an FA). The current 'terminology' preferred by the PR for the procurement of commodities (at least where e-reverse auctions are not used) – eg 'framework agreement' – may have been influenced by the fact that 'pre-qualification for a number of contracts', having been recognised under the 2011 Procurement Guidelines for any types of items other than consulting services (and not just commodities),[114] does not appear to be envisaged any longer by the PR.

Whichever way it is to be regarded, procurement of commodities under the WB system provides a good example of adaptation to the particular features and structure of the specific market, allowing purchasers flexible, 'agile supply' approaches that traditional procurement methods (including a 'standard' type of FA) would not offer.

3.2.2.2. *Call-Off Processes*

An important control over the use of FAs is included in the requirement that 'FAs shall only be used between the Borrower's procuring entity/s and the FA firm/s'.[115] This applies to both demand and supply sides of an FA. Namely no purchaser other than that/those identified in the RFP/RFB for the FA is entitled

---

[109] Point 6.7 Annex XII PR.
[110] ibid.
[111] Section 2.68 (n 44).
[112] Point 6.7 Annex XII PR.
[113] Point 6.8 Annex XII PR.
[114] Section 2.10 (n 44).
[115] Point 3.2 Annex XV PR.

to buy under the FA. Similarly, a call-off process can only involve firms which were admitted to the FA (and were not removed therefrom). The requirement does not only concern closed frameworks. It would also apply to an open FA[116] in the sense that a call-off could only involve firms already admitted to the framework (and which have not been removed from the framework) by the time of that call-off process.

As a general approach to call-offs, it is clarified that 'the Borrower does not need to openly advertise individual contract opportunities to be awarded as call-offs'.[117] Indeed, the open advertisement of the establishment of the FA should suffice, for closed and open FAs alike. A requirement to re-advertise openly each call-off would be unnecessary and defeat the intended efficiency at the call-off stage, as the EU experience with dynamic purchasing systems under the previous (2004) directives clearly indicates.[118] Call-off processes are described at point 5.2 of Annex XV, and are also addressed in the Guidance on Frameworks and SPDs. They can take the form of 'mini-competition' or 'direct selection'. Both types of processes must 'be based on objective criteria ... that have been described in the FA'. As a matter of good practice, such criteria (including details thereof, such as the ranges of weighting for them, where applicable) should be pre-disclosed from the initial procurement documents for the award of the framework, and then carried forward into the actual FA upon its conclusion. This is implied in point 4.2(e) of Annex XV that requires 'the secondary procurement method or methods' to be included in the RFB/RFP for the framework, and it is indeed reflected in SPDs, though an express requirement to specify weightings for criteria would be a very useful addition in the interests of transparency and objectivity (for instance in the case of consulting services).

Call-offs under an FA could involve mini-competition, or direct selection. An FA could involve 'as an option both' forms of call-off processes,[119] certainly subject to this having been pre-disclosed.[120] Again, as a matter of good practice, objective conditions under which each of the processes would apply under the same FA should also be pre-disclosed,[121] but no such requirement has been identified in the available WB instruments. Where mini-competition is used, the PR provide that offers[122] are requested 'from some or all of the panel members'.[123] This is significantly reinforced in SPDs that require invitations to be sent to 'all

---

[116] In the rather unlikely event of being implemented under PR, as discussed.
[117] Point 4.1 Annex XV PR.
[118] See Chapter 5, section 5.3.3.3.2 of this book.
[119] Point 5.2 Annex XV PR.
[120] Points 5.1 and 4.3 Annex XV PR; also reflected in relevant SPDs (the option is not available for consulting services frameworks where financial proposal is invited only at secondary stage, for which the only call-off method is mini-competition).
[121] See, for instance, in EU context, Chapter 5, section 5.3.2.4 of this book.
[122] ie quotes, bids or proposals.
[123] Point 5.2 Annex XV PR.

eligible' framework suppliers, with eligibility being defined in PR and SPDs,[124] which is likely to reduce the risk of unjustified limitations of competition among panellists and enhance transparency. As for the criteria to be applied in the mini-competition itself, these could involve 'lowest evaluated cost' (where quotations are used) or 'expertise, proposed solutions and value for money' (where bids or proposals are used).[125] Where direct selection is used for call-off processes, examples of criteria provided in the PR include the location 'where call-off contracts are awarded to the firm that is best able to deliver based on their location' and the delivery location of the items.[126] Also, 'balanced division' of requirements involving rotation among suppliers is mentioned subject to some conditions.[127] SPDs bring valuable clarifications, linking such rotation to lowest evaluated costs as at the first stage (or applicable ranking for consulting services) and to an upper limit on total/upper value or quantity of aggregated call-offs to be awarded to each framework supplier: thus, the supplier with the lowest evaluated cost (or best ranking) is first awarded call-offs to the upper aggregated value/quantity; then the second lowest (or second best ranking) receives call-offs to the aggregated limit, etc. Whilst SBDs are silent on direct selection based on location, where more than one framework supplier are able to deliver to the specific location, I stress that a balanced division (as described above) should also be seriously considered, or any other objective and pre-disclosed mechanisms and criteria to identify the supplier that is 'best' able to deliver, in order to avoid arbitrary awards.

Irrespective of the type of call-off process used, 'The price for individual call-off contracts shall be based on the fees, charge rate or pricing mechanism detailed in the FA'.[128] This is an important safeguard for an appropriate use of FAs[129] and, again, SPDs provide a valuable stage-consistency control, relating to mini-competitions, by stating that framework suppliers are not permitted to quote/propose prices (or rates) in mini-competition that are higher than those provided for in the framework itself (as adjusted in accordance with the framework, as applicable). On the other hand, the criteria and selection method at the call-off stage need not be the same as those used for the establishment of the FA,[130] but some relation would need to exist in practice to secure value. Whilst the options provided for call-off processes potentially offer significant flexibility

---

[124] Proof of 'continued qualification and eligibility' may be required during secondary procurement (eg SPD Goods, ITT 48.1).

[125] Point 5.2(a) Annex XV PR. For instance, SPDs for goods and SPD for non-consulting services provide for quotations (lowest evaluated cost).

[126] Point 5.2(b)(i) Annex XV PR.

[127] Point 5.2(b)(ii) Annex XV PR.

[128] Point 5.3 Annex XV PR.

[129] As discussed, it need not apply in the case of commodity frameworks, or some consulting services (where financial proposals are only required during secondary procurement).

[130] In some cases, the criteria would be the same, for instance SPDs for goods and non-consulting services refer to lowest evaluated cost both at the primary stage and at secondary stage where mini-competition is used.

for purchasers and efficiency at the call-off stage, there may also be problematic aspects in the approach of the PR.

Thus, first, the choice of call-off process for an FA is not linked to whether all terms for future purchases are set, or otherwise, at the establishment of the FA. Where not all terms are set (with precision) in the FA, the question that arises at the call-off stage is how to establish (or refine) the outstanding terms – in addition to choosing an appropriate framework contractor for the specific call-off (under multiple-supplier FAs). If mini-competition is not used for this purpose the only alternative solution appears to be negotiating those terms with the selected supplier. In some cases, this might leave an undesired area of subjectivity in placing call-offs, in particular as the PR do not indicate whether or to what extent the general conditions applicable to direct selection (outside the context of FA)[131] are to apply to call-offs. Conversely, where all terms are set in the FA, reopening competition may be redundant, unless further discounts (or improvement of terms) can realistically be expected. It might have been preferable if some preferences for call-off processes were stated in the PR to guide users, such as: for mini-competition where not all terms are established in the FA (with possible exceptions or limitations for small-value orders, or as otherwise justified); and for direct award to the framework contractor offering best terms for the specific call-off based on its original offer for admission to the FA when the FA establishes all terms (again with possible exceptions when reopening competition may be appropriate, or when using other objective criteria could be desirable).

Second, the PRs are silent as to any transparency requirements concerning call-off processes. It is not specified whether, in the case of a mini-competition not inviting all FA firms (if at all permitted since, as shown, available SPDs require inviting all eligible FA suppliers), those not invited are to be informed of an envisaged call-off.[132] Similarly, it is not provided whether a notification of the decision on the evaluation of mini-competition submissions is to be issued at least to participants. Equally, it is not stated whether any transparency requirements apply at all for call-offs not involving a mini-competition. On the other hand, standstill notices (and standstill periods) as well as publication of public award notices are explicitly not required for any type of call-offs.[133] If any transparency requirements are implied (other than those explicitly not required) then it seems incongruous to expect Borrowers to 'anticipate' them, when it is assumed that the limited capacity in the domestic procurement system in question required the use of the WB procedures in the first place. Conversely, if no transparency requirements are envisaged at the call-off stage (which could be 'consistent' with the PR approach that regards FAs as a 'particular type of contractual arrangement', rather

---

[131] Paras 6.8–6.10 and 7.13–7.15PR.

[132] Also, in such cases it is not clear what criteria would apply for inviting or not inviting an FA supplier.

[133] Paras 5.80 and 5.95PR.

than a 'method' or 'procedure') most call-off processes are likely to remain outside any bidder complaint mechanism. Even where a complaint were lodged, SPDs explicitly state that the submission of the complaint shall 'not prohibit' the award of the contract (or 'pause' the process). This overall approach[134] does not appear to be 'compensated' for by specific measures concerning Bank oversight of call-offs, which could anyway be quite inefficient given that FAs usually involve large numbers of potentially low-value call-offs, but whose aggregated value becomes significant.

Still, nothing should prevent the Borrower from proposing at the project planning stage, or a relevant Bank officer from requiring, for example for larger call-offs, transparency measures, as well as potential interim measures in light of the risks involved in lack of oversight at the call-off stage.[135] But stronger requirements in the PR could have enhanced confidence in FAs by Bank officers, Borrowers, and suppliers alike.

3.3. Conclusions

Overall, the 2016 regulations have expanded the potential uses of FAs, though this expansion is nuanced. Notably, the limitations on aggregated value/volume of purchases under an FA, and to specific types of items, which were applicable under the previous 2011 guidelines, have been removed. On the other hand, the 2016 regulations include restrictions on committing or exclusive FAs, types which were not precluded by the 2011 Guidelines.

Open arrangements are not 'promoted' by the 2016 regulations, possibly on a view that these are inherently linked to 'electronic procurement systems' and thus their use must be subject to the Bank's satisfaction 'with the adequacy of the system, including its accessibility, security and integrity, confidentiality, and audit trail features'.[136] In effect there is no substantive progress in the area of open arrangements. At the same time 'pre-qualification' for a group of contracts to be awarded at the same time or subsequently, which was provided for under the 2011 Guidelines (for items other than consulting services), is not envisaged any longer under the regulations. This could have proven a useful 'vehicle' for subsequent purchases where terms could not be established in advance, including, but not limited to commodities.

The main focus of the current regulations, and of the available SPDs, is on non-committing/non-exclusive closed FAs. Many of the provisions are to be welcome and represent good progress by comparison to the previous Guidelines.

---

[134] Which favours to some extent procurement efficiency at the call-off stage.

[135] That such risks are real and significant is clearly shown from the US experience; see Chapter 4 of this book.

[136] Para 5.8PR.

They allow for flexible design of framework 'vehicles', apparently with many available options, as may be needed depending on circumstances, consistent with fitness-for-purpose and value-for-money principles. From this perspective, the approach to FAs is similar to the more general approach of the PR.[137] However, an appropriate use of FAs in this context hinges, to a large extent, on the knowledge and experience of the Borrowers and Bank officers involved. An approach more articulated on regulation preferences (subject to exceptions where justified) and on transparency requirements and oversight at the call-off stage might have rendered FA more 'self-sustainable'.

On a distinct level, looking forward, the eventual setting up by the Bank itself of frameworks for use by Borrowers (or their agencies implementing projects) in relation to emergencies and also possibly more generally, could bring significant efficiency and value across projects, as well as provide Borrowers with direct 'learning' experience on frameworks by actually purchasing through such framework(s) to implement projects. Whilst such a course of action would imply a 'major change' in the 'current governance arrangements' of the Bank, as explained by Moss in a somewhat related context,[138] it seems worth investigating it.

---

[137] But significantly different, for example, from that concerning e-reverse auctions, for which only a very simple type is contemplated involving the lowest bid price (paras 6.1–6.3 of Annex XII of the PR).
[138] Moss (n 9) 289 (and see more generally section XII in relation to section IX of that piece).

4

The United States Federal
Procurement System

4.1. Procurement Context

4.1.1. Background and History

There are several reasons why the US federal procurement system has been included as a case study in this book: the size of the US federal procurement market, its multi-faceted experience including with purchasing uncertain or indefinite requirements (PUIR), its historical evolution, and its influence on other procurement systems, particularly at international level. The sheer volume of the US federal procurement system and its tendency to increase make this system both attractive and relevant: over US$500 billion is being spent yearly on government procurements, 'an amount that increased during the Clinton and George W Bush Administrations'.[1] In terms of coverage, it deals with both civilian and defence procurement in quite a consistent fashion, in accordance with the responsibilities of the US federal Government. Still, quite a lot of civilian procurement is dealt with by individual states (within the US), according to their local regulations, which may differ, in some ways significantly, from federal regulations.[2] The main focus of the federal procurement system relates to ensuring efficiency, effectiveness and practicality of procurement processes in order to serve as best possible the interests and agenda of the US federal Government, rather than establishing targets or providing guidance for procurement regulation by individual states. The scope of this case study is limited to the US *federal* procurement system, namely procurement carried out by federal agencies as defined in Titles 10 and 41 of the US Code (USC)[3] and in the Federal Acquisition Regulation (FAR), and it does not include the procurement systems of any individual states that form the US.

---

[1] DI Gordon and GM Racca, 'Integrity challenges in the EU and U.S. procurement systems' in GM Racca and CR Yukins (eds), *Integrity and Efficiency in Sustainable Public Contracts: Balancing Corruption Concerns in Public Procurement Internationally* (Brussels, Bruylant, 2014) 117, 121.

[2] CR Yukins, 'Emergency Procurement and Responses to COVID-19: The Case of the US' in S Arrowsmith et al (eds), *Public Procurement in (a) Crisis: Global Lessons from the Covid-19 Pandemic* (Oxford, Hart Publishing, 2021) 393, 395.

[3] Dealing with defence procurement (USC 10) and, respectively, civilian procurement (USC 41).

As regards its long history, one of the main 'players' of the system, ensuring an independent, third-party review of award procedures, the Government Accountability Office (GAO) has provided an 'independent administrative forum for the relatively quick resolution of disputes concerning the award of federal contracts' since as early as the mid-1920s,[4] which means almost 100 years of experience in reviewing bid protests. The history of the US system involves an evolution of the trade-offs between the various values of public procurement and, consequently, of the balance between rigidity of regulation and flexibility in decisions that procurement officers could take. While the early days displayed a certain degree of rigidity, the focus shifted, starting with the 1990s, on efficiency and speed of supply, rather than on observing strict, transparent and competitive rules,[5] or open and efficient review systems. This was in line with the US Government objectives at that time and a tendency towards business-like procurement.[6] However, there have been more recent developments, after 2008, possibly triggered by the GAO's reports emphasising a relatively large number of cases when competition or transparency requirements were not fully observed, and/or by the lessons of Hurricane Katrina.[7] For example, additional transparency requirements were included for larger orders (over US$5 million) under certain types of task/delivery order contracts (see below).

There appear to be at least two main international 'dimensions' of the US federal procurement system. One dimension consists of the US's participation in, and influence on, international instruments, such as the GPA or the UNCITRAL Model Law on Procurement. For instance, Wang, writing on China's accession to the GPA, indicates that the first step taken by China towards the GPA 'was largely a result of the immense pressure asserted by the US'.[8] On the other hand, the US Department of State Advisory Committee on Private International Law participated in the Working Group that revised the 1994 UNCITRAL Model Law on Procurement of Goods, Construction and Services,[9] and the introduction of rules concerning framework arrangements, including of the open type, was one of the major elements of novelty of the 2011 Model Law on Public Procurement that

---

[4] NB Bleicher et al, 'Accountability in Indefinite-Delivery/Indefinite-Quantity Contracting: The Multifaced Work of the U.S. Government Accountability Office' (2008) 37 (3) *PCLJ* 375, 376.

[5] SL Schooner, 'Desiderata: Objectives for a System of Government Contract Law' (2002) 11 *PPLR* 103.

[6] S Kelman, *Procurement and Public Management: The Fear of Discretion and the Quality of Government Performance* (AEI Press, 1990).

[7] eg, the report of the US House of Representatives, The Committee on Government Reform – Minority Staff, Special Investigations Division, from August 2006, titled 'Waste, Fraud and Abuse in Hurricane Katrina Contracts'.

[8] In P Wang, 'China's Accession to WTO's Governement Procurement Agreement: Domestic Challenges and Prospects in Negotiation' (The University of Nottingham, China Policy Institute, Briefing Series, Issue 48, March 2009) 8.

[9] Federal Register, June 15, 2007 (Volume 12, Number 115), page 33273, Public Notice 5808 of the US Department of State. See also, PM Lalonde et al, 'ABA SIL International Procurement Committee Year in Review' (2007) 42 (2) *The International Lawyer* 479.

replaced the 1994 Model Law. A second international 'dimension' consists in the use of indefinite-delivery/indefinite-quantity (ID/IQ) arrangements by the United States Agency for International Development (USAID) in providing development and humanitarian assistance worldwide.[10]

An important feature of the US federal procurement system is that it relies heavily on what I refer to as PUIR arrangements, particularly for (but not limited to) standard items. Some of these arrangements are remarkably complex (multi-agency/multi-supplier ones) and of high value. The history of such arrangements started in the 1950s when the General Services Administration (GSA) launched the so-called Federal Supply Schedule (FSS), initially intended as an efficient, procedurally streamlined and simplified mechanism for the purchasing of office supplies by other agencies as well. While the Economy Act of 1932 permitted procurement by one agency through another agency, this was not common before 1990s.[11] FAR16.5, which became effective in 1984, provided for three separate regular purchasing arrangements referred to as 'indefinite-delivery' contracts: definite-quantity contracts, requirements contracts, and indefinite-quantity contracts (or ID/IQ). FASA[12] 1994 encouraged multiple-award contracting, while the Clinger-Cohen Act of 1996 introduced the so-called 'Governmentwide Acquisition Contracts' for IT purchasing[13] (GWAC). These too are task order or delivery order contracts, being operated by agencies designated by the Office of Management and Budget (OMB) or under a delegation of authority issued by the GSA.[14] The extensive use of ID/IQ contracts, GWACs and/or federal supply schedules was consistent with the 'more business-like procurement' approach of the 1990s, in the sense of providing agencies with efficient and simplified purchasing arrangements by placing orders in already existing ID/IQ or schedule contracts, as well as a wider degree of discretion in the selection of contractors.

An interesting recent development, of 2020, concerns the possibility for federal users (rather than the procurement function) to purchase directly from established electronic marketplaces, such as Amazon.com, through a GSA online portal and arrangement.[15] However, it exceeds the scope of this book since the subject of direct exercise of 'user choices' deserves distinct analysis in a

---

[10] eg, J Jin and M McLaughlin, 'Procurement and Distribution of Critical COVID-19 Supplies: The Experience of USAID' in S Arrowsmith et al (eds), *Public Procurement in (a) Crisis: Global Lessons from the Covid-19 Pandemic* (Oxford, Hart Publishing, 2021) 291, 299.

[11] D Gordon and JL Kang, 'Task-Order Contracting in the U.S. Federal System: The Current System and Its Historical Context' in S Arrowsmith (ed), *Reform of the UNCITRAL Model Law on Procurement: Procurement Regulation of the 21st Century* (Thomson Reuters/West, 2009) 215, 217.

[12] The Federal Acquisition Streamlining Act (1994) (FASA 1994).

[13] Bleicher et al, 'Accountability in Indefinite-Delivery/Indefinite-Quantity Contracting' (n 4) 384. For some criticism, see J Kucharski, 'Modernising IT Procurement: One Small Step Towards Progress, One Giant Leap for Federal Contracting' (2022) 51 *PCLJ* 299, mainly at 309–10.

[14] FAR2.101.

[15] See eg CR Yukins, 'GSA's Commercial Marketplace Initiative: Opening Amazon and Other Private Marketplaces to Direct Purchases by Government Users', George Washington University Law School, *GW Legal Studies Research Paper No 2021–04*.

wider context,[16] and the new GSA mechanism is only available for purchases below the micro-purchase threshold.

4.1.2. Institutional Framework

Executive Agencies are the federal institutions or certain corporations, wholly owned by Government, to which the federal procurement regulations apply, namely institutions that award procurement contracts in accordance with federal procurement regulations.[17] The Office of Federal Procurement Policy (OFPP) provides 'overall' procurement direction in relation to Governmentwide procurement policies and promotes 'economy, efficiency, and effectiveness' in the federal procurement system.[18] The OFPP's functions include unification of procurement practice, and formulation of laws, policies, regulations, procedures and forms, providing the Administrator of the Office with wide capabilities to shape the federal procurement system.[19] The OFPP is also involved in the development of the acquisition workforce, particularly by directing the Federal Acquisition Institute; it is a policy body and it does not interfere with individual contract award processes conducted by agencies.

Legal review bodies, though, are entitled to look into the legality of decisions issued by agencies in their conduct of individual contract award procedures. It is relevant to outline some features of the US federal procurement review system, such as: (i) the lack of what the EU law (or indeed UNCITRAL) calls 'standstill periods';[20] (ii) a 'stay' of contract award or performance pursuant to lodging an application for review that may be overridden by determination of the head of the agency;[21] and (iii) a preoccupation with minimising possible disruption(s) to the procurement process caused by the review process. Of particular relevance to the operation of the federal procurement system is the GAO's activity. There are three main lines of GAO activity described in the literature:[22] appropriation law decisions and opinions, bid protest decisions, and audit reports on procurement activity. The GAO provides for an administrative forum for bid protest resolution in a relatively quick and less formal fashion, and it also has specific and exclusive jurisdiction for reviewing certain orders under indefinite-quantity contracts, as

---

[16] See eg Recital 61 in Directive 2014/24.

[17] ibid. Also 41 USC 133 (2011). The concept appears quite similar, mutatis mutandis, to 'contracting authorities' in the EU procurement system.

[18] 41 USC 1101 (2011). Further on OFPP see eg Yukins, 'Emergency Procurement and Responses to COVID-19' (n 2) 394.

[19] AWH Gourley and A Cliffe, 'United States' in H-J Prieß (ed), *Getting the Deal Through Public Procurement: An overview of regulation in 37 jurisdictions worldwide* (Global Competition Review/ Law Business Research, 2013) 242.

[20] ibid, 247.

[21] Requirement introduced by the Competition in Contracting Act (CICA) 1984. See FAR33.103(f) and 33.104(b).

[22] See further, Bleicher et al (n 4).

will be discussed later. The GAO started this activity in the 1920s and in 1984 it received statutory entitlement for the review activity under the Competition in Contracting Act (CICA). The 'head' of the GAO is the Comptroller General and the main function of the institution is to monitor that the appropriations made by Congress to Executive Agencies of the Federal Government are actually used for their intended purpose and in accordance with the applicable statutes.[23] This is where the bid protest resolution function arose from, as a mechanism for oversight of the budgetary execution. Bid protests may also be filed with the Court of Federal Claims, whose decisions can be appealed at the US Court of Appeals for the Federal Circuit.[24]

Thus, as pointed out in literature, the US federal system 'attempts to provide, a balance between allowing contracting officials to exercise their discretion and judgment in spending public funds ... and ensuring integrity of public procurement through effective accountability',[25] namely through bid protests[26] and audits.

4.1.3. Legal Framework

The Armed Services Procurement Act (1947) and the Federal Property and Administration Services Act (1949), as amended from time to time, have been described by the GAO as the 'main statutes controlling public procurements'.[27] Major amendments of the two main statutes, generating significant shifts in the regulation of federal procurement, included the aforementioned Competition in Contracting Act (CICA 1984), the Federal Acquisition Streamlining Act (FASA 1994), as well as the Federal Acquisition Reform Act (FARA 1996).[28] CICA 1984 introduced at least three major changes worth noting: (i) the concept of 'full and open competition' as a norm in federal purchasing; (ii) provision of an explicit statutory basis for the bid protest system at the GAO; and (iii) provision that submission of protests triggers a stay of proceedings or performance (see preceding section). In connection with ID/IQ contracts though, the 'full and open competition' test only applied to the award of the 'umbrella' arrangements, and the award of orders under the 'umbrella' arrangement was simply not covered by statutory regulations.[29]

---

[23] ibid, 375.

[24] FAR33.105. Gourley and Cliffe, 'United States' (n 19) 247. For concise highlights concerning history of bid protests and competent fora for hearing protests see DI Gordon, 'Bid Protests: The Costs Are Real, But the Benefits Outweigh Them' (2013) 42 *PCLJ* 489.

[25] Gordon and Racca, 'Integrity challenges in the EU and U.S.' (n 1) 128.

[26] Gordon, 'Bid Protests' (n 24).

[27] GAO, 'Bid Protests at GAO: A Descriptive Guide', 10th edn (GAO-18-510SP, 2018) 5.

[28] Additional acts relevant to federal procurement were issued, but here we will focus only on acts triggering major shifts in the US federal procurement system.

[29] Gordon and Kang, 'Task-Order Contracting in the U.S. Federal System' (n 11) 221.

The 1994–96 reform brought relevant measures in connection with ID/IQ contracting.[30] First, as shown, FASA 1994 provided the 'statutory basis' for a preference for multiple-supplier ID/IQ contracts ('multiple-award contracting'). Secondly, following growing concern over the non-competitive award of orders, FASA required that 'for orders above $2,500, every one of the multiple contract holders was to receive "a fair opportunity to be considered" for award of each order'. Thirdly, an explicit ban on protests against the award of orders was imposed, except for protests against the award of orders exceeding the scope of the 'umbrella' contract. Instead, 'task and delivery order ombudsmen' were established at each agency to hear complaints in connection with the award of orders; however, this was not the most effective way to deal with such protests.[31] A development of 2008, possibly triggered by reports of abuses of ID/IQ contracting, showed further concern[32] regarding the need for enhanced competition and transparency in connection with the award of orders, in particular those of high value. The National Defense Authorisation Act for Fiscal Year 2008, section 843,[33] provided for 'greater transparency and review' in connection with the award of orders over US$5 million while orders of US$10 million (or above) could be protested exclusively with the GAO.[34]

A relevant feature of the US federal regulatory system is codification/consolidation. The Acts mentioned above are codified/consolidated under the US Code, Titles 10 and 41. Codification provides for systematisation and organisation of legislation, and for comprehensive links and references. Implementing regulations are codified in the FAR (Title 48 of the Code of Federal Regulations, Chapter 1).

Also noteworthy is the potential use of PUIR arrangements in emergency situations, in light of the experience faced by the US federal procurement on the occasion of Hurricane Katrina when there was an urgent need for certain supplies and services to relieve the consequences of the disaster. The literature[35] emphasised that the response to the effects of the hurricane was slower than and not as efficient as expected, and even in some instances it brought about dangerous solutions. Thus the concept of 'emergency procurement' emerged. Starting from the assumption

---

[30] Bleicher et al (n 4) 384–86.

[31] For further details on federal procurement legislation in the 1980s and 1990s, see JF Nagle, *History of Government Contracting*, 2nd edn (Washington DC, The George Washington University, 1999) 495–518. Also, concerning the approach to ID/IQ contracts in that period, see GL Albano and C Nicholas, *The Law and Economics of Framework Agreements: Designing Flexible Solutions for Public Procurement* (Cambridge, CUP, 2016) 100–104.

[32] CR Yukins, 'Are IDIQs Inefficient? Sharing Lessons with European Framework Contracting' (2008) 37 *PCLJ* 545.

[33] Bleicher et al (n 4) 399–400.

[34] See also FAR16.504 and 505; and Albano and Nicholas, *The Law and Economics of Framework Agreements* (n 31) 112–14.

[35] W Sims Curry, 'Contracting during Emergencies' in W Sims Curry, *Government Contracting: Promises and Perils* (New York, CRC Press, 2010) 209–35.

that such catastrophic events are to happen inevitably, and items usually needed to deal with such events are known in advance, albeit that exact quantities or delivery places are not known beforehand, indefinite-delivery contracts or schedule contracts seem to be adequate arrangements to be established in advance, in order to allow for orders to be placed efficiently and effectively, as and when needed.[36] Fast-forward moving onto the Coronavirus pandemic, it seems that at federal level procurement 'worked well' (under the circumstances) given its maturity and the fact that adjustment for crisis is factored into its design, though one should bear in mind that the federal level has been 'largely outside the immediate health demands of the pandemic'.[37] Indeed, flexibilities are 'identified' under Part 18 of FAR, that can be either 'generally available flexibilities' ('when certain conditions are met') or 'emergency flexibilities' that can only be used in 'prescribed circumstances', such as to 'facilitate defence against or recovery from … attack' or in the event of an 'emergency declaration' by the President of the United States.[38] Amongst generally available flexibilities, specific reference is made for example to 'Federal Supply Schedules' and 'multi-agency, indefinite-delivery contracts' that 'may offer agency advance planning, pre-negotiated line items, and special terms and conditions that permit rapid response'.[39] However, the situation at state level (and the extent to which authorities at this level could use or coordinate with federal procurement mechanisms, including relevant schedules under the FSS programme) appears to be a different story for various reasons beyond the scope of the case study.[40]

4.2. Relevant Arrangements

4.2.1. Overview

The US federal procurement system implements a number of different regular purchasing arrangements, of various degrees of complexity, classified into two main categories: indefinite-delivery contracts, mainly regulated under FAR16.5, and Federal Supply Schedules, mainly regulated under FAR8.4 and FAR38. These arrangements cover a wide range, from rather straight-forward ones (single agency, single contractor) to very sophisticated ones involving one agency organising an arrangement with more suppliers or very many suppliers, and very many agency buyers accessing the arrangement and placing task or delivery orders to their

---

[36] See JI Schwartz, 'Katrina's lessons for ongoing US procurement reforms efforts' (2006) 15 *PPLR* 362.

[37] Yukins (n 2) 412.

[38] FAR18.000 and 18.001.

[39] FAR18.105.

[40] eg, Yukins (n 2); L Hendrix, 'Lessons from Disaster: Improving Emergency Response through Greater Coordination of Federal, State, and Local Response Efforts' (2021) 51 *PCLJ* 69.

purchasing needs. While all such arrangements are generally referred to as 'task or delivery order contracts',[41] there are significant differences between indefinite-delivery contracts and schedules (or schedule contracts), such as the manner of joining them, ordering regulations, and protest mechanisms.

4.2.2. Definite-Quantity Contracts

A definite-quantity contract[42] may be regarded as the simplest and most straight-forward regular purchasing arrangement in the US federal procurement system. Basically, purchasers and bidders go through a standard procurement procedure (as a first-stage process), following which a supplier is selected and a definite-quantity contract is concluded. This first stage is not different procedurally from 'traditional' forms of procurement under the US federal procurement system, as provided for in the US Code (USC) and the FAR.

At the time of contracting, all elements are certain for parties under a definite-quantity contract, including the period of the contract and quantity of supply or services to be provided.[43] The agency guarantees the purchase of a specified quantity of items over the contract period, and, failing to do so triggers its liability. The only aspects not known when launching the procurement and at the time of contracting are the particulars of deliveries, ie the time, precise location (among 'designated' locations) and fractions of total quantity forming the subject of individual orders. The second stage of the arrangement, namely placing orders once the definite-quantity contract is concluded, is also straight-forward as there will only be one contractor and no competition involved when issuing orders. As and when a need materialises, the agency simply issues an order stating specific quantities, locations and times, and the contractor has to make deliveries as per all contractual or order conditions.

The simplicity of this regular purchasing arrangement and level of certainty it provides for the parties involved might call into question whether it can be called a PUIR arrangement. In the EU, for example, such an arrangement would not normally be regarded as a 'framework' arrangement. However definite-quantity contracts are at a 'confluence' or transition area between 'traditional' contracts and PUIR, being the closest arrangement to 'traditional' purchasing, and from a conceptual perspective it is relevant to consider it in the context of this book. A definite-quantity contract provides advantages when the total quantity to be procured over a period of time is certain at the start of the procurement and

---

[41] But see specific definitions in the context of indefinite-delivery contracts in FAR16.501-1.
[42] FAR16.502.
[43] RC Nash Jr, KR O'Brien-Debakey and SL Schooner, *Government Contracts Reference Book: A Comprehensive Guide to the Language of Procurement*, 4th edn (Wolters Kluwer Law & Business/ CCH Incorporated, 2013) 167.

where the items 'are regularly available or will be available after a short lead time.'[44] Nonetheless, where there is a risk that the full and precise quantity will not be required by the agency, then other, more flexible arrangements will be needed, that do not trigger the responsibility of the agency if the fixed and precise quantity is not ordered, such as requirements contracts or ID/IQ contracts.

4.2.3. Requirements Contracts

Compared to definite-quantity contracts, requirements contracts provide more flexibility regarding the total quantity to be supplied under the contract, but less flexibility in buying items covered by a requirements contract outside that contract. At the risk of over-simplification, a requirements contract grants an 'exclusivity' status for the successful bidder with whom the contract is concluded for the period of that requirements contract.[45] Buying the same items outside the contract is only allowed in exceptional circumstances, such as an inability of the contractor to deliver urgently needed goods earlier than could 'be specified under this contract' and subject to a request for an accelerated delivery (under the requirements contract) being issued by the agency and refused by the contractor.[46]

Under FAR16.503,

> A requirements contract provides for filling all actual purchase requirements of designated Government activities … with deliveries or performance to be scheduled by placing orders.

However, 'all requirements' is not an absolute statement, as further clarified in FAR, since the agency has an obligation to include in the solicitation and in the contract a 'realistic estimated total quantity'. Without such an estimate of total quantity, bidders would miss essential information that is absolutely necessary to enable them to put forward a bid. For example, in the absence of a total quantity estimate, bidders would not be able to assess whether they have the capacity to deliver what will be required, nor will they have any realistic basis for submitting a (meaningful) financial proposal. Consequently, the agency would not have a basis for evaluation of bids. Since requirements contracts can be of high dollar value, the total quantity estimate can also serve as a business plan for the bidders, for example, to change their production methods, management systems or supply systems to meet the increased requirements, reduce lead-times or prices, thus enhancing value for money for the agency.

---

[44] FAR16.502(b)(2).

[45] MW Kipa, KR Szeliga and JS Aronie, 'Conquering Uncertainty in an Indefinite World: a Survey of Disputes Arising under IDIQ Contracts' (2008) 37 *PCLJ* 415, 418.

[46] FAR52.216-21 providing for standard clauses for requirements contracts (letter e).

Similarly, the estimate has to be a realistic one; certainly, if the estimate is unrealistic or completely unrealistic, then the procurement is unlikely to be successful as regards value for money, or contractual problems may even arise. The FAR gives few indications as to what should generate a realistic estimate, ie one that is based on 'previous requirements and consumption' or on 'other means' and that uses 'the most current information available'.[47] In litigation other elements may also be considered. Still, in requirements contracts the estimate does not guarantee (it is not a 'representation')[48] to the contractor that the estimated quantity will be required or ordered. Normally, this means that there will be no compensation ('no equitable price adjustment') if the total quantity ordered under the contract is below the estimated or the maximum estimated quantity.[49] However, there will be compensation if the contractor proves that the estimate was not realistic. Case law has clarified that the estimate can be challenged successfully and compensation awarded if the contractor proves that the estimate has been prepared with negligence, since estimated quantities are the only indication on the basis of which contractors prepare their quotes and the agency selects the successful contractor.[50]

With a 'captive client' for a long period of time, particularly if the client buys large quantities of items under a requirements contract, contractors may have a tendency to become complacent and less interested in enhancing value for money and competitiveness. Having a 'captive' client for large sales and for long periods of time, could also trigger temptations toward fraud and corruption. Further, the sheer volume of sales or purchases might distort the market. These are some reasons that legislators might consider limiting the use of this type of arrangement either in time[51] or in terms of value. However, the US federal procurement system has taken an additional approach. Thus, no requirements contract with an estimated value over US$ 100 million can be awarded to a single source unless specific circumstances are met.[52] Such circumstances are dealt with under FAR16.504 regarding indefinite-delivery/indefinite-quantity (ID/IQ) contracts and include the impossibility to separate tasks, contracts that provide for fixed unit prices, situations when only one offeror is qualified and capable of doing the work at

---

[47] FAR16.503(a)(1).

[48] ibid.

[49] FAR16.503(a), FAR52.216-21. J Cibinic Jr, RC Nash Jr and CR Yukins, *Formation of Government Contracts*, 4th edn (Washington DC, The George Washington University; Wolters Kluwer, 2011) 1350–51.

[50] See cases quoted by Kipa, Szeliga and Aronie, 'Conquering Uncertainty in an Indefinite World' (n 45); also Cibinic, Nash and Yukins, *Formation of Government Contracts* (n 49) 1351–54.

[51] In the US federal system a 10-year time-limit applies to task or delivery order contracts issued by the Department of Defense, whereas a 5-year general limit applies to all contracts under FAR; Cibinic, Nash and Yukins (n 49) 1343.

[52] FAR16.503(b)(2). Note that amounts provided throughout FAR (and referred to in this book) are amended from time to time.

prices acceptable to the Government, or public interest.[53] Also, no requirements contract for advisory and assistance services in excess of three years' duration and US$ 15 million in value can be awarded to a single source unless a determination is made by a relevant procurement officer (or other official) that the requirements 'are so unique or highly specialized that it is not practicable to make multiple awards' under an ID/IQ contract.[54] This approach is consistent with the statutory multiple-award preference introduced by FASA 1994.

The explicit language of the FAR that refers to filling all needs 'from one contractor', might suggest, prima facie, that requirements contracts are envisaged as single-agency, single-contractor arrangements.[55] However, from the provisions in the preceding paragraph it can be inferred, and in the literature it has been discussed, that multi-contractor requirements contracts may be permitted since 'the government can obtain more competition by dividing the requirement among two or more contractors', particularly when smaller contractors could be interested and 'the government's requirements are large'.[56] As shown below (under ordering), standard clauses for requirements contracts explicitly recognise that requirements contracts may involve two contractors in some circumstances. The first stage of the arrangement, namely selecting the contractor(s) and awarding a requirements contract, follows the general/'traditional' procurement procedures of the US federal procurement system. Selecting the right contractor(s) is particularly important since the arrangement is likely to close the market during its term and requirements contracts may generate a certain degree of reciprocal dependency between agency and contractor(s). The second stage of the arrangement, ie awarding orders under the requirements contract, is straight-forward as there usually is only one contractor. If a requirements contract is concluded with more than one supplier, then, when allocating successive orders, the agency should 'maintain as close a ratio as is reasonably practicable between the total quantities ordered from the two contractors'.[57]

Requirements contracts represent one more step further away from traditional procurement. In definite-quantity contracts, when starting the procurement and contracting, all elements are known (and set) except for the actual delivery schedule. In requirements contracts, there is one additional element that is not known with certainty, but only as a realistic estimate: the total quantity to be supplied or delivered under the contract. Definite-quantity contracts guarantee a certain total quantity of items to be procured while requirements contracts guarantee that all requirements for certain Government activities will be purchased from the contractor(s), unless exceptional circumstances arise.

---

[53] FAR16.504(c)(1)(ii)(D).
[54] FAR16.503(d)(1).
[55] FAR16.503(a).
[56] Cibinic, Nash and Yukins (n 49) 1346.
[57] eg, Alternate III under FAR52.216-21 where the 'requirements contract involves a partial small business set-aside'.

4.2.4. Indefinite-Delivery/Indefinite-Quantity Contracts (ID/IQ)

A step even further away from traditional procurement, providing increased flexibility to agencies, is represented by ID/IQ contracts.[58] An ID/IQ contract only guarantees that the agency will purchase from the contractor, through task or delivery orders, a minimum quantity of items over the contract period. This minimum can be very low in order to be deemed contractual consideration.[59] According to FAR16.504, in order to be binding the minimum must be 'more than a nominal quantity, but it should not exceed the amount that the Government is fairly certain to order'. The agency will be bound to purchase through orders only the nominal minimum; and it will be entitled to order during the contract period, and the contractor will be bound to supply, any quantity of items above the nominal minimum up to a maximum stated in the contract, defined in terms of quantity or value. Further, above the nominal minimum, the agency can order not only from the contractor but it can also purchase outside the ID/IQ contract[60] from other suppliers or providers.

Thus, it can be easily seen that ID/IQ arrangements provide increased flexibility and convenience for the agency. But flexibility and convenience may have a price and may also mean increased complexity or challenges. If the defined nominal minimum quantity is very low and the potential maximum quantity is very high, bidders may tend to quote high unit prices or rates, corresponding to the low guaranteed minimum quantity. If the agency then decides to order from the same contractor, above the nominal minimum, large quantities of items up to the potential maximum established in the contract, there is a risk that the same or similarly high unit prices will continue to be quoted or used, potentially affecting value for money over the contract duration. Clearly, if a need arises that could not have been predicted when initiating the procurement, then ordering under the ID/IQ contract in the conditions described (over the nominal minimum) provides for flexibility and convenience. But if the need could have been better predicted when initiating the procurement and it was not included in the nominal minimum, then orders above the minimum may become an extravagance. As in requirements contracts, the making of the right estimates by the agency before initiating the procurement is essential for such arrangements if they are to achieve value for money. However, the consequences of failing to meet estimates, and the standard of assessment, are different under ID/IQ contracts and requirements contracts.

---

[58] FAR16.504.

[59] Kipa, Szeliga and Aronie (n 45).

[60] ibid, 418, quoting the Court of Federal Circuit in case *Travel Ctr v Barram* 236 F.3d 1316 (Fed. Cir. 2001), as well as *Abatement Contracting Corp v United States* 58 Fed. Cl. 594, 604 (2003).

In many cases, because of the diligence standard of assessment in preparing the estimate, some contractors preferred, in litigation, to support the allegation that the contract was actually a requirements contract and not an ID/IQ contract. This is so because in a requirements contract contractors have a better chance of obtaining remedy if the agency ordered below the estimated maximum (which in requirements contracts coincides with estimated quantity), and the estimate has been prepared negligently.[61] By contrast, in an ID/IQ contract only the nominal minimum quantity is guaranteed for purchase by the agency, and the potential maximum anticipated under the contract basically creates no obligation for the agency, irrespective of negligence in the agency's preparation of the estimated potential maximum. Even in the context of allegations of bad faith in the preparation of the potential maximum estimate under ID/IQ contracts, aggrieved parties might be unsuccessful in obtaining remedy. The logic behind this approach is that 'the contractor does not have a reasonable expectation that the Government will order more than the minimum quantity' and the potential maximum does not have 'legal significance'.[62] Case law was also pretty much consistent considering that the nominal minimum guaranteed purchase quantity, as identified in the solicitation and the contract, is the drawing line for contractual obligations and liability of the agency. If the agency does not order the nominal minimum, through task or delivery orders issued during the contract period, then the aggrieved contractor is likely to be granted remedy.

As shown, because of a statutory preference, the 'usual' form of ID/IQ involves multiple-award contracting, whereas single-supplier ID/IQ arrangements are only possible under certain circumstances defined in the FAR that a procurement officer is able to justify. Thus, under FAR16.504(c)(1)(i),

> Except for indefinite-quantity contracts for advisory and assistance services … the contracting officer must, to the maximum extent practicable, give preference to making multiple awards of indefinite-quantity contracts under a single solicitation for the same or similar supplies or services to two or more sources.

Indeed, having more contractors able and willing to supply upon order toward satisfying a certain need of the agency, without the agency being bound to purchase from a certain contractor above the nominal minimum, provides not only for flexibility and convenience but also for security of supply. In arrangements with only one contractor, and in particular in requirements contracts because of the 'exclusivity' status of the contractor, if the contractor gets into difficulties, or does not perform satisfactorily, these difficulties will very likely have an impact on supply and on fulfilling the agency's needs. By contrast, in multiple awards ID/IQ contracts, the agency will have more supply alternatives, to whom the agency can turn to satisfy its needs (as they materialise).

---

[61] ibid, 428.
[62] ibid, 428 et seq.

Another reason for preferring multiple-award ID/IQ contracts is to avoid the concentration of too much business in a single supplier's 'yard', since this may distort the market or even competition in future procurements of the same agency or in similar procurements of other agencies. Actually, as in the case of requirements contracts (section 4.2.2 above), no task or delivery order contracts (including ID/IQ contracts) whose estimated value is in excess of US$ 100 million may be awarded to a single source unless specific conditions are met.[63] Distinct criteria apply to ID/IQ contracts for advisory and assistance services exceeding three years' duration and US$ 15 million in value.[64] Where the relevant circumstances apply then the head of agency / procurement officer has to make a written determination to this effect and keep it on file.[65]

Some elements are provided in the FAR that procurement officers should consider when planning the acquisition in order to decide on the appropriate number of contractors in a multiple-award ID/IQ exercise. These include the scope and complexity of requirement, the expected duration and frequency of orders to be placed, the mix of resources the contractor must have to perform orders, and ability to maintain competition between contractors throughout the contract's duration.[66] Circumstances when multiple-awards 'must not' be used are also listed, including:[67] (i) only one contractor being able to supply because the items to be procured are highly specialised; (ii) the connection between tasks dictates that only a single contractor can perform them; (iii) the expected costs of administering multiple awards outweigh the benefits of making multiple awards; (iv) based on the procurement officer's knowledge of the market, more favourable terms and conditions will be achieved if a single award is made; (v) the total estimated value of the contract is less than or equal to the simplified acquisition threshold;[68] (vi) multiple awards would not be in the best interest of the Government. It is relevant to note the nuanced considerations that procurement officers are required to weigh when planning ID/IQ contracts. These matters are discussed in a wider context in Chapter six, section 6.4.2.2.1.

After the elements above have been considered and a decision made as to whether an ID/IQ contract with a single source will be placed, or whether a multiple-award ID/IQ arrangement will be organised, a written determination by the procurement officer justifying the decision will be prepared and kept on the procurement file.[69] Following this, a 'standard' bidding procedure will be launched as the first stage of the ID/IQ procurement, ie selecting among

---

[63] FAR16.504(c)(1)(ii)(D).
[64] FAR16.504(c)(2).
[65] nn 63–64.
[66] FAR16.504(c)(1)(ii)(A).
[67] FAR16.504(c)(1)(ii)(B).
[68] In accordance with FAR2.101 this threshold usually is US$ 250,000; however, higher thresholds can apply in specific circumstances, including in crisis situations (see section 4.1.3 above).
[69] FAR16.504(c)(1)(ii)(C).

interested bidders and concluding the ID/IQ contract(s) with one or more suppliers. The FAR provides for a few specific elements that a solicitation must include in case of ID/IQ procurement.[70] These apply to both single-source and multiple-award ID/IQ procurements. Firstly, the solicitation must include the duration of the contract, and the period or periods for which the Government may extend the contract. Secondly, the solicitation must specify the minimum and the maximum quantities the Government will acquire under the contract. Thirdly, a statement of work needs to be included describing the general scope, complexity, and purpose of the supplies or services to be supplied under the contract, allowing bidders to decide whether to bid or not, and to prepare a bid. Also, the solicitation must include the procedures that will be used once the ID/IQ contract is in place, such as 'ordering media', and in case of multiple awards, 'the procedures and selection criteria' that will be used for the selection of suppliers for specific task or delivery orders; such procedures or criteria must ensure that each ID/IQ contractor will be given 'a fair opportunity to be considered for each order' above the micro-purchase threshold.[71]

Two inter-related elements require special attention in the case of multiple awards, as literature and case law have emphasised, since such elements can raise a number of practical issues: the procedures for selection of contractors to whom individual orders are to be awarded, and protesting against such awards by aggrieved contractors who believe their rights to receive orders have been ignored or breached. As shown, as a matter of principle, when awarding orders (above the micro-purchase threshold),[72] the procurement officer must ensure that all contractors within the ID/IQ arrangement are given a fair opportunity to be considered.[73] Unless specific circumstances are involved 'the contracting officer does not synopsize',[74] meaning that normally there is no need to publish calls for orders, or in any event not necessarily in the media where 'traditional' procurements are published. However, the appropriate media for making orders must be provided for in the contract.

Actually, the contracting officer does not need to 'contact' all ID/IQ contractors to submit offers for individual orders if the value of the order is below the simplified acquisition threshold[75] and provided that by doing so they do not affect the right of any contractors to be given a fair opportunity to be considered.[76] But specific conditions apply to order calls, which must be 'within the scope' of the ID/IQ

---

[70] FAR16.504(a)(4).

[71] FAR16.505(b)(1). The micro-purchase threshold, defined in FAR2.101, is usually US$ 10,000 but it can vary depending on specific circumstances.

[72] Basically, orders below the micro-purchase threshold can be placed as is most convenient for the agency.

[73] FASA attempted to introduce in this way enhanced competition among contractors at the second stage of ID/IQ procurements.

[74] FAR16.505(a)(1).

[75] See n 68.

[76] FAR16.505(b)(1)(ii).

contract, issued within the contract performance period and 'within the maximum' contract value or quantity provided for by the contract.[77] Similarly, a clear description of the services or supplies must be included, allowing for the cost or price to be established when the order is being placed,[78] since cost or price must always be considered in the selection decision.[79] At the same time, contracting officers should keep submission requirements to a minimum when calling for orders, and may use streamlined procedures or oral presentations.[80] It is relevant to note that contracting officers are required to 'Develop placement procedures … that reflect the requirement and other aspects of the contracting environment' and to 'Tailor the procedures to each acquisition'[81] within the limits imposed by 'fair consideration being given to all awardees'.[82]

Two additional conditions apply to orders exceeding the simplified threshold but not exceeding US$ 6 million.[83] First, a 'fair notice of intent' concerning the purchase must be issued to 'all contractors offering the required' items, which must state 'a clear description' of such items and the basis 'upon which the selection will be made'. Second, all contractors responding to the notice of intent must be provided with 'a fair opportunity to submit an offer and have that offer fairly considered'. Further competition requirements apply to orders to the value of over US$ 6 million,[84] which include a reasonable period for contractors to reply to the notice of the order (sent to all contractors); disclosure of 'the significant' evaluation factors and sub-factors, and their relative importance; and 'an opportunity for a post-award debriefing' regarding the outcome of the exercise.[85] While increased procedural and competition ('fair opportunity') requirements apply to higher value orders, as shown above, contracting officers 'may exercise broad discretion in developing order placement procedures'[86] in multiple-award ID/IQ contracts. In so doing, very relevant aspects are recommended by FAR to be considered by contracting officers, such as previous performance 'under the contract', whether a new order could affect 'other orders placed with the contractor', the time needed by contractors to respond to order calls, or (as appropriate) processes involving 'exchanges of information' with contractors (consultations on specification, and/ or a 'multiphased approach' involving further selection amongst all contractors followed by discussions).[87]

---

[77] FAR16.505(a)(2).
[78] ibid.
[79] FAR16.505(b)(1)(ii)(E).
[80] n 76.
[81] FAR16.505(b)(1)(ii)(A) and (C).
[82] FAR16.505(b)(1)(ii)(B).
[83] FAR16.505(b)(1)(iii).
[84] These were originally introduced in 2008 for orders above US$ 5 million following 'serious concerns about the use of task order[s] to conduct major acquisitions' and about the need for increased 'transparency and review': Acquisition Advisory Panel Report to Congress, as quoted in Bleicher et al (n 4) 399.
[85] FAR16.505(b)(1)(iv).
[86] FAR16.505(b)(1)(ii).
[87] FAR16.505(b)(1)(v).

Where providing a fair opportunity to be considered is not possible or desirable in order to select a contractor for placement of an order within a multi-contractor ID/IQ arrangement, the FAR provides for specific circumstances that allow for an exception to fair opportunity.[88] Such circumstances include: extreme urgency (which can be particularly useful in cases of crises); 'unique or highly specialized goods' or services; 'logical follow-on' from an older order (provided that for such previous order fair opportunity to be considered was given to all contractors under the arrangement); meeting a 'minimum guarantee'; orders set-aside for small businesses; and others. Specific rules apply to the preparation and approval mechanism for a justification for exception to the fair opportunity rule, depending on the value of the order.[89] Further, contract award notices (synopses) *as well as* justifications of exceptions to fair opportunity are required to be published for orders exceeding the simplified acquisition threshold (and awarded without fair competition), unless specified circumstances apply such as small business set-aside orders.[90] Publication occurs via the 'Governmentwide point of entry' which is 'where Government business opportunities ... can be accessed electronically by the public'.[91] It is relevant to note that the FAR addresses expressly both circumstances that justify exceptions to fair opportunity as well as the detailed procedures for approval of such course of action and any transparency requirements over the award of such orders. In contrast, in some systems or instruments, for instance under the EU directives, the regulation is silent on these matters, thereby creating some areas of legal uncertainty.[92]

Returning to the US federal procurement system, as shown, FASA 1994 introduced a ban on protesting orders under ID/IQ contracts, except where an order exceeded the scope of the ID/IQ contract,[93] which was intended to ensure the convenience and practicality of ID/IQ contracting. This provided an even wider area of discretion for contracting officers, which brought about case-law interpretations of the ban on ID/IQ order protests and, possibly in light of abuse concerns, the ban was then softened, as shown below. But under those circumstances many protests had to be dismissed without a review on the merits, because of lack of jurisdiction. In an attempt to maintain a certain level of oversight over the award of orders under ID/IQ contracts, the GAO employed two other exceptions to the FASA ban that were not explicit in FASA: first, down selections, ie 'reductions in the group of potential vendors', for example, narrowing 'the field of eligible vendors for future orders under a multiple award ID/IQ

---

[88] FAR16.505(b)(2)(i).

[89] FAR16.505(b)(2)(ii).

[90] FAR16.505(b)(2)(ii)(D) and FAR5.301. Small business set asides are also exempt from justification under FAR16.505(b)(2)(ii).

[91] FAR2.101 specifying it can be accessed at www.sam.gov. Justifications may (also) be posted on the agency's website (FAR16.505(b)(2)(ii)(D)).

[92] For wider perspectives see Chapter 6, section 6.6.2.3 of this book.

[93] This is currently located in FAR16.505(a)(10)(i)(A).

contract to a single vendor';[94] and, second, the award of orders under the federal supply schedules[95] that we discuss in the following section. There was certainly proper justification for these implicit exceptions to the ban. 'Down selections' were quite rightly considered practices against the spirit of the regulation of ID/IQ arrangements, as it would not make sense to have a multiple-award ID/IQ contract if the order or orders awarded to a contractor would basically prevent all other potential contractors in the ID/IQ arrangement from being awarded future orders. On the other hand, since the ban only relates to ID/IQ contracts and federal schedules are dealt with separately in the regulations, the award of orders under federal supply schedules was not considered to fall within the scope of the ban.

Beyond these exceptions, many awards of orders under ID/IQ contracts remained 'below the radar' of GAO review. However, the changes in the procedures for the award of orders valued at over US$ 5 million (currently over US$ 6 million) and also extension of the GAO's jurisdiction to the award of orders above US$ 10 million suggest that increased competition and oversight were needed in connection with the award of orders.[96] Still, this threshold was subsequently increased to US$ 25 million in the case of defence agencies (Department of Defense, NASA, or the Coast Guard), whilst it remained at US$ 10 million for civilian agencies.[97] This extension of jurisdiction, compared to the original provision in FASA, means that the GAO can review on merits the protests of orders above the value thresholds shown in the preceding *sentence*, and not only if such protests fall within the exceptions described in the preceding *paragraph*.

However, for orders below these thresholds the ban still applies, with the exceptions discussed above. Therefore, an independent, third-party review on the merits of a protest against such an order continues to be difficult.[98] Instead, FASA took the view that the GAO's jurisdiction to review order protests would be replaced with an alternative system whereby a task or delivery order ombudsman was established in each agency to deal with complaints (according to the procedures provided for in the contract) and to ensure that such contractors are provided with a fair opportunity to be considered. This was not necessarily the most effective way to review such complaints, since, even if the ombudsman may be independent from the contracting officer, they cannot possibly be fully independent of the agency that designated them and whose official the ombudsman is. Thus, a fully independent review cannot be achieved through the ombudsman.

[94] Bleicher et al (n 4) 390.

[95] ibid, 392.

[96] National Defense Authorization Act for Fiscal Year 2008, section 843.

[97] See: GAO Civilian Task and Delivery Order Protest Authority Act of 2016; National Defense Authorization Act for Fiscal Year 2017, section 835; 10 USC 3406(f); 41 USC 4106(f); FAR16.505(a)(10)(i)(B).

[98] Further on this, GM Ebert, 'Protests of Orders: A Drizzle or a Downpour: Examining the Results of the Government Accountability Office's Exclusive Protest Jurisdiction Following the NDAA Amendments to FASA' (2016) 45 *PCLJ* 613.

As can be noticed, FASA tried to find some middle-ground between the need for more transparency and competition in the award of orders on the one hand, and the likely disruptions that submission of task order protests would bring to procurement through orders, on the other hand.

ID/IQ contracting, and particularly multi-award contracting remains one of the main vehicles of procuring for recurrent needs in the US federal procurement system. Practicality, speed and convenience appear to outweigh transparency and contestability in the second stage of a multiple-award ID/IQ arrangement, for many orders, in particular smaller ones, but also to some extent quite large ones. It is relevant to note in particular the (detailed) provisions concerning the multiple-award preference and the ordering process (second stage of the arrangement), which provide for a nuanced approach and significant flexibility. Whilst being very informative on multi-phased aspects of 'framework' arrangements, regulations on ordering appear perhaps overly complex and/or insufficiently precise in some respects to secure proper compliance in their implementation,[99] for instance in comparison with the UNCITRAL Model Law or the EU directives. Conversely, additional express provisions or nuancing may be desirable in those latter instruments, for example concerning potential limitations on or exceptions to second-stage competition (in frameworks involving reopening of competition) or simplified procedures for smaller call-offs, and the FAR might provide some inspiration on such matters that could be adapted as needed.[100] However, a ban on protesting orders seems unlikely to promote an appropriate use of frameworks.

4.2.5. Federal Supply Schedules

Another vehicle aiming at a quick and convenient procurement process for 'commercial supplies and services'[101] is the Federal Supply Schedule (FSS) Program – also referred to as the GSA Schedules Program, or the Multiple Award Schedule (MAS) Program – directed by the General Services Administration (GSA).[102] This programme has a long history starting in 1949. In the 1990s it experienced an explosive development, with more and more schedule contractors being involved in the programme and with more and more orders being placed. Various reports and literature emphasised the expansion of MAS sales, as

---

[99] From this perspective, describing those regulations as 'amount[ing] to nothing more than "purely generalized suggestions"' seems too harsh (MJ Lohnes, 'Attempting to Spur Competition for Orders Placed under Multiple Award Task Order and MAS Contracts: The Journey to the Unworkable Section 803' (2004) 33 *PCLJ* 599). But the suggestion of these authors concerning the need for additional guidance and rules appears adequate.

[100] See further Chapter 6, sections 6.4.2 and 6.6.2 of this book.

[101] FAR38.101(a).

[102] FAR8.402(a).

well as the MAS contracts.[103] One article accounted for the significant growth in terms of sales volumes from $US 4 billion in 1992 up to $US 34.8 billion in 2008, and in terms of the number of schedules contracts administered, from 1,817 in 1994 to 17,683 in 2006.[104] Indeed, the sales continued at similar levels annually from 2016 to 2020.[105]

Schedules are lists of suppliers, items and services they provide, and prices offered, following a selection process carried out by the GSA[106] or by other agencies authorised by it, such as the Department of Veteran Affairs (DVA).[107] Such lists are established and administered by the GSA (or DVA) in a catalogue that is available online to Government agencies as *e Library*.[108] Schedule contracts are contracts concluded between the GSA (or DVA) with interested contractors willing to be included in the e Library catalogue and to supply products or provide services to various Government agencies, upon orders or based on blanket purchase agreements (BPAs).[109] Whilst originally the use of GSA Schedules was compulsory for 'all federal agencies', this changed after the 1990s when 'GSA lost its role as a mandatory source of supply'.[110]

The process of entering the MAS Program, namely the first stage of selecting contractors and establishing schedule contracts, has some specific features and, notably, terms are *not* established through a comparison *amongst* offers received. Thus, upon a solicitation of offers for certain goods or services, issued by the GSA, interested vendors submit proposals. More vendors can submit proposals for similar or like products or services, while other contractors may already have been included in the MAS Program at the time of a specific solicitation. The relevant MAS centre analyses the proposal as to its eligibility/qualification (contractor responsibility) and completeness.[111] Before including a contractor in the programme, if the offer is determined as eligible and complete, an essential step is to establish whether prices offered by that contractor are fair and reasonable for the Government agencies to purchase such items.[112] This basically means, in terms of MAS, to ensure that the prices offered (or further negotiated, or maintained during the duration of the schedule contract) for MAS are at least as

---

[103] eg, GAO 'Contract Management: Opportunities to Improve Pricing of GSA Multiple Award Schedule Contracts' (GAO-05-229, February 2005) 5–7.

[104] RR Hutchinson, 'Oversight of GSA Federal Supply Schedule Contracts: From Internal Compliance Programs to Civil False Claims Actions' (2008) 37 *PCLJ* 569.

[105] FEDSched, 'GSA MAS Schedule Contract: Fiscal Year 2020 Sales Stats' at https://gsa.federalsched-ules.com/resources/a-first-look-at-fy-2020-gsa-contract-sales/, with over $US 36 billion in FY2020.

[106] Cibinic, Nash and Yukins (n 49) 1144.

[107] eg, FAR38.101(d).

[108] FAR8.401, stating that the relevant web address is www.gsa.gov/elibrary, though the link actually leads to https://www.gsa.gov/tools-overview/buying-and-selling-tools (and e library can be accessed via this site).

[109] Cibinic, Nash and Yukins (n 49) 1184–88.

[110] Gordon and Racca (n 1) 137. FAR38.101(b) and (c).

[111] GAO, 'Contract Management' (n 103) 11.

[112] ibid, p 2.

advantageous as the most privileged (discounted) price offers the contractor uses in their business for their other clients.[113]

To support achieving this in practice, a number of instruments can be used by GSA officers, such as market research, documents relating to vendors' sales history, pre-award audits and post-award audits. For instance, in pre-award audits vendors' documents may be inspected at the vendor's head-office to ensure that the information submitted by the vendor is accurate and complete, and therefore that the basis for establishing the fair and reasonable price is correct. However, not all assessments of vendors' offers for entering MAS are subject to audit. The literature has emphasised that a significant reduction of the number of such audits took place in particular after 1996, combined with a reduction of other controls during the schedule contract period.[114] In many cases, this had resulted in excessive spending by Government, with contractors abusing the system and failing to provide appropriate information either to enter the system, or to maintain the most privileged price offers during the contract period.[115] Whilst these types of issue have persisted (and have continued being reported and approached),[116] beyond pros and cons, MAS carries on as a big success in terms of the value of sales, convenience, and not least, in terms of the commissions charged for such sales.[117] Basically, MAS is a huge centralised PUIR arrangement, where GSA enters into and administers a very large number of schedule contracts with many suppliers. The first stage of the arrangement, when schedule contractors are selected and schedule contracts concluded is started by the GSA before the needs of agencies are actually known (or have materialised), and the GSA initiates the process based on the assumption that Government agencies will always need various commercial items.[118]

Once a contractor is awarded a schedule contract, it will have the chance of being awarded task or delivery orders, or BPAs, that Government agencies can employ to procure items, under the second stage of this purchasing mechanism.[119]

---

[113] See eg Albano and Nicholas (n 31) 105–06; GAO (n 103).

[114] GAO (n 103) 14–18.

[115] On criticism about the process of establishing/maintaining fair and reasonable prices in GSA schedules, see further Gordon and Racca (n 1) 137–38; AE Woodward, 'The Perverse Effect of the Multiple Award Schedules' Price Reductions Clause' (2012) 41 *PCLJ* 527.

[116] Albano and Nicholas (n 31) 134–35, and documents referred to therein; CL Vacketta and S Curley, 'An Effective Compliance Program: A Necessity for Government Contractors under IDIQ Contracts and Beyond' (2008) 37 *PCLJ* 593; and see also GSA, 'GSA Strategic Plan Fiscal Years 2022–2026', strategic objective 2.2 (p 18) via www.gsa.gov/reference/reports/budget-performance/gsa-fy-20222026-strategic-plan.

[117] The commission is also known as 'the industrial funding fee' (IFF). It is charged to GSA contractors on a quarterly basis as 'a percentage of the total quarterly sales'. See Cibinic, Nash and Yukins (n 49) 1142; see also the Industrial Funding Fee and Sales Reporting Clause 552.238-80 in the General Sevices Acquisition Manual (GSAM) via www.acquisition.gov/gsam.

[118] See the definitions of 'commercial supplies' and 'commercial services' in FAR2.101 (such items form the subject matter of schedules, see eg FAR8.402(a)).

[119] The applicable ordering rules are described in FAR8.4.

As shown, one of the main differences between ID/IQ multiple-award orders and orders issued against schedules is that the protest ban does not apply to the latter.[120] For each category of similar or like products or services, there are many schedule suppliers, so that competition among them can be achieved when agencies award orders or BPAs to existing GSA schedule contractors. Orders are used for filling one-off needs, while BPAs are used 'to fill repetitive needs for supplies or services'.[121] BPAs may be placed against one or more schedule contractor(s), can be 'used by multiple agencies, and may be for five years',[122] though a preference applies for multiple-award BPAs[123] (somewhat similar to that under ID/IQ contracts). In case of BPAs, the procurement actually involves a third stage, namely placing orders under the BPA. It should be noted that the GAO held that BPAs are not contracts, that orders under BPAs are placed on the basis of the 'main' schedule contract and, in effect, orders under BPAs can only be placed by the time the schedule contract has expired, it thus being suggested in the literature that a more adequate 'name' for BPA would have been 'blanket orders'.[124]

The provisions concerning procedures that must be followed by ordering activities (entities eligible to order) intending to purchase items from schedules are quite detailed and complex.[125] The FAR structures these procedures by: (i) the nature of the purchase, namely order or BPA; (ii) the value of the purchase; and (iii) the nature of the item(s) being procured, ie, items requiring a statement of work (SOW) or items not requiring such description. A statement of work defines the features, performance, and/or other characteristics of a service, and must be used 'when ordering services priced at hourly rates as established by the schedule contracts';[126] whereas items not requiring a SOW refer to 'supplies and services that are listed in the schedules contracts at a fixed price for the performance of a specific task ... (*e.g.*, installation, maintenance, and repair)'.[127]

Since 'fair and reasonable' prices have been pre-determined by the GSA with schedule contractors during the first stage of schedule procurement (when selecting schedule contractors), procedures during the second stage, for awarding orders or BPAs, generally require some level of competition, though not the 'full and open competition' standard applicable to 'traditional' procurements, consistent with the approach that schedules should be a vehicle for quick and convenient purchases. But orders placed or BPAs established under MAS, according to FAR8.4, 'are considered to be issued using full and open competition'.[128] Along this line of thinking, 'ordering activities are not required to make a separate determination

[120] Section 4.2.4 above.
[121] FAR8.405-3(a)(1).
[122] Nash, O'Brien-Debakey and Schooner, *Government Contracts Reference Book* (n 43) 59.
[123] FAR8.405-3(a)(3).
[124] Cibinic, Nash and Yukins (n 49) 1187.
[125] FAR8.405 et seq.
[126] FAR8.405-2(a); and see also FAR8.405-2(b).
[127] FAR8.405-1(a).
[128] FAR8.404(a).

of fair and reasonable pricing, except for a price evaluation' in the case of services requiring a SOW.[129] In any event, before placing an order or BPA, contracting officers may – and, where the order or BPA exceeds the simplified acquisition threshold,[130] they must – seek further discounts from schedule contractors by comparison to listed schedule prices, although contractors are not bound to offer such further discounts.[131]

Ordering procedures follow somewhat similar approaches, which are determined by the value of the exercise, and are addressed in the FAR distinctly depending on whether or not the items require a SOW,[132] since this entails some significant differences, such as the requirement for a determination of price reasonableness and fairness within the financial evaluation referred to in the preceding paragraph.[133] In any event,

> By placing an order against a schedule contract … the ordering activity has concluded that the order represents the best value … and results in the lowest overall cost alternative (considering price, special features, administrative costs, etc.) to meet the Government's needs.[134]

Under FAR2.101 '*Best value* means the expected outcome of an acquisition that, in the Government's estimation, provides the greatest overall benefit in response to the requirement'.

For orders below the micro-purchase threshold[135] the order can be awarded to any schedule contractor able to fill the agency's need and 'Although not required to solicit from a specific number of schedule contractors, ordering activities should attempt to distribute orders among schedule contractors'.[136] As can be seen, the approach resembles the one employed for orders under that threshold in multiple-award ID/IQ contracting. For MAS orders between the micro-purchase threshold and the simplified acquisition threshold, where a SOW is not required, the contracting officer must review 'at least three schedule contractors through *GSA Advantage!*' online facility (or otherwise document and consider catalogues or pricelists of such contractors) or request 'quotations from at least three schedule contractors' that can provide the required supply or service.[137] Where a SOW *is* required, a Request for Quotations (RFQ) comprising SOW and evaluation criteria must be provided to 'at least three schedule contractors that offer services

---

[129] FAR8.404(d) referring FAR8.405-2(d). See also FAR8.405-3(b)(2)(vi).

[130] n 68.

[131] RJ Sherry, GM Koehl and SA Armstrong, 'Competition Requirements in General Services Administration Schedule Contracts' (2008) 37 *PCLJ* 468, 475. See also FAR8.404(d) and FAR8.405-4.

[132] FAR8.405-1 et seq.

[133] See text to n 129.

[134] FAR 8.404(d).

[135] n 71.

[136] FAR8.405-1(b). Quite similar wording is provided in FAR8.405-2(c)(1).

[137] FAR8.405-1(c). '*GSA Advantage!*' is available via www.gsa.gov/tools-overview/buying-and-selling-tools.

that will meet the agency's needs'.[138] Alternatively, in both situations above, if there are reasons for restricting the number of sources, ordering activities must document the circumstances and in some cases publish relevant data;[139] this provision also somewhat resembles that applied under ID/IQ multiple-award contracting.[140]

Proposed orders exceeding the simplified acquisition threshold are to be awarded competitively, unless a limitation of sources applies, and the procedural requirements are described distinctly depending on whether a SOW is applicable or otherwise.[141] Basically, the contracting officer must provide an RFQ describing the requirement and the basis for selecting the offer (or, as applicable, comprising the SOW and evaluation criteria), or publish the RFQ on *e-Buy*, an electronic site allowing for all interested schedule contractors to take notice of the opportunity and submit an offer.[142] Where publication on *e-Buy* is not pursued, the ordering activity officer must provide the RFQ to 'as many schedule contractors as practicable', according to the market research conducted, so as 'to reasonably ensure' *receipt* of at least three quotes from 'contractors that can fulfil the requirements'.[143] Also, the contracting officer must ensure that all quotes are fairly considered and that the successful quote is selected based on the RFQ.[144]

Establishment of BPAs follows procedures set forth distinctly in the FAR,[145] resembling in broad-brush those for orders, though with specific features and approaches. These procedures are also structured mainly by the applicability or not of SOW, and by the estimated value of the BPA. As regards orders from BPAs, if the BPA arrangement is with one contractor, then orders are placed directly, as and when the needs for supply or services within the scope of the BPA arise. If the BPA is with more contractors then placement of orders will need to observe the BPA ordering procedures, which, again, will depend on the value of order, and on the type of items required.[146] The regulations provide for a determined duration of BPAs,[147] and for (at least) an annual review of BPAs.[148]

The above gives 'a flavour' of, and some 'key' features concerning, the intricacies of ordering procedures in relation to schedules. Whilst there is no room or scope here to discuss full procedural details, overall, somewhat similar to those on ID/IQ ordering, the provisions on procedures appear perhaps overly complex and/or insufficiently precise in some respects to secure proper compliance

[138] FAR8.405-2(c)(2)(ii).
[139] As provided under FAR8.405-6.
[140] Compare with FAR16.505(b)(2).
[141] FAR8.405-1(d) and FAR8.405-2(c)(3), each referring to FAR8.405-6.
[142] FAR8.402(d). The web address is www.ebuy.gsa.gov/ebuy/.
[143] FAR8.405-1(d)(3)(ii). Similar provision is made in FAR8.405-2(c)(3)(iii)(B).
[144] FAR8.405-1(d)(4); FAR8.405-2(c)(3)(iii)(C).
[145] In FAR8.405-3(a) and (b).
[146] FAR8.405-3(c).
[147] As described in FAR8.405-3(d).
[148] FAR8.405-3(d).

in implementation. It is important, though, to recall that, unlike ID/IQ orders, MAS orders and BPAs are not exempt from protest.[149] From another angle, it is relevant to note the 2011 development of provisions concerning BPAs and ordering under them, which confirms the need to regulate carefully such a 'three-stage' purchasing arrangement.[150]

Beyond advantages and shortcomings, or potential criticism, GSA schedule procurement represents the furthest step away from 'traditional procurement'. The MAS Program is, by its very nature, a centralised multiple-agency multiple-contractor arrangement. The process is started on the assumption that commercial items of all kinds are going to be needed by agencies at some point. Interested contractors then enter schedule contracts. They commit to the most privileged (discounted) price offers for being listed in schedules, which provides opportunities for sales to a wide range of Government agencies, through orders or BPAs. There are no guaranteed scales of sales to ordering entities but there is an indefinite potential. Whilst the size of the US federal procurement market appears to be a significant enabler of the programme, motivating firms to agree to offering the most privileged (discounted) prices, the question arises whether a somewhat similar core purchasing mechanism (adjusted as appropriate) might be developed to operate, for instance, at EU level for use by Member States, or at the level of an international development organisation such as the World Bank for its project operations.[151]

4.3. Conclusions

US federal procurement relies to a great extent on what I define as PUIR arrangements' recurrent purchasing arrangements. Practical experience demonstrates that purchasing standard items needed regularly, or on an ongoing or indefinite basis, requires specific purchasing arrangements providing for quick and convenient acquisition methods, whereas going through a full 'traditional' procurement each and every time a need for standard items materialises is likely to be inefficient and time-consuming. The arrangements of the US federal procurement system analysed in this chapter provide the example of a very experienced system that has developed a wide range of mechanisms to suit various

---

[149] FAR8.404(e).

[150] As to which, in wider perspective, see further eg Chapter 5, section 5.3.2.4.2 and, in particular Chapter 6, section 6.6.3 of this book.

[151] On the idea of potentially coordinating procurement strategy and demand at such levels, in relation to emergency procurement in light of the coronavirus pandemic experience, but not addressing the method for formation of terms in such procurement mechanisms, see GL Albano, 'Homo Homini Lupus: On the Consequences of Buyers' Miscoordination in Emergency Procurement for the COVID-19 Crisis in Italy' (2020) 29 *PPLR* 213, 219.

procurement circumstances, each representing one or more step(s) away from 'traditional' public procurement, toward 'business-like procurement'.

Such approaches naturally tend to be very specific and geared tightly to the features and objectives of the US federal procurement market. Nonetheless, *some* elements of those approaches may also be particularly informative and potentially inspiring for other procurement systems – in a wider perspective, not 'imported' as such, but thoroughly selected and adapted to the relevant context of that other procurement system. These elements include, as shown, considerations in deciding amongst establishing a single- versus a multiple-supplier 'framework' arrangement, or the desirable number of 'framework' suppliers, or addressing expressly potential justifications for limitation of competition in frameworks that involve reopening of competition at the call-off stage. Similarly, MAS is an arrangement uniquely of its kind amongst those reviewed in this book; it uses a distinct mechanism for establishing prices during its first stage (formation of schedule contracts), and regulations address comprehensively orders or BPAs placed against schedules (second stage), as well as, if applicable, orders based on BPAs (third stage). Conversely though, the US federal experience also suggests that overly complex or too lax call-off procedures, and/or precluding protests on a significant share of call-offs is likely to affect value for money and/ or integrity. Transversal perspectives in Chapter six discuss these aspects in the context of all the procurement systems and instruments analysed in this book, thereby supporting relevant actors to balance their approaches in light of the prevailing circumstances.

5

EU Law, Selected EU
Member States, and the UK

5.1. Scoping and Organisation

This chapter examines, jointly, EU law and policy toward purchasing uncertain or indefinite requirements (PUIR) as regards purchases conducted by covered purchasers from EU Member States, three national public procurement systems of Member States – France, Romania, and the UK *before* Brexit – as well as the UK *post*-Brexit public procurement reform outside the EU. This organisation of the material permits the avoidance of unnecessary repetition that would have been inherent given the significant commonalities arising from EU regulation, whilst at the same time including, in appropriate sections throughout the chapter, specific domestic approaches and experiences (of the EU Member States examined, in relation to margins of discretion envisaged by EU law) that are significant in the wider context of the book. Furthermore, addressing and incorporating developments in the UK *post*-Brexit procurement reform in appropriate places throughout this chapter provides the net advantage of a fluid analysis of evolutions in context. It is relevant to bear in mind that, at the time of writing, the UK continues to use PUIR rules that are quite similar to the EU rules, with adjustments ensuring operation outside the EU, whilst the envisaged changes to PUIR pursuant to the UK Public Procurement Reform can currently be regarded as 'work in progress' and yet to be detailed and nuanced during the legislative process of the UK Procurement Bill and upcoming secondary legislation and guidance. In this way, this chapter is significantly more concise and revealing as to the main themes and trends, having addressed each of the case studies it refers to in other separate chapters.

At EU law level, public procurement, including PUIR, is regulated through specific legal instruments imposing obligations on Member States. These legal instruments are, mainly, the EU procurement *directives*: the public sector (or 'classic') directive,[1] the utilities directive,[2] and the defence and security directive.[3]

---

[1] Directive 2014/24/EU of the European Parliament and of the Council of 26 February 2014 on public procurement and repealing Directive 2004/18/EC [2014] OJ L94/65 (hereinafter 'PSD').

[2] Directive 2014/25/EU of the European Parliament and of the Council of 26 February 2014 on procurement by entities operating in the water, energy, transport and postal services sectors and repealing Directive 2004/17/EC [2014] OJ L94/243 (hereinafter 'UD').

[3] Directive 2009/81/EC of the European Parliament and of the Council of 13 July 2009 on the coordination of procedures for the award of certain works contracts, supply contracts and service

These are supplemented by two procurement remedies directives (and other instruments referred to here as appropriate). Since the majority of public procurement rules at EU law level are enacted by using the legal instrument of directives, their norms must be coordinated among the EU Member States. Whilst national legislators of Member States must ensure that the requirements of the EU public procurement directives are transposed into their legal systems, they are allowed to issue or follow their own public procurement procedures and regulations to the extent that such procedures or regulations do not contradict the requirements of EU law.[4] Thus, among Member States there are certain common procurement approaches, principles and requirements, as imposed by EU law, but there are also national differences, as permitted within the 'limits' or 'framework' provided for by the EU public procurement law.

The rules in the EU directives apply only to procurements whose value exceeds certain thresholds specified in the directives,[5] and the scope of the current chapter does not include procurements below those thresholds in Member States, or procurements otherwise excluded from the remit of the EU procurement directives. As regards the UK, to which EU law no longer applies since January 2021 pursuant to its departure from the EU, the chapter refers to the Westminster jurisdiction, and not to devolved jurisdictions.

5.2. Relevant Procurement Contexts

5.2.1. EU Public Procurement Law

5.2.1.1. Approach

The EU law shapes to a significant degree public procurement systems of all (currently 27) EU Member States. Almost all substantive procurement norms are found in directives, noting also that relevant case law of the European Court of Justice (Court of Justice of the European Union (CJEU)) is compulsory for Member States. The nature of directives as a legal instrument explains to a considerable degree the approach and features of the public procurement system. Whilst a regulation, as an EU legal instrument, is directly applicable and binding in all respects for all Member States,[6] a directive 'shall be binding, as to the result to

---

contracts by contracting authorities or entities in the fields of defence and security, and amending Directives 2004/17/EC and 2004/18/EC [2009] OJ L216/76 (hereinafter 'DD').

[4] See S Arrowsmith and S Treumer, 'Competitive Dialogue in EU law – A Critical Review' in S Arrowsmith and S Treumer (eds), *Competitive Dialogue in EU Procurement* (Cambridge, CUP, 2012) 9–13; also, P Trepte, *Public Procurement in the EU: A Practitioner's Guide* (Oxford, OUP, 2007) 1–3.

[5] Art 4PSD; art 15UD; art 8DD, as amended – see also the revision of thresholds through Implementing Regulations, eg, under art 6PSD (or as relevant for each sector).

[6] Treaty on the Functioning of the European Union (TFEU), art 288.

be achieved ... but shall leave to the national authorities the choice of form and methods'.[7] Transposition of a directive into national law takes the form of either enacting new domestic legislation of the appropriate level, or amending existing legislation so as to ensure that the results provided for in the directive are met. In effect, some degree of discretion is allowed to Member States. A directive provides for flexibility, allowing not only for harmonisation of legal norms among Member States but also within each Member State's own legal, administrative and institutional environment. This instrument takes into account that in some areas of EU legislative intervention there may be a need to adapt approaches to different national contexts. Public procurement has been perceived as one such subject that requires a flexible approach.

It is also important to look at the legal basis of the procurement directives in the Treaty on the Functioning of the European Union (TFEU). All three procurement directives 'were adopted under the EU's internal market provisions',[8] as it results from their preambles.[9] It follows that the directives are mainly concerned with maintaining and enhancing the good functioning and openness of the EU internal market, defined in TFEU article 26(2) as 'an area without internal frontiers in which free movement of goods, persons, services and capital is ensured.' Recital 1 of the 2014 Public Sector Directive states:

> The award of public contracts ... has to comply with the principles of the Treaty ... and in particular the free movement of goods, freedom of establishment and the freedom to provide services, as well as the principles deriving therefrom, such as equal treatment, non-discrimination, mutual recognition, proportionality and transparency.

The procurement directives are less concerned with provision of detailed rules or guidance as to how procuring entities should achieve efficiency or value for money in their individual procurement processes, and focus on coordination and harmonisation of measures supporting development of the internal procurement market of the EU at macro-level, as well as other EU objectives.[10] The main 'addressees' of the directives are Member States (and not the covered purchasers). It is for Member States to pursue efficiency and value for money in public procurement, as well as other (domestic) objectives to the extent not conflicting with EU law. These issues are particularly relevant not just for understanding the approach of EU law in public procurement and interpreting it, but also as regards the UK's procurement reform objectives after Brexit.[11]

---

[7] ibid. However, under the 'direct effect' doctrine, 'individuals may enforce in national courts the rights conferred by the directives' subject to certain conditions: OECD, Sigma, *Brief 1 Public Procurement – Public Procurement in the EU: Legislative Framework, Basic Principles and Institutions* (OECD, Sigma, 2016) 4.

[8] S Arrowsmith, 'The Purpose of the EU Procurement Directives: Ends, Means and the Implications for National Regulatory Space for Commercial and Horizontal Procurement Policies' (2012) 14 *Cambridge Yearbook of European Legal Studies* 1, 5.

[9] Referring to TFEU, arts 53(1), 62, 114 (or their predecessors).

[10] Arrowsmith and Treumer, 'Competitive Dialogue' (n 4).

[11] See section 5.2.3 below.

EU regulation of public procurement mainly through directives has been a constant since the 1970s, when public procurement was initially regulated explicitly using secondary law. However, with every 'generation' of directives over the decades the margin of discretion of Member States has narrowed in many respects, and the 2014 Public Sector Directive has introduced an additional 'layer' of constraint which may generate transposition and interpretation issues, including with regard to framework agreements, as will be discussed in this chapter.

Thus, the EU public procurement system as mainly regulated through directives can be described as an 'indirect' procurement system to a large degree, in that its provisions and instruments mainly address EU Member States, rather than their purchasers. In contrast, the US federal procurement system is actually intended as a comprehensive public procurement system for purchasers under its own jurisdiction. As shown in Chapter two, the UNCITRAL Model Law on Public Procurement (like the EU directives) is also addressed to States and legislators, rather than to purchasers. However, while the adoption of the UNCITRAL Model Law is entirely voluntary for States, the flexibility provided by the EU directives for Member States is limited in that the EU directives impose legal obligations on EU Member States concerning the results to be achieved through domestic legal instruments.

5.2.1.2. History and Coverage

In the early days of the construction of the European Community (EC), it did not take long for EC institutions to come to the conclusion that specific measures were needed to ensure establishment and proper functioning of the internal market, and that such measures had to address, inter alia, public sector buying. An initial concern related to discrimination on grounds of nationality in public procurement and this was addressed, as early as the 1960s, in two General Programmes which were then partly implemented through the so-called 'liberalisation' directives, whose main focus was to eliminate restrictions on the free movement of goods and freedom to provide services.[12] But those measures proved insufficient to secure the freedoms provided for in the Treaty establishing the European Economic Community (Treaty of Rome, 1957), and the need for further positive action was perceived, namely to coordinate the laws of Member States concerning public contract award procedures. 'Coordination' directives were a qualitative move; the initial ones were Directive 71/305/EEC[13] concerning public works and Directive 77/62/EEC[14] concerning public supply contracts. Whilst repealed in 1993, these instruments had set the foundation stones for the current EU public procurement law.

---

[12] Trepte, *Public Procurement in the EU* (n 4) 27–29.
[13] [1971] OJ L185/5.
[14] [1977] OJ L13/1.

The 1980s were a period of review and analysis of the integration of the public procurement market. Notable developments ensued towards the end of the decade when Directive 89/665/EEC[15] came to regulate review mechanisms concerning public procurement, namely making available means for aggrieved tenderers to challenge procurement acts and decisions of covered purchasers. The objective of this directive was to establish a specific public procurement review mechanism, including legal standing, competence of a review body independent from the purchaser, availability of quick and specific measures (suspension), other reparatory measures as appropriate, and enforceability of the decisions delivered by the review bodies. Together with initial procurement coordination directives, Directive 89/665/EEC set another 'building block' of the EU public procurement law system.

An additional impetus to the regulation of public procurement was brought by the Single European Act (1986), with its ambitious agenda of establishing a 'single market' by 1992. First, the utilities sector was brought into a procurement regulatory regime through Directive 90/531/EEC.[16] Extension of the regulatory regime to the utilities sector was relatively quickly followed by a corresponding extension of the remedies regime to this sector, through Directive 92/13/EEC.[17] One further extension of the regulatory regime, in July 1992, concerned inclusion of public sector (non-construction) services, the procurement of such services being initially regulated through Directive 92/50/EEC.[18] The next 'legislative action' of the 1990s was a consolidation exercise concerning some of existing directives.

The first decade of the new millennium brought new changes to the procurement regulatory regime. In 2004 a new consolidated directive was adopted for the public sector, which covered, for the first time together, supply, services and works contracts (substantive procurement rules): Directive 2004/18/EC[19] (hereinafter '2004PSD'). At the same time a new directive on utilities substantive rules was adopted: Directive 2004/17/EC[20] (hereinafter '2004UD'). These 2004 directives were driven by a perceived need for modernisation, simplification and increased flexibility.[21] It is important to note that the 2004PSD specifically recognised and regulated framework agreements in the public sector. Also, the 2004 directives introduced in both sectors 'dynamic purchasing systems', a specific type of open arrangement for repeat procurement of 'common use' items. As a consequence of the new substantive procurement rules and case law of CJEU, the two remedies directives were also 'up-dated' in a coordinated fashion in 2007, through a single amending act which covers remedies in both sectors, Directive 2007/66/EC.[22]

---

[15] [1989] OJ L395/33.
[16] [1990] OJ L297/1.
[17] [1992] OJ L76/14.
[18] [1992] OJ L209/1.
[19] [2004] OJ L134/114.
[20] [2004] OJ L134/1.
[21] See, for example, MK Larsen, 'The New EU Public Procurement Directives' in R Nielsen and S Treumer (eds), *The New EU Public Procurement Directives* (Copenhagen, Djøf Publishing, 2005) 10.
[22] [2007] OJ L335/31.

In 2009, the regulatory regime was further extended to include defence and security procurement, which was addressed through Directive 2009/81/CE[23] (hereinafter 'Defence Directive' (DD), which includes both substantive and remedies provisions).

The 2004 public and utilities directives were in force for a decade. In 2011 a consultation and review were initiated[24] and, following the drafting process, the current 2014 public and utilities directives were enacted,[25] and the 2004 directives were repealed. The roots of the 2014 directives lie in the Europe 2020 Strategy for smart, sustainable and inclusive growth.[26] The main strategic directions envisaged for procurement were supporting innovation, protection of the environment, and SMEs. At the same time the objectives of procurement policy concerned ensuring 'the most efficient use of public funds' and keeping procurement markets 'open EU wide'.[27] Certainly, the 2014 procurement package has generated wide debate and analysis concerning the extent to which the simplification and flexibility agenda has actually been met, whether legal certainty was improved or otherwise, as well as the impact of the package on specific aspects of procurement.[28] It can, however, be noticed that (i) consolidation of public and utilities sector rules (into a single instrument) did not take place, (ii) the remedies directives were not reviewed jointly with the revision of substantive procurement rules,[29] and (iii) a distinct regulatory regime was introduced for concessions, which increase complexity in transposing and interpreting or applying the rules in some respects.

It needs mentioning that the total estimated volume of procurement market regulated at EU level accounted for €670.31 billion in 2018.[30] The use of framework agreements has become increasingly popular after the coming into force of 2004 directives; between 2006 and 2010 'the number of framework agreements increased by a factor of almost four'.[31] In 2010 'framework contracts accounted for about one-seventh of the value of all the contracts published in the OJEU', which

---

[23] [2009] OJ L216/76 (n 3).

[24] European Commission, 'Green Paper on the Modernisation of EU Public Procurement Policy Towards a More Efficient European Procurement Market' (Brussels, 27.1.2011) COM(2011) 15 final.

[25] See nn 1 and 2 above. Also, Directive 2014/23/EU of the European Parliament and of the Council of 26 February 2014 on the award of concession contracts [2014] OJ L94/1.

[26] European Commission, Communication from the Commission 'Europe 2020: A Strategy for Smart, Sustainable and Inclusive Growth', COM(2010)2020 of 3 March 2010.

[27] European Commission, 'Green Paper on the Modernisation of EU Public Procurement' (n 24) at 3.

[28] See, eg S Arrowsmith, *The Law of Public and Utilities Procurement: Regulation in the EU and UK*, vol 1, 3rd edn (London, Sweet & Maxwell, 2014); C Bovis, *The Law of EU Public Procurement*, 2nd edn (Oxford OUP, 2015); F Lichère, R Caranta and S Treumer (eds), *Modernising Public Procurement: The New Directive*, European Procurement Law Series vol 6 (Copenhagen, Djøf Publishing, 2014).

[29] See, eg, A Sanchez-Graells, '"If It Ain't Broke, Don't Fix It"? EU Requirements of Administrative Oversight and Judicial Protection for Public Contracts' in S Torricelli and F Folliot Lalliot (eds), *Contrôle et Contentieux des Contrats Publics – Oversight and Challenges of Public Contracts* (Brussels, Bruylant, 2018) 495.

[30] European Commission, DG Grow, 'Public Procurement Indicators 2018' (17 December 2021) via http://ec.europa.eu/growth/single-market/public-procurement/studies-networks/.

[31] European Commission, 'Annual Public Procurement Implementation Review 2012' (Brussels, 9 October 2012, SWD(2012)342 final) 26.

meant about 14 per cent of the total EU directives' purchase volume, with the most intensive user countries being (in 2009) the UK, France, Germany and Denmark; in 2009 Romania was one of the seven EU Member States where 'framework agreements covered more than a quarter of all contract notices'.[32]

5.2.1.3. Current Directives

The 2014 Public Sector Directive (PSD or 2014PSD) applies to public institutions falling under the definition of 'contracting authorities' in the instrument,[33] in respect of covered procurements above certain value thresholds,[34] and unless specific conditions are met for the application of a different regime, such as utilities or defence procurement. This directive provides for developments in the area of 'techniques and instruments for electronic and aggregated procurement'.[35] Framework agreements continue to be covered where the total value of expected orders under a framework exceeds thresholds, and irrespective of whether the value of individual orders is below the thresholds. However, PSD brings an end to the discretion of Member States as to whether purchasers are permitted or not to use frameworks. Member States must now allow *all* purchasers to use frameworks, and it can also be argued that under the new directive Member States could not limit the use of frameworks to certain types of configurations thereof,[36] which might create implementation complexities (however, the position on this is not entirely clear; see, for example, section 5.3.2.2.1 below). The rules concerning dynamic purchasing systems have been streamlined and simplified, particularly regarding the second stage of the arrangement for awarding specific contracts.[37] Also, express provisions as regards structuring and content of electronic catalogues have been provided,[38] including their potential uses under framework agreements and dynamic purchasing systems. At the same time the rules concerning centralised and joint procurement have been developed to clarify the responsibilities of parties establishing or using these arrangements,[39] and specific rules have been introduced for centralised or joint procurement 'involving contracting authorities from different Member States'.[40] Official lists of approved economic operators and certification by designed bodies[41] have been adjusted. However, a 'mandatory list' type of arrangement somewhat similar to the qualification systems in the utilities sector continues to be prohibited for the public sector.

---

[32] ibid.
[33] Art 2(1)1PSD.
[34] Art 1(1)PSD.
[35] Language of the directive (Title II, Ch II).
[36] Art 33(1)PSD. Arrowsmith, *The Law of Public and Utilities Procurement*, vol 1 (n 28) 1110–12.
[37] Art 34PSD.
[38] Recitals 55, 68; art 36PSD.
[39] Arts 37, 38PSD.
[40] Art 39PSD.
[41] Art 64PSD.

Turning to the 2014 Utilities Directive (UD), its application is determined by a quadruple 'qualification' (as for its 2004 predecessor) consisting of: (i) nature of the purchasing organisation, (ii) type of sector and activity in pursuit of which a specific procurement is being carried out, (iii) nature of the specific national market sector/activity, and (iv) value of the procurement exceeding specific thresholds for the utilities sector. Traditionally, utilities rules have provided for additional flexibility compared to the public sector, taking account of the more 'commercial-like' environment in which utilities operate,[42] an approach which has also always manifested in respect of arrangements falling under our definition of PUIR. Besides the less prescriptive rules concerning framework agreements, the utilities regime is the only EU procurement regime that permits and regulates qualification systems[43] – a 'mandatory list' type of arrangement, which can prove particularly useful for purchasers in situations where neither dynamic purchasing systems (under their current regulation) nor framework agreements would adequately fit the circumstances of the envisaged procurements. It is argued here that the continued reservations concerning 'mandatory list' arrangements – not just in the EU public sector regime but also under the UNCITRAL Model Law on Public Procurement, and the IBRD regulations – appear unjustified, since the risks such arrangements may pose can be efficiently mitigated through suitable regulation, and it is likely that the UK post-Brexit procurement reform could address this gap to some extent with the arrangement called 'dynamic markets'.[44] Returning to the EU Utilities Directive, rules concerning dynamic purchasing systems have been streamlined similarly to the public sector[45] and provisions concerning electronic catalogues and centralised/joint procurement[46] are pretty much along the lines of those in the public sector.

The two remedies directives, for the public sector and the utilities sector, were significantly amended through Directive 2007/66/EC (see preceding section 5.2.1.2). The latter effected two major developments in the review rules by formalising standstill periods, and introducing the remedy of ineffectiveness (and/or of alternative penalties). A standstill period consists of a mandatory 'stay' of an award procedure following communication of an award decision, and gives 'tenderers and candidates concerned' an opportunity to analyse whether that decision should be challenged for illegality, before the conclusion of a contract. It seeks to secure that where procurement legislation has been breached, remedial action can be effectively taken before a contract is concluded. Conversely, ineffectiveness involves that a contract concluded in breach of procurement law

---

[42] Further on utility procurement, eg, T Kotsonis, 'The 2014 Utilities Directive of the EU: Codification, Flexibilisation and other Misdemeanours' (2014) 23 *PPLR* 169; S Torricelli, 'Utilities Procurement' in M Trybus, R Caranta and G Edelstam (eds), *EU Public Contract Law: Public Procurement and Beyond* (Brussels, Bruylant, 2014) 223.

[43] Art 77UD.

[44] See section 5.4 below.

[45] Art 52UD.

[46] Arts 54–57UD.

should, under certain circumstances, not be enforceable and not be performed. The remedies directives refer explicitly to framework agreements and dynamic purchasing systems. The process of awarding (or admitting suppliers onto) such arrangements is covered by the scope of the remedies rules. As regards contracts awarded based on a framework agreement and/or dynamic purchasing system, Member States may replace standstill periods with the remedy of ineffectiveness.[47] Further amendments to the remedies directives were effected, rather convolutedly, in 2014.[48] The 2017 Report from the European Commission on the effectiveness of the remedies directives[49] concludes that 'the Remedies Directives, in particular the amendments introduced by Directive 2007/66/EC, largely met their objectives in an effective and efficient way'.[50] Whilst it was recognised that some provisions still need clarification,[51] those do not appear to include any specific remedies aspects concerning PUIR. Nevertheless, it is argued here that some adjustments in this connection might be usefully considered in the future.[52]

Finally, the regulatory regime was extended in 2009 with specific material rules coordinating the award procedures in the fields of defence and security, through the Defence Directive (DD). Both material and review provisions are included in the same instrument. Whilst some procurement in the field of defence had always been subject to the public sector regime, Member States tended to rely on an excessive interpretation of the exception provided for in Article 296 TEC (currently Article 346 TFEU) to exclude 'often even non-sensitive procurement in the field of defence ... from EU public procurement rules'.[53] This, in conjunction with other aspects of the defence sector, caused a very fragmented defence procurement market in the EU that was characterised as consisting of a number of individual 'national markets fenced off with regulatory barriers to entry aimed at protecting national defence industries'.[54] The Defence Directive only applies if the subject-matter of procurement concerns specific items, such as military equipment, or sensitive equipment,[55] and if the procurement exceeds specific value thresholds for the defence sector.[56] As regards PUIR, this procurement regime only provides for framework agreements, and not for dynamic purchasing systems or any other 'mandatory list' type of arrangement. But unlike the other procurement sectors,

---

[47] Recital 9 to Directive 2007/66/EC (n 22).
[48] Through Directive 2014/23/EU on concessions (n 25).
[49] European Commission, Brussels, 24 January 2017 COM(2017)28 final (accompanied by Commission Staff Working Document 'Evaluation of Modifications Introduced by Directive 2007/66/EC ...'), Brussels, 24 January 2017 SWD(2017)13 final.
[50] Report COM(2017)28 final (n 49) 8.
[51] Commission Staff Working Document (n 49), eg at 8, 9, 43.
[52] See also A Sánchez-Graells, 'If it ain't broke' (n 29).
[53] OECD Sigma, *Brief 23 Public Procurement – Defence Procurement* (OECD, Sigma, September 2016) 3.
[54] ibid.
[55] Art 2DD.
[56] More generally on EU defence procurement see, eg, M Trybus, *Buying Defence and Security in Europe: The EU Defence and Security Procurement Directive in Context* (Cambridge, CUP, 2014).

this directive includes provision for potential use of framework agreements as a means for subcontracting by a 'successful tenderer'.

5.2.2. The Member States Examined

France was a founding member of the European Communities. It also has a long tradition of regulating public procurement through detailed 'hard law' national rules,[57] namely binding and enforceable legal norms that are subject to judicial review, such as decrees, ordinances or codes.[58] For example, in the past there were several versions of the '*Code des Marchés Publics*' (CMP), the first one dating from 1964. Whilst naturally involved in the drafting of the Community law on public procurement, France has also encountered difficulties in integrating EU law concepts into its domestic law.[59] On the occasion of transposing the 2014 directives, France also engaged in a procurement reform and codification effort. Originally the 2014 directives were implemented in French law mainly through five domestic instruments: two ordinances (primary legislation) and three decrees (secondary legislation) adopted in 2015–16, but these have been incorporated, together with many other legal texts from various domestic instruments relevant to public procurement, into the '*Code de la commande publique*' (CCP), in its turn adopted through one ordinance[60] and one decree.[61] The CCP entered into effect in April 2019; it covers the public, utilities, and defence procurement sectors, as well as concessions.

In contrast, Romania is one of the newest Member States, having joined the EU in 2007. Thus, its experience with EU law is more limited, which also reflects less coherently a long-term public procurement strategy. Legislative changes have been very frequent and in general the regulation tends to be detailed and prescriptive, and includes primary, secondary, and tertiary legislation. When transposing the EU directives, their norms or the selected options tend to be supplemented with additional 'layers' of legal provisions, which increases complexity, sometimes generating issues of consistency and interpretation, which can in turn also affect legal

---

[57] See, eg, L Folliot-Lalliot, 'The French Approach to Regulating Frameworks under the New EC Directives' in S Arrowsmith (ed), *Reform of the UNCITRAL Model Law on Procurement: Procurement Regulation for the 21st Century* (Thomson Reuters/West, 2009) 193, 195; M Frilet and F Lager, 'France', in R Hernández García (ed), *International Public Procurement: A Guide to Best Practice* (London, Globe Business Publishing, 2009) 217.

[58] Lichère clarifies the meaning of code in the French context as 'a gathering of different binding texts linked with the same subject matter': F Lichère, 'Award of contracts covered by the EU Public Procurement rules in France' in ME Comba and S Treumer (eds), *Awards of Contracts in EU Procurements* (Copenhagen, Djøf Publishing, 2013) 69.

[59] Folliot-Lalliot, in 'The French Approach to Regulating Frameworks' (n 57) 195, emphasises the 'inspiration' role that the 1964 French Public Procurement Code had for 'the first EC Directive on public works contracts'.

[60] No 2018–1074.

[61] No 2018–1075.

certainty. The current public, utilities and remedies directives are implemented in Romanian legislation, mainly, through three distinct laws of 2016: the Public Procurement Law (PPL),[62] the Utilities Procurement Law (UPL),[63] and the Procurement Remedies Law (PRL).[64] The PPL and UPL are each completed with implementing norms approved through Government Decisions (GD),[65] which in some respects are inconsistent with the laws they seek to implement. Regarding the defence sector, the relevant directive was transposed, with some delay, through the Government Urgency Ordinance 114/2011, as amended by Law 195/2012 (DSL).[66]

A different approach and experience are brought by the UK, which joined the European Communities in 1973 and left the EU at the end of 2020. A very distinctive feature of the UK public procurement system, as emphasised by Arrowsmith, is that it does not have a 'longstanding tradition of regulating public procurement through detailed rules that are binding and enforceable.'[67] Instead, the system preferred 'to rely on the judgment of individual procurement entities and officials who have traditionally been given significant discretion'.[68] This also influenced, historically, its approach to transposing the EU directives while it was a Member State. Generally, the UK implementing regulations were 'minimalist' in approach[69] in that they reproduced much of the text of the directives, usually without adding further conditions or details[70] and without limiting the options that the directives provided for Member States. These options were normally 'cascaded' to contracting authorities or entities so as to afford wide flexibility and discretion to purchasers,[71] consistently with the UK's traditional approach. The 2014 EU directives were transposed into domestic law through the Public Contracts Regulations 2015[72] (PCR), the Utilities Contracts Regulations 2016[73] (UCR), and the Defence and Security Public Contracts Regulations 2011[74] (DSPCR). PCR and UCR apply to England,

---

[62] Law 98/2016 (MO 390/23.5.2016).

[63] Law 99/2016 (MO 391/23.5.2016).

[64] Law 101/2016 (MO 393/23.5.2016).

[65] GD 395/2016 (MO 423/6.6.2016) for public sector (procurement implementing norms – PIN); GD 394/2016 (MO 422/6.6.2016) for utilities (utilities implementing norms – UIN).

[66] MO 932/29.12.2011 and, respectively, MO 753/8.11.2012.

[67] S Arrowsmith, 'Methods for Purchasing On-Going Requirements: The System of Framework Agreements and Dynamic Purchasing Systems under the EC Directives and UK Procurement Regulations' in S Arrowsmith (ed), *Reform of the UNCITRAL Model Law on Public Procurement: Procurement Regulation for the 21st Century* (Thomson Reuters/West, 2009) 131, 141.

[68] ibid.

[69] P Telles, 'Awarding of Public Contracts in the United Kingdom' in ME Comba and S Treumer (eds), *Award of Contracts in EU Procurements* (Copenhagen, Djøf Publishing, 2013) 251.

[70] With some exceptions, such as Part 4 of the Public Contracts Regulations that provided for additional domestic obligations.

[71] In some cases, not pursuing an option under the directive offered enhanced flexibility, for example not imposing a shorter time-limit for 'the mandatory use of full e-communications': A Gatenby, B Gillian and L Dobson, 'United Kingdom' in J Davey and A Gatenby (eds), *The Government Procurement Review* (Law Business Research, 2017) 240.

[72] SI 2015/102, replacing the Public Contracts Regulations 2006 (SI 2006/5).

[73] SI 2016/274, replacing the Utilities Contracts Regulations 2006 (SI 2006/6).

[74] SI 2011/1848.

Wales and Northern Ireland. DSPCR, in contrast, applies 'throughout the United Kingdom (including Scotland) but excluding Gibraltar'.[75] Before leaving the EU, the UK procurement regulations were amended, but rather minimally so as to ensure their operation outside the EU, for example by removing the requirement to publish notices in the OJEU and replacing this with domestic dedicated media, without generally affecting substantive provisions.[76] This approach is intended to secure continuity of procurement activities until completely reformed post-Brexit procurement legislation and policy will be put in place.

5.2.3. The Public Procurement Reform in the UK after Leaving the EU

For public procurement, Brexit is seen by the Westminster Government as an opportunity to reform the UK system and legislation significantly in line with a redefined balance of domestic objectives, beyond (outside) the requirements of EU law, focusing on value, sustainability, integrity, transparency, fairness and non-discrimination. This perspective was articulated in the Green Paper called 'Transforming Public Procurement'[77] (hereinafter referred to as the 'Green Paper') issued by the Cabinet Office shortly before the UK's formal departure date from the EU. The Green Paper also initiated consultations concerning the proposals it included, with a view to developing upcoming new legislation. The transformations contemplated appear far-reaching, though it needs pointing out that they would still need to be confined to the realm of the World Trade Organization's Government Procurement Agreement to which the UK has become a party as of 2021, and of other trade agreements concluded by the UK, including with the EU. Substantive reforms and simplification are envisaged in the Green Paper by replacing the different regimes (such as public, utilities, defence or concessions) with 'a common set of rules with a single, uniform set of rules for all contract awards' that 'will be supplemented with sector-specific parts or sections' as appropriate.[78]

This approach goes significantly deeper than other 'codification' exercises such as those in France,[79] which inevitably, as a Member State, has to implement the somewhat analogous but complex regimes for the public sector, utilities, defence and concessions. The UK post-Brexit transformation also envisages substantive streamlining and additional flexibility in respect, for example, of the award

---

[75] J Falle and C Dwyer, 'United Kingdom' in J Davey and J Falle (eds), *The Government Procurement Review* (Law Business Research, 2013) 230.

[76] eg, The Public Procurement (Amendment etc.) (EU Exit) Regulations 2020 (SI 2020/1319).

[77] Cabinet Office, 'Transforming Public Procurement', December 2020 (CP 253), at: https://assets.publishing.service.gov.uk/government/uploads/system/uploads/attachment_data/file/943946/Transforming_public_procurement.pdf.

[78] 'Green Paper', ibid, 7.

[79] Section 5.2.2 above.

procedures, proposing that just three such procedures will apply across the consolidated regime. Materially, the post-Brexit procurement approach promises to pursue primarily the UK national objectives as well as to streamline and significantly improve the legislation, outside the requirements of EU law. But it is relevant to point out, as Arrowsmith emphasises,[80] that the UK appears to intend using legally binding and enforceable rules in pursuit of its post-Brexit balance of objectives, including value for money, something that was rather alien to its traditional approach. This could be regarded as an EU post-Brexit influence with potentially beneficial consequences in the long run.

The Green Paper addresses what we refer to as PUIR in its Chapter five, titled 'Using the best commercial purchasing tools', which proposes legislating 'for a new Dynamic Purchasing System (DPS+) that may be used for all types of procurement (not just commonly used goods and services)' and 'for new options in framework agreements including an option for an "open framework" with multiple joining points'.[81] However, the proposal that DPS+ would replace both the current dynamic purchasing system *and* qualification system raised concerns that PUIR in the UK utility sectors could become less flexible than it is currently under the EU directive, whereas the frameworks proposals seemed to be equivalent to the EU provisions, and in general this area appeared to be in need of significant developments.[82]

In December 2021, the Cabinet Office issued its response to the public procurement reform consultations[83] arising from the analysis of the feedback received during the consultations. Some clarifications were provided concerning commercial purchasing tools,[84] for example that continued use of qualification systems for utilities is considered (point 201) and that DPS+ are to be called 'dynamic market'. Nevertheless, this area still appears to be a work in progress even after the publication of the Procurement Bill for its first reading in the House of Lords on 11 May 2022, with some aspects, including substantive ones, to be developed and nuanced during the legislative process, in future secondary legislation, or through official guidance, as is discussed in section 5.4 below. As in the case of the pre-Brexit regime, this book discusses procurement above relevant thresholds in the contemplated post-Brexit regime of the Westminster jurisdiction (covering mainly England, Wales, and Northern Ireland), and not devolved jurisdictions or procurement under relevant thresholds.

---

[80] S Arrowsmith, 'Transforming Public Procurement Law after Brexit: Early Reflections on the Government's Green Paper' (15 December 2020), http://dx.doi.org/10.2139/ssrn.3749359, section 2. This piece provides comprehensive explanations on the logic of the matters contemplated in the Green Paper. But see also A Sanchez-Graells, 'The UK's Green Paper on Post-Brexit Public Procurement Reform: Transformation or Overcomplication?' (2021) 16 *EPPPL* 4.

[81] Green Paper (n 77) 42 (with ideas then developed to some extent at 45–47).

[82] S Arrowsmith, 'Transforming Public Procurement Law' (n 80) sections 2–3.

[83] Cabinet Office, 'Transforming Public Procurement: Government response to consultations', December 2021 (CP 556).

[84] ibid, ch 5, pp 46–49.

5.3. Relevant Arrangements in EU Directives and Specific Approaches in Selected Member States

5.3.1. Summary

There currently are three 'major' or 'generic' types of PUIR arrangement provided for in the EU public procurement system: framework agreements, dynamic purchasing systems, and qualification systems. The table below illustrates the 'distribution' of relevant arrangements among the three procurement sectors regulated by the directives.

Arrangement Type / Regulatory Regime	Framework Agreements	Dynamic Purchasing Systems	Qualification Systems
Public	Yes	Yes	No
Utilities	Yes	Yes	Yes
Defence	Yes	No	No

Framework agreements are recognised and regulated in all three sectors, though different rules apply in some respects for each sector. As the name suggests, these can be classified as framework 'arrangements' since the first stage involves establishing certain terms for future procurements. Under the 2014 directives providing for dynamic purchasing systems (public and utilities), this arrangement can be organised either as a framework arrangement or as a 'list' type of arrangement, as is discussed in section 5.3.3.1 below. In contrast, qualification systems continue to be provided for only in the utilities sector. This type of 'mandatory' list arrangement is not permitted in the other two regimes. However, 'optional' list type of arrangements will be discussed, including in the public and defence sectors, though not explicitly regulated. Because of their potential relationship with optional lists, official lists of approved economic operators and certification (in the public and defence sectors) are also addressed, though official lists and certification cannot be regarded as specific PUIR arrangements per se.

5.3.2. Framework Agreements

5.3.2.1. General

The main provisions concerning framework agreements are at articles 33PSD, 51UD, 3(1) and 29DD. However, specific rules concerning certain aspects relating to frameworks are spread throughout the text of each directive. Many of the general rules on awarding contracts also apply to frameworks, though in some cases a degree of 'adaptation' is needed. It is important to note the varying degrees of discretion allowed by each of the directives to Member States regarding regulation of framework agreements. Thus, 2014PSD has effected what could be a signifi-cant change. Under the previous 2004PSD, framework agreements were optional, meaning that Member States had the discretion to decide through domestic legis-lation whether to permit the use of these arrangements to purchasers within their jurisdiction or not,[85] or to limit the permitted uses.[86] Whilst all three Member States examined here provided for framework agreements in their domestic legis-lation under 2004PSD, two of them (France and Romania) did choose to limit their use.

In contrast, under the 2014PSD, Member States do not appear to retain such discretion,[87] though the boundaries of such curtailing could be debatable. It is noteworthy that France and Romania appear to manifest some 'inertia', in that their current domestic regulations continue to provide for certain limitation of the use of framework agreements to certain configurations thereof. It is theoreti-cally possible that a purchaser in these countries might pursue a configuration of framework not envisaged in domestic legislation but permitted by the relevant directive, seeking to invoke inappropriate transposition by the Member State; however, in practice it seems unlikely that a purchaser would be prepared (or have the time) to defend the case in potential legal proceedings. Similarly, in the utilities sector frameworks are not 'optional' for Member States.[88] From a Member State perspective, the safest approach as regards transposition of framework provisions in the 2014 directives appears to be 'copy-out', supplemented by guidance, as did the UK whilst an EU Member State. But it needs recognising that in some Member States, depending on their administrative culture, non-binding guidance alone could prove insufficient to instil an appropriate use of frameworks. While in the defence sector frameworks are optional under EU law,[89] all three Member States examined have provided for frameworks in their domestic legislation.

5.3.2.2. Definition and Types

The directives provide for a unitary definition of a framework agreement,[90] that is

> an agreement between one or more contracting authorities and one or more economic operators, the purpose of which is to establish the terms governing contracts to be awarded during a given period, in particular with regard to price and, where appropri-ate, the quantity envisaged.

Whereas this definition per se seems to focus on the outcome of the first stage of a 'framework arrangement', the substantive provisions dealing with framework

[85] Art 32(1) of 2004PSD.
[86] Arrowsmith (n 28) 1110–12.
[87] Art 33(1)1PSD.
[88] Art 51(1)UD.
[89] Art 29(1)DD.
[90] Art 33(1)2PSD. Similar definitions are provided under art 51(1)2UD, and art 1(11)DD.

agreements clearly take a 'framework agreement procedure' approach.[91] They differentiate between the two stages of such an arrangement, which comprises a first stage aimed at establishing a 'framework agreement' as described above, and a second stage for the award of contracts under the 'framework agreement'.

In literature it has been argued that frameworks 'are not a procedure, they are a type of technique and instrument for aggregated procurement'.[92] Such categorical repudiation seems unnecessary. Whilst the main provisions on framework agreements are included in the structure of the PSD and UD under a chapter on 'Techniques and instruments', the Defence Directive includes provisions on framework agreements precisely under the 'Procedures' chapter. On the other hand, the content of the provisions does not link any effect to the denomination of 'technique' or 'instrument'. For example, while framework agreements are mainly used for aggregate procurement, nothing in the actual rules prevents frameworks from being used for other purposes,[93] such as to deal with indefinite requirements, and the procedural content of a framework agreement purchasing process is more prominent.

It can be noticed that both single-contractor and multiple-contractor frameworks, as well as single-agency and multiple-agency frameworks, are explicitly envisaged by the legal definition of framework agreements. Framework agreements must be established for a 'given period', namely, they must not be concluded for indefinite periods of time. Depending on circumstances, particular attention is usually given to avoiding excessively long-term framework agreements that are likely to negatively affect competition.[94] The legal definition per se makes no distinction between closed arrangements or open arrangements. However, procedural rules under PSD and DD do clarify that only closed framework agreements are permitted by providing that call-off procedures for the award of contracts under framework agreements are to be applied 'only between those contracting authorities clearly identified for this purpose ... and the economic operators party to the framework agreement as concluded'.[95]

The directives provide for flexibility in that framework agreements do not have to be mandatory (or committing, or exclusive). A purchaser is allowed to procure outside an established framework,[96] for instance if it is unsatisfied with the contractors' performance or simply if it has identified better terms elsewhere on the market. Recital 61(3)PSD now explicitly states that purchasers 'should not be obliged ... to procure works, supplies or services that are covered by a framework

---

[91] Trepte (n 4) 375.

[92] M Andrecka, 'Framework agreements, EU procurement law and the practice' (2015) 2 *Upphandlingsrättslig Tidskrift* 127, 146, referring to C Risvig Hamer, 'Chapter II: Techniques and instruments for electronic and aggregated procurement' in M Steinike and PL Vesterdorf (eds), *Commentary on EU Public Procurement Law* (Baden-Baden, Nomos, 2015).

[93] Section 5.3.2.3 below.

[94] ibid.

[95] Art 33(2)2PSD. Similar provisions are in art 29(2)2DD.

[96] Unlike, for example, requirements contracts in the US federal procurement system.

agreement, under that framework agreement.' Such flexibility may be particularly useful, for example, in the case of sub-optimal closed framework arrangements, or as a 'preventive' tool against collusive practices among framework contractors. Being aware of the possibility for the purchaser to procure outside an established arrangement might act to some extent as a deterrent for framework contractors from offering terms that do not reflect the market during the call-off stage.

But nothing prevents a purchaser from taking on additional commitments, such as sourcing all its requirements for the subject-matter of the procurement from an established framework arrangement,[97] where it considers that this approach may generate better terms and increased value from expected aggregate demand. In principle, the decision on a mandatory or non-mandatory framework appears best placed at purchaser level, on a case-by-case basis. As defined in the directives, a framework agreement, as the outcome of the first stage of a 'framework agreement procedure', does not necessarily imply binding obligations between parties. However, this might be the case depending on the intent of the parties as well as the applicable national law,[98] reflecting the nature of the EU supra-national regime to some extent.

Still, a clear distinction should be made between a 'binding framework agreement' and a 'procurement contract'.[99] With the exception of single-contractor framework agreements where all terms and conditions are established, including commitments to buy and sell,[100] the conclusion of a framework agreement does not normally itself trigger the effect of any supplies being delivered or work being performed, or of any payment obligations. Such effects are generated by call-off contracts issued under the framework agreement and according to the terms established under it.[101] Consequently, all phases of a framework up to reaching a 'procurement contract' with such effects should in principle be considered and treated as framework procedural stages, with full oversight and monitoring requirements being applicable. This is irrespective of whether a framework agreement per se is deemed to form a 'binding contract' or otherwise.

For the public and defence sectors, a distinction is made in the relevant directives between frameworks that *do not* establish all terms and those that *do* establish all terms. In the former case the award of call-offs involves reopening of competition amongst framework contractors, whereas in the latter case call-off awards are made on the basis of 'the terms and conditions of the framework without reopening competition',[102] though provision is also made in the public sector for reopening competition in this case, subject to some requirements.

---

[97] Or commit to buy a certain minimum volume.

[98] See Trepte (n 4) 208–11.

[99] From this perspective, the European Commission's Explanatory Note on Frameworks, 2005 (Ref. ARES(2016)810203–16/02/2016) section 1.1, seems insufficiently nuanced.

[100] With only the realisation of committed obligations taking place at the 'call-off' stage.

[101] S Arrowsmith, *The Law of Public and Utilities Procurement*, 1st edn (London, Sweet & Maxwell, 2005) 1062–65.

[102] Art 33(4)PSD; similarly, art 29(4)DD. See further section 5.3.2.4 below.

5.3.2.2.1. Specific Approach in Romania: Limitation to Committing Frameworks

The Romanian legislation provides for some useful clarifications and controls for ensuring an appropriate and efficient use of frameworks. However, the very tight commitment to buy the subject-matter of a framework – including in frameworks of the type that involve reopening competition – under that framework, as provided for in the secondary legislation (implementing norms), could in fact exacerbate collusion risks at the call-off stage and affect value. Under that national legislation, by concluding a framework agreement, the purchaser commits not to conclude a procurement contract with any other contractor for the subject-matter of the framework throughout its duration, as well as to 'award contracts' to framework contractors 'each and every time it intends to procure' the subject-matter of the framework 'by observing the essential conditions established upon its conclusion' (article 108(1)PIN[103]). Exceptionally, the purchaser is permitted to procure the subject-matter of the framework outside it where the framework contractor(s) are 'not capable any longer of honouring the requests of the purchaser' (article 108(2)PIN).

Certainly, in frameworks not establishing all terms, and thus involving reopening of competition, there is the possibility that framework contractors may not attend call-off competitions, or they could make uninteresting offers for call-offs. This type of framework is less amenable to being committing for the supply side, whereas frameworks that establish all terms are much more so, since all terms are set at the first stage, including the rules concerning which of the framework contractors is to perform a call-off. But the Romanian implementing norms 'force' committing frameworks, including for frameworks of the type involving reopening of competition. It needs emphasising in this context that, under Romanian legislation, framework contractors are only permitted to improve the terms that are subject to the reopening of competition at call-off stage.[104] If no such improved terms are offered during the call-off stage, the purchaser has the obligation to award the contract to the framework contractor who ranked first during the initial stage of awarding the framework agreement 'by taking into consideration the conditions and elements provided for in its initial offer as updated'.[105] This might be an option where all terms have been established at least provisionally at first stage, but the norms do not clarify what the position should be for frameworks in which competition reopening is also 'based on ... other terms' than those 'applied for the award of the framework agreement'.[106] In this case it would seem that negotiation of the outstanding terms with the first ranking contractor (as at the first stage) is the only option, but there might be little to negotiate since the purchaser *must* award the contract to this contractor.

---

[103] See text to n 65.
[104] Art 110(5)PIN.
[105] Art 110(7)PIN.
[106] Art 33(5)PSD as implemented in art 119PPL.

If the framework contractor selected for award of a call-off 'does not have the capacity' to perform the call-off 'because the quantity for the call-off exceeds the estimated quantity', the purchaser must award the 'difference' to the other framework contractors, and is allowed to procure it outside the framework *only* if none of the framework contractors 'has the capacity'.[107] Further, if the framework contractor selected for award of a call-off is unable/unwilling to supply, without justification, the purchaser must also award the call-off to the other framework contractors and is allowed to procure it outside the framework *only* if none of the framework contractors 'has the capacity'.[108] In this case the defaulting framework contractor(s) is to 'suffer the consequences provided for in the framework agreement for failing to meet its obligations', but the Romanian norms do not elaborate here.[109]

In light of these heavy restrictions for the purchaser, framework contractors could be tempted – if not 'invited' – to circumvent substantive competition by 'agreeing' amongst themselves not to offer any improvements of the terms in call-off competitions, and to 'share the pie' on the basis of the terms tendered to enter the framework at first stage, possibly subject to minimal improvements. The collusion risk that is inherent in closed frameworks involving reopening of competition is elevated where such frameworks are also committing for the purchaser (see further on collusion in frameworks, section 5.3.2.4.2). The effort in the PIN to 'paint' a committing framework involving reopening of competition could be regarded as an example of a possible configuration. But restricting the use of frameworks involving reopening of competition to this configuration appears not only inconsistent with the approach of the (2014)PSD, including recital 61 – specifically stating that 'Contracting authorities should not be obliged pursuant to this Directive to procure works, supplies or services that are covered by a framework agreement, under that framework agreement' – but also impractical for purchasers.

France also used to require that frameworks be committing for purchasers in the past, subject to different requirements from those applicable in Romania, but this does not apply any longer under the 2016 French regime (codified in the 2019 CCP).

5.3.2.2.2. Specific Approach in France: Regarding the Framework as a 'Contract'

The CCP describes a framework agreement (*'accord-cadre'*) as a procurement 'technique' for 'preselecting' suppliers, specifying that its purpose is 'concluding a *contract* establishing all or part of the rules concerning the purchases to be made during a certain period' (author's translation; emphasis added).[110] Describing or

---

[107] Art 111(1)PIN.
[108] Art 111(2)PIN.
[109] Art 111(3)PIN.
[110] Art L2125-1CCP.

defining a framework agreement as a 'contract' seems to be an element of domestic tradition, and it was also included in the definition of frameworks in the French ordinance of 2015 originally transposing the 2014 directives.[111] To the extent that any framework agreement within the scope of the definition in the 2014 directives can be organised as a 'contract' under French law, there is no harmonisation issue. However, if qualification as a 'contract' under French law excludes certain types of frameworks as defined in the 2014 directives – for whatever reasons, for example an insufficiently defined object, lack of required commitments, or lack of other contractual elements – then the French legal definition might not 'fit the bill' in so far as the public and utilities sectors are concerned. As shown, EU Member States do not appear to have the option any longer to limit, through domestic law, the use of frameworks to certain purchasers or certain types of frameworks. The position used to be different under the previous (2004) directives and Member States had the option to limit uses of frameworks. This is still the case under the 2009 Defence Directive. Under the previous (2006) French regime, framework agreements were also defined as contracts,[112] consistent with this option allowed in the 2004 directives for the Member States.

The 2019 French Guidance on framework agreements explains that a framework agreement 'is a contract comprising obligations and commitments for each party', it should not just 'summarily outline its needs', or consist of 'an empty shell which does not engage any of the parties' (author's translation).[113] This suggests that an arrangement where, for example, none of the parties commit to buy or sell – which would be perfectly valid under the directives if all other requirements were met – is not envisaged by French law. It needs to be recognised that classifying (in law) a framework agreement as a contract is likely to offer, in some (but not all) cases, certain advantages in terms of responsibility and enforceability.

5.3.2.3. Selecting This Arrangement

5.3.2.3.1. Conditions

None of the current EU procurement directives provide for any conditions for use of framework agreements. Thus, under the directives, frameworks can be employed for recurrent, indefinite, or emergency requirements. The main provisions on frameworks are located in the PSD and UD in a chapter on 'electronic and aggregated procurement', which suggests that repeat procurement is the main use envisaged. However, nothing in the directives prevents purchasers from employing frameworks in other circumstances. Also, the directives do not require them to prepare a justification concerning the use of a framework agreement,

---

[111] Ordinance 2015-899, art 4(3), repealed in 2019.
[112] Art 1(I)3 of the 2006 *Code des Marchés Publics* (2006CMP) and art 1(3) of Ordinance 2005-649.
[113] Thematic fiche via www.economie.gouv.fr/daj/accords-cadres-2019, p 3.

rather than a 'traditional' contract or a different type of PUIR arrangement. Consequently, no justification for a particular type of configuration of framework is required either.

A requirement applies to multi-contractor frameworks under the defence regime and concerns the minimum number of parties to a framework agreement, which 'must be at least three'.[114] It also applied in the past under the 2004PSD. While this condition is likely to be aimed at ensuring a sufficient degree of competition at call-off stage, the legal text does not distinguish between frameworks involving second-stage competition and frameworks not involving such competition. Imposing an obligation for three contractors could be counter-productive for the latter type of framework. The 2014PSD does not maintain this requirement for the public sector. This is considered a positive development, permitting purchasers to establish the number of contractors according to circumstances of individual procurements.

Specific Experience in France: Conditions – Past and Present

As discussed, under the 2014 EU directives, purchasers appear to be given full discretion to design their frameworks so long as they observe EU law, though the domestic law of some Member States continues to envisage some limitations. In any event, Member States or their specialised agencies can certainly issue non-binding guidance highlighting the potential advantages and pitfalls of various uses or types of frameworks. At the same time, the history of French regulation can offer some orientation. Under the current (2016/2019) and the previous (2006) French regimes the decision to procure through framework agreements is/was at the discretion of purchasers. However, prior to the 2006 regime specific conditions did apply in France to the use of the various framework arrangements. Folliot-Lalliot provides a brief but comprehensive overview.[115]

From 2001, unlike before, purchasers did not have full liberty to procure by way of a framework arrangement. Under article 72 of 2001CMP, purchase order contracts could only be used 'When for economic, technical or financial reasons, the ordering rate or scope of the requirements to be met cannot be completely finalised in the contract'.[116] The same requirement can be found in article 71(I) of 2004CMP. This was the 'general' condition allowing the shift from a traditional/ classic procurement to a framework type of arrangement – in the legal language of the time, to 'split contracts' ('*marchés fractionnés*'). But this condition alone only offered access to what Folliot-Lalliot referred to as the regular type of 'purchase order contract per se', namely a single-supplier framework contract which determined the quantity or value of the procurement by way of a minimum *and* a maximum, the specifications, the object of the procurement, and the price or the

---

[114] Art 29(4)DD.
[115] Folliot-Lalliot (n 57) 198–208.
[116] As translated by Folliot-Lalliot, ibid, 198. The text of that author refers to art 71, which is probably an editing error.

method for its calculation.[117] The maximum limit could not exceed the minimum by four times.[118] A specific type of single-supplier 'framework' was the purchase order contract without minimum and maximum. To use this arrangement an additional condition applied under article 71(II) of 2004CMP, which needed to be duly justified by the purchaser, namely that: 'the amount of the requirements and the rate at which purchase orders are to be issued cannot be determined by the public entity in advance'.[119] In slightly different language, a similar condition had applied under the 2001CMP.[120]

Additional conditions had to be fulfilled in order to use a multiple-supplier purchase order contract. These conditions were, first, the inability of a single supplier to carry out the entire requirement, or the need to ensure security of supply.[121] The 'standard' type of multiple-supplier arrangement to which these conditions offered access was one without reopening of competition for the issue of orders. In fact, this type included two sub-types corresponding to single-supplier arrangements discussed above. Thus, one sub-type was a 'standard' multiple-supplier arrangement with minimum and maximum (sub-type A), while the other was a 'standard' multiple-supplier arrangement without minimum and maximum (sub-type B). In order to use sub-type A two sets of conditions had to be met: the general condition for any 'framework' arrangement and also, one of the conditions for 'standard' multiple-supplier frameworks referred above. To use sub-type B three sets of conditions had to be met: those for sub-type A, plus those corresponding to the single-supplier arrangement without minimum and maximum. The procurement of 'standard' multiple-supplier frameworks involved tendering for different lots with identical requirements. The contract stipulated the way in which orders were issued, without reopening of competition among the suppliers who were awarded the various lots.[122]

On the other hand, a multiple-supplier arrangement with reopening of competition (without a minimum or maximum) was only permitted when rendered necessary by: the high volatility of product prices, rapid obsolescence of products, or emergency situations not attributable to the purchaser and incompatible with the time required by the preparation of a (separate) procurement.[123] A similar arrangement was also permitted for products or materials for which certain features could only be established as a result of the carrying out a scientific or technologic research mission.[124]

In light of the liberal approach of the current directives as regards the use of framework agreements, or indeed of the tradition in countries like the UK,

---

[117] ibid, 200.
[118] Art 71(I)(1) of 2004CMP.
[119] As translated by Folliot-Lalliot (n 57) 202.
[120] Art 72(I)2 of 2001CMP.
[121] Art 72(I)3 of 2001CMP and art 71(III) of 2004CMP.
[122] Folliot-Lalliot (n 57) 203.
[123] Art 71(IV) of 2004CMP and art 72(I)4(a), (b), (c) of 2001CMP.
[124] Art 71(V) of 2004CMP and art 72(I)4(d) of 2001CMP.

the older French provisions referred to above might appear (excessively) restrictive. However, bearing in mind the time of their 'action',[125] they were remarkable in regard to the legal 'articulation' of various categories of frameworks. In particular, the gradual nuancing of the circumstances for the use of each type of 'framework arrangement' is something that might have deserved to outlive the legal norms that initially expressed them by transforming those norms, after their repeal into flexible, non-binding guidance. However, this has not been done so far.[126] That 'wisdom' which in some form saw light by way of the 2001 and 2004CMP might be lost, potentially giving way to a predominant use of frameworks for administrative convenience. In the absence of substantive guidance as to framework design and decisions, purchasers may like to use as a source of inspiration, mutatis mutandis, the Guide to Enactment of the 2011 UNCITRAL Model Law on Public Procurement,[127] and in particular the specific conceptual framework for decisions and design of PUIR arrangements provided in this book at Chapter six, section 6.4.

5.3.2.3.2. Controls

Controls relate to requirements mainly intended to ensure an appropriate use of framework agreements once they have been established, rather than affecting directly the decision to establish, or otherwise, such an arrangement. In the EU directives, at a general level, under article 51(2)3UD and article 29(2)DD it is prohibited to 'use framework agreements improperly or in such a way as to prevent, restrict or distort competition.'

As regards the public sector, a similar statement can be found in recital 61PSD. Since it represents an application of general principles of the directive to the specific subject of frameworks, the alternative location in recitals should not affect its strength.[128] Specific controls are discussed below.

Limitation in Time
A first control is a limitation of the duration of any framework agreement.[129] This is important particularly because framework agreements, as regulated under

---

[125] ie, before the recognition of frameworks in the 2004 Public Sector Directive and at a time when the European Commission was quite reluctant to accepting multiple-supplier arrangements.

[126] The updated 2017 and 2019 Guidance, similarly to the previous guidance concerning the 2006 regime, limits itself, in this connection, to providing brief descriptions of some relevant aspects: some examples of when the use of frameworks could be appropriate; stating that frameworks without reopening competition can offer a quick and efficient response to needs as they arise, whereas frameworks involving reopening of competition offer adaptability to needed adjustments to the requirement; and explaining that frameworks that do not guarantee a minimum order or the exclusivity of supplier(s) will not incite tenderers to make attractive proposals.

[127] Chapter 2 of this book.

[128] Arrowsmith suggests that the CJEU is likely to consider the prohibition as applying to PSD (n 28 at 1178).

[129] See A Geddes, *Public and Utility Procurement: A Practical Guide to the UK Regulations and Associated Community Rules*, 2nd edn (London, Sweet & Maxwell, 1997) 31.

the EU procurement regimes, are closed arrangements where contractors not initially a party to the agreement may not later join the agreement. An indefinite (or excessive) period would seriously affect competition on the market. Other negative effects may involve framework contractor complacency or collusive practices. The definition of framework agreements clearly refers to 'a given period', by this meaning that frameworks have to be limited in time as an essential aspect of their operation. Additionally, a maximum duration is also explicitly provided for in each of the sectors: four years for the public sector, eight years for utilities, and seven years for defence.[130] However, in some circumstances, where justified, a longer period may be used, for example where contractors 'need to dispose of', and 'must make available' throughout the period of the framework, equipment whose 'amortisation period' is longer than that of the usual regulatory limit for the framework.[131] But enforcing these controls through supplier review mechanisms (alone) could prove inefficient, since suppliers would probably prefer to be part of a longer-term arrangement. Thus, they are unlikely to challenge a longer duration or the justification therefor, particularly at the start of an award procedure for a framework agreement.[132] Alternative oversight and/or enforcement mechanisms appear to be needed in this respect.

The duration of a framework agreement refers to the period within which call-offs can be made. This means that the actual duration of the framework 'arrangement' or 'process' is likely to actually be longer than that of the framework agreement per se, as the last call-offs may extend beyond its duration.[133] Similarly, the duration of a call-off 'does not need to coincide' with that of the framework in question.[134] Nonetheless, excessively large or long orders placed towards the end of a framework agreement may be regarded as abuses of the framework and purchasers should maintain a fine balance in this respect.[135] Certainly, the duration of any given framework agreement is to be established on a case-by-case basis by the purchaser and it need not coincide with the maximum duration provided for in the applicable procurement regime. Such duration may be shorter than the 'general' maximum provided in an applicable directive. Although there is no legal requirement for shorter durations to be justified, it would be good practice for a purchaser to satisfy itself that the set duration of a framework agreement is an appropriate one.[136]

Prohibition of Substantial Amendments
Another specific control prohibits 'substantial' amendments to the terms of a framework agreement, whether made directly to the framework agreement itself,

---

[130] Arts 33(1)3PSD; art 51(1)3UD; art 29(2)4DD.
[131] Recitals 62(2)PSD, 72(2)UD.
[132] Publication of the justification is usually required in the contract notice, despite some inconsistencies in the provision.
[133] Recitals 62(1)PSD, 72(1)UD.
[134] ibid.
[135] Trepte (n 4) 437.
[136] On this matter, see discussion in Chapter 2, section 2.2.1.1 of this book.

or entailed by contracts awarded under that framework.[137] This derives from the principle of equal treatment, since 'substantial' amendments are 'capable' of (retrospectively) affecting the outcome and conditions of first-stage competition, and therefore the decisions concerning admittance of suppliers onto the framework. Other amendments may be permitted, allowing for some flexibility, and the 2014 directives include express provisions in this connection.[138] The UD does not include express provision prohibiting substantial amendments to the terms of a framework agreement being entailed by contracts awarded under that framework. However, this is clearly covered both by the general requirement that frameworks shall not be used 'improperly or in such a way as to prevent, restrict or distort competition',[139] and by general rules on 'modifications'.

Stage Consistency

A wider control could be referred to as stage consistency. This includes the prohibition of making substantial amendments discussed above, but encompasses additional measures seeking to ensure that the scope of a framework, as established at the outset, is not 'hijacked' during its implementation, and that what has been achieved at the first stage is not denied or contradicted at the call-off stage. Some aspects of stage consistency are not regulated explicitly and can be inferred from general principles and policy. A notable aspect of 'stage consistency', not addressed expressly in the directives, concerns the relation between criteria for the award of the framework agreement itself and criteria used for the award of contracts under it. In literature, this element was analysed by Arrowsmith.[140] Some variation in criteria used at each stage of a framework agreement is possible, or even necessary in some cases, for commercial considerations. However, that relationship between the criteria used at each stage needs to take account of securing equal treatment in a wider sense: providing any interested supplier an equal chance to offer the most efficient proposals for the *objective* needs of the purchaser.[141] I submit that in case of frameworks this concept should concern the overall arrangement. This, in turn, requires a degree of consistency between the two stages. In other words, the criteria used at the first stage should not result in selecting framework suppliers that are irrelevant for the future call-offs and/or in denying access to suppliers that could be better placed to meet the call-offs.

An example could be selecting framework contractors for consultancy projects based on lowest price, followed by the award of orders under that framework using

---

[137] Art 72PSD and art 89UD; art 33(2)3PSD and art 29(2)3DD.

[138] Art 72PSD and art 89UD, codifying existing CJEU case law. See S Treumer, 'Contract Changes and the Duty to Retender under the New EU Public Procurement Directive' (2014) 23 *PPLR* 148; also, C Risvig Hamer, 'Regular Purchases and Aggregated Procurement: The Changes in the New Public Procurement Directive regarding Framework Agreements, Dynamic Purchasing Systems and Central Purchasing Bodies' (2014) 23 *PPLR* 201, 205–6.

[139] Art 51(2)3UD.

[140] Arrowsmith, 'Methods for Purchasing On-Going Requirements' (n 67) 171–72; Arrowsmith (n 28) 1161–63.

[141] See Trepte (n 4) 13–15.

the criterion of the most economically advantageous tender. In effect, the use during the call-off stage of factors that were not taken into consideration during the first stage may easily result in the selection of framework contractors that are not particularly relevant for call-offs. It is suggested that the introduction of an explicit statement in the directives as to the importance of criteria consistency may serve as an additional (and deserved) safeguard for the principle of equal treatment in operating framework agreements.

An additional substantive aspect that could affect stage consistency may involve defining the object of procurement in too broad terms, making it difficult to ensure that selection of framework contractors during the first stage will be relevant for second-stage orders. Recent case law of the CJEU (Case C-23/20, *Simonsen & Weel A/S v Region Nordjylland og Region Syddanmark*, ECLI:EU:C:2021:490) incorporates this aspect in relation to a single-contractor framework by clarifying that the contract notice

> must indicate the estimated quantity and/or the estimated value as well as a maximum quantity and/or a maximum value of the … [requirements] under a framework agreement and that that agreement will no longer have any effect once that limit is reached.

A 'formal' or 'documentary' aspect of consistency has also been identified in the course of this research; this involves that all relevant terms and conditions should be included in tender documents for the award of a framework agreement (of any type), then carried forward to the actual framework agreement, and then further on to the second-stage awards. Whilst this is implicit in transparency requirements, the 2014 directives have strengthened to some extent the explicit provisions on this point.

Specific Approach in Romania: Price Adjustment Clauses

An important control is provided for in the Romanian legislation concerning the price tendered for the purposes of entering a framework agreement. Under article 117(1)(b)PPL, in the case of single-supplier frameworks, the framework agreement must stipulate 'the unitary price that the economic operator provided in his offer and on the basis of which the price of each subsequent contract will be determined.'[142] For any type of framework agreement, including multiple-supplier frameworks, 'unitary price … other financial or commercial promises' are also to be included in the actual framework,[143] as well as price adjustment formulas as appropriate.[144] At the same time, in the case of multiple-supplier frameworks involving reopening of competition, framework contractors are only permitted to improve during the call-off competition the terms they had offered at the first stage to enter the framework.[145] Where price adjustment was provided for, 'the improvement of this element relates to the updated value obtained from the

---

[142] A similar provision can be found in art 112(1)(b)DSL.
[143] Art 109(1)(b)PIN. See also art 115(1)(b)DSL.
[144] Art 109(1)(c)PIN.
[145] Art 110(5)PIN.

application of the adjustment coefficients'.[146] These are very useful controls. The prices tendered during the award of the first stage not only serve to gain entry onto the framework: they become limits (or bases) for prices that framework contractors can offer in call-off competitions. This provides a strong link between the first and the second stage of a framework agreement. It is also an effective measure against collusion among contractors at the call-off stage.

5.3.2.3.3. Specific Configurations

Price Element in the First Stage

One aspect that has been subject to some debate is whether establishment of terms as to price (or a pricing mechanism) during the first stage of setting up a framework is essential for the existence of a framework agreement under the EU directives, or whether it is permitted for this element to be left (entirely) for the call-off stage. The directives provide some indication in this connection in the definition of frameworks. It is also clear from the overall provision that most of competition should take place during the first stage. Also, price (pricing mechanism) is one of the main elements of competition in any procurement, at least from a value-for-money perspective.[147] These arguments suggest that the price or pricing mechanism must usually be established in the framework agreement.[148] The only possible exception could be for the procurement of commodities, where the specific features of the markets in question make it objectively impossible to establish any pricing mechanism in advance of orders. However, using a dynamic purchasing system might be more appropriate for such situations.[149]

'Generic' Multiple-Agency Frameworks

Specific issues can arise relating to the so-called 'generic' frameworks

> that do not identify all user authorities by their exact name, but provide that the framework is set up for use by a generic group of authorities, such as 'universities', 'local authorities' or even 'the public sector' or 'contracting authorities'.[150]

Recital 60PSD clarifies that

> framework agreements should not be used by authorities which are not identified in them. For that purpose, the contracting authorities that are parties to a certain framework agreement from the outset should be clearly indicated either by name, or by other

---

[146] Art 110(6)PIN.

[147] See also M Bowsher QC and LE John, 'The use (and abuse?) of framework agreements in the United Kingdom', in HR Garcia (ed), *International Public Procurement – A Guide to Best Practice* (London, Globe Business Publishing Ltd, 2009) 357.

[148] Despite an inadequate statement in the European Commission's 2005 Explanatory Note (n 99).

[149] Arrowsmith (n 28) 1133–34.

[150] S Arrowsmith, 'Implementation of the New EC Procurement Directives and the Alcatel Ruling in England and Wales and Northern Ireland: A Review of the New Legislation and Guidance' (2006) 15 *PPLR* 95.

means, such as a reference given to a certain category of contracting authorities within a clearly delimited geographical area, so that the contracting authorities concerned can be easily and unequivocally identified.

Where a central purchasing body (CPB) maintains a register of purchasers entitled to use frameworks placed by that CPB, such register should also record the date from which those purchasers obtain 'the right to have recourse' to the procurement devices placed by the CPB (ibid). This is to prevent the retrospective inclusion of purchasers in already existing frameworks.[151]

However, the directives do not make explicit a requirement for involving all individual users / potential purchasers of a (planned) framework from the planning stage, though recent CJEU case law suggests that such approach could be required mainly for single-supplier frameworks. The PSD appears to be satisfied of the 'closed nature' of the arrangement to the extent that user-purchasers 'are clearly identified in the call for competition or invitation to confirm interest'.[152] This, in conjunction with a view that rules in the directives concerning the estimated value of a framework could be applied in a more relaxed manner once it is clear that the aggregated value of the framework in question exceeds the applicable EU threshold,[153] could offer flexibility for centralised frameworks intended for 'government-wide' use or otherwise very large numbers of users (though, again, as shown above, recent CJEU case law might curtail this approach to some extent). Consulting or involving all intended users, particularly when large numbers of potential framework users are involved, could be inconvenient. But practical problems can also arise from a 'vague' estimation of the value (and, more generally, of requirements) as a consequence of not having involved potential users in the preparation of the frameworks, such as actual call-offs exceeding the estimation, or being significantly lower than the estimation. It should be borne in mind that, because a framework establishes terms competitively at the first stage, it is particularly important that requirements be realistically estimated[154] and made known to tenderers, since they 'calibrate' their offers in light of certain expectations of sales.

---

[151] Risvig Hamer, 'Regular Purchases and Aggregated Procurement' (n 138) 203. However, in extreme crises, such as during the coronavirus pandemic, not being able to include additional users of a framework could hamper relief efforts; see S Arrowsmith, 'Recommendations for Urgent Procurement in the EU Directive and GPA: COVID-19 and Beyond' in S Arrowsmith et al (eds), *Public Procurement in (a) Crisis: Global Lessons from the Covid-19 Pandemic* (Oxford, Hart Publishing, 2021) 63, 70.

[152] Art 33(2)2PSD. See also Case C-216/17, *Autorità Garante della Concorrenza e del Mercato – Antitrust and Coopservice Soc. coop. arl v Azienda Socio-Sanitaria Territoriale della Vallecamonica – Sebino (ASST) and Others*, ECLI:EU:C:2018:1034.

[153] In the literature it was supported that the rule on aggregating the value of all contracts that could be placed under a framework agreement (or dynamic purchasing system) should be considered in relation to the 'rationale for requiring aggregation ... namely that the size of the transaction as a whole means that it is likely to be of cross-border interest', see further S Arrowsmith, 'Dynamic Purchasing Systems under the New EC Procurement Directives: A Not So Dynamic Concept?' (2006) 15 *PPRL* 16, 28.

[154] The 'estimate of the likely size of the requirement' (the total/maximum estimated value/quantity of the framework) should probably be a 'bona fide and plausible estimate to be made', rather than a 'guess', Arrowsmith, 'Implementation of the New EC Procurement Directives' (n 150) 98. See also, Case C-216/17 (n 152) and Case C-23/20, *Simonsen & Weel A/S v Region Nordjylland og Region Syddanmark*,

On the other hand, very 'wide' frameworks could negatively affect competition on the market in question.[155]

A type of arrangement that appears more amenable to being organised as a 'generic' arrangement is the dynamic purchasing system,[156] since in this case the terms of future purchases are not established (competitively) at the first stage, and the overall estimated value or size of the requirement is thus less relevant.

Specific Domestic Experience: 'Generic Frameworks' in the UK

'Generic frameworks' as described above, have been of particular interest in the UK because of their intensive use for many years. In some cases, certain bodies first placed a 'generic' framework and then sought to persuade potential users to make purchases under them against a commission. This has reflected an optional approach towards centralised procurement, though, starting with 2010, the central Government moved towards mandatory centralised procurement to some extent through the Crown Commercial Service (CCS).[157] As has been customary, the UK regulations have generally followed the directives and have not provided for any specific conditions or rules concerning the use of multiple-agency frameworks, including 'generic' ones. The 2016 Guidance on Framework Agreements issued by the CCS for the public and utilities sectors includes the identification of contracting authorities in the call of competition as a key point, providing some examples of how potential users could be identified.[158] Similarly, and potentially in a rather more restrictive way, the Ministry of Defence Guidance on DSPCR (updated August 2021) indicates, amongst other possibilities, that 'wherever possible you must aim to identify each [potential user] individually by name'.[159]

However, as discussed in the preceding section, the issue of the way in which the identities of the users of a framework agreement are to be presented in a call for competition should not be detached from other substantive matters, such as the rules for estimating the value of a framework agreement, or indeed the 'mechanics' of establishing terms at the first stage of a framework agreement that should be

---

ECLI:EU:C:2021:490; and see recent discussion in M Andhov and R Vornicu, 'A Comparative View of the Use of Procurement Techniques and Electronic Instruments by Central Purchasing Bodies' in C Risvig Hamer and M Comba (eds), *Centralising Public Procurement: The Approach of EU Member States* (Cheltenham, Edward Elgar Publishing, 2021) 36, 44–48.

[155] See further, A Sanchez Graells, *Public Procurement and the EU Competition Rules*, 2nd edn (Oxford, OUP, 2015) 347–63.

[156] See section 5.3.3 below.

[157] See 'Centralised Procurement' at www.gov.uk/guidance/public-sector-procurement-policy#handbooks-and-guidance. For an overview, see A Manzini, L Butler and M Trybus, 'Central Purchasing Bodies in the United Kingdom' in C Risvig Hamer and M Comba (eds), *Centralising Public Procurement: The Approach of EU Member States* (Cheltenham, Edward Elgar Publishing, 2021) 316, 316–22. Also, National Audit Office (NAO), 'Cabinet Office – Crown Commercial Service. Report by the Comptroller and Auditor General' (HC786, Session 2016-17, NAO 2017).

[158] At https://assets.publishing.service.gov.uk/government/uploads/system/uploads/attachment_data/file/560268/Guidance_on_Frameworks_-_Oct_16.pdf (p 4).

[159] At: www.gov.uk/government/publications/the-european-union-defence-and-security-public-contracts-regulations-dspcr-2011/dspcr-chapter-11-framework-agreements, para 35(b).

'geared' to the extent possible to a realistically estimated usage of the framework. It is clear that the process of estimating the value of a multiple-agency framework will inevitably need to include an estimation of

> all the potential call-offs over the lifetime of the agreement that may be made by all contracting authorities that are permitted to use the framework, *not just the intended call-offs by the contracting authority which is procuring the framework agreement* (emphasis added).[160]

But no further indication is given as to what the estimation of other purchasers that may use a framework should involve. That this aspect is likely to present certain difficulties in practice arises from a recommendation to the effect that 'the risk of exceeding the advertised scope of the framework agreement' with multiple users 'can be mitigated further by providing a range of the estimated value for the framework'.[161] Whilst expressing a 'maximum' (as requested by the directives and the regulations) as a range could seem inappropriate, it is nevertheless practical where, as in 'generic' frameworks, there can be quite a significant degree of uncertainty as regards actual use. It seems preferable that potential tenderers are given an estimate as 'accurate' as possible, rather than creating an unjustified over-expectation. However, the breadth of such range might in some cases fail to offer a meaningful basis for establishing, at the first stage (through competitive bids), terms reflecting an expectation of sales from tenderers.[162]

In cases of optional use of centralised frameworks, the simultaneous availability of a plurality of 'generic' frameworks for the same items and for the use of the same entities, usually placed by different central purchasing bodies, could have some undesired effects on the relevant markets. In particular, a tendency to 'maximise' the estimation of the overall purchases to be made under a framework could easily become manifest, for a variety of reasons: seeking to ensure that all users and all orders can be accommodated; the hope of obtaining larger savings; or the hope that a larger number of users will be convinced to use the framework (among those 'generically' included, potentially without having been consulted in advance) resulting, where applicable, in proportional charges being thus levied. Caution should be exercised, as the lack of more detailed planning and thorough estimation – which, as shown, might be inherent to placing frameworks in this way – presents the risk that the estimated size of the requirement(s) could be manifestly detached from reality, in the sense of (serious) overestimation. This may be unfair to potential tenderers, as their offers are likely to take account of this element when preparing their tenders to access the framework. The older frameworks guidance issued by the former Office of Government Commerce (OGC),

---

[160] CCS Frameworks Guidance (n 158) 6. For a similar recommendation, see Defence Frameworks Guidance (n 159) para 32.

[161] Defence Frameworks Guidance (n 159) para 32.

[162] eg, OJEU Contract Notice – CCS Framework Agreement for Advertising and Marketing Services (OJ/S S170/03/09/2016 306636-2016-EN), estimated total value: range between £11,400,000 and £42,000,000 (Framework RM3796).

currently not applicable and archived, warned that 'Having too many frameworks for the same product or service will not encourage the market to bid or offer value for money if bidders are not convinced about the likely level of take up'.[163] Where suppliers are not convinced that the estimated size is realistic, they are unlikely to offer best value. Where they have initially trusted the estimate and offered best terms to enter the framework in relation to the overall estimated size, but then find that the actual orders are abruptly below expectations, they might refrain from honouring call-offs. Any losses or unrealised profits on a framework agreement will inevitably be internalised by suppliers in their tenders for other framework agreements or other public contracts and thus (re)charged to the public sector. The same will apply to the costs of tendering for a large number of parallel frameworks.

A further implication of multiple-agency framework purchasing, in particular in the form of generic arrangements, could be that the same entity may be entitled to procure the same items from a number of different frameworks running in parallel (placed by different CPBs or other consortia). The question then is which framework the entity in question should choose. The directives and the regulations are silent on this situation. It might be argued that the terms for each framework had already been subject to transparency and competition requirements, and thus there would be no need for further assessment. However, in the literature it has been pointed out, rightly, that: 'Based on the transparency principle ... an obligation is arguably implied for the purchaser to show objective commercial grounds for choosing one particular framework, to ensure that the discretion to choose between frameworks is not abused for illegitimate reasons'.[164] Value for money should also probably require objective commercial judgement when choosing among the frameworks. Where the frameworks in question establish all terms for the future purchases and do not involve second-stage competition, a comparison between the terms offered by framework contractors in relation to the purchaser's requirement should be straight-forward. However, where they do not establish all terms, and finalisation of terms requires second-stage competition, a comparison between the options available, prior to actually conducting a competition could be more difficult, simply because the terms that would be offered cannot be known in advance.

In such cases, an additional burden for a purchaser who is entitled to use a number of parallel frameworks may be first to ascertain which actually are all the frameworks that that purchaser is entitled to purchase from (if some of these are 'generic' ones and the purchaser in question was not individually identified, specifically consulted, etc). Thus, whereas centralised framework purchasing should have provided entities with a simple and efficient vehicle for making orders, they might instead find themselves in a rather uncertain situation, as described above.

---

[163] Section 3.5 of that Guidance, accessible via: http://webarchive.nationalarchives.gov.uk/20110601212617/http:/ogc.gov.uk/documents/OGC_Guidance_on_Framework_AgreementsSept_08.pdf.
[164] Arrowsmith, *The Law of Public and Utilities Procurement* (n 101) 692.

In the author's view, some methodology for choosing among frameworks in such cases should be provided for, or at least suggested in guidance. As shown, dynamic purchasing systems appear more amenable to be used as 'generic' arrangements, since they do not establish terms competitively at the first stage. In any event, because of the numerous legal and practical implications, multiple-agency framework contracting, in particular involving optional use and 'generic' configurations, represents a complex area, as shown here. The UK experience is extremely valuable, and it suggests that specific guidance or even dedicated rules may be desirable, not just in the UK but also in other procurement systems contemplating such arrangements.

5.3.2.4. Procedures

5.3.2.4.1. First-Stage Procedures

Procedures for awarding a framework agreement under the EU directives are the general procedures normally used for 'traditional' procurements. There are variations amongst the three EU procurement sectors as regards the 'general' award procedures that can be used by purchasers in all circumstances and without a need to justify their choice, as well as 'special' award procedures that can only be used under specific circumstances. Usually, the 'general' procedures are those providing for the widest degree of transparency and competition, such as open or restricted procedures. In practice, as discussed in the UNCITRAL chapter (Chapter two), in many cases award procedures other than open or restricted procedures are less likely to be appropriate for purposes of establishing framework agreements.

Generally, first-stage procedures for award of framework agreements and for selection of the framework contractor(s) do not differ from those used for 'traditional' procurements. The transparency requirements and challenge procedures are also very similar to those provided for 'traditional' procurement. However, there are some matters specific to framework agreements. Thus, there is specific information that needs to be provided in the contract notice or solicitation, for example that a framework is envisaged, whether this is a single- or multiple-supplier framework, the duration of the framework (together with justification where this is longer than the recommended maximum duration for the regime in question), and others.[165] Also, there are specific rules for estimating the overall value of a framework agreement which is 'the maximum estimated value net of VAT of all the contracts envisaged for the total term of the framework agreement.'[166] For frameworks involving reopening of competition there are specific rules

---

[165] eg, the estimated quantity or value and the maximum quantity or value of procurements under the framework overall (Case C-23/20 *Simonsen & Weel A/S v Region Nordjylland*, see n 154), whether second-stage competition is involved, the terms that are to be refined or established during second-stage competition, or the award criteria to be used during second-stage competition, the anticipated value or frequency of call-offs, where known, etc.

[166] Art 5(5)PSD; art 16(5)UD; art 9(9)DD.

concerning the minimum yearly turnover required as a selection criterion, which is not to 'exceed two times … the expected maximum size of specific contracts'.[167] However, where this is not known the maximum ceiling will be twice the estimated value of the framework. On the other hand, in both cases the maximum can be exceeded 'in duly justified cases'.[168]

One of the elements that need to be stated in the call for competition is the number of framework contractors contemplated to be admitted onto the framework. Certainly, the actual number is likely to be influenced by market response. In all cases there will need to be objective justification for variations in the number of admitted suppliers compared to the number envisaged. A related question is whether it would be possible for a framework agreement to be awarded to all tenderers who meet all relevant (qualitative selection and award) criteria, but without a 'competitive' reduction of the number of framework contractors at this stage.[169] This would permit a wider competition at the call-off stage, which might be appropriate in certain cases, when it may not be possible (or appropriate) to establish terms in advance of an actual order, for example on volatile price or commodity markets. Such a configuration might be achievable by providing for a (very) large maximum number of framework contractors in conjunction with very relaxed (low) criteria. This could be regarded as being against the 'spirit' of the framework 'concept', which involves establishing most terms during the first stage. Also, it would not be really efficient at the call-off stage, since reopening of competition would be significant, rather than 'mini'. Thus, even if permitted under the rules, the arrangement seems 'imperfect' from a number of angles. Again, dynamic purchasing systems under the 2014 directives could be far more appropriate for such procurements, since they do not involve a competitive reduction of suppliers at the first stage and remain open for the supply side throughout their duration.

In the 2014 directives there is also express provision for the use of electronic catalogues in the context of framework agreements.[170] An electronic catalogue is described as 'a format for the presentation and organisation of information in a manner that is common to all the participating bidders and which lends itself to electronic treatment'.[171] Tenders for the award of a framework agreement may be required 'in the form of electronic catalogues'[172] (under certain conditions) and, in this case, electronic catalogues are to be prepared by tenderers 'in accordance with the technical specifications or format established by the contracting authority'.[173] For multiple-supplier framework agreements the use of electronic catalogues at the first stage also enables (as an option to purchasers, provided it is stated from

---

[167] Art 58(3)PSD.
[168] ibid.
[169] Arrowsmith (n 67) 161.
[170] Art 36(4)PSD; art 54(4)UD.
[171] Recital 68PSD; recital 77UD.
[172] n 170.
[173] Arts 36(2)PSD; art 54(2)UD.

the outset) the use of electronic catalogues also at call-off stage, under specific rules that are discussed in the section below.

5.3.2.4.2. Call-Off Procedures

Overview

In the public and defence sectors contracts awarded under single-supplier frameworks must be 'awarded within the limits of the terms laid down in the framework agreement'.[174] Explicit provision is also included to the effect that the purchaser 'may consult' the framework supplier 'in writing, requesting it to supplement its tender as necessary'.[175] It follows that where all terms are established in the framework itself with sufficient precision, consultation is not needed and call-off procedures could consist of issuing an order to the framework contractor. But where not all terms are established with precision, further consultation at the call-off stage is a necessary step towards completing a call-off contract.

As regards multiple-supplier frameworks in these sectors, a distinction is explicitly made between frameworks establishing all terms and those which do not establish all terms, and this distinction has implications for call-off procedures. In the latter case, the purpose of call-off procedures is twofold: to refine or settle the terms not completed at the first stage and to establish which of the framework contractors performs a specific call-off. Where all terms had already been set with precision in the framework itself (at the first stage) the purpose of call-off procedures is (mainly) to establish which of the framework contractors is awarded a specific call-off. However, it could also include improvement/adjustment of terms established in the framework. In the case of frameworks that do not establish all terms, the PSD and DD provide that the award of call-offs involves reopening of competition amongst the framework contractors on the basis of the terms and using the criteria provided for in the framework agreement (and having been carried forward from the procurement documents for that framework agreement). Whilst the award criteria to be used in the mini-competition have to be those generally provided in the directives for the award of contracts,[176] they need not be the same as those used during the first stage, though some relationship among them will be inherent, in light of stage consistency, as well as commercial considerations.

Basically, second-stage competitive procedures involve: (i) an approach in writing to all framework contractors capable of performing the contract, that includes the provision of a reasonable time-limit for submission of tenders; (ii) a requirement that tenders must be submitted in writing and by the deadline for submission; (iii) a requirement that the content of the tenders is to remain

---

[174] Arts 33(3)1PSD; art 29(3)1DD.
[175] Arts 33(3)2PSD; art 29(3)2DD.
[176] Arrowsmith (n 28) 1152–53.

confidential 'until the stipulated time-limit for reply has expired'; and (iv) the award of each contract 'to the tenderer that has submitted the best tender on the basis of the award criteria set out in the procurement documents for the framework agreement'.[177] The provision for competitive second-stage awards seems to reasonably 'fit the bill'. Still, there appear to be a number of weaknesses in the existing provisions. First, the publicity requirements may need additional attention, since some decisions and processes seem to remain below the 'radar' of potentially interested bidders or framework contractors. For example, the provisions are silent on the issue of objectively establishing which of the framework contractors are to be deemed 'capable of performing the contract'. Presumably, this determination is to be made on the basis of the 'qualification' criteria (and the corresponding data and documents provided by the framework contractors during the first stage), as applied specifically to the requirements of each individual contract to be awarded under a framework agreement. However, there is no explicit provision in this connection, which may leave a 'grey' area of subjectivity as to potential limitations (or exceptions) to call-off competition. Also, there is no transparency requirement to inform each and every framework contractor of an up-coming opportunity (as there is in the UNCITRAL Model Law),[178] as well as of the determination concerning the contractor's capability or otherwise of performing the contract. Such a requirement would allow the concerned contractors of the framework agreement to challenge unjustified decisions that may subjectively limit second-stage competition(s). Additional transparency issues at the call-off stage are discussed later in this chapter.

Another aspect that could be regarded as a weakness concerns the fact that the risks of collusion in call-off competitions are not referred to. Such risks are elevated in this context since the arrangement is closed and the admitted suppliers may be just a few, knowing each other's identities as well as the estimated requirements on the demand side. Framework contractors could thus be seeking to impose less advantageous conditions than those generally available on the market, or than those that would normally result from a genuine mini-competition within the framework agreement in question. Whilst managing collusion risks involves many aspects[179] (rather than just regulatory ones), it might be that procurement regulation could also assist this process,[180] at least by pointing out to purchasers or even to Member States that such risks may be a real concern in closed frameworks

---

[177] Art 33(5)PSD; similar provisions are under art 29(4)DD.

[178] Chapter 2, section 2.2.3.3.2 of this book.

[179] GL Albano and C Nicolas, *The Law and Economics of Framework Agreements: Designing Flexible Solutions for Public Procurement* (Cambridge, CUP, 2016), in particular ch 9 (212–52). But see also, P Arden, 'Legal Regulation of Multi-Provider Framework Agreements and the Potential for Bid Rigging: A Perspective from the UK Local Government Construction Sector' (2013) 22 *PPLR* 165.

[180] A Sánchez-Graells, 'Prevention and Deterrence of Bid Rigging: A Look from the New EU Directive on Public Procurement' in GM Racca and CR Yukins (eds), *Integrity and Efficiency in Sustainable Public Contract: Balancing Corruption Concerns in Public Procurement Internationally* (Brussels, Bruylant, 2014) 171–98.

involving reopening of competition. It should also be noted that the 2014PSD addresses collusion more generally and in the context of irregular tenders,[181] something that was not present in the 2004PSD. Whilst it can be argued that a duty for purchasers to seek to prevent collusion may be implied in the requirement not to use frameworks in a way that prevents, distorts or restricts competition, a more explicit approach to collusion in this context could have been useful. The literature has discussed the possibility to address potential collusion by providing less detailed information concerning the anticipated requirements, namely by reducing transparency, so that collusion 'strategies' are more difficult to prepare and implement.[182] However, in the current author's view, transparency needs to be maintained or even expanded in some respects as is suggested above (and see also the sections below). It is submitted that the key is using closed frameworks involving reopening of competition only when this type of arrangement is really appropriate in light of the specific requirements of the procurement(s) in question and market circumstances.

As regards multiple-contractor framework agreements that do establish all terms, second-stage procedures do not usually involve reopening of competition since there is no need to establish or refine terms. However, under the 2014PSD (but not DD) provision is also made for the possibility to reopen competition for certain call-offs under such frameworks.[183] Where competition is not reopened (and all terms are set in the framework itself) the PSD provides that call-offs are awarded 'following the terms and conditions of the framework agreement'.[184] It also provides that 'the objective conditions for determining which' of the framework contractors 'shall perform them' must have been 'indicated in the procurement documents for the framework' and (then) 'set out' in the framework itself.[185] The DD simply states that call-offs are to be awarded 'by application of the terms laid down in the framework agreement'.[186] It thus appears that call-offs should be awarded by applying the criteria that are pre-established, from the procurement documents for the framework, to the actual requirements of each specific call-off.[187] Such criteria clearly include the award criteria provided generally for contract awards.[188] However, the language of article 33(4)(a)PSD seems to contemplate that 'objective conditions', other than the award criteria provided generally for contract awards, could also be used for framework call-offs without reopening of competition, certainly observing the principles of equal treatment and transparency.[189]

---

[181] Recital 59PSD; art 26(4)(b)PSD; art 35(5)3PSD.
[182] n 179.
[183] Art 33(4)(b)PSD.
[184] Art 33(4)(a)PSD.
[185] ibid.
[186] Art 29(4)DD.
[187] See further discussion by Arrowsmith (n 28) 1141–46.
[188] In art 67PSD.
[189] n 187.

In this connection, Recital 61PSD states that such objective conditions 'may ... include the needs or the choice of the natural persons concerned', an approach which seems inconsistent with the 'general' award criteria. The 'objective conditions' may also permit 'aleatory' awards, that is to say award methods not related to the terms offered (such as rotation, or alphabetical order); however, I submit, as is discussed in relation to the UNCITRAL Model Law (Chapter two), and notably in Chapter six, section 6.2.2.2, that these should be treated with great attention since they can easily foster favouritism and affect value.[190] Additional clarifications, or even limitations, concerning 'objective conditions', in the directive itself would have been desirable.

As already mentioned, the 2014PSD also provides for the possibility to reopen competition for certain call-offs, even where all terms had been set at the first stage.[191] In this case, the choice between reopening competition or making a call-off 'directly on the terms set out in the framework agreement shall be made pursuant to objective criteria, which shall be set out in the procurement documents for the framework agreement'.[192] All other rules for reopening competition or awards based directly on the terms set at the first stage must be observed accordingly. This option seems adequate for situations when it is anticipated that improvements in the terms generally offered for the framework might be obtained for certain orders, such as larger orders over a specified value. Recital 61PSD also refers to 'the need for a higher degree of service or ... developments in price levels compared to a predetermined price index'. However, care should be exercised. Contractors might not be prepared to offer their best possible terms at the first stage knowing that further competition may take place for some call-offs, but the terms offered by them at first stage will apply anyway to call-offs awarded without reopening competition.

Finally in contrast to the public and defence sectors, the provision in the utility sector does not distinguish, for the purposes of call-off procedures, between single- and multiple-supplier frameworks, or between frameworks establishing all terms and frameworks not establishing all terms at first stage. In all cases call-offs 'shall be awarded on the basis of objective rules and criteria' that 'shall be set out in the procurement documents for the framework agreement'[193] and 'shall ensure equal treatment'[194] of all framework contractors. For multi-supplier frameworks

---

[190] See also, Andhov and Vornicu, 'A Comparative View of the Use of Procurement Techniques and Electronic Instruments by Central Purchasing Bodies' (n 154) 40–41. But for a different view, see F Lichère and S Richetto, 'Framework Agreements, Dynamic Purchasing Systems and Public E-procurement' in F Lichère, R Caranta and S Treumer (eds), *Modernising Public Procurement: The New Directive* (Copenhagen, Djøf Publishing, 2014) 185, 217.

[191] Art 33(4)(b)PSD.

[192] ibid.

[193] Art 51(2)1UD.

[194] Art 51(2)2UD.

call-off procedures 'may include reopening the competition'.[195] In this case, the purchaser

> shall set a time limit which is sufficiently long to allow tenders ... to be submitted and ... shall award each contract to the tenderer that has submitted the best tender on the basis of the award criteria set out in the specifications of the framework agreement.[196]

It follows that all procedural options available in the public sector are also available here and, additionally, flexibility is offered concerning call-off negotiations with framework suppliers for the purposes of establishing or refining terms not set with precision at the first stage, or for improving/refining terms even where all terms had been set at first stage.[197] Certainly, whatever the design of the call-off procedures, they must observe the principle of equal treatment and requisite transparency.

Specific Approach in France: Explicit Exception to Call-Off Competition in Frameworks that Do Not Establish All Terms

The 2019 French Public Procurement Code includes provisions which may appear to derogate from the general rules on framework mini-competitions in the public and defence sectors. It is thus stated that a framework agreement not establishing all terms may stipulate that the award of certain call-offs is not to involve reopening of competition.[198] This only applies where 'for technical reasons' a subsequent purchase can only be entrusted to a specific contractor, a typical example given being where the subject-matter of that procurement cannot be substituted by other (alternative) items and there is only one contractor that is able to supply the required items. In reality, rather than derogation, such a situation appears to provide an explicit application of the provision in the directives according to which the reopening of competition requires purchasers to 'consult in writing the economic operators capable of performing the contract'.[199] Where only one economic operator is *objectively* capable of supplying the *objectively* required items, it would make no sense to invite any other contractor.

Could a Call-Off Consist of a (Secondary) Framework?

The EU directives do not include express language in this connection, but no reason could be identified to preclude such call-offs. Two interpretations are possible. One interpretation involves a limitative approach, revolving around a literal interpretation of the directives, which refer to call-offs as 'contracts', according to which a call-off consisting of a 'sub-framework' (under a primary framework) is only permitted where the 'sub-framework' qualifies as a 'contract'. However, an

---

[195] n 193.
[196] n 194.
[197] Kotsonis, 'The 2014 Utilities Directive' (n 42) 179.
[198] Art R2162-10CCP (last para); art R2362-7CCP.
[199] Art 33(5)(a)PSD; art 29(4)(2)(a)DD.

open interpretation of this point of the directive, favoured by the current author, is also possible. Under this approach, the focus of the relevant EU provisions is on ways to perform a framework agreement and they do not exclude establishment of a 'sub-framework' under the main framework agreement, as an 'intermediary' stage between the main framework agreement and actual procurement contracts being awarded. It is irrelevant whether or not such sub-framework qualifies as a 'contract', and what type of 'sub-framework' is involved (ie, establishing all terms, involving reopening of competition, single- or multiple-supplier, etc) so long as: (i) the terms and conditions of the main framework agreement are fully observed; (ii) the award of contracts under the sub-framework fully observes all legal rules concerning the award of call-offs; and (iii) the award of a 'sub-framework' is not an abusive way of performing the main framework, for example by way of 'reserving', through the sub-framework, a disproportionate part or the totality of the orders only to some (or one of the) contractors of the main framework.[200] Call-offs in the form of a 'secondary' framework arrangement can be efficient and effective purchase mechanisms, notably where a purchaser seeks to satisfy some of its recurrent requirements under a multiple-agency framework agreement.

Specific Approach in France: 'Frameworks within Frameworks'
An 'addition' brought by the French instruments to the provisions of the EU directives in the public and defence sectors concerns the possibility for framework agreements that do not establish all terms to award call-offs that themselves take the form of a (secondary) framework agreement, provided that the latter does establish *all* terms governing performance of the purchase in question.[201] As discussed in the preceding section, the directives do not include express language in this connection. The explicit clarification in French law of the possibility for call-offs to be organised as framework arrangements is to be welcome. As shown, a somewhat similar (mutatis mutandis) concept, referred to as 'blanket purchase arrangement', exists in the US federal procurement system.[202]

Among the EU Member States investigated in this book, France is the only one explicitly recognising this option in legislation and it is not a recent development: the provision was also present in the 2006CMP.[203] In that previous regime, '*marchés à bons de commande*' (purchase order contracts, ie, frameworks establishing all terms) were inadvertently classified in the CMP as procurement contracts, which might provide a historical explanation for permitting call-offs to take this form – but not the form of a framework arrangement not establishing all terms and involving a further, secondary, mini-competition.

[200] For 'abusive' orders, see also 'down-selections' in US federal purchasing (Chapter 4, section 4.2.4 of this book).
[201] Art R2162-8CCP; art R2362-7CCP.
[202] See Chapter 4, section 4.2.5 of this book.
[203] Art 77(VI); art 250(VI).

Further Electronic Avenues

The 2014 EU directives include specific provisions concerning the use of electronic catalogues in the context of framework call-off procedures involving reopening of competition.[204] The first situation envisaged is where tenderers are invited 'to resubmit their electronic catalogues, adapted to the requirements of the contract in question'.[205] On the occasion of the 'resubmission', the 'adapted' electronic catalogues will include the (improved) terms offered by contractors, which were subject to the reopening of competition. The second situation envisaged is where purchasers 'notify tenderers that they intend to collect from the catalogues which have already been submitted the information needed to constitute tenders adapted to the requirements of the contract in question'.[206] This appears to relate to an intention for the initially submitted catalogues to be complemented by contractors with regard to certain terms, for which competition is reopened for a particular call-off. While not expressly provided in the directives for framework agreements, the e-catalogue complementing aspect would seem somewhat similar to what is provided there for dynamic purchasing systems.[207]

In other words, the purchaser first 'generates' an adapted offer for the call-off in question on the basis of the electronic catalogue submitted during the first stage of the framework, ie, on the basis of the terms established in the framework. Then it calls for competition with regard to certain terms, either terms established in the framework but subject to reopening of competition as per the procurement documents for the framework, or terms not yet established by the framework but referred to in the procurement documents for the framework. A potential application of the e-catalogue collection of information method could be for a framework that provides for call-off awards under it, both with and without competition, under article 33(4)(b)PSD: collection of information could then be used for establishing the basis for competition, where call-offs are awarded through reopening of competition, and for establishing the best terms offered in relation to a specific call-off directly on the basis of the initial submissions (at the stage when the framework agreement was set), where reopening of competition is not envisaged.

Finally, a specific way of organising a second-stage mini-competition under a framework agreement is by conducting an electronic auction.[208] This possibility is provided for under all three regimes,[209] subject to certain specific conditions.

Notices and Transparency

Arrowsmith notes that transparency requirements in the EU directives concerning call-off procedures under framework agreements are in some respects unable

---

[204] Art 36(4) and (5)PSD; art 54(4) and (5)UD.

[205] Art 36(4)(a)PSD; art 54(4)(a)UD.

[206] Art 36(4)(b)PSD; art 54(4)(b)UD.

[207] Art 36(6)PSD; art 54(6)UD.

[208] The use of electronic auctions is not limited to the award of contracts under a framework agreement though.

[209] Art 35(2)2PSD; art 53(2)2UD; art 48(2)2DD.

to support proper monitoring and review of such awards.[210] Whilst Arrowsmith refers to the public sector, similar considerations apply to defence and utilities sectors. As shown above, where the call-off stage involves reopening of competition, and not all framework suppliers are invited – when only some of them are deemed 'capable' for the specific call-off – there is no requirement in the directives, as there is in the UNCITRAL Model Law, to inform suppliers not invited that a call-off is underway. This is likely to prevent the framework contractors in question from being able to challenge (where appropriate) a decision not to be invited in the call-off competition, since they might not be aware that a call-off is intended.

But this is not the only problem. Contract award notices regarding call-offs, informing the public that a call-off has been awarded,[211] are not required either. Instead, for call-offs under a framework agreement it is provided expressly that purchasers 'shall not be bound to send a notice of the results of the procurement procedure for each contract based on that agreement'.[212] In the public and utilities sectors an option is nevertheless provided for Member States to require purchasers to 'group notices' concerning the award of call-offs under a framework agreement 'on a quarterly basis', in which case 'the grouped notices' are to be sent for publication 'within 30 days of the end of each quarter'.[213] The option is implied in the DD as well, since it would not involve sending individual notices for each call-off. The approaches of the Member States examined are varied. For example, in the public sector, Romania requires quarterly grouped contract award notices for call-offs;[214] France does not require contract award notices for call-offs;[215] whereas the UK has taken (since 2015) a different approach to publishing information on call-offs, as is described in the section following.

On the other hand, the directives are not explicit as to the application of the provisions on informing candidates or tenderers of call-off award decisions.[216] In respect of 'traditional' procurement contracts and the award of framework agreements (ie, first-stage procedures), it is provided that purchasers must 'as soon as possible inform each candidate and tenderer of decisions reached concerning the conclusion of a framework agreement, the award of the contract or admittance to a dynamic purchasing system'. Also, upon request from an unsuccessful tenderer, the purchaser must within 15 days provide 'reasons for the rejection of its tender'. Analysing possible interpretations, Arrowsmith asserts that the correct legal interpretation is that those information obligations apply to call-off award

---

[210] Arrowsmith (n 67) 174–81.

[211] As provided for contracts and framework agreements in general – to be published within 30 days of conclusion in the public and utilities sectors (art 50(1)PSD; art 70(1)UD); and within 48 days of award/conclusion for the defence sector (art 30(3)1DD).

[212] Art 50(2)2PSD; art 70(2)2UD. Very similar provision is also in art 30(3)2DD.

[213] Art 50(2)2PSD; art 70(2)2UD.

[214] PPL, art 145(2).

[215] Art R2183-3CCP.

[216] Art 55PSD; art 75UD; art 35DD.

decisions (in any event, to decisions concerning call-offs above EU thresholds), whether or not the call-off procedures involve reopening of competition, since 'orders are public contracts under the directives'.[217] From a good practice perspective too, we suggest that this approach is desirable. But the matter may be further confused by the rather convoluted provisions in the public sector remedies directive on the communication of intended contract award decisions to candidates or tenderers concerned in the context of standstill periods.[218] That communication involves similar information as discussed above, though it must be sent together with information on the applicable standstill period. Nevertheless, the standstill communication may not apply at all where Member States use the derogation from standstill obligations in respect of call-offs under framework agreements[219] (see section 5.3.2.5 below).

The 'aggregated' effect of these provisions is that certain call-offs can be affected by a significant deficit of 'visibility', notably call-offs awarded without reopening of competition, or call-offs awarded under a limitation of competition (when not all framework contractors are deemed 'capable' for a certain call-off). In these cases, abusive or illegal awards may be difficult to spot for fellow framework contractors, or other potentially interested suppliers. It is thus suggested *de lege ferenda* that call-off visibility requirements should be both strengthened and expressly clarified.

Specific Approach in the UK (before Brexit): Publishing Information about Call-Off Awards

As shown, the approach in the directives permitting Member States the option not to require the publication of any contract award notices in respect of any call-offs under frameworks is questionable from a monitoring perspective. Whilst the 2014 directives provide for an option for Member States to require quarterly publication of grouped contract award notices for call-offs, the UK regulations have not opted for this.[220] Instead, the 2015 PCR included provision, not stemming from EU law,[221] for certain information to be made available through the UK Government's specialist public procurement opportunities website ('Contracts Finder') concerning call-offs placed under a framework agreement,[222] including call-offs below the EU thresholds.[223] These provisions continue to apply after Brexit pending the adoption of the new Procurement legislation emerging from the post-Brexit procurement reform.

---

[217] Arrowsmith (n 67) 176–77.
[218] Directive 89/665/CCE as amended, art 2a(2).
[219] ibid, art 2b(c).
[220] Reg 50(4)PCR; reg 70(4)UCR.
[221] In Part IV of PCR.
[222] Reg 108(1)(b)PCR.
[223] Reg 112PCR.

5.3.2.5. *Legal Review and Remedies*

Review procedures in EU directives (in all three sectors) cover both the first stage of a framework agreement,[224] as well as, in principle, call-offs. All review measures required for 'traditional' procurement also apply to the award of the framework itself. However, as regards the second stage of a framework agreement, there may be potential 'fractures' in the proper operation of remedial mechanisms. These arise both from insufficient transparency at the call-off stage, as discussed, and from an imbalanced regulation of review procedures in connection with certain call-offs.[225]

Thus, Member States are permitted to provide for derogation from the application of standstill periods for the award of (any) call-offs under framework agreements.[226] This supports the efficiency envisaged for the call-off stage, but could affect the review of call-off decisions. All three Member States examined have made use of this option. Where the derogation is invoked, Member States are obliged to provide for the remedy of ineffectiveness of the call-off contract; however, this only applies where 'there is an infringement' of the provisions concerning the *reopening of competition* and the call-off value exceeds the EU thresholds.[227] It follows that there is no obligation to 'enforce' ineffectiveness in the case of call-offs whose award has not involved second-stage reopening of competition. This seems an incongruent approach since multiple-supplier frameworks without second-stage competition still involve, at the second stage, the selection of a supplier (amongst those admitted onto the framework) to actually perform the call-off in question, and it is particularly important that such selection fully observes the rules and criteria provided in the framework agreement. However, weaknesses in transparency combined with waiving ineffectiveness for call-offs not involving reopening of competition makes these call-offs particularly vulnerable to fostering abuse or favouritism.

Returning to call-offs awarded by reopening competition (and above the EU value thresholds), Member States may provide, as in the case of 'traditional' contracts, for retroactive ineffectiveness (*ex tunc*), that is to say 'retroactive cancellation of all contractual obligations', or for prospective ineffectiveness (*ex nunc*), namely a limitation of 'the scope of cancellation to those obligations which still have to be performed'.[228] In the latter case, provision is also made for alternative

---

[224] In the literature it was suggested that the approach of the CJEU in Case C-410/14, *Dr. Falk Pharma GmbH v DAK-Gesundheit*, ECLI:EU:C:2016:399 might call into question the scope of the remedies directive to cover the first stage of awarding a framework agreement; Sanchez-Graells (n 29) section 4. Nevertheless, Sanchez-Graells rightly concedes that such interpretation would be unreasonable. Whilst that highly questionable CJEU approach is exacerbated in Case C-9/17, *Tirkkonen*, ECLI:EU:C:2018:142, these cases relate to very specific schemes and circumstances.

[225] Arrowsmith (n 67) 180–81.

[226] Directive 89/665/CEE as amended, art 2b(c); similarly, art 58(c)DD.

[227] ibid.

[228] Directive 89/665/CEE as amended, art 2d(2)(1).

penalties that are to be applied.[229] Such penalties are also to be applied when a Member State provides review bodies with the option of not considering

> a contract ineffective, even though it has been awarded illegally … if the review body finds, after having examined all relevant aspects, that overriding interests relating to the general interest require that the effects of the contract should be maintained.[230]

Alternative penalties may consist of 'fines on the contracting authority' or 'shortening of the duration of the contract'.[231]

Where a Member State invokes the derogation from standstill periods for framework call-offs, a purchaser may still voluntarily apply the standstill period for a call-off involving reopening of competition, to avoid the consequences of ineffectiveness.[232] In this case a standstill notice must be provided to the 'tenderers concerned' including the relevant reasons for the decision (as required in article 55(2)PSD) and 'a precise statement of the exact standstill period applicable'.[233]

It is suggested *de lege ferenda* that review provisions for call-offs under frameworks would benefit from clarification and strengthening, in correlation with transparency requirements, whilst also bearing in mind procurement efficiency envisaged for framework call-off awards. Potentially leaving certain call-offs below the 'radar' of review mechanisms can seriously undermine the values that both substantive and review procurement rules (in the directives) seek to protect and promote, such as equal treatment. It would clearly be insufficient to monitor through appropriate review procedures the first stage of awarding the framework itself, but then neglect – in particular in the case of multiple-supplier frameworks – the second (call-off) stage when actual procurement contracts are awarded thereby 'allocating' business to a specific supplier who might be favoured for example on grounds of nationality, to the disadvantage of the other suppliers admitted to the framework. Inadequate review mechanisms at the call-off stage may also affect value or even foster corruption, though the framework itself may have been awarded perfectly legally. It should also be recalled that individual call-offs can exceed EU thresholds and be of very high value.

Further, because frameworks under the EU directives are closed arrangements, some aspects in their operation (at call-off stage) could be insufficiently safeguarded simply through providing information and legal standing to framework contractors. It seems unlikely, for example, that framework contractors will challenge call-offs exceeding the scope of the framework, in the hope each will have to get that order. Even less so, colluding framework suppliers, possibly operating in conjunction with the purchaser, are unlikely to challenge

---

[229] ibid, art 2e(2) in conjunction with art 2d(2)2.
[230] ibid, art 2d(3).
[231] ibid, art 2e(2).
[232] ibid, art 2d(5).
[233] ibid, art 2a(2).

(themselves).[234] Apart from such instances, framework suppliers could, quite often, also be reluctant to challenge eventual breaches of law in the award of call-offs, to avoid what may be perceived as a deterioration of relationship with the purchaser, bearing in mind that frameworks tend to be quite long-term arrangements. Thus, consideration could be given *de lege ferenda* (or at national level) to providing information on call-offs, and legal standing in relation to call-offs, not just to suppliers admitted onto the framework,[235] but also under certain conditions to tenderers who participated in the first stage of awarding the framework but were not admitted to it, and who may be more willing to tackle collusive practices and/or orders exceeding the scope of the framework at the call-off stage. Additionally, at national level, procurement enforcement/ oversight authorities could consider monitoring (ex-ante and/or ex-post) the implementation of certain frameworks.

5.3.2.5.1. Specific Approach in the UK (before Brexit): Call-Offs Awarded before Declaration of Framework Ineffectiveness

Under the UK regulations only prospective ineffectiveness applies,[236] even where a declaration of ineffectiveness is made by a court. In the case of some call-offs this may mean that by the time a challenge is lodged and resolved, the call-off contract may have already been executed entirely, for example if it is of a relatively short duration. In such circumstances damages may remain an option if conditions are met.

The UK regulations also address a matter which the directives are silent about: the implications of a declaration of ineffectiveness concerning a framework agreement for call-offs already awarded under that framework agreement.[237] In this case, the regulations specifically apply the prospective concept to ineffectiveness. Thus, a call-off contract entered into before a declaration of ineffectiveness was made in respect of the framework in question 'is not to be considered ineffective merely because a declaration of ineffectiveness has been made in respect of the framework agreement'.[238] Ineffectiveness of a framework agreement does not automatically render ineffective call-off contracts awarded before the framework is declared ineffective. Ineffectiveness may apply to those contracts only if a specific claim has been lodged for each such specific contract, within the relevant time-limits applicable to them, and irrespective of whether this was made simultaneously with a claim concerning ineffectiveness in respect of the actual framework

---

[234] See DI Gordon, 'Bid Protests: The Costs Are Real, but the Benefits Outweigh Them', The George Washington University Law School, *GW Legal Studies Research Paper No 2013–41*, fn 148 and the text it relates to, referring more generally to procurement oversight in connection with collusive practices.
[235] See further discussion in Arrowsmith (n 67) 181; and wider considerations in Chapter 6, section 6.7.3 of this book.
[236] Reg 101PCR; reg 116UCR; reg 62DSPCR.
[237] Reg 103PCR; reg 118UCR; reg 64DSPCR.
[238] Reg 103(2)PCR.

agreement.[239] Where overriding reasons relating to a general interest relate specifically to any such contract, the court must not make a declaration of ineffectiveness in respect of that particular call-off contract.[240]

It appears likely that a similar approach concerning the implications of a declaration setting aside a framework for call-offs already made under that framework would apply in the post-Brexit procurement system as well, as shown in section 5.4.2 below.

5.3.3. Dynamic Purchasing Systems

5.3.3.1. *Description Instead of Legal Definition*

Dynamic purchasing systems (DPSs), as vehicles for recurrent purchases, are provided for under the EU public sector and the utilities directives. Unlike framework agreements, DPSs are not envisaged in the defence procurement regime. This appears to be the case because DPSs are intended for off-the-shelf (standard items) – as will be shown below – and such requirements are not envisaged as much by the defence regime. Nevertheless, in the literature it has been pointed out that 'there are some contracts for which they could be used' (in the defence sector).[241] The 2014 directives do not provide a legal definition per se for DPS, unlike the predecessor (2004) directives.[242] Instead, certain essential features of the arrangement are evidenced in the current legislation. It is thus provided that a DPS 'shall be operated as a completely electronic process, and shall be open throughout the validity of the purchasing system to any economic operator that satisfies the selection criteria'.[243] It is also emphasised that 'All the candidates satisfying the selection criteria shall be admitted to the system, and the number of candidates to be admitted to the system shall not be limited'.[244] In order to award a contract under a DPS, the purchaser must 'invite all admitted participants to submit a tender' and 'shall award the contract to the tenderer that submitted the best tender on the basis of the award criteria set out' in the relevant procurement documents for the establishment and operation of the DPS.[245] Such criteria may 'where appropriate, be formulated more precisely in the invitation' to the call-off competition.[246]

---

[239] Reg 103(4)PCR.
[240] Reg 103(5)PCR referring to reg 100PCR.
[241] Trybus, *Buying Defence and Security in Europe* (n 56) 350–51.
[242] See art 1(6) of 2004PSD; art 1(5) of 2004UD.
[243] Art 34(1)PSD; art 52(1)UD. For some discussion on the meaning of 'fully electronic process' see, eg, European Commission (The Multi-stakeholder Expert Group on eProcurement (EXEP)), *Dynamic Purchasing Systems: Use Guidelines* (Publications Office of the European Union, 2021) 13, and practical examples at 39–48. See also section 5.3.3.2 below.
[244] Art 34(2)1PSD; art 52(2)1UD.
[245] Art 34(6)PSD; art 52(6)UD.
[246] ibid.

From a legal drafting perspective, the regulation of the DPS might have been conceptually assisted by a clear legal definition of it, as a specific type of open 'non-traditional' recurrent procurement arrangement, involving two distinct processes: (i) an on-going admission process, where any interested suppliers meeting the selection requirements can apply for, and be granted in an expeditious fashion, admission to the system at any time during the existence of the arrangement; and (ii) the award of call-offs where all contractors already admitted onto the system by the time of each individual call-off are invited to tender for the procurement. The existence and purpose of the two stages of a DPS emerge from the substantive provisions of the directives concerning this type of procurement arrangement, though in a rather convoluted way.

In the past, DPSs have been described as 'essentially multiple framework agreements conducted through electronic means'.[247] This was consistent with the regulation of DPSs by the 2004 directives, under which admittance onto a DPS involved meeting selection criteria *and* 'an indicative tender' complying 'with the specification'.[248] The latter requirement suggested that at least some terms and conditions of future purchases were likely to be set on the occasion of the establishment of the DPS and/or on the occasion of admittance of each contractor onto the system, though not on a competitive basis, but as requirements imposed by the purchaser. As shown above, the 'standard' configuration for DPS under the 2014 directives only involves at the first stage an assessment of whether applicants for admission onto the system satisfy qualitative selection criteria. The requirement for indicative tenders has been removed, recital 63PSD[249] explaining that this had been 'identified as one of the major burdens' (under the 2004 directives). Since only selection criteria are assessed, it follows that terms are not established at the first stage, suggesting that this 'configuration' of DPS could be described as being closer to the concept of a 'supplier list' type of arrangement, rather than a 'framework' arrangement. Nonetheless, a different 'configuration' of DPS is implied in the context of the electronic catalogues. Under article 36(6)2PSD,[250] a purchaser may require that requests for participation in a DPS 'be accompanied by an electronic catalogue in accordance with the technical specifications and the format established' by that purchaser. Since an electronic catalogue is a form of presentation of a tender,[251] it follows that some terms are likely to be established at the first stage of this configuration of DPS.[252] This is confirmed by the fact that, at the call-off stage, the purchaser may, under certain conditions, collect information from those catalogues in order to 'constitute tenders adapted to the requirements'

---

[247] Trepte (n 4) p xxviii.
[248] Art 33(2) of 2004PSD; art 15(2) of 2004UD.
[249] And recital 73UD.
[250] And art 54(6)2UD.
[251] Art 36(1)PSD; art 54(1)UD.
[252] Though, again, through requirements imposed by purchasers, and not through a competitive reduction of number of contractors at first stage.

of the call-off that are to be 'completed subsequently by the candidates'.[253] This configuration of DPS could be regarded as closer to the concept of an open type of 'framework' arrangement.

Overall, the nature of DPS might be described as 'hybrid',[254] since any configuration involves the provision of estimated quantities at the first stage[255] and predetermined procedures for the award of contracts within the system. Whilst it is positive that a variety of configurations of DPS may be organised under the current directives, it would have been preferable if the provisions concerning them were more integrated and contained, with enhanced clarity.

5.3.3.2. Selecting This Arrangement

The directives do not include any provisions concerning procurement planning and decisions to embark on carrying out a DPS. From a practical point of view, a DPS offers the benefits of maintaining an open communication channel with the 'real' market outside the system in question, thereby reducing the risks of collusion and complacency significantly by comparison with (closed) framework agreements. On the other hand, the prospects of achieving better value from expected aggregate demand are less promising in the case of DPSs, because of the increased fragmentation of requirements and uncertainty over the actual number of competitors during each round of call-offs.

Certain prerequisites for the use of a DPS apply under the directives. First, the subject-matter of the procurement must consist of 'commonly used purchases the characteristics of which, as generally available on the market, meet the requirements of the contracting authorities'.[256] This long-winded way of expressing it was criticised in the literature for introducing an unnecessary degree of complexity without delimiting precisely the scope of covered items, it being noted that covered items should probably not be subject to 'adaptation for the entity's use', although minor customisation such as inscribing the organisation's name or logo on various items of stationery could be provided for.[257] Covered items may include, for example, office supplies, standard spares, or non-complex services such as cleaning or maintenance services.

It is likely that this provision is meant to serve a threefold purpose: (i) that the arrangement is mainly used for meeting on-going requirements; (ii) that meaningful competition is attracted for call-offs, the lack of which might not justify the use of a dynamic purchasing system; and (iii) that the assessment of admissibility to the system during the first stage does not involve a complex technical evaluation (for the configuration involving electronic catalogues at this stage), which could

---

[253] Art 36(6) and (4)(b)PSD; art 54(6) and (4)(b)UD.
[254] Term used by Trybus (n 56).
[255] Art 34(4)(b)PSD; art 52(4)(b)UD.
[256] Art 34(1)PSD; art 52(1)UD.
[257] Arrowsmith, 'Dynamic Purchasing Systems' (n 153) 18.

delay the overall assessment and affect the efficiency of the process. However, this limitation concerning the subject-matter of procurements under DPSs seems unnecessary[258] and could be counter-productive in certain situations. Whilst using DPSs for 'common' purchases as defined above could be one of the useful situations for implementing such a system, precluding DPSs for more complex items or those involving adaptations may 'push' purchasers into framework agreements (for such items), which may not always be an appropriate approach, for example depending on the type of relevant market and the potential dynamics of terms on that market.

The second prerequisite is that the process must be 'completely electronic'.[259] This involves not just the publication of relevant notices[260] and securing to any interested suppliers 'unrestricted and full direct access … to the procurement documents' throughout the duration of the DPS[261] but, apparently, all other steps involved in the process. In this connection, it is provided that 'All communications … shall only be made by electronic means'.[262] The legal obligation concerns both ways of communication with the purchaser, including the electronic submission of tenders at both stages, and there does not appear to exist a binding obligation concerning an automatic (electronic) assessment of submissions. However, such an electronic assessment would be required if an electronic auction is conducted in order to award contracts under a DPS.[263]

The third prerequisite in the operation of dynamic purchasing systems concerns a prohibition of billing any charge to interested suppliers or to suppliers that are parties to the system.[264] The scope of this provision is probably to eliminate any barriers to the free access of suppliers to such systems if they meet the other admittance requirements. Such barriers could result in failure to ensure meaningful competition at the second stage which is regarded as of the essence by the directives, since DPSs involve competition at that stage only.[265]

Because DPSs are open arrangements on the supply side, the main controls for their operation are permanent advertising,[266] short time-limits for assessing

---

[258] Arrowsmith (n 80) section 3, under 'Principle 5'. See also section 5.4.1 below.

[259] Art 34(1)PSD; art 52(1)UD.

[260] The Publications Office of the EU ensures that the full text of any call for competition for a DPS shall continue to be published 'for the period of validity of the dynamic purchasing system' (art 51(4)(b)PSD; art 71(4)(b)UD).

[261] Arts 34(4)(d) and 53PSD; arts 52(4)(d) and 73UD.

[262] Art 34(3)PSD; art 52(3)UD.

[263] Art 35PSD; art 53UD.

[264] Art 34(9)PSD; art 52(9)UD. However, in centralised purchasing, commissions may be charged to contracting authorities using a DPS, or to suppliers being awarded contracts: European Commission, *Dynamic Purchasing Systems* (n 243) 35.

[265] As shown, the first stage of a DPS does not involve a comparison among submissions received from various applicants, but only an assessment of each individual submission against the selection criteria (and specifications, where electronic catalogues are used) established by the purchaser as admission conditions.

[266] See n 260.

applications for admittance to the system,[267] the requirement to invite all admitted contractors to call-off competitions,[268] and awarding call-offs on the basis of criteria pre-disclosed in the call for competition for the establishment of the DPS. The duration of a DPS is less relevant than in the case of a (closed) framework agreement, since new suppliers can join at any time. Whilst the 2004 directives imposed limitations on the maximum duration of a DPS, the 2014 directives have removed such controls, though they do, rightly, require that the duration be stated in the call for competition.[269] Any change in the validity period is to be notified to the European Commission.[270] For similar reasons, the possibilities of harming competition under a DPS appear more limited than in the case of framework agreements.[271] Using selection criteria during the first stage that are not relevant for the actual call-offs might still result – deliberately, or otherwise – in allowing into the system contractors that are not properly 'equipped' to perform call-offs, or in preventing fully capable contractors from entering the system. Nonetheless, this risk is seen by the current EU legislator as low, since the explicit provision in the 2004 directives that DPS should not be used so as to affect or distort competition has also been removed.

Finally, it should be noted that, because terms are not established (competitively) at the first stage, DPSs appear more amenable than framework agreements to being used as 'generic' multiple-agency arrangements: a detailed and accurate estimation of the aggregated requirements of future purchases is less relevant for the purposes of admittance during the first stage.

5.3.3.3. Procedures

5.3.3.3.1. First-Stage Procedures

The current directives approach the entire DPS process as an adjusted form of restricted procedure.[272] It is accurate that there will be similarities between the latter procedure and a DPS, since the outcome of the initial stage consists only of the admission to the system of candidates who meet selection criteria (with no contract or agreement per se being awarded or concluded), and it is only selected candidates that are then to be invited to tender for specific procurements. However, there is also something 'fictional' in the approach, and it might have been more straight-forward to address the DPS as a specific, stand-alone, procurement vehicle. Thus, selection assessment under DPS is an on-going process throughout the duration of the arrangement, at any time when interested suppliers request

---

[267] Section 5.3.3.3.1 below.
[268] Where the system was divided into categories of items objectively defined, all contractors admitted for the category corresponding to the call-off in question must be invited.
[269] Art 33(8)PSD; art 52(8)UD.
[270] ibid.
[271] Sanchez Graells, *Public Procurement and the EU Competition Rules* (n 155) 365–66.
[272] Art 34(2)1PSD; art 52(2)1UD.

admission to the system, as a result of a permanently live advertisement. Similarly, all candidates meeting the selection criteria must be admitted, and their number cannot be reduced as permitted for the restricted procedure per se.[273] These features, in conjunction with multiple call-offs contemplated throughout the duration of the system, are important differences from the restricted procedure with significant implications for the overall process.

Some specific provisions concern first-stage procedures. In order to establish a DPS, the purchaser shall cause the publication of a call for competition, clearly stating that a DPS is involved,[274] and shall show in the procurement documents 'at least the nature and estimated quantity of the purchases envisaged' together with operational and technical details concerning the operation of the system.[275] Where applicable, 'the division into categories' of items to be purchased is to be indicated, and the 'characteristics defining' such categories of items,[276] which 'may include reference to the maximum allowable size of the subsequent specific contracts or to a specific geographic area' where call-offs 'will be performed'.[277] If categories are used, then the purchaser must specify the selection criteria for each category.[278] As regards calculating the estimated value of a DPS, the same rules apply as for framework agreements.[279] However, the rules concerning the ceiling for yearly turnover requirements (as part of the selection criteria) diverge from those applicable to frameworks. The language concerning DPSs is not entirely clear in this connection[280] and, in light of the objective of SMEs' participation, we submit that the ceiling is to be construed as twice the estimated value of largest call-off envisaged under the DPS, unless 'duly justified cases' dictate otherwise.[281]

Initially, a fixed time-limit applies, of a minimum of 30 days after sending the contract notice[282] for the dynamic purchasing system, for receipt of requests to participate, but 'No further time limits for receipt of requests to participate shall apply once the invitation' for the first call-off is issued.[283] The initial period is thus 'reserved' for setting-up the DPS. Normally, the assessment of requests to participate must be completed within 10 working days of receipt, though the period may be extended in certain circumstances.[284] Once a decision on the admission, or otherwise, of an applicant has been reached the purchaser must

---

[273] ibid.
[274] Art 34(4)PSD; art 52(4)UD.
[275] ibid.
[276] ibid.
[277] Art 34(1)PSD; art 52(1)UD.
[278] Art 34(2)PSD; art 52(2)UD.
[279] Art 5(5)PSD; art 16(5)UD.
[280] Art 58(3)PSD.
[281] See also A Eyo, 'Evidence on the Use of Dynamic Purchasing Systems in the United Kingdom' (2017) 26 *PPLR* 237.
[282] Or invitation to confirm interest, if relevant.
[283] Art 34(2)2(a)PSD; art 52(2)2(a)UD.
[284] Art 34(5)PSD; art 52(5)UD.

inform the 'operator concerned at the earliest possible opportunity',[285] which has been criticised for lack of specificity[286] (and is particularly important in cases of inappropriately denying admission onto the system).

A distinct aspect of the first stage of a DPS concerns the option for purchasers to re-check 'qualification' of suppliers admitted onto the system 'at any time during the period of validity' of the DPS.[287] This may be needed or desirable in particular in a DPS with very long duration, and the lack of specific rules in this connection has also been identified as a weakness.[288] Related to this, it is provided that the purchaser 'may require admitted participants to submit a renewed and updated self-declaration' concerning exclusion and selection criteria 'within five working days'.[289] However, the consequences of missing this time-limit are not clarified and it is optional in nature anyway, since the purchaser 'may' require (or otherwise) the renewal of the self-declaration. The time-limit appears in fact to be a minimum recommended time-limit in case the purchaser considers such renewal is needed. If the purchaser is not bound to require renewed self-declaration in the first place, it should also be able to accept it after the time-limit, but only to the extent that equal treatment is not affected.

Finally, as shown, no explicit provisions are included in the directives as to what first-stage procedures should involve where an electronic catalogue is required to accompany each application for admission. In light of the general approach toward DPSs it is inferred that such an electronic catalogue will be assessed for compliance with the requirements of the purchaser. Given the silence of the instrument, purchasers might take the view that the terms in electronic catalogues are binding to the extent they meet the purchaser's requirements. However, it seems also possible to regard all terms in an electronic catalogue as binding for the supplier in question – even where these exceed the requirements of the purchaser – and as minimum terms for future call-off competitions. This might be an (implied) hypothesis for the option where the purchaser 'constitutes' call-off 'tenders' that are then to be completed by suppliers in the system during second-stage competitions.[290] It would have been preferable if the instruments elaborated on these methods.

5.3.3.3.2. Call-Off Procedures

Call-off procedures represent a main area of simplification and improvement of the regulation of DPSs under the 2014 directives in comparison to their predecessor (2004) directives. Under the latter, the initiation of each call-off was conditional

---

[285] ibid. The requirement is also stated in arts 55(1)PSD and 75(1)UD.
[286] Eyo, 'Evidence on the Use of Dynamic Purchasing Systems' (n 281).
[287] Arts 34(7)PSD and 52(7)UD.
[288] Eyo (n 281) 246.
[289] n 287.
[290] Art 36(6)PSD; art 54(6)UD.

upon the publication of 'a simplified contract notice inviting all interested economic operators' to apply for admission to the DPS, and upon completion of the evaluation of all applications for admission received pursuant to the publication of that simplified contract notice.[291] It was only after this exercise that tenders for the specific call-off in question could be requested (from all suppliers admitted to the system). This was an unnecessary hindrance to the efficiency of the call-off stage, which resulted in infrequent use of this procurement method.[292]

Fortunately, that 're-run' of the first stage on the occasion of each call-off has now been eliminated by the 2014 directives, significantly improving the 'take-up' of the DPS in some Member States, such as the UK.[293] Thus, under the 2014 directives, once a specific need arises for items covered by a DPS, the purchaser simply proceeds to invite tenders from 'all admitted participants'.[294] In general, call-off procedures should not raise major issues. The use of electronic means should ensure that *all* tenderers are indeed invited simultaneously.[295] A minimum time-limit for receipt of tenders is established at '10 days from the date' when the invitation is issued.[296] Certainly, the actual time-limit should be adequate to allow tenderers to properly prepare their tenders. An electronic auction can also be organised at this stage for the award of contracts.[297] A call-off is to be awarded to the best tender received in accordance with the criteria established in the contract notice for the DPS, and 'Those criteria may, where appropriate, be formulated more precisely in the invitation to tender'.[298]

As in case of frameworks, the rules concerning the provision of information to tenderers as to the 'result' of the award procedure[299] do not specifically refer to call-offs under DPSs. Nevertheless, for the reasons shown in section 5.3.2.4.2, it is submitted that those requirements *do* apply to the award of DPS call-offs. It should also be noticed that *contract award notices* are required for call-offs under DPSs, either in the form of individual notices (for each call-off) or as quarterly grouped notices.[300] This position is more appropriate than that concerning call-offs under frameworks, where Member States may elect not to require the publication of any contract award notice.

---

[291] Art 33(5) of 2004PSD; art 15(5) of 2004UD.

[292] Arrowsmith, 'Dynamic Purchasing Systems under the New EC Procurement Directives' (n 153) 29; Arrowsmith (n 67) 185–86; S Arrowsmith, 'Modernising the EU's Public Procurement Regime: A Blueprint for Real Simplicity and Flexibility' (2012) 21 *PPLR* 71, 79.

[293] Eyo (n 281).

[294] Or, as applicable, from all participants admitted for the category of items relevant for the call-off (art 34(6)PSD; art 52(6)UD).

[295] As required under art 54(1)PSD or art 74(1)UD.

[296] Art 34(2)2(b)PSD; art 52(2)2(b)UD. In certain cases the time-limit (including a shorter one) may be established by mutual agreement with the candidates (art 28(4)PSD; art 46(2)2 and 3UD).

[297] Art 35(2)PSD; art 53(2)UD.

[298] Or other relevant procurement document for the DPS, depending on the call for competition used (art 34(6)2PSD; art 52(6)2UD).

[299] Art 55PSD; art 75UD.

[300] Art 50(3)PSD; art 70(2)3UD.

Specific Provision in Romania Concerning 'Frameworks' Awarded within Dynamic Purchasing Systems?

An interesting provision, included in Romanian legislation,[301] refers to 'contracts or framework agreements awarded through a dynamic purchasing system'. It is, however, unclear whether DPS call-offs consisting of framework agreements are indeed envisaged. It could be just a drafting error, since the only place in the instruments where this appears is in the context of publishing contract award notices (for call-offs under a DPS). The use of DPSs in Romania is still very limited,[302] as searches on the specialised domestic website,[303] or indeed on Tenders Electronic Daily,[304] demonstrate. It is possible that limited experience of more novel procurement methods contributed to this wording in the legal instrument.

Nevertheless, the discussion in section 5.3.2.4.2 above concerning interpretation of provisions in the EU directives so as to permit framework agreement call-offs consisting of sub-framework agreements seems relevant, mutatis mutandis, for potentially permitting call-offs consisting of framework agreements under dynamic purchasing systems. Such configurations can prove useful, under certain conditions, in the case of some centralised (multiple-agency) DPSs, and provisions in this sense are included in Italy and Hungary (European Commission, *Dynamic Purchasing Systems: Use Guidelines*, pp 30–31).[305]

5.3.3.4. Legal Review and Remedies

As concerns legal review mechanisms, DPSs should not usually raise major issues, both stages being reasonably covered by the general rules and measures in the EU directives. For the purposes of the remedies directives, 'contracts include public contracts … and dynamic purchasing systems'.[306] There are some particularities though.

With regard to first-stage procedures, it can be noticed that standstill periods are not relevant because there is no contract award decision or conclusion

---

[301] Art 145(3)PPL; art 155(3)UPL.

[302] As at May 2022; however, there has been some use of DPSs (including, apparently, a few ones below the EU value thresholds) in particular after the new electronic facilities became available in 2021, as to which see also a post by the current author: Ş Filipon, 'Opening the Door for Operating Dynamic Purchasing Systems in Romania: Are We Ready to Use the Additional Flexibility and Convenience in a Balanced Way?' (March 2021) at https://in-in.ro/news/dynamic-purchasing-systems-romania-are-we-ready-to-use/.

[303] www.e-licitatie.ro.

[304] Supplement to the Official Journal of the EU. See also R Vornicu and D Dragos, 'Central Purchasing Bodies in Romania' in C Risvig Hamer and M Comba (eds), *Centralising Public Procurement: The Approach of EU Member States* (Cheltenham, Edward Elgar Publishing, 2021) 266, 271, who link the scarce use of DPSs to 'the immaturity of the Romanian public procurement system'.

[305] See n 243.

[306] Art 1(1) of Directive 89/665/CEE (as amended). Similar provision is included in Directive 92/13/CEE (as amended). In the literature it has been suggested that the approach of the CJEU in the *Falk Pharma Case* C-410/14, ECLI:EU:C:2016:399 might call into question the scope of the remedies directive to cover the first stage of DPSs; Sanchez-Graells (n 29) section 4. Nevertheless, rightly, the author concedes that such interpretation would be unreasonable.

involved. Consequently, the remedy of ineffectiveness[307] also appears irrelevant in connection with the admission stage of a DPS. However, an interested supplier could challenge the contract notice (or relevant invitation) for a DPS, the relevant procurement documents, or the decision concerning its own application for admittance. Thus, any interested supplier will be 'protected' against abusive behaviour by a purchaser concerning the rejection of its application for admission[308] and/or delaying unjustifiably a decision on the application.[309] But interested suppliers wishing to apply for admittance, or contractors already admitted may be less 'protected' against decisions that may favour admittance to the system of suppliers that do not meet the required criteria and conditions, simply because no information in connection with the admittance (or otherwise) of other suppliers is required to be made available to the former.[310] In light of full competition at the call-off stage, this risk and its potential effects appear moderate. Still, it is suggested that decisions of admission (of suppliers) in DPSs may benefit from increased attention from alternative review mechanisms (at national level or in future EU legislation), including ex-post controls by procurement audit or a supervision body.

Review avenues for the call-off stage are generally thorough and comprehensive. The entire range of remedies may be applicable in a straight-forward fashion, depending on the circumstances. Member States are given the option to derogate from the application of standstill periods for call-offs under DPSs and to replace this measure with ineffectiveness for both public and utilities regimes.[311] As in the case of call-offs under frameworks involving reopening of competition, where the derogation is invoked, ineffectiveness would still not apply where a purchaser voluntarily observes the standstill period (and associated information requirements).[312]

Because of the ongoing nature of the first stage, there might be situations of interaction between stages in terms of remedies sought. For example, a supplier challenging a decision rejecting his application to join the system might also request the cancellation or suspension of a call-off procedure carried out by the purchaser whilst this legal review is underway. Such interaction situations are not addressed explicitly in the current instruments and might benefit from increased attention in future revision/streamlining of both the procedural and review rules.

---

[307] And/or alternative penalties.
[308] If notified promptly by the purchaser of the decision; see section 5.3.3.3.1 above.
[309] And, also, against illegal provisions in procurement documents for the DPS.
[310] Art 34(5)3PSD. But note good practice examples and recommendations for increased transparency on qualified (admitted) suppliers: see European Commission (n 243) 34, 36.
[311] Art 2b(c) of Directive 89/665/CEE; art 2b(c) of Directive 92/13/CEE.
[312] Art 2d(5) of Directive 89/665/CEE; art 2d(5) of Directive 92/13/CEE.

5.3.4. Qualification Systems

Qualification systems are recognised and permitted in the utilities sector only. They are provided for mainly under article 77UD, though the directive deals with various aspects that are relevant to qualification systems in a number of different provisions, such as those concerning publication of notices, means of calling for competition, or use of exclusion grounds.

A legal definition of qualification systems is not included in the directive. Chapter one showed that two major types of arrangement arise from our definition of PUIR arrangements: 'framework arrangements', which at the first stage involve the assessment of 'suitability' of interested suppliers *as well as* the establishment of some terms of future purchases; and 'supplier lists' which at the first stage *do not* involve the establishment of terms for future purchases. As regards the latter, Arrowsmith distinguishes between 'mandatory' supplier lists, where registration on the list is a condition of participating in any procurements under it, and 'optional' lists where registration is not compulsory for participating in procurements.[313] From the relevant provisions of the UD it can be inferred that a qualification system is a contracting entity-driven mechanism for establishing mandatory lists of suppliers[314] whose 'suitability'/'qualification' has been assessed, at least in part, for various types of contracts or procurement needs. The suppliers who are registered in a qualification system, ie, those who meet the applicable criteria (which must be objective), will 'then form a pool from which the utility may draw those who are to be invited to bid or negotiate on future contracts'.[315] The 'mandatory' (or 'exclusive') nature of the arrangement arises from article 77(5)UD, which states:

> When a call for competition is made by means of a notice on the existence of a qualification system, specific contracts ... covered by the qualification system shall be awarded by restricted or negotiated procedures, in which *all* tenderers and participants are selected among the candidates *already* qualified in accordance with such a system. (emphasis added)

The same seems to apply when specific contracts are awarded by competitive dialogue and innovation partnership under a qualification system.[316]

A qualification system is an open arrangement. Thus, 'entities ... shall ensure that economic operators are at all times able to request qualification', under article 77(1)UD. Also, in order to establish a qualification system, an entity must publish (in the OJEU) a notice on the existence of a qualification system 'indicating the purpose of the qualification system and how to have access to the rules concerning its operation'.[317] The notice also acts as a means for calling for

---

[313] eg, Arrowmith (n 28) 1311–12. See also Chapter 2, section 2.2.5, fn 181 of this book.
[314] See also Trepte (n 4) 366 and subsequent.
[315] Arrowsmith (n 101) 970.
[316] Arts 44(4)(b), 48(1) and 49(1)UD in conjunction with art 68UD.
[317] Art 68(1)UD. Annex X to UD states the additional information required for this notice.

competition for subsequent contracts,[318] and the EU Publications Office ensures its permanent publication throughout the 'period of validity' of the system.[319] On the other hand, a qualification system can be a single- or multiple-purchaser arrangement, and it is argued that it could be an open arrangement on the demand side as well. In this connection, article 77(3)UD states that where a purchaser considers that the qualification system organised by another entity 'meets its requirements, it shall communicate to interested economic operators' the identity of that entity. Consistent with the open nature of the arrangement, its duration is not limited by the directive. The period of validity is to be indicated in the notice on the existence of a qualification system,[320] whereas 'any change' to that period must be notified to the EU Publications Office by using specific forms.[321]

The term 'qualification' in the context of assessment for entry onto a qualification system potentially includes a range of aspects concerning a supplier, as considered relevant by a purchaser in light of its planned procurement(s). The requirement in article 77(2)UD is for contracting entities to establish 'objective rules and criteria for the exclusion and selection of economic operators requesting qualification'.[322] These 'objective criteria and rules' *may* include exclusion and selection criteria referred to under the public sector regime[323] and/or technical specifications.[324] Thus, 'qualification systems' may cover a wide range of 'first-stage' assessments, from mere registration of interest, to partial or full 'qualification', to an assessment of specifications, or even to the possibility of reducing the number of those qualified, as the system 'may involve different qualification stages'.[325]

Procedurally, it seems surprising – if not disappointing – that the (2014)UD has carried forward the provisions in the previous (2004)UD[326] concerning the six-month time-limit for contracting entities 'to inform applicants of their decision as to qualification'[327] (ie, as to the admittance or otherwise to the system). This appears excessively long, potentially leading to abuses, as does the 'shorter' four-month time-limit for reaching a decision.[328] Within this lax period a procuring entity could, for example, deliberately delay a decision concerning the admission of an applicant to avoid its participation in a certain procurement exercise.

---

[318] Annex X, point 7 (UD).
[319] Art 71(4)(c)UD. This is an improvement compared to publication rules in the previous (2004)UD.
[320] Art 68(2)UD (and point 6 of Annex X).
[321] Art 68(2)UD.
[322] And also for the operation of the system, including 'inscription' in it or 'periodic updating of qualifications'.
[323] Art 80UD referring to arts 57 and 58PSD. But certain utility entities must use some of the exclusion criteria in art 57PSD.
[324] Art 77(2)UD.
[325] ibid.
[326] Art 49(3) of 2004UD.
[327] Art 75(4)UD.
[328] ibid. In most cases a (much) shorter period is needed to complete a full evaluation of competitive tenders. It is thus puzzling why the assessment of interest and/or of compliance with a number of 'suitability' or 'capability' criteria should be allowed to drag on for so long.

During the same period, it could quickly assess a preferred supplier and grant admission to it, in time to 'catch' a procurement exercise based on that qualification system. Clearly, these provisions on time-limits appear unlikely to facilitate wise admission decisions, in particular in the context of 'interactions' between 'newcomer' applications and calls for specific procurements under the system in question. It would have been preferable to include much shorter time-limits for decisions and information on admission in the system, or even a prohibition to delay a decision on admission where the contracting entity is aware of up-coming procurements that the applicant might be interested to participate in. On the other hand, once admitted to a qualification system, bringing the qualification of a supplier to an end during the duration of a qualification system appears to be subject to adequate procedural safeguards against abuse.[329] However, these provisions cannot compensate for the 'damage' potentially caused to a qualification system by the long time-limits for deciding on admission of applicants.

As regards remedies in the context of a qualification system, the interaction and overlaps between stages are not addressed specifically. In this connection, somewhat similar matters may arise, as in the case of DPSs.[330] In fact, in particular in the UD, a number of similarities can be identified more widely between qualification systems and DPSs,[331] such as permanent advertising, open access throughout the validity, and notifying changes in the validity. The possibility to specify the criteria for the award of contracts in the notice on the existence of a qualification system[332] is also relevant. Certainly, there are significant differences as well, notably the fact that DPSs are confined to 'common use' purchases, whereas this is particularly not the case with qualification systems. Also, the 'second-stage' award procedure can be significantly different, for example where contracts are awarded through negotiated procedures.[333] It is likely that a DPS type of arrangement could be organised under the rules of qualification systems, though the reverse may not apply in many cases.

Perhaps in the future the 'common' areas between qualification systems and DPSs could be built on to substantiate the recognition of a mandatory list type of arrangement in the public sector, somewhat similar to qualification systems in the utilities sector, subject to conditions and coverage provided for in the Government Procurement Agreement of the World Trade Organization.[334] I submit that qualification systems in the EU utilities sector, as currently regulated, would just need some adjustments to 'fit' relevant coverage of the public sector, mainly: (i) a drastic reduction of the time permitted to assess applications for admission and for informing applicants on the decision reached, (ii) confining the selection and

---

[329] Art 75(6)UD.
[330] Section 5.3.3.4 above.
[331] Notably the 'standard' DPS configuration, not involving establishment of terms at the first stage.
[332] Annex X, point 10 of UD.
[333] Other differences apply, for example charges may be billed to applicants in case of qualification systems (art 77(6)UD), whereas this is not permitted in the case of the DPS.
[334] Which the EU is a party to. See, in particular, art IX(7)–(13), and EU annexes 2 and 3 to GPA(2012).

exclusion criteria to those specifically provided for in the PSD, (iii) some express provision and increased transparency over selecting participants among suppliers, and (iv) certain clarifications concerning review mechanisms. Since 'mandatory list' arrangements are (still) not permitted in the public sector[335] their recognition seems long overdue. Arrowsmith noted back in 2005 that 'in light of the potential advantages of mandatory lists' their introduction in the 2004 directive would have been useful.[336] However, this has not even occurred in the 2014 directive.

5.3.5. Official Lists of Approved Economic Operators and Certification by Bodies Established under Public or Private Law (Official Lists)

Under this title the public sector and the defence regimes[337] recognise and regulate certain mechanisms intended to facilitate the assessment of supplier 'suitability' (referring, in the language of the directives, to criteria for qualitative selection) in any type of procurement procedure. The mechanisms involve 'standardisation' and simplification of documentary evidence and verification of how candidates or tenderers meet those criteria or certain aspects of them, relating to the personal situation of candidates or tenderers (exclusion grounds), the suitability to pursue a professional activity, their technical and professional ability, economic and financial standing, quality assurance standards, and environmental management standards.[338] The main purpose of the provisions on official lists appears to be preventing unjustified restrictions on accessing procurements by suppliers from other Member States (than that of the purchaser) that may result from an improper operation of such documentary evidence mechanisms. Establishing or maintaining an official list is optional for Member States.[339] Where an official list exists, the Member State in question must notify the Commission and the other Member States of the address of the 'body ... to which applications shall be sent'.[340]

These mechanisms have the role of 'hubs' and 'repositories' for various proofs that suppliers would otherwise have to provide to purchasers as part of the qualitative selection requirements for procurements. When regulating qualitative selection, the directives also define the proof that will have to be considered sufficient by a purchaser in respect of various aspects or criteria. Rather than having to supply the various and possibly numerous pieces of documentary evidence for each procurement contract or purchaser, official lists may reduce this burden by

---

[335] Other than to the extent that a DPS falls in this category.
[336] Arrowsmith (n 101) 770.
[337] The relevant provisions are in art 64PSD and art 46DD.
[338] Arts 57–63PSD; arts 39–44DD.
[339] Art 64(1)PSD; art 46(1)DD.
[340] Art 64(1)PSD; a similar requirement is found in art 46(8)DD.

requiring submission of such documentation only once to the 'official list body'. That body verifies the evidence and data in it, in accordance with the provisions of the directive – which are the exact same provisions concerning qualitative selection, as they would apply to purchasers – and, where satisfied, records the data.[341] Then, for each contract, suppliers registered on an official list may submit to relevant purchasers a certificate of registration on the official list to prove fulfilment of the relevant qualitative criteria.[342] Official lists may not completely simplify all documentary evidence issues, but they can streamline some of them. Thus, official lists may only cover certain elements of those that qualitative selection may refer to. On the other hand, some of the qualitative selection aspects may be so comprehensive and/or specialised that a general registration on a list or certification system may not be particularly helpful (eg, in specialised consulting services).

In order to ensure that, where introduced, official lists are not used in a discriminatory way, the directives institute a number of compulsory provisions concerning their operation. Thus, as shown, the conditions for registration must observe the conditions that a purchaser would have to fulfil when requesting/ assessing qualitative selection criteria and proofs.[343] Similarly, certificates issued 'shall state the references which enabled' the registration of a supplier.[344] Registration on an official list constitutes 'a presumption of suitability with regard to requirements' covered by the list in question and information resulting from registration 'shall not be questioned without justification'[345] (by a purchaser). However, these rules operate only in favour of economic operators established in the Member State holding the official list in question.[346] It is inferred that this may include the State of the purchaser. On the other hand, suppliers from other Member States 'shall not be obliged to undergo' registration in the country of the purchaser as a condition of participation in a procurement exercise; instead, the purchaser will have to 'recognise equivalent certificates from bodies established in other Member States' or other equivalent documentary evidence concerning the qualitative selection criteria.[347] It appears *a contrario* that registration of suppliers established in the Member State holding the list could be made compulsory, for example through a general requirement by the Member State in question that is applicable to any national supplier wishing to participate in public procurement.[348] Another very relevant rule concerning the operation of official lists is that they must be open to suppliers at any time and the decision

---

[341] Art 64(2)PSD; art 46(1)DD.
[342] Art 64(3)PSD; art 46(2)DD.
[343] Art 64(2)PSD; art 46(1)DD. Also, art 64(6)PSD.
[344] Art 64(3)PSD; art 46(2)DD. But see also the expansion of information requirements concerning 'documents produced as evidence' by suppliers in art 64(8)PSD.
[345] Art 64(4) and (5)PSD. See also art 46(3) and (4)DD.
[346] Art 64(5)PSD; art 46(4)DD.
[347] Art 64(7)PSD; similar provisions are in art 46(5)DD.
[348] Arrowsmith (n 28) 1303.

regarding registration (or otherwise) is to be issued 'within a reasonably short period of time'.[349] Finally, for registration of economic operators from other Member States, where they wish to register, the same proof or statements shall be required of them as from national suppliers.[350]

The distinctive point that, it is submitted, draws a line between 'official lists' and PUIR as defined in this book is that the organisation of official lists is not entrusted to individual purchasers but to assigned bodies 'established under public or private law' that are 'complying with European certification standards'.[351] Purchasers are only players and not 'managers' of the official list, and it is argued that they are secondary players. This is because purchasers are bound to accept registration on official lists as a presumption of 'suitability' (under the conditions discussed) but they cannot require such registration as a means of proof of suitability, at least as regards economic operators from other Member States. From this perspective, suppliers should be regarded as the main players of the system since they have the option and initiative of using for the purposes of individual procurements the registration on an official list as a presumption of suitability. They will also have the option, but not the obligation, to register on a list in the country of the purchaser. Thus, official lists are not purchaser driven and, in effect, they are unlikely to assist purchasers specifically by structuring potential suppliers by 'specialities' as a first step towards approaching *their envisaged* but uncertain or indefinite requirements within an articulated arrangement geared to their needs. On the other hand, mandatory lists (organised by the purchaser) are implicitly prohibited by the directives in the public and defence sectors in that these instruments clearly prescribe the permitted proof that may be required by the purchaser concerning qualitative selection requirements, but such proof does not include (pre-)registration on a list organised by the purchaser – with CJEU case law clarifying that under certain circumstances registration may be required *during* the award procedure in question if the registration requirement does not prevent participation in the procurement and subject to other conditions.[352]

In light of the above, it appears that purchasers may organise *optional* lists, not in the sense of 'official' ones, if they observe all applicable rules concerning 'qualitative selection'[353] and the general award rules for the procurements in question, and if such lists are advertised.[354] In this case, participation in award procedures would be open both to suppliers registered on such a list – which would benefit from a presumption of being 'qualified'/'suitable' in connection with the aspects

---

[349] Art 64(6)PSD; art 46(6)DD.
[350] Art 64(6)PSD; art 46(5)DD.
[351] Art 64(1)PSD.
[352] Arrowsmith (n 28) 1312–13. See also Case C-74/09, *Bâtiments et Ponts Construction SA and WISAG Produktionsservice GmbH v Berlaymont 2000 SA*, ECLI:EU:C:2010:431, which the author refers to (ibid and p 1201).
[353] Including those concerning 'official lists', mutatis mutandis.
[354] A requirement that appears to stem from TFEU; see Arrowsmith (n 28) 1319.

referred to by the list in question[355] – as well as to non-registered suppliers who are interested and whose 'qualification'/'suitability' is to be fully assessed during the award procedure in question. Participation of both 'categories' of suppliers for each specific procurement carried out must be ensured under equal terms with no 'advantages' for already registered suppliers other than a presumption of suitability, as discussed above.[356]

However, the use of optional lists as a vehicle for PUIR remains of relatively limited practical relevance under EU law. The fact that the permitted use of such lists is implicit in the text of the directives, rather than addressed explicitly, leaves a potential area of legal uncertainty, which is unlikely to encourage purchasers to organise optional lists. This seems particularly surprising given the express provision for a certain type of (optional) multi-use list in GPA(2012)[357] and its general coverage including for the public sector.

5.4. Arrangements Contemplated in the UK Post-Brexit Procurement Reform

5.4.1. Dynamic Markets

As shown in section 5.2.3 above, the Green Paper outlining the view of the Westminster Government to reform public procurement in the UK after Brexit envisaged legislating for a new arrangement then called the 'new Dynamic Purchasing System (DPS+)'.[358] It was proposed that, unlike the 'old' dynamic purchasing system in the EU directives, the application of the new tool in the UK's reformed procurement system would not be limited to 'common use' items[359] and, instead, any type of requirement could be procured through this tool, which is a very desirable and forward-looking approach. At the same time, however, it was also proposed that this new tool, described as 'a form of GPA multi-use list', would, under the new post-Brexit UK legal framework, replace both dynamic purchasing systems *and* qualification systems[360] in the UK's 'pre-reform' procurement regulations. This last element, in conjunction with a lack of clarity over the operation of DPS+, raised serious concerns regarding the potential for significant limitation of flexibility for utilities using qualification systems. The issue was initially raised by

---

[355] They may need, though, to complete or update that evidence.
[356] Arrowsmith (n 28) 1315, referring to Case C-71/92, *Commission of the European Communities v Kingdom of Spain*, ECLI:EU:C:1993:890, [1993] ECR I-05923.
[357] Art IX(7)–(11).
[358] In chapter 5: Using the Best Commercial Purchasing Tools (42–47). See also n 77.
[359] For this requirement in the EU directives, see section 5.3.3.2 above.
[360] Green Paper (n 77), point 146.

Arrowsmith,[361] and then confirmed by feedback received from wide consultations with stakeholders (users of the reformed laws), arising from the Green Paper.[362]

Consequently, in its response to consultations and taking note of the concerns, the Government proposed to 'maintain the effect of qualification systems as a separate tool for utilities under similar terms to the UCRs', specifically permitting utilities to 'exercise a choice to use a Tender Notice (which replaces the notice on the existence of a qualification system) as a call for competition'.[363] However, in the Procurement Bill[364] (PB), such provision could not be identified. It could be included via a separate Act, but the approach seems unclear at the time of writing (May 2022). On the other hand, a return to the original approach where dynamic markets would replace qualification systems appears unlikely to provide a similar degree of flexibility to utilities as exists under the current UCR, given the distinction that the GPA makes between multi-use lists as regards utilities and sub-central authorities on the one hand, and central authorities on the other hand.[365] From this perspective, pursuing the objective of flexibility and bearing in mind the familiarity of UK purchasers with existing arrangements, it might have been preferable if a qualification system type of arrangement were not just maintained in the utilities sector but also extended to sub-central authorities, perhaps subject to certain improvements (as compared to the provision in the EU directive) that I pointed out in section 5.3.4 above.

The apparent lack of provision concerning the fate of qualification systems is not the only issue in the PB. To further evidence that a different arrangement is contemplated than the EU dynamic purchasing system, the DPS+ in the Green Paper has been renamed as the dynamic market (DM), and there seem to be good reasons for this. These are not just that the new tool is not limited to common use items (like the EU one), but it is also designed around the competitive flexible procedure – in the PB named 'competitive tendering procedure other than open procedure'[366] – which provides significant flexibility in the award of contracts under the DM, during the second stage of the proposed arrangement, such as using negotiations where and as appropriate. Nevertheless, in the initial version of PB, the lack of clarity over the type of notices involved in procuring under the dynamic market[367] still appears to need addressing. Whilst section 39PB is to require a purchaser to publish a notice concerning their intention of establishing a dynamic market, before such establishment, and a notice concerning the establishment of a dynamic market, it is unclear if any of these could also act as, and thereby

---

[361] Arrowsmith (n 80), section 3, under 'Principle 5'.
[362] Cabinet Office (n 83), point 74.
[363] ibid, point 82.
[364] As introduced in the House of Lords on 11 May 2022 [HL Bill 4].
[365] See GPA, art IX(7)–(11) and art IX(12)–(13).
[366] s 34(1)PB.
[367] Explanatory Notes to the PB (available via https://bills.parliament.uk/bills/3159/publications) do not shed further light on this matter either.

substitute, a tender notice referred to in section 20PB for each of the procurements made by reference to the DM (and above the value thresholds in the PB), and how the approach will fit the relevant provisions of the GPA. Similarly, no provisions could be identified in the PB concerning permanent (electronic) publication of notices relating to dynamic markets.

Presumably, these aspects are left to be detailed in the regulations to be issued in the future, under quite wide prerogatives conferred by sections 86, 110(3) and 113PB, but given the prominence afforded to statements in the Green Paper, and the importance of 'commercial tools' for an efficient public procurement system, it seems rather disappointing that major lines are not effectively set in the Bill. The situation may not be particularly surprising though: it is a complex area and some aspects of the proposals in the Green Paper were, correctly, criticised for falling short of providing a proper and substantive basis for consultations.[368] Thus, dynamic markets continue to represent a 'work in progress' even with the PB as introduced. Nevertheless, the *express* availability of supplier list types of arrangements in all sectors and for all types of items is a very welcome development if subject to appropriate terms and conditions.

Apart from these considerations, the provisions included in the original version of the Bill generally follow (adapting as needed) those concerning GPA multi-use lists, as well as the predecessor dynamic purchasing systems and features of qualification systems. Thus, a purchaser may establish 'conditions for membership of a dynamic market … only if it is satisfied that the conditions are a proportionate means of ensuring that members' are suitable legally, financially and/or technically 'to perform contracts awarded by reference to membership of the market'.[369] These conditions appear to relate to 'conditions for participation' and specify that 'When considering whether a condition is proportionate … a contracting authority must have regard to the nature, complexity and cost of the public contract',[370] and may also refer to technical specifications.[371] From the language of the PB it can be inferred that dynamic markets may include a rather wide range of assessment from merely intention to furnish items referred to by the system, to intention plus various aspects of suitability, including specifications. Conditions for participation 'may require the provision of evidence that is verifiable by a person other than the supplier',[372] and applications for admission onto the market can be submitted by interested suppliers 'any time during the term of the market'.[373] The purchaser must admit onto the dynamic market any supplier meeting the conditions for membership and not falling into exclusion grounds.[374] However, consideration by the

---

[368] Arrowsmith (n 80) section 3, under 'Principle 5'.
[369] s 36(1)PB.
[370] s 21(4)PB.
[371] s 21(3)b subject to rules in s 24PB.
[372] s 21(5)PB.
[373] s 36(2)(a)PB.
[374] s 36(2)(c)PB and see also ss 54–55PB on excluding suppliers, as well as s 36(2)(d)PB in relation to applications from excludable suppliers (subject to discretionary rather than mandatory exclusion grounds).

purchaser of applications for admission is to be done within 'a reasonable period', and informing an applicant of the result of assessment ('together with reasons') is to be performed 'as soon as reasonably practicable'.[375] Provision of specific and relatively short maximum time-limits could be preferable, regarding which, refer also to the current author's criticism in section 5.3.4 above in relation to qualification systems under the EU directives.

The PB includes some useful controls for the open, proper and fair operation of DM. Thus, the number of suppliers to be admitted onto the arrangement may not be limited (ie, all suppliers applying and meeting the requirements must be admitted),[376] and the 'conditions for membership' cannot be changed 'during the term of the market'.[377] Also, rules are set out concerning removal of suppliers from a dynamic market, including obligations to inform the relevant supplier of the decision and reasons for it before the removal,[378] though without the provision of specific time-limits for assessing circumstances for removal or informing relevant suppliers, which might affect the correct operation of the arrangement or potential challenges.

Further, following the GPA rules on multi-use lists, the PB permits participation of a supplier in a procurement under the dynamic market even if such supplier had not been a member of the market when the specific procurement was initiated, provided that the supplier has submitted an application for membership at the time of the submission of its tender. In this case, the purchaser must consider the application and, if admitted, the purchaser must also consider the tender.[379] However, this would not apply where 'due to exceptional circumstances arising from the complexity of the particular procurement, a contracting authority is unable to consider the application' until the deadline for receipt of requests to participate or of tenders, whichever is first, as applicable.[380] This last provision is likely to require further detailing and clarification. If 'the particular procurement' in this context refers to the subject-matter of an overall dynamic market (or part/category thereof), for instance critical railway safety supplies or equipment, which requires specialised analysis, testing, homologation, etc, then performing such operation within the timeframe for an award procedure for a specific contract (under the dynamic market) could be unreasonable or unrealistic. In such cases, in the current author's view, the notice concerning the dynamic market should clearly specify that only suppliers who are members of that dynamic market at the time when a specific award process is initiated for a contract under that market may attend that award procedure. Also, a specific maximum time-limit for assessing applications for admission should be included in the notice concerning the DM so that interested suppliers can plan their action, and also in order to avoid potential

---

[375] s 36(2)(b) and s 36(2)(e)PB.
[376] s 36(3)(a)PB.
[377] s 36(3)(b)PB.
[378] s 37PB.
[379] s 34(4)PB and see also Explanatory Notes to the PB (n 367), point 226.
[380] s 34(5)PB.

misuse or abuse of the arrangement. However, conversely, if the subject-matter of the DM is not (particularly) complex, or if the assessment involved for admission onto the DM is not (particularly) complex, it would seem preferable that suppliers be permitted to apply for membership even together with their request for participation or tender for a specific contract under the DM.

As shown, being designed around the competitive tendering procedure other than an open procedure, DM provides very significant flexibility for second-stage procedures of arrangement, which, by implication of section 19(4)(a)PB 'may limit the number of participating suppliers, generally or in respect of particular tendering rounds or other selection processes'.[381] It is relevant to point out here that the PB generally provides a wide discretion to purchasers in designing procedures 'appropriate for the purpose of awarding the public contract', whether or not by reference to a DM, ensuring that the said procedure 'is a proportionate means of awarding the public contract, having regard to the nature, complexity and cost of the contract'.[382] In other words, the second stage of the arrangement may consist of 'a multi-stage procedure to include a limited number of participants in any of the stages'.[383] But this is not compulsory: if appropriate, the purchaser could simply request tenders for competitive evaluation and without negotiation, from all suppliers admitted onto the DM (a concept including those admitted as a result of applying together with the submission of their tender, where applicable). In this case, the process would resemble closely to the ancestor dynamic purchasing system in the public sector. However, where the second stage of DM accommodates multi-stage procedures, as those referred to in section 19(4)PB, then the arrangement appears closer to ancestor qualification systems. Still, in the absence of clear provisions concerning notices and transparency (or other) requirements for the operation of the DM, it is not possible at this stage to consider whether sufficient safeguards of fair treatment and against misuse or abuse would apply.

After a contract award decision by reference to a dynamic market has been reached (pursuant to the second stage of the arrangement), as per the general rules governing competitive awards, the purchaser 'must provide an assessment summary to each supplier that submitted an assessed tender' and publish a contract award notice (for contracts above thresholds referred to by the Bill).[384] In the literature it is maintained though that at least quarterly 'aggregated' award notices should be required for under-threshold call-offs as well, in light of the increased transparency agenda.[385] I would add that this should apply at a minimum when the aggregated value of call-offs reaches the relevant threshold, and I agree that in the context of electronic procurement even individual notices for

---

[381] See also s 19(4)(c).
[382] s 19(3)PB.
[383] Explanatory Notes (n 367), point 142.
[384] s 48PB.
[385] A Sachez-Graells, 'Initial Comments on the UK's Procurement Bill: A Lukewarm Assessment' (19 May 2022): http://dx.doi.org/10.2139/ssrn.4114141, point 17, 11–12.

every call-off might not be a significant burden. Standstill periods are optional in respect of contracts awarded by reference to dynamic markets, but the minimum duration of any voluntary standstill period for such contract appears unclear in the PB.[386] However, in light of the consequences of voluntarily applying and observing a standstill period with all relevant publicity – namely ensuring that the contract is not subject to potential setting aside (ineffectiveness)[387] – it would seem normal that such voluntary standstill period should be of a minimum duration equal to that of the mandatory duration or longer, and the language of the PB would benefit from revision to state this expressly. Conversely, if a (proper) standstill period is not applied and observed in relation to a contract awarded by reference to a dynamic market, then the contract could be subject to setting aside if a breach of law occurred in its award. Once a contract has been entered into, a contract details notice, and, depending on contract value, the actual contract, must be published.[388]

Overall, the Procurement Bill as published for First Reading in the House of Lords, includes very useful elements, as described above, of what could become various PUIR arrangements, expressly extends the scope of arrangements we refer to as 'supplier lists' to all sectors and all types of items, and appears to offer significant procedural flexibility. However, as it stands, given the lack of crucial provision on notices concerning a dynamic market and its operation, there are limited possibilities at the time of writing to anticipate how precisely the arrangement is to be used in various contexts, or its full and exact features. The PB may be amended during its legislative course through Parliament, and it already envisages that essential aspects such as notices and substantive transparency requirements are to be addressed via separate, future, secondary legislation.

For purposes of clarity and of supporting implementation, a few matters would have been preferable in my view. First, providing in the same act for all the main rules concerning a DM, including those on notices and transparency discussed in this section, would permit users to reflect on them in advance and could facilitate interpretation and application of the rules once in force. In comparison, a contracting authority in the public sector wishing to establish and operate a dynamic purchasing system under the PCRs would find all the main rules in the PCRs. Second, it could have been useful if the Bill provided a definition or overall description of the new arrangement to provide some orientation for interpreting the rules on dynamic markets. Third, more generally, it would be desirable for the provisions for the DM to be more articulated in the PB, covering directly and expressly the overall purchasing mechanism across its two main stages as a PUIR arrangement, thereby offering a clearer view on its purpose and potential uses. It is perhaps relevant that during the Second Reading of the Bill in the House of Lords,

---

[386] s 49PB and see also Explanatory Notes (n 367), points 300–03.
[387] s 94PB.
[388] s 51PB.

in the transcript of the debates, the term 'dynamic markets' only appeared in two places, mentioning either that the concept was not understood or that it will be explored as a vehicle supporting SMEs' participation in public procurement.[389]

By strengthening and articulating further, in a balanced way, the approach of the Bill along the lines discussed, there is a real chance for the procurement law reform package to provide a break-through in recognising, extending and promoting an appropriate use of supplier list arrangements in the UK that could also then motivate other procurement systems in this direction. It should be mentioned though that, being so intrinsically embedded in the overall conduct of a competitive procedure other than an open procedure, dynamic markets could also be influenced by eventual changes of the envisaged rules in that regard. In any event, Chapter six provides useful perspectives and orientation in implementing such arrangements when the new package becomes live.

5.4.2. Closed and Open Frameworks

The Green Paper contemplated providing 'contracting authorities a framework tool that has two options for all types of contracts including utilities: closed and open'.[390] It is important to point out from the outset that open frameworks, as envisaged in the UK's post-Brexit reform, appear as a significantly different type of arrangement from open framework agreements under the 2011 UNCITRAL Model Law on Public Procurement.[391]

As for closed frameworks, these seem somewhat similar to framework agreements in the pre-Brexit (EU derived) regulations, leaning closer to the pre-Brexit utilities regulations. Whilst the Green Paper had proposed that closed frameworks be limited to four years,[392] pursuant to consultations as well as criticism against including shorter limits to the duration of frameworks in comparison to the EU derived rules,[393] the Government's Response submitted that utilities would be able to conclude frameworks with a 'longer term' and, also, that 'a longer term than the relevant maximum term can be set provided the justification is published in the tender notice and is related to the framework itself'.[394] These renewed proposals have been carried forward into the Procurement Bill; note that in doing so the 'standard' maximum duration for defence and security frameworks has been extended from seven years (as in the DSPCR and the Defence and Security Directive) to eight years, and that the justification for a longer than standard

---

[389] *Hansard*, HL, Vol 822, cols 921 and 929 (25 May 2022).

[390] Green Paper (n 77), point 150.

[391] As will result from discussion in this section, and see also, in comparison Chapter 2, section 2.2.4 of this book.

[392] Green Paper (n 77), point 151.

[393] Cabinet Office (n 83), point 204; Arrowsmith (n 80) s 3, under 'Principle 5'.

[394] Cabinet Office (n 83), point 208.

duration (ie, more than four years for public sector and more than eight years for the utilities and defence sectors) must relate to the 'nature' of the items to be procured.[395]

A framework is defined in the PB as 'a contract between a contracting authority and one or more suppliers that provides for the future award of contracts by a contracting authority to the supplier or suppliers'.[396] This seems to be a synthetic definition focusing on the 'interim' outcome of a framework process, rather than the overall process, an approach that seems similar to that in the pre-Brexit regulations. However, certain elements need some consideration. First, the concept of a 'closed framework' in the Green Paper and Response to Consultations appears to have been renamed simply as a 'framework'. Second, the qualification of a framework as a 'contract' rather than, as previously, an 'agreement' in pre-Brexit regulations, deserves careful review during the legislative process, in particular if such qualification could involve a limitation on the types of frameworks permitted under the new law (as this might affect flexibility as an objective of the reform).

Third, under section 2(3)PB, a framework that is not an excluded framework, and that exceeds a relevant value threshold also qualifies as a 'public contract', which, as the Explanatory Notes clarify, means that a framework 'must be awarded in accordance with the legislation'.[397] This is an important statement on 'first stage' procedures, and even though it can be inferred from other provisions of the Bill,[398] it deserves express and articulated provision in the legal text, including additional elements in the award of a framework that need to be factored in, such as the specific information requirements (see further below). That a framework can be awarded by competitive procedure, or by direct award (should the conditions for this be met), is also implied incidentally in section 45(3)PB, referring to the reasons for any longer-than-standard period of a framework needing to be stated in 'the tender or transparency notice for the framework'.[399] It certainly follows that choosing an appropriate procedure, or designing it if a procedure other than an open one is used, will be a matter for the purchaser to decide upon, depending on the relevant circumstances of the foreseen procurements, notably the features of the purchaser's needs and those of the relevant market segment. This is an area that would benefit from guidance, or possibly from legal preferences (with requirements for justifications for cases other than the preference), and the guidance requested by stakeholders and proposed by Government on 'selecting the best tool for different requirements'[400] could consider addressing these matters, since a wide range of possible configurations are covered by the concept of framework. Orientation on first-stage procedures for closed framework arrangements from a

---

[395] s 45PB.
[396] s 44(2)PB.
[397] Explanatory Notes (n 367), point 270.
[398] PB ss 2(3), 10(1)–(3), 18(1), 40(1), 42(1).
[399] And see also s 20 and s 43PB on such notices.
[400] Cabinet Office (n 83), point 214.

wider perspective can be found in Chapter two, section 2.2.2.3.1 and Chapter six, section 6.6.1.

Fourth, whilst the definition of frameworks in section 44(2)PB refers to 'a contracting authority', this needs to be read in conjunction with section 10(4)PB relating to joint or centralised procurement, being thus clear that both single- and multiple-purchaser frameworks are envisaged and permitted. In this connection, and bearing in mind the phenomenon and potential implications of what were referred to as 'generic frameworks' in the UK, discussed at section 5.3.2.3.3, the proposal in the Green Paper and Response to Consultations concerning the creation of a central register of 'all commercial tools … making it easier to find and compare' is to be welcomed.[401] According to the Government, the proposal was supported by respondents, though some noticed that 'often frameworks overlapped … leading to increased bidding costs for suppliers and potential duplication of available supply'.[402] In its response, the Government stated that: 'The central register of commercial tools will provide a list of frameworks and Dynamic Markets. Bringing greater transparency to the frameworks available to contracting authorities should reduce the current duplication of frameworks'.[403] Time will tell whether this last argument proves correct, but greater transparency would facilitate identifying the frameworks (and/or dynamic markets) through which a purchaser is entitled to procure and thus, importantly, facilitate comparing the potentially available supply and, as applicable, the terms offered. As discussed, such comparison should be quite straight-forward when comparing frameworks that establish all terms (or 'core terms' in the language of the PB), and might be more complex when frameworks that do not establish all terms come into play, and/or dynamic markets. But the central register would clearly facilitate consideration of options for the award of a contract that best fits the purchaser's objectives – such as value for money and maximising public benefit – and observing equal ('same') treatment.[404] On a connected line of thinking, whilst duplication of frameworks and/or dynamic markets is likely to lead to internalising within the terms offered by suppliers the increased transaction costs (inherent in registering in multiple arrangements) and potential uncertainty over actual demand on each such arrangement, it may also result in increased availability of potential supply avenues, and convenience, which can be crucial in crisis situations. Here, again, the central register would facilitate quick access to relevant data about such potential procurement vehicles that have been intensively used in the UK in relation to the Covid pandemic, notably awards under frameworks not involving mini-competition,[405] which is logical given the additional speed and convenience in placing orders in this way.

---

[401] Green Paper (n 77), point 155.
[402] Cabinet Office (n 83), point 206.
[403] ibid, point 215.
[404] s 11PB.
[405] See National Audit Organisation, *Investigation into Government Procurement during the COVID-19 Pandemic*, HC 959, Session 2019–2021, 26 December 2020. For reflections on how call-off methods on

Returning to the definition on frameworks in the Bill, it is self-evident that both single- and multiple-supplier frameworks are envisaged. Single-supplier frameworks would (naturally) involve award of public contracts 'without competition between suppliers'.[406] No further provisions on single-supplier frameworks could be identified at the time of writing, and it is suggested that potential scope of such frameworks should be more clearly qualified in the legislation and/or guidance to avoid situations of unjustified market closure. Multiple-supplier frameworks 'may only' involve 'a competitive selection process' (amongst framework suppliers) for the award of a public contract,[407] unless the framework provides 'the core terms of the public contract, and ... an objective mechanism for supplier selection'.[408] In this context, the Explanatory Notes give examples of what 'core terms' could involve and also state that 'additional terms on matters which are specific to that contract' can be included at call-off stage.[409] We suggest that similar conditions on core terms are relevant for single-supplier frameworks. The language of the Bill appears to permit multiple-supplier frameworks that involve call-offs with *and* without a 'competitive selection process' if the core terms for future purchases are established in the framework.

Some important controls are provided in the Bill, intended to safeguard a correct use of frameworks, such as rules concerning potential exclusion of suppliers during the duration of the framework where they fail to meet mandatory or discretionary exclusion grounds, notably a prohibition of awarding a public contract to a supplier that fails to meet mandatory grounds in such a way that it becomes an 'excluded' supplier.[410] Also, the Bill requires inclusion in the framework of relevant information concerning the description of items to be supplied in call-off contracts, the price or mechanism for determining the price of call-offs, the selection process for awarding call-offs, purchasers that 'are entitled' to use the framework for awarding contracts, the duration and estimated value of the framework, and other matters.[411]

However, the PB appears to miss the opportunity to require that these important pieces of information be provided also in the tender documents for the award of the framework itself, and then carried forward in the framework (as applicable) to secure stage consistency of the overall framework purchasing process. This potential weakness of the provisions in the PB is likely to have arisen from the fact that substantive rules concerning notices and procurement documents, including the content thereof, are to be put forward via separate

---

various types of arrangement could facilitate addressing crises under existing or reformed systems, see, eg, Arrowsmith, 'Recommendations for Urgent Procurement in the EU Directive and GPA' (n 151) 68–73 and 98–99.

[406] s 44(4)(a)PB.
[407] s 44(3)PB.
[408] s 44(4)(b)PB.
[409] Explanatory Notes (n 367), point 273.
[410] s 46 and s 44(6)PB (see also s 54PB for the notion of 'excluded supplier').
[411] s 44(5)PB.

secondary legislation (under section 86PB). The Government's Response referred specifically to 'a requirement' to state 'in the tender notice or in the procurement documents' certain information concerning contracts to be awarded under the framework, with the objective 'To discourage contracting authorities from putting in place extremely broad and poorly defined frameworks'.[412] If this is still the intention, whilst an articulated provision for all controls in the PB would have been preferable in the interest of clarity, it should also be noted that some relevant pre-disclosure requirements appear to be missing and would benefit from being considered and included during the legislative process. These comprise: the number of (envisaged) suppliers in the framework; the terms for future purchases that are to be established during the first stage and the terms that may be refined or established during the call-off stage; details of what would (or may) involve a competitive selection process at the call-off stage (if applicable); whether and under which conditions call-offs would be awarded with or without a competitive selection process in cases when the framework does set out the core terms for call-offs (and if there is an intention to use both types of call-off awards). We refer mostly to the advanced provisions on closed framework agreements in the 2011 UNCITRAL Model Law on Public Procurement, and its attending instruments, which could inspire, mutatis mutandis, the overall UK reformed provision for closed frameworks, notably in respect of controls for their appropriate use. The Government's Response proposes to issue guidance 'on designing framework agreements so that they contain all of the relevant terms',[413] which is to be welcomed, but we submit that the requirements discussed above are better addressed through legislation.

As regards call-off procedures, the PB states as a general rule that 'a framework may only provide for the future award of a public contract following a competitive selection process'.[414] However, there are two stated exceptions when call-offs may be awarded 'without competition between suppliers': one concerning (naturally) single-supplier frameworks, and a separate one concerning multiple-supplier frameworks establishing 'the core terms' for future purchases.[415] In the latter case, the PB states that the framework needs to include 'an objective mechanism for supplier selection'.[416] It remains to be seen if and how this requirement will be circumstantiated during the legislative process or through guidance.[417] Orientation on this type of framework arrangement and call-off method, from a wider perspective, can be found, eg, in section 5.3.2.4.2 above and, notably, in Chapter six, section 6.6.2.2.

Returning to awarding call-offs through a 'competitive selection process', it can be inferred from the PB that the provision for such a call-off method is compulsory

---

[412] Cabinet Office (n 83), point 213.
[413] ibid, point 214.
[414] s 44(3)PB.
[415] s 44(4)PB.
[416] s 44(4)(b)PB.
[417] Cabinet Office (n 83), point 214.

in frameworks that do not set 'the core terms' for future purchases, and optional for frameworks that *do* set the said terms. Again, it remains to be seen whether further, more detailed, transparency and procedural requirements will be included during the legislative process or in guidance as safeguards for fairness and non-discrimination in awarding call-offs via a competitive selection process. So far, it could not be identified expressly in the Bill, for example, whether negotiations can be contemplated at this stage and/or whether, and under what conditions, only some (or one) rather than all of the framework suppliers could be invited to submit offers for a specific call-off (ie, whether a further reduction in the number of eligible framework contractors could be operated in relation to specific call-offs). I submit that these matters ought to be carefully and expressly provided for in the legislation. Distinctly, it would seem logical that direct awards may be made under such frameworks, subject to strict conditions under sections 40–41, 43PB and, as applicable, Schedule 5PB, though some of the grounds for direct award may be less relevant in the case of properly designed frameworks, and, consequently, guidance would be beneficial on such special cases.

From a connected perspective, concerning the criteria for this call-off method (through a competitive selection process), the Government's Response provided that:

> Where mini-competitions are used the contracting authorities will need to evaluate the mini-competition on the same basis as was applied for the award of the framework, including the evaluation criteria, but they can set out more detailed terms such as detailed sub-criteria within an existing criterion, if they wish.[418]

It does not appear that this approach has been carried forward into the PB.[419] In fact, a distinction should be made between 'terms' on the one hand, and 'criteria' used for establishing such 'terms' on the other hand. Further, requiring that evaluation criteria for the award of call-offs be 'the same' as those used for the award of the framework would go against the flexibility agenda of the reform. Depending on the type and circumstances of the procurements under a framework it may well make sense, for example, to award the framework on the basis of quality and price, but award call-offs via competition on the basis of price alone (though the reverse would not normally make sense). So, it is indeed crucial that the relationship between first-stage criteria and call-off criteria secures consistency between the two (main) stages of a framework, but the way the Government's Response approached this appears too tight. For orientation from a wider perspective on such issues, and more generally on competitive call-off procedures see Chapter two, section 2.2.2.3.2, and Chapter six, sections 6.6.2.3–5 and 6.5.

It can be inferred from the PB that a call-off could be, itself, a sub-framework under a (main) framework, since a framework is defined as a 'contract' and also

---

[418] ibid, point 210.
[419] s 23PB on refining award criteria does not seem to be intended for framework call-offs.

qualifies as a 'public contract'.[420] As shown, this configuration could be useful in particular for centralised or joint procurement. But certain requirements should also expressly accompany such option, to safeguard an appropriate and beneficial use; for orientation in a wider perspective see section 5.3.2.4.2 and Chapter six, section 6.6.3.

It is also clear from the definition of a 'public contract' as including a framework that the usual rules on transparency and standstill periods would apply to the award of a framework.[421] Also, the award of a framework is subject to remedies in Part 9 of PB, just like call-off contracts (if above the value thresholds). Contract award notices apply to such call-off contracts, but an exception is provided for call-offs under frameworks in the defence and security sector.[422] However, it would seem that framework call-offs are not covered by the requirements on assessment summaries,[423] which would be a weakness of the legislation since aggrieved contractors may not have a substantive basis for appreciating the legality of a call-off awarded under a multiple-supplier framework, whether or not involving mini-competition. Standstill periods are optional in respect of framework call-offs,[424] but voluntary observance of a standstill period (including associated transparency) excludes potential setting aside of that call-off contract,[425] as in the case of contracts awarded by reference to dynamic markets. It is relevant to point out that the PB carries forward the approach in pre-Brexit regulations that an order 'setting aside a framework' does not affect call-offs 'already awarded' under that framework,[426] whilst the Explanatory Notes specify that 'separate orders may be applied for in relation to those contracts',[427] an addition that might benefit from being included in the actual legal text.[428]

Moving on to 'open frameworks' under the PB, these are defined as 'a scheme of frameworks that provides for the award of successive frameworks on substantially the same terms',[429] such award meaning 'an award that could be made by reference to the same tender or transparency notice without substantial modification'.[430] The total period covered by such successive frameworks must be a maximum of eight years, with a first framework having a maximum duration of three years and the second, a maximum of five years.[431] There can be a larger number of successive frameworks within the eight-year (maximum) overall period, for example in case

---

[420] s 44(2) in conjunction with s 2(3); and see also s 10(3).
[421] ss 48(1)–(5) and 49(1)–(2)PB.
[422] ss 48(1) and 48(6)(a)PB.
[423] ss 48(2)–(5)PB.
[424] s 49(1)(3)(c).
[425] ss 94(1)(d) and 94(2)PB.
[426] s 93(7)PB.
[427] Explanatory Notes (n 367), point 551.
[428] See section 5.3.2.5.1 above for the relevant provision in pre-Brexit regulations.
[429] s 47(1)PB.
[430] s 47(8)PB referring also to s 31PB.
[431] s 47(2)(c)PB and s 47(2)(a).

of reopening the framework annually, but an open framework 'is also not permanently open to new suppliers'.[432]

The purpose of the provision for such arrangement is not yet very clear, since quite similar outcomes could be obtained by applying the rules on (closed) frameworks, discussed above, to successive frameworks with similar subject-matter.[433] Some marginal efficiency benefits might arise from rules permitting a supplier to be retained or 're-admitted' to the open framework (ie, to the next framework) 'on the basis of the supplier's tender submitted when it first applied or inviting a new tender', for cases when the number of suppliers on a framework is limited.[434] The Green Paper explained how this could work on reopening: 'Suppliers already on the framework should be given the option of remaining on the framework based on their original bid or submitting an updated bid',[435] whilst new suppliers from the market would be permitted to bid as well, and the purchaser evaluates all such bids to establish which suppliers will be parties to the framework. Given the risk of being removed from the framework in light of improved terms arising from opening competition to the wider market, suppliers already on the framework may well submit updated bids. Irrespective, the purchaser would still have to compare the same number of bids as if a new closed framework was initiated.

In cases when the number of framework suppliers is not limited, in addition to the two options above for retaining suppliers wishing to remain on the next framework, there is also the possibility to retain the supplier based on the fact that it was a party on a previous framework, without needing to reconsider a tender from that supplier.[436] The fact that frameworks without a limit on the number of suppliers is considered seems a rather peculiar approach given that dynamic markets are to be available for all sectors and all types of items under the reformed regime; in the past such frameworks were 'forced' in the public sector because no adequate supplier list type of arrangement was permitted, notably under the 2004PSD. Whilst the Government remained adamant to 'open frameworks', consideration should still be given by the time the reform is complete as to whether a dynamic market arrangement could be more practical for the intended scenario[437] or, failing that, if a truly (permanently) open framework agreement type of arrangement, as outlined in the 2011 UNCITRAL Model Law on Public Procurement would be preferable.[438]

---

[432] Explanatory Notes (n 367), point 287.

[433] eg, Arrowsmith (n 80) s 3, under 'Principle 5'. Also, Sanchez-Graells, 'The UK's Green Paper' (n 80).

[434] Explanatory Notes (n 367), point 289; s 47(4)PB.

[435] Green Paper (n 77) point 153.

[436] Explanatory Notes (n 367), point 288; s 47(3)PB.

[437] See, eg, Sachez-Graells, 'Initial Comments on the UK's Procurement Bill' 19 (in table re s 47PB) (n 384). See also the Italian approach to the possibility of awarding successive frameworks under a DPS, which 'could be particularly useful for Italian CPBs (Consip and regional ones) in order to ensure timeliness and continuity in the offering of centralised FAs for CAs': European Commission (n 243) 31–32.

[438] See Chapter 2, section 2.2.4 of this book.

Returning to 'open frameworks' in the PB, it is not entirely clear whether all successive frameworks could be awarded under a single (initial) tender notice and tender documentation or whether each successive framework would require distinct tender notices. If it is the former – which could bring about some benefits in terms of efficiency – then permanent electronic publication is strongly advised. Overall, however, the potential benefits of 'open frameworks' as provided for in the first version of the PB appear modest. For instance, the requirement that the previous framework is to expire 'on the award of the next'[439] could be easily accommodated outside the rules on open frameworks, through good planning. Also, the provisions on open frameworks need further articulation with those on frameworks. It seems quite unclear why in the event that only one supplier becomes a party to a framework under an open framework, the framework then becomes automatically converted to a closed framework that, if it is the first framework under the open framework, might be capable of gaining a longer duration (of up to four years) than a first 'usual' framework under an open framework (which is limited to three years).[440] Similarly, the express exclusion, in section 44PB, of the application of all substantive rules on frameworks from the award of an open framework[441] seems ambiguous since no specific provision concerning the process of awarding an open framework could be identified (and an open framework contains frameworks).

Generally, the provision on frameworks deserves further substantive work if it is to reach the intended standard in light the vast experience in using frameworks in the UK so far. Further, the provision on open frameworks requires thorough consideration going along the legislative/reform process.

5.5. Conclusions

There currently is a high level of sophistication of the rules concerning PUIR arrangements both in EU law and in that of the Member States reviewed and the UK. So far, framework agreements have enjoyed a great success since their recognition in the 2004 directives. Whilst dynamic purchasing systems have been quite rarely used in practice under those directives, they have become, under the 2014 directives, significantly more attractive. There certainly is potential for further streamlining the rules concerning these methods, as well as those on qualification systems and on legal review, as discussed.

The three parallel EU regimes (public, utilities and defence) include many similar provisions, while the differences among them may not always be justified

---

[439] s 47(2)(b)PB.
[440] s 47(5) and (6). Whilst a limitation in time might have been intended, it fails to specifically address the situation of a first framework under an open framework.
[441] s 44(8).

by pragmatic considerations, and some of them may just be reflections of sectorial 'inertia'. For example, there appears to be no reason why public sector or defence procurement should not be able to use an arrangement quite similar to 'qualification systems' for recurrent or indefinite requirements that do not fully meet the conditions for framework agreement or dynamic purchasing systems.[442] In fact, the approach of the 2014PSD on this point appears particularly unbalanced: an 'ultra-liberal' approach to frameworks and a continuing prohibition on mandatory lists.

Whilst an opportunity for consolidation of the EU public and utilities directives into a single instrument was not used in 2014, it is submitted that efforts in that direction (for all sectors and including procurement legal review) should be considered in the future.[443] The post-Brexit procurement reform emphasises both the challenges and potential benefits of such consolidation and streamlining. As regards PUIR, the Procurement Bill has great merit in pursuing an expansion of 'supplier lists' types of arrangements across all sectors and for all types of items. But, as discussed, further substantive work in drafting and policy guidance appears needed, in particular towards addressing the proposed arrangements as *strategic* procurement methods for indefinite or recurrent needs, in their own right, rather than merely convenient award avenues for individual contracts. As shown, this needs significant focus on articulating expressly, including in legislation, the *two* main stages of a PUIR arrangement and the potential implications of specific features of such arrangements.

Overall, the EU law, the reviewed Members States, and the UK provide a very comprehensive approach to PUIR. EU law shapes to a significant degree the procurement systems of Member States. But the latter 'enrich' the overall EU public procurement system not only through involvement in the drafting of directives, but also, notably, through specific approaches and experiences. The pre-Brexit UK regulations provided an innovative interpretation of the rules of the directives, probably offering the widest flexibility to purchasers permitted under EU law. Similarly, interpretations that promote procurement efficiency have been sought, for example the prospective ineffectiveness and its application to call-offs based on an ineffective framework. On the other hand, France and Romania 'contribute' with specific controls or clarifications supporting an appropriate use of frameworks, such as binding rules on price revision at the call-off stage, or France's explicit recognition of 'frameworks in frameworks'. Even where certain aspects of the directives are not pursued in Member States this also enriches the overall experience. Romanian practice shows that simply regulating complex tools

---

[442] If GPA provisions on multi-use lists, and their applicability to various types of authority are seen as an obstacle, this matter could be approached at that level: see also Arrowsmith (n 151) 99. However, as discussed, the EU approach in the public and defence sectors seems overly restrictive as regards lists, even in relation to the 2012GPA rules.

[443] Certainly, tailored provisions concerning certain aspects that would require specific sectorial 'treatment' are not excluded from this approach.

like dynamic purchasing systems and qualification systems, without being accompanied by appropriate guidance and training, could easily result in long-term unfamiliarity with these useful tools.

Things move on … It seems the time for an EU law procurement reform should draw near, including in light of the experiences during the coronavirus pandemic, and the post-Brexit procurement transformation should provide some inspiration in broad lines.[444] Certainly, the balance of objectives of EU law has been and will continue to be different; some approaches would thus inherently be different, and tailoring to procurement environments of varied Member States would need to be factored in but, beyond this, further modernisation and conceptual streamlining is needed.

---

[444] Although – or maybe precisely because – our case studies have not recorded significant changes in the legislation concerning PUIR following the pandemic (still, the UK post-Brexit reform will also have been influenced more generally by experiences during the pandemic).

PART II

Developing a Conceptual Framework for the Regulation, Policy, and Implementation of Arrangements for Procurement of Uncertain or Indefinite Requirements

6

A Transversal Perspective on Procurement of Uncertain or Indefinite Requirements Across Public Procurement Systems and Instruments

6.1. Arrangements Identified: Nuances of a Phenomenon,[1] Rather than Separate Concepts

Previous chapters mainly provided a vertical analysis, by procurement system or instrument, and within each of these, by purchasing arrangement. They also involved some 'intra-system' horizontal comparisons, among the various arrangements identified in each system or instrument. The current chapter provides a comprehensive horizontal analysis. Using the general structure used for the main individual arrangements identified in case studies, this chapter compares all purchasing arrangements that are the subject of this book, by way of their essential elements, such as definition, types, design, controls, procedures, and remedies. Each of the following sections deals with such an essential element and provides a synthesis of relevant matters for the entire range of arrangements investigated in the book.

Chapter one defined arrangements for purchasing uncertain or indefinite requirements (PUIR) in public procurement as those arrangements designed and/or implemented to meet on-going, recurrent, uncertain or indefinite requirements for a long-term period through purchasing items from the free market, and whereby the parties, at the initiative of the purchaser, seek to go through a number of procedural stages and/or to establish a number of contractual terms, but not all, in advance of the moment when an actual need for specific items arises; this

---

[1] Similar terminology is used by S Arrowsmith, eg in 'Framework Purchasing and Qualification Lists under the European Procurement Directives: Part I' (1999) 8 *PPLR* 115, 116. On the other hand, GL Albano and C Nicholas, in *The Law and Economics of Framework Agreements: Designing Flexible Solutions for Public Procurement* (Cambridge, CUP, 2016) 13–14, appear to have reservations on this approach, but their argument might not consider certain types of arrangements.

is followed by placement of subsequent contracts or orders whenever the actual needs for items arise, based on the procedural stages conducted in advance, or based on the terms agreed beforehand.

On this basis, the preceding chapters identified and discussed arrangements existing in selected case studies. Looking at them jointly, as procurement mechanisms, a wide variety of arrangements and some very significant differences among them, including the way they are regulated, can easily be noticed. Beyond this apparently heterogeneous picture, though, the underlying process – namely establishing purchasing arrangements (or a part thereof) where some elements concerning the envisaged purchases are uncertain or indefinite at the time when the process is initiated – is common. This commonality provides an essential perspective for understanding the PUIR phenomenon and developing a conceptual framework for it.

From the angle of a 'traditional' procurement exercise, PUIR arrangements could be looked at as 'incomplete' transactions.[2] In the case of 'traditional' procurement, three main elements of a transaction – requirement, terms, and commitments (to buy and sell) – are all present and fully defined. In the case of PUIR arrangements an incomplete transaction emerges first for the overall estimated or predicted requirement (first stage). This is then followed by a number of 'complete' transactions concluded based on the first stage, covering parts or certain 'segments' of the overall requirement (second stage), when such 'partial' requirements materialise. It should be noted that intermediary stages are not excluded in some cases though (see section 6.6.3 below).

A varying degree of 'incompleteness' at the first stage characterises the specific types of PUIR arrangements. The 'incompleteness' relates to the uncertain or indefinite aspect(s) among those aspects constituting a 'complete transaction'. At one end of the spectrum, some PUIR configurations are very similar (or close) to a 'traditional' procurement, possibly with just one aspect being affected by some uncertainty. In this 'confluence area' the distinction between 'traditional' procurement and PUIR may not always be straight-forward, since a 'traditional' contract may also involve the supply of successive tranches of similar items, and might accommodate some adjustment of terms.

An illustration of this point is offered by 'definite-quantity contracts' in the US federal procurement, which are regarded in the Federal Acquisition Regulation (FAR – at 16.501-2) as a type of 'indefinite-delivery' contract. However, the total quantity to be supplied under such 'definite-quantity contract', the price(s) and delivery locations are all set at the time of contracting, while orders express specific timings and quantities to be supplied to 'designated' delivery locations (FAR 16.502). In the EU directives this type of arrangement does not receive separate treatment and it would not be considered a framework agreement. This

---

[2] See also Albano and Nicholas, *The Law and Economics of Framework Agreements* (n 1) 18–19, referring to incomplete master agreeements in relation to frameworks involving call-off competition.

already suggests a continuum of possible arrangements with some indefinite or 'open' aspects.

Just one step further from 'traditional' procurement, indefinite areas of arrangements become more significant. Again, the US federal procurement system provides a good illustration of the gradual departure from 'traditional' procurement. Thus, in 'requirements contracts' the total quantity under the arrangement is not guaranteed, but a realistic estimate is. The next arrangement in the order of 'distance' from 'traditional' procurement in the US federal system consists of ID/IQ contracts. Here, the purchaser's commitment to buy is limited to a minimum quantity guaranteed under the contract, which can be very low. ID/IQ contracts could be single-supplier arrangements, but the preference is for multiple-contractor arrangements. There are also multi-agency ID/IQ configurations.

In other procurement systems or instruments, similar or different nuances in the spectrum are present, though they might be less immediately visible, because they are not treated separately. Under the EU directives for example, arrangements that would be quite similar to a US requirements contract (or ID/IQ contract) could be organised as specific 'configurations' of framework agreements. On the other hand, an 'EU' framework agreement need not commit the purchaser to buy anything (as the US arrangements referred above require), whereas the World Bank frameworks *must not* commit either party to buy/sell.

The more aspects, or elements, are affected by uncertainty (or left open) at the first stage, the further away in the spectrum the PUIR configuration in question will be from 'traditional' procurement. In some circumstances it is impossible or undesirable to establish in advance any terms for future purchases. However, it may still be possible to take some steps in advance toward meeting future needs, for example by establishing a list of potentially interested suppliers whose 'suitability' is assessed prior to a procurement requirement materialising. This category includes arrangements like qualification systems in the EU utilities procurement directive, or 'optional lists' that were discussed in the context of EU public and defence procurement directives.

Similarly, it may be undesirable to limit the pool from which the contractor(s) will be selected for future purchases to the group of suppliers which were admitted onto an arrangement at the time it was established.[3] In this case, the two stages of the PUIR arrangement go in parallel throughout its duration and may overlap at the points of individual purchases under the arrangement. These can be described as 'open' arrangements and include 'open framework agreements' under the UNCITRAL Model Law on Public Procurement (2011), 'dynamic purchasing systems' in the EU public and utilities sectors, 'qualification systems' in the EU utilities sector, 'optional lists' in the EU public and defence sectors, and GSA (MAS) Schedules in US federal procurement.

---

[3] On the other side of the coin, a somewhat similar matter can arise with regard to purchasers who may be interested to use an existing arrangement when they were not involved in its establishment.

Open arrangements can include arrangements that establish terms, such as UNCITRAL open framework agreements or GSA Schedules, and arrangements that do not establish terms, such as EU qualification systems, (some) dynamic purchasing systems, and optional lists. The last of these could actually be regarded, among the arrangements identified in this book, as being the furthest away from 'traditional' procurement since it does not establish any terms (or commitment) and its use is not a condition for access to the purchase(s) it relates to.

At a practical level PUIR arrangements involve managing uncertainties surrounding certain procurement needs, on the basis of some prediction. At a policy level those arrangements involve regulating the management of such uncertainties. The following sections map out a world of 'indefinite purchasing' resulting from the juxtaposition of the arrangements identified in the research (over 20 'types') against the structure developed for the analysis.

6.2. Defining an Arrangement for Procurement of Uncertain or Indefinite Requirements

In most cases (legal) definitions of PUIR arrangements are 'synthetic', namely they focus on the outcome of the first stage of an arrangement. This kind of definition usually summarises distinctive features of an arrangement (as compared to 'traditional' contracting), but fails to provide an overview of the entire purchasing mechanism involved.[4] The need to complete a 'formal' definition with other features or requirements relevant to the arrangement in question but stipulated in other provisions, to obtain an accurate 'picture', is not unusual. In some cases there is no explicit legal definition of an arrangement at all, such as for dynamic purchasing systems in the 2014 EU procurement directives.

Providing an accurate and complete legal definition in the relevant legal instrument offers an increased level of legal certainty over the 'essentials' of an arrangement, and guides interpretation of the other rules concerning that arrangement. It is submitted that a definition along the lines of my overall definition of PUIR arrangements,[5] as applied to a given arrangement, would contain those beneficial features. The definition of framework agreements in the 2011 UNCITRAL Model Law on Public Procurement does this, first by distinguishing between 'framework procedure' and 'framework agreement' and clarifying their meaning. Second, the Model Law provides definitions for sub-types of possible configurations of frameworks, thus bringing additional legal certainty.

Conceptually, regarding a framework arrangement as a contractual arrangement, rather than a procedure (or procurement process), may have inherent implications for an arrangement, as the World Bank, US and France case studies

---

[4] For example, framework agreements in EU procurement directives.
[5] See section 6.1 above.

indicate. These could involve limitations of certain types of arrangement, or transparency and review at the call-off stage.

Similarly, supplier list types of arrangement could benefit from explicit legal definitions. However, no such definitions were identified in the case studies examined.

6.3. Classification of Arrangements

6.3.1. General

The wide variety of PUIR configurations identified call for a comprehensive classification. The classification below expands classic taxonomies by Arrowsmith[6] with types or features of arrangements analysed in this book.

6.3.2. 'Framework' Arrangements and 'Supplier List' Arrangements

A first distinction results from my definition of PUIR and employs the criterion of the outcome of the first stage of an arrangement. Thus, one 'type' of arrangement, referred to in this book as 'framework' *arrangements*,[7] involves that some terms of future purchase(s) are established at the first stage. This aspect differentiates them from supplier lists.[8] Such terms could include firm, adjustable or maximum prices; minimum, maximum or indicative quantities; delivery places and/or time-limits; insurance; warranties; etc. In the systems reviewed, US requirements and ID/IQ contracts, US GSA schedules, EU (and Member States) frameworks agreements, UNCITRAL framework agreements, and World Bank (WB) framework agreements would fall in this 'category'.

On the other hand, in other arrangements, referred to in this book as 'supplier lists', the outcome of the first stage is not the establishment of terms governing future purchases but merely the identification of suppliers who might

---

[6] S Arrowsmith, 'Framework Purchasing and Qualification Lists' (Part I) (1999) 8 *PPLR* 115 and 'Framework Purchasing and Qualification Lists under the European Procurement Directives' (Part II) (1999) 8 *PPLR* 161; S Arrowsmith, *The Law of Public and Utilities Procurement: Regulation in the EU and UK* (3rd edn, vol 1) (London Sweet & Maxwell, 2014) 1106–10 and 1112–13. Also S Arrowsmith and C Nicholas, 'The UNCITRAL Model Law on Procurement: Past, Present, and Future' (ch 1), and 'Regulating Framework Agreements under the UNCITRAL Model Law on Procurement' (ch 2) in S Arrowsmith (ed), *Reform of the UNCITRAL Model Law on Procurement: Procurement Regulation for the 21st Century* (Thomson Reuters/West, 2009) 58–70 and 102–16.

[7] Not to be confused with 'framework agreements' in specific procurement systems.

[8] For a somewhat different approach to the distinction between 'frameworks' and 'lists' see Albano and Nicholas (n 1) 13–14.

be interested in supplying certain (types of) items and/or whose 'suitability' is partially or fully assessed. Qualification systems in the EU utilities directive are an arrangement falling into this category. EU official lists of approved economic operators (or certification by certification bodies)[9] also 'intersect' this type of 'scheme' in a wide sense, though they are not 'purchaser driven' and not designed to meet procurement needs as envisaged by a specific purchaser.

The distinction should not be regarded as absolute, since many nuances are possible. There will be differences between a framework arrangement which sets most of the terms at the first stage[10] and an arrangement which only concerns a ('generic') type of items and only establishes, say, a (maximum) delivery period from issuance of an order. The latter would be closer to a 'supplier list'. At a practical level, a dynamic purchasing system under the EU public and utilities systems can be a 'supplier list' but it may also be a 'framework' type of arrangement where electronic catalogues are submitted at the first stage, and then completed at the call-off stage.[11]

The level of specification of the requirement in the 'outcome' of the first stage of PUIR is not a net differentiator between 'frameworks' and 'supplier lists'. For certain 'frameworks', particularly those that set most (or all) terms during the first stage, the requirement can be expected to be specified in quite some detail. However, a 'framework' arrangement may only establish some terms at the first stage, which leaves room for more flexibility as regards specification as well. Similarly, a 'supplier list' may concern 'generic' categories of items, or items specified to varied degrees, but the subject-matter of a 'list' could also be fully specified.[12]

Beyond possible interference, the distinction between 'framework' and 'supplier list' types of arrangements is very useful since it influences the approaches needed for an adequate design and use of an arrangement. Where terms are being set at the first stage, it is particularly important to ensure that these remain relevant for the future purchases made during the second stage. Where terms are not set at the first stage an arrangement offers increased flexibility but the award of call-offs at the second stage is likely to be less efficient and less expeditious, since *all* terms need to be established 'from scratch'.

6.3.3. Singularity and Plurality of Parties on the Supply Side and Demand Side, Including Closed and Open Plurality

Sub-classifications of PUIR arrangements usually start from the distinction between 'frameworks' and 'supplier lists'.[13] Nevertheless, there are criteria which

---

[9] Under the public and defence procurement sectors.
[10] Such as a requirements contract in the US federal system.
[11] Chapter 5, section 5.3.3.1 of this book.
[12] See qualification systems in the EU utilities sector.
[13] See pieces by Arrowsmith (n 6).

can be applied to both categories of arrangement, such as the singularity or plurality of parties on the demand or supply side of an arrangement. Thus, an arrangement can involve one purchaser (single-agency arrangements) or a plurality of purchasers (multiple-agency arrangements). Similarly, it can involve one supplier (single-supplier arrangements) or a plurality of suppliers (multiple-agency suppliers). Combinations like single-agency-multiple-supplier, and multiple-agency-multiple-supplier can apply to both 'frameworks' and 'supplier lists'. Single-supplier configurations can apply to frameworks but they seem very unlikely for 'supplier lists'.

Where a plurality of parties on each side of an arrangement is present, the arrangement may be closed or open, depending on whether suppliers and/or purchasers which were not originally a party to, or involved in the establishment of the arrangement can join it later, throughout the duration of the arrangement. For example, an EU framework agreement will in principle be closed both on the demand side and on the supply side. In contrast, arrangements like EU dynamic purchasing systems or qualification systems, or UNCITRAL open framework agreements are open on the supply side, since interested suppliers can apply to join at any time during the life of the arrangement.

On the other hand, the 'openness' of an arrangement on the demand side has received less explicit attention in the systems reviewed. However, it can be inferred that an EU qualification system may present this feature. In the UK, a practical development concerns 'generic' framework agreements. These are arrangements that may be used through awarding call-offs by purchasers which might not have actually been involved in their establishment, but which have been envisaged as parties, generically, by the entity organising the arrangement.[14]

The closed or open 'aspect' of an arrangement has significant practical consequences. On the supply side, closed arrangements may generate, for the purchases in question, a 'micro-market' that is isolated from the real market outside the arrangement. In the systems reviewed, closed 'framework' arrangements[15] usually involve a competitive exercise at the first stage, aimed at obtaining good (competitive) terms and reducing the number of suppliers to what is appropriate.[16] However, for closed frameworks not establishing all terms, the smaller the number of framework contractors, the higher may be the risk of collusion among framework suppliers at the call-off stage regarding the setting of the outstanding terms for individual orders.[17] Hence the need to provide for stage consistency controls in this type of arrangement, meaning that the terms offered by framework contractors

---

[14] Chapter 5, section 5.3.2.3.3 of this book.

[15] eg US requirements contracts and ID/IQ contracts, UNCITRAL closed framework agreements, EU (and Member States') framework agreements.

[16] Under the EU directives it is debatable whether a framework agreement involving no or very lax competition at the first stage could be permitted.

[17] See eg discussion in the EU / Romanian context in Chapter 5, sections 5.3.2.2.1 and 5.3.2.4.2 of this book. This risk is exacerbated in the case of 'commiting' frameworks on the demand side.

at the call-off stage must be consistent with those that allowed them to access the framework in the first place, namely, terms that are more advantageous for the purchaser than (or at least equally advantageous to) those originally offered at the first stage, or within margins of an adjustment mechanism also established during the first stage.

On the other hand, arrangements that are genuinely open on the supply side – meaning that suppliers may apply to join anytime during the duration of the arrangement – do not involve a competitive exercise at the first stage aimed at limiting the number of suppliers to be admitted.[18] Indeed, it appears difficult to imagine a proper competitive exercise without a common time-limit for the submission of competitive tenders.[19] Irrespective of whether terms are established[20] or not[21] in an arrangement that is genuinely open on the supply side, the assessment of 'bids' or 'applications' at the first stage only involves a comparison of each of them with the conditions or standards requested by the purchaser, and not a comparison among the 'bids' or 'applications' received. The risk of collusion is lower in the case of arrangements that are open on the supply side, since it is likely that many suppliers will be involved in the arrangement, and there is always the possibility of newcomers who could derail any collusive 'scheme' amongst pre-existing suppliers in the arrangement.

There seems to be equivalence on the demand side. An arrangement permitting purchasers not originally involved to join later seems to fit well with first-stage procedures which do not involve a competitive exercise amongst interested suppliers. Thus, arrangements that are open on the supply side seem more easily amenable to being open on the demand side as well. Conversely, arrangements that are closed on the supply side also tend to close the demand side. Since arrangements that are genuinely open on the supply side do not involve a competitive exercise at the first stage, an 'accurate' estimation of the overall requirement to be covered by the arrangement is not vital. A 'rough' estimation is likely to suffice and a further increase of that estimation by new purchasers should not affect the terms of future purchases, since most of the competition for an actual (specific) purchase shifts towards the second stage of the arrangement (in the case of EU dynamic purchasing systems, EU qualification systems and UNCITRAL open framework agreements). On the other hand, an alternative mechanism is used for the establishment of terms, and in particular prices, in the case of US GSA Schedules, where each supplier interested in being included in the programme (at the first stage of the arrangement) is required to demonstrate that the price it offers is at least as

---

[18] Exceptionally, the number of suppliers might be limited in certain circumstances in UNCITRAL open framework agreements.

[19] As shown, 'open' frameworks under the UK post-Brexit Procurement Bill, and some configurations of 'open frameworks' under the IBRD regulations rather appear as a series of subsequent closed frameworks for the same subject-matter (Chapter 5, section 5.4.2 and Chapter 3, section 3.2.1 of this book).

[20] As in UNCITRAL open framework agreements or some EU dynamic purchasing systems.

[21] As in EU qualification systems or some EU dynamic purchasing systems.

advantageous as its 'most privileged' (discounted) price offered to any of its other clients.[22]

It should also be noticed that ensuring best chances for good procurement through a 'supplier list' arrangement makes it necessary for it to be kept open (on the supply side) throughout its duration, involving inter alia permanent or regular advertising, objective criteria for admittance, a reasonable time-limit for finalising the assessment and appropriate transparency. To the contrary, supplier lists that become closed bear significant risks of fostering complacency and/or collusion among the suppliers admitted, potentially resulting in poor terms being proposed at the call-off stage, favouritism or corruption.[23] In light of such risks, none of the procurement systems reviewed in this book recognises closed 'lists'. Such 'arrangements' should not be contemplated since they would not appear to bring any (legitimate) benefits to the demand side.

6.3.4. 'Framework' Sub-Categories

Under this heading we look at sub-categories of 'framework' arrangements that were not covered in the preceding sections. Using a commitment / an obligation to buy and/or, respectively, to sell under the arrangement as a criterion, frameworks may be committing or non-committing for the parties.[24] Four combinations are thus possible: (i) committing on both the supply and demand sides; (ii) non-committing on both the supply and demand sides; (iii) committing on the demand side and non-committing on the supply side; (iv) non-committing on the demand side and committing on the supply side.[25]

The approaches of the various systems/instruments differ. The EU directives and UNCITRAL Model Law allow in principle for all combinations. This is consistent with the scope of these systems/instruments. Countries adopting the UNCITRAL Model Law can certainly decide whether they wish to cascade all those options to their purchasers, or whether they will only permit some types of frameworks. Similarly, under the 2004 Public Sector Directive, EU Member States could limit, if they so wished, their purchasers to using only certain types of framework agreements. The UK did not introduce any limitations in this connection. On the other hand, France *did* impose a condition for both types of (closed) framework arrangements recognised in the 2006 *Code des marchés public* (2006CMP) to be committing on the purchasers. Romania still requires

---

[22] Chapter 4, section 4.2.5 of this book.

[23] These risks are higher in the case of a 'mandatory' list (see below).

[24] Sometimes called 'mandatory' or 'non-mandatory'.

[25] For an analysis of such categories in the context of EU and UK public procurement (prior to the post-Brexit reform), see Arrowsmith, *The Law of Public and Utilities Procurement* (n 6) 1106–10. For an analysis of commitments (and their potential impact on terms and prices) in centralised purchasing frameworks in a wider context, see Albano and Nicholas (n 1) 287–91.

frameworks to be committing.[26] The US federal procurement system presents a mixed picture in terms of 'commitment' in 'framework arrangements'. At the more 'traditional' end of the US spectrum of PUIR, definite quantity contracts and requirements contracts are committing 'frameworks' both for the purchaser and for the supplier. Moving into ID/IQ contracts, these are committing too for both sides, but only partly and to different degrees. In contrast, under the current WB regulations, only frameworks that are non-committing on both sides are permitted.

Committing to purchase under a 'framework' arrangement is likely to generate better terms in a competitive exercise at the first stage. At the same time such an arrangement assumes that the purchaser remains pretty much 'locked' within that framework, which might exacerbate 'collusion' amongst framework contractors. Unless the framework supplier(s) are bound to supply at the call-off stage, terms set during the first stage may remain simple abstractions. Thus, a configuration that is committing on the demand side and non-committing on the supply side should only be used in very exceptional circumstances, such as shortage of supply. Nevertheless, enforcing 'commitment to supply' may be less than straight-forward in frameworks involving reopening of competition.

Single-supplier committing 'frameworks' are usually straight-forward to implement. For multiple-supplier frameworks, depending on whether a framework establishes all terms at the first stage and/or the call-off mechanism it involves, enforcing the commitment of the suppliers may be a complex matter. Frameworks that establish all terms at the first stage *and* which do not involve a reopening of competition at the call-off stage should not pose any significant issues in terms of commitment. However, where some terms are not set at the first stage, or where competition is reopened at the call-off stage, framework suppliers could avoid the 'commitment to supply' by not participating in the second-stage competition. If participation in mini-competitions is compulsory under the framework, suppliers may propose 'unattractive' or non-conforming bids. Thus, where call-offs cannot be issued directly or 'constructed' on the basis of the terms set at the first stage, *without further involvement from framework suppliers*, it could be preferable to regard the framework as non-committing on the supply side (since commitment to sell might be eluded).

Commitments to buy and/or, respectively, to sell in open frameworks have received little attention so far. As regards the demand side, it should in principle be possible for the purchasers to commit to purchase the subject-matter of an UNCITRAL open framework agreement or EU dynamic purchasing system exclusively under that arrangement. However, the impact on the terms offered by the suppliers at the first stage is likely to be marginal. As regards the supply side, commitment appears difficult to realise in these arrangements. The standard 'mood' for these arrangements appears to be non-committing on both sides.

---

[26] Chapter 5, section 5.3.2.2.1 of this book.

It should be noted that an arrangement establishing terms at the first stage without a competitive exercise and by reference to the applicants' most favourable price/terms offers (as offered to any of its other clients),[27] is also likely to be pretty much 'commitment neutral'.

Other categories of frameworks are self-explanatory. By using the criterion of the type of procedure used at each stage of the arrangement, there could be: frameworks involving a competitive exercise at the first stage,[28] or not involving a competitive exercise at the first stage;[29] frameworks involving a competitive exercise at the second stage, or not involving a competitive exercise at the second stage. By using the criterion of terms established at the first stage, frameworks could set all terms at the first stage,[30] or could set only some of the terms then.[31] Finally, a framework arrangement could be expressly regarded by a domestic system as a contract,[32] or – where this is not the case – a framework could, or it could not, meet the general legal criteria in the relevant legal system for being determined as a contract. As discussed, at policy level it seems preferable for the concept of a framework arrangement to be considered distinctly from that of a contract.

6.3.5. 'Supplier List' Sub-Categories

Under this heading we look at categories of 'supplier list' not covered by sections 6.3.2 and 6.3.3 above. A preliminary aspect is the extent to which commitment might apply to the 'list' type of arrangement. Since no terms are established during the first stage of 'lists' it appears illogical to 'commit'. The standard 'mode' for the 'supplier list' type of arrangement is thus non-committing for both the demand and the supply side.

By the criterion of the 'organiser' of a 'supplier list', these can be organised by the purchaser, or by a third party who is not a purchaser. Qualification systems in the EU utilities sector fall under the first category, whereas official lists of approved economic operators[33] in the EU public and defence sectors fall under the second category. Being organised by a purchaser, qualification systems allow for, and can support, a strategic and streamlined approach toward future requirements that are

---

[27] Like US GSA Schedules (see Chapter 4 of this book).

[28] eg US requirements contracts and ID/IQ contracts, EU or IBRD framework agreements.

[29] eg UNCITRAL open framework agreements, EU dynamic purchasing systems or US GSA Schedules.

[30] When call-offs may be awarded directly based on those terms without reopening competition. However, in some cases reopening competition may still be preferred (an option provided for explicitly in the 2014 Public Sector Directive).

[31] When some form of reopening competition is usually needed for setting or refining the reminder of the terms.

[32] See framework agreements in France; also US requirements or ID/IQ contracts.

[33] Or certification by bodies established under public or private law.

related in some way. In contrast, however, official lists do not have that capacity since they are not organised in view of any concrete estimation of future needs. Instead, they 'assess', or rather record, 'suitability' generally and abstractly. Thus, approved lists can be used both for 'traditional' purchasing as well as for 'non-traditional' purchasing.

A major distinction in the context of 'supplier lists' has been addressed by Arrowsmith. This concerns an option that suppliers might or might not have to participate in a specific procurement by using an existing list, or by expressing interest to participate and proving suitability in alternative ways without the need to have been registered on the list.[34] Where a supplier is not permitted to partici-pate in a procurement unless already registered on the relevant 'supplier list', such a list is referred to as a 'mandatory list'; instead, where a supplier may participate in a procurement even if not registered on a relevant 'supplier list', that is referred to as an 'optional list'. The differences between the two types, delineated as above, are significant but they should not be regarded in absolute terms since, in some configurations of list, variations may fade away to some extent as in the case of GPA multi-use lists, or the post-Brexit Procurement Bill.

A mandatory list provides increased procedural efficiency since at the time a specific purchase is started the aspects covered by the list need not be revisited for any participant in the specific procurement. This type of list has been regarded by legislators as involving potential risks like favouring suppliers already on the list over 'new entrants'. In effect, the 2011 UNCITRAL Model Law and the 2009 EU Defence Directive have not recognised mandatory lists, whereas in the 2014 EU Public Sector Directive some dynamic purchasing systems fall into this cate-gory, where terms are not established at the first stage, though this arrangement appears a specific and rather limitative type of list as regards items that can be procured under it and the procedural requirements involved. In contrast, quali-fication systems in the EU utilities sector can be regarded as a 'generalist', wide in scope, and nuanced (versatile) mandatory list type of arrangement. Under the previous (2011) WB Guidelines, pre-qualification lists for a number of subsequent contracts could be regarded as 'mandatory lists'. However, the current 2016 WB Regulations do not appear to envisage such pre-qualification lists any longer. In the author's view this reluctance is not justified where the list is maintained genu-inely open, which can be ensured by appropriate transparency, objective criteria and rules for admission applied equally to all interested suppliers, appropriate (fair) second-stage procedures that are transparent for all suppliers admitted onto the list, and appropriate review mechanisms for both stages. Subject to the observations in Chapter five, section 5.4.1, it is indeed very positive that the UK post-Brexit Procurement Bill envisages supplier lists under its novel 'dynamic markets' concept, which may under certain circumstances include 'mandatory list'

---

[34] eg, Arrowsmith, *The Law of Public and Utilities Procurement* (n 6) 1311–12.

per se type of configurations, of wide scope and providing for procedural flexibilities, including for the public sector.

Risks presented by 'optional lists' appear lower, since interested suppliers can in principle access specific procurements that such a list relates to without needing to register on it. Whether the risks would indeed be lower in practice may depend, though, on the award method for the procurement in question.[35] Procedural efficiency of optional lists may be limited since a full suitability assessment is needed for those suppliers who are interested in tendering for a specific procurement to which the optional list relates, but who are not interested in registering on that list. In procurement systems recognising mandatory lists it can probably be assumed that optional lists are also permitted for purchasers, even though not explicitly (eg, the EU utilities sector). Conversely, under the EU public and defence sectors procurement directives or under the UNCITRAL Model Law, which implicitly prohibit mandatory lists (other than the dynamic purchasing systems in the EU public sector), nothing appears to preclude purchasers from using optional lists, but the lack of express recognition is likely to affect their up-take in practice. As regards the UK post-Brexit Procurement Bill, the 'usual' type of dynamic market permits suppliers to apply for membership until the time-limit for tendering, provided they also submit a tender, for that specific procurement (and obliges purchasers to consider such application), which places this configuration of dynamic market somewhere between truly mandatory type of lists and optional lists. The mandatory per se configuration of dynamic markets seems rather an exception, permitted in relation to complex procurements.

6.4. Decisions and Design

6.4.1. 'Traditional' Procurement or Arrangement for Procurement of Uncertain or Indefinite Requirements?

When a purchaser considers PUIR, a proper analysis of the procurement need envisaged should be conducted. In principle, as a starting point, a PUIR arrangement is likely to make sense when uncertainties surrounding the procurement need are real and objective or indefinite aspects are desired and justified. In the first case, the procurement need cannot be defined (objectively) with sufficient precision so as to enable the establishment of all terms for the purchase(s) in a way that is responsive and appropriate for the need (which might be evolving). In the second case, the procurement need might be amenable to establishing all terms at the time of initiating the procurement process, but external factors, such as the estimated evolution of market conditions, make this undesirable. PUIR

---

[35] ibid.

arrangements require an increased planning effort. They are not a substitute for good planning. Their success is likely to depend on market dynamics over that period, market knowledge, and how the framework adapts to the market conditions.

Some of these arrangements tend to be (significantly) more complex than 'traditional' purchasing, meaning that their establishment and administration may involve additional costs and require more experienced personnel to handle both the setting up and the call-off stage. A cost-benefit analysis exercise appears thus desirable to support the decision-making process. This could help the purchaser to appreciate, where repeat purchases are envisaged, whether the additional cost and effort involved by a PUIR arrangement would be outweighed by overall savings which can arise from better prices being offered in light of expected aggregation of demand. However, excessive aggregation under closed arrangements may significantly restrict competition on the market for the subject-matter of the arrangement throughout its duration.[36]

Even where a procurement need could be defined so as to organise a 'traditional' purchase, it may be preferable to put in place a PUIR arrangement in order to facilitate SMEs' participation in public procurement (by 'fragmenting' the requirements, and subject to 'suitability' criteria that are proportional to the 'fragments'). On the other hand, not using a PUIR arrangement for recurrent purchases could result in small and repeated procurements, which individually could fall below the thresholds for transparent and competitive purchasing. This may bring significant disadvantages, such as increased transaction costs (from repeating a full-cycle procedure for each 'segment') and less advantageous terms (from lack of aggregation), and it could facilitate favouritism and affect competition.

In the systems reviewed in this book, the position concerning decisions between 'traditional' procurement and PUIR arrangements varies. The UNCITRAL Model Law defines conditions for use of framework agreements, related to the fact that the need for the subject-matter of the procurement is expected to arise on an indefinite or repeated basis, or that the need may arise on an urgent basis. The Model Law also requires the justification of a decision to embark on a framework agreement, and of the type of framework chosen, to be recorded. That decision could be challenged by aggrieved suppliers (though this may not be a straightforward process).

A requirement for purchasers to record their decisions to embark on a PUIR arrangement, together with the reasons therefor, appears good practice in that it alerts purchasers to analyse the procurement need in order to establish an appropriate way to tackle it. Where this requirement is accompanied by general conditions for use of PUIR arrangement(s) and the possibility for suppliers to challenge that decision, the analysis could be treated more seriously and in depth,

---

[36] Also, collusion or even corruption could be facilitated.

though this may depend on the maturity of the procurement system in question. Consideration could also be given to requiring justification and reasons for embarking on traditional procurement (rather than on PUIR).

In the WB system quite similar 'parameters' for the decision to embark on a framework arrangement seem to apply. Namely, such an arrangement may be used where the anticipated need is recurrent, indefinite, or likely to arise in emergency situations. However, here the reasons (justification) for the decision to use a framework are included in project documents that are prepared by the Borrowing agency and subject to the Bank's approval. This approach is consistent with the nature of procurement under development programmes by international donors/lenders.

In the US federal system, the 'hallmarks' of both the requirements contracts and ID/IQ contracts, provided for under the FAR, concern an uncertainty[37] over the precise quantities that will be needed as well as the recurrent nature of the estimated requirement. Indefinite needs or those that may arise in emergency situations are not explicitly covered. Nevertheless, the potential use of task order contracting for emergency situations was addressed in the literature by using the argument of the recurrent nature of 'disasters' and, in effect, of certain items being needed to cope with them.[38] Decisions to use an indefinite-delivery contract are part of acquisition planning, a (predominantly) internal process of the purchasing agency.[39]

Under the EU directives, the use of PUIR arrangements is rather a 'discretionary option' for purchasers. The directives do not require a justification for embarking on PUIR. Also, there are no conditions provided concerning the use of framework agreements (or qualification systems in the utilities sector) relating to the features of the procurement need. As regards dynamic purchasing systems, the 'standard items' and 'electronic process' conditions exist, but there is no requirement to justify the decision.[40] While this 'liberal' approach may be justified under the directives, in light of their role at EU level,[41] it could be more problematic for Member States. None of the EU Member States reviewed in this book include, at the domestic law level, conditions for use of frameworks (as in the directives).[42] In the past, the French public procurement law (the older versions of the CMP) *did* include strict conditions for use of certain 'framework'

---

[37] Of a different degree for each of the mentioned arrangements.
[38] Chapter 4, section 4.1.3 of this book.
[39] FAR Part 7.
[40] European Commission, *Dynamic Purchasing Systems: Use Guidelines* (September 2021), at https://op.europa.eu/en/publication-detail/-/publication/9b5394f7-3219-11ec-bd8e-01aa75ed71a1, and Local Government Association (UK), 'A Guide to Dynamic Purchasing Systems within the Public Sector: Is It Right for You and Your Suppliers' (May 2017) offer some orientation.
[41] ie maintaining and enhancing the good functioning of the EU internal market by opening public procurement markets of Member States (see Chapter 5, section 5.2.1 of this book).
[42] Guidance is also limited.

arrangements. Under the previous (2004) Public Sector Directive, the margin of discretion of Member States allowed them to limit uses of framework agreements as deemed appropriate. But under the 'ultra-liberal' approach of the 2014 Directives it is questionable whether Member States would still have such possibilities (should they wish to).[43]

In some cases, a purchaser may be entitled to procure by using an arrangement set up by another entity, whether or not that purchaser has been involved in the preparation or setting up of that arrangement.[44] Such situations include the so-called 'generic frameworks' as used in the UK, the use of a qualification system set up by another entity in the EU utilities sector, or US GSA Multiple Award Schedules. In such cases, or similar, an initial step for addressing the procurement need should be for the purchaser to identify any (pre)existing arrangements established by other entities which might be used for that purchase. For this purpose, a central register of all available arrangements, such as that envisaged in the UK post-Brexit reform, appears particularly useful.[45]

A thorough analysis of the procurement need, of the relevant market segment, and of the best way to satisfy that need (ie, through 'traditional' procurement vs designing and implementing a PUIR arrangement vs where applicable, using an existing arrangement) would always need to be done at the purchaser's level on a case-by-case basis, in light of the specific circumstances of each procurement need. Whilst the regulatory framework and policy cannot secure quality of such assessment (that would also depend on available capability), some 'aid' in this process may be useful at policy or/and legal level, encouraging an appropriate use of PUIR arrangements, for instance by providing balanced conditions for use. Certainly, this should not include any excessive or arbitrary limitations.

6.4.2. Selecting an Appropriate or Desirable Type of Arrangement

6.4.2.1. General

Similarly to decisions between 'traditional' purchases and PUIR arrangements, a requirement at law/policy level for the purchaser to justify and record its choice of a specific type/sub-type of PUIR can be found in the UNCITRAL, World Bank and the US federal procurement instruments. Under the UNCITRAL Model Law this choice may be subject to scrutiny from interested suppliers, whereas under the

---

[43] eg Chapter 5, sections 5.2.1.3 and 5.3.2.1 of this book. Still, Romanian secondary legislation requires some background information concerning procurement planning decisions, including for PUIR arrangements (art 9PIN).

[44] eg multiple-agency arrangements (in centralised procurement).

[45] Chapter 5, section 5.4.2 of this book.

WB system it is subject to approval by the Bank. In the US federal procurement system the choice between multiple-supplier and single-supplier indefinite-delivery contracts must be documented by the purchaser, as part of acquisition planning. In contrast, in the EU directives, there is no requirement to justify and record the decision to embark on any type or sub-type of PUIR arrangement.

Regarding specific conditions for use of certain types of PUIR, the picture is even more diverse. The UNCITRAL Model Law does not include conditions for use of each of the *specific* types of frameworks, but guidance is provided in this connection in the Guide to Enactment. States implementing a UNCITRAL-based system may choose to include in their national legislation some of the recommended circumstances when a certain type of framework could be appropriate from the Guide.

The WB Regulations do not state conditions for use of specific configurations of *framework agreements*, though they do provide for an 'adapted' form of framework that is available for commodity items only. While in the US federal procurement the FAR provides conditions concerning the use of various types of indefinite-delivery contracts, the EU has taken pretty much the opposite approach as no conditions apply in the directives to the use of the various framework agreement 'configurations'. The Member States reviewed have followed the same 'trend' under the 2004 and 2014 Directives.

6.4.2.2. *Options among Categories or Sub-Categories of Framework Arrangements*

Options among types or sub-types of framework arrangements can be quite complex. They are very common, too, in the systems reviewed, since quite similar types (and sub-types) of framework arrangements can be found in almost all case studies.[46]

Where purchasers determine that a framework arrangement (rather than traditional purchasing) is necessary to address a procurement need, they face similar questions: single- or multiple-supplier framework?; if multiple-contractor framework, then closed or open?; if closed framework, then with or without second-stage competition, and how many suppliers?

For the US federal procurement system the question concerning a closed or open 'framework' is not relevant, since GSA (MAS) Schedules (the only open arrangement in this system) are an already existing centralised arrangement. Similarly, the question as to whether the call-off stage should involve competition or otherwise is less relevant in the US system, since in ID/IQ contracts call-off procedures are determined by the size (ie, value) of each order.[47]

---

[46] Certainly, this is not to say that those 'configurations' are identical in various systems.
[47] FAR16.505(b).

6.4.2.2.1. Single- or Multiple-Supplier Framework?

The US federal procurement provisions in the FAR provide potential answers to the question concerning the use of a single- or multiple-supplier framework arrangement, and to the question of establishing an appropriate number of suppliers for a closed arrangement. Among the systems reviewed this is the only one that currently addresses, in a legal/regulatory instrument, circumstances which could justify those decisions. It is noteworthy they are provided in the context of a wider US policy preference towards multiple-supplier task order (ID/IQ) contracting.[48]

The FAR places a 'cap' on the maximum value of a single-supplier framework arrangement. This may have some benefits but there are limitations on intended effects. Framework arrangements being longer-term arrangements, their (aggregated) value tends to be high and corruption temptations are also likely to be high, particularly as regards closed frameworks. Where single-supplier frameworks are envisaged, temptations may be even higher, since whoever wins gets in principle the entire 'cake'. Excessively large single-supplier frameworks may also affect competition in the relevant market. In some cases though, even where a multiple-supplier arrangement is initially envisaged, it may turn out during the first-stage that only one supplier among those attending is capable or qualified for that framework, or that only one supplier attends, so the framework could end up being a single-supplier arrangement.

An opposite approach to establishing a ceiling value up to which certain types of 'framework' arrangement *can* be used might be to set a threshold below which they *must not* be used. This could secure better chances that the higher administration costs of a framework are outweighed by the economies of scale from expected aggregate demand and/or repeat purchases.[49] In the US federal system, multiple-supplier 'framework' arrangements are not permitted where 'the total estimated value of the contract is less than the simplified acquisition threshold',[50] which is usually US$250,000 and can be higher in some circumstances.[51] The 'multiple award preference'[52] – relevant for indefinite-delivery contracts where their estimated amount exceeds certain amounts, eg US$100 million for items other than advisory and assistance services – applies in fact only to cases when the use of multiple awards is not prohibited. Wrapped up in a multiple-award preference, the rules up to the ceiling for single-supplier arrangements will lead in many cases to single-supplier arrangements. It might even be argued that, to a significant extent, there is a preference towards single awards. This actually makes sense and it is in fact consistent in broad-brush with both the suggestions in the UNCITRAL

---

[48] FAR16.504(c).

[49] eg the previous regime in France did not seem to envisage dynamic purchasing systems below the EU thresholds.

[50] FAR16.504(c)(1)(ii)(B)(5).

[51] FAR2.101.

[52] n 48.

Guide to Enactment and the conditions that were applicable in France in the past. Since award procedures for closed frameworks are competitive (at the first stage), it is likely in many cases that single-supplier frameworks result in better terms and prices due to higher expected aggregated demand and more certainty for the supplier in getting business under the arrangement.

However, single-supplier arrangements are permitted in the US federal procurement system above the ceiling in a number of situations, such as where 'The contract provides only for firm-fixed price'[53] for call-offs, in the form of unit price for products or price for specific tasks. This suggests that abusing large single-contractor frameworks without firm/fixed prices are of concern. Where full consistency among call-offs is required or only 'one source is qualified and capable of performing the work at a reasonable price' single supplier arrangements are permitted over the ceiling.[54] Embarking on a single-supplier arrangement over the ceiling requires a written determination by the head of the agency (purchaser) that the relevant condition(s) are met.

Another perspective on the matter concerns the potential for a supplier to specialise exclusively in certain specific aspects of work under a framework arrangement, which could then result in the need for call-offs to be awarded to that supplier only, whether on that framework or in a subsequent one. On this point, the FAR quite rightly advises that such situations should be avoided.[55] An obvious way to do this might indeed be to have a multiple-supplier arrangement to start with. However, this in itself might not ensure that exclusive specialisation does not arise, since much depends on the call-off award procedures and their outcome, for example, where during second-stage competitions the same supplier offers best terms for most or all orders. In the US federal system, purchasers enjoy more flexibility in establishing call-off procedures, in particular for smaller orders, which is likely to facilitate accommodation of the requirement to avoid excessive specialisation. However, in other systems, such as the EU or UNCITRAL, where such flexibility in call-off procedures is not available, a potential solution might be a framework establishing all terms as well as a guaranteed minimum quantity for each of the suppliers. Under such systems a concern regarding excessive specialisation could fall under an obligation not to use frameworks in such a way as to restrict, distort or prevent competition.

For multiple-supplier arrangements FAR provides for a number of aspects that should be considered when deciding an appropriate number of contractors to be engaged in a closed 'framework' arrangement.[56] These include: 'the scope and complexity' of the subject-matter of the arrangement, the expected duration

---

[53] FAR16.504(c)(1)(ii)(D)(1).

[54] An additional situation when single-contractor frameworks are permitted over the ceiling concerns public interest due to exceptional circumstances (ibid). In this case the Congress must be notified. FAR16.504(c)(1)(ii)(D)(2).

[55] FAR16.504(c)(1)(ii)(a).

[56] ibid. See also, more generally, Albano and Nicholas (n 1) 263–64.

and frequency of call-offs, 'the mix of resources' that a supplier needs in order to carry out the expected call-offs, and the ability to maintain competition among suppliers during the duration of the framework. The relevance of these aspects to other procurement systems is self-evident.[57] This certainly implies a thorough analysis on a case-by-case basis of both the expected requirement *and* the relevant market players. While a single-supplier arrangement or an arrangement involving a small number of suppliers is likely to result in better terms in view of higher expected aggregated demand,[58] it may fail to provide for security of supply, or to fill the expected need. For example, where a number of (large) orders overlap in time, a small number of suppliers might not have the capacity or resources to cope with those orders. Similarly, in the case of non-committing arrangements, an insufficient number of suppliers may result in lack of interest in (ie non-attendance for) certain call-offs.[59]

At the same time, the extent to which the 'scope' of the requirement can be determined at the planning stage is also likely to influence the number of framework contractors. If most, or all, terms governing future purchases under the arrangement can be established at the first stage of the arrangement it could then make sense to concentrate competition at this stage of the procedure,[60] which means a single contractor or as small as possible a number of contractors. On the other hand, if only a few terms can be established at the first stage, or the subject-matter of the requirement cannot be determined in detail or with precision, it then makes sense to secure an adequate level of competition at the call-off stage, once the estimated needs become actual and specifiable.[61] This, in turn, involves a larger number of suppliers being admitted onto the arrangement at the first stage. But where relevant market conditions are unpredictable and/or unstable it could also be preferable to focus the competition closer to the moment when the need becomes actual, and this is likely to involve admitting a larger number of suppliers during the first stage, irrespective of how closely the scope of requirement can be determined when planning the framework. Certainly, fine-tuning among inter-linked elements is needed on a case-by-case basis, for balancing potentially conflicting aspects. For example, whereas a closed framework with a small number of suppliers may result in better terms (from higher expected aggregated demand), the risks of collusion during the call-off stage are also likely to be higher.

As shown, in the EU directives there is no requirement to document and record a decision-making process as regards embarking on a specific type of

---

[57] However, the need to ensure a sufficient number of framework contractors received an inadequate and inflexible application in the previous (2004) EU Public Sector Directive and in the (2009) EU Defence Directive (see Chapter 5, section 5.3.2.3.1 of this book).

[58] It could also offer a 'lighter' administration effort and cost.

[59] The risk of non-attendance is not eliminated by a larger number of suppliers, but it is likely to be lower.

[60] See eg Chapter 2, sections 2.2.1.2 and 2.2.3.2 of this book.

[61] ibid.

framework agreement, and there are no conditions applicable for such decision. Under the 2014 Directives Member States might not even be permitted to introduce such conditions.[62] Thus, the way to guide purchasers through the various types/sub-types/configurations of frameworks, and choosing one that meets specific needs seems to be through written guidance. However, on this subject guidance is scarce. In the past the legislation in France did provide for strict conditions under which certain types of framework arrangements could be used. Thus, under article 71 of the 2004CMP,[63] 'task order contracts' could only be used where, 'because of economic, technical or financial reasons, the extent or rhythm of the need to be satisfied cannot not be fully established in the purchase deal'.[64] The standard configuration for such a 'framework' was a single-supplier arrangement, with certain features. In the cases mentioned above, but only for reasons duly justified by the inability of a single supplier to 'carry out all the requirements' or by 'the need to ensure security of supply', the purchaser was permitted to pass a multiple-supplier arrangement (of the type that establishes all terms and not involving reopening of competition).[65]

Finally, a multiple-supplier closed framework arrangement configuration involving reopening of competition at the call-off stage was only permitted where such a procedure was necessary because: 'of the high volatility of product prices', 'or of the rapid product obsolescence', or where issuance of an order was rendered necessary by a situation of imperative emergency not attributable to the purchaser.[66]

It can be noticed that the French instrument at the time provided for a very subtle, gradual but direct relationship between the indefinite or uncertain features of an envisaged procurement need, on the one hand, and the permitted configuration of a (closed) framework arrangement to address that need, on the other hand. That approach might seem nowadays excessively prescriptive and inflexible, in particular in some systems. It does not seem to attend to the potential negative consequences that an excessively large single-supplier arrangement may have for competition, or to the risk of exclusive specialisation of a single supplier. However, the old French legislation cited does provide for a wise general 'mechanism' for analysis of the options between various configurations of closed framework arrangement, which, it is submitted, could be turned and further adapted into useful guidance, not just for France but for other Member States as well. It would guide purchasers through relevant framework options while allowing purchasers to do otherwise where justified.

---

[62] Arrowsmith, *The Law of Public and Utilities Procurement* (n 6) 1112.

[63] Similar provisions were also in art 72 of the 2001CMP. See Chapter 5, section 5.3.2.3.1 of this book.

[64] My translation.

[65] Art 71(III) of 2004CMP. That reopening of competition was clearly not envisaged here results from analysing art 71(III) jointly with art 71(IV) and (V) of 2004CMP.

[66] Art 71(IV) of 2004CMP.

6.4.2.2.2. Framework Involving Reopening of Competition at
Call-Off Stage versus Direct Orders Based on the Framework,
and Committing versus Non-Committing Framework

While the EU directives' approach offers full flexibility as to the type of framework agreement to be used by a purchaser, consistent with its envisaged procurement need, it could also lead to an inappropriate use of framework agreements. The potential advantages that these arrangements could offer – such as better prices from expected aggregation of demand, security of supply, administrative convenience[67] and/or flexible supply arrangements[68] – may not be convergent, and might require different types of frameworks. For example, the simplest ordering procedures, potentially involving shortest lead-times between materialisation of needs and delivery, are likely to be offered by frameworks establishing all terms at the first stage. These allow, under both the EU directives and the UNCITRAL Model Law on Public Procurement, for orders to be issued directly based on the terms of a (closed) framework agreement, without the need to reopen competition among framework contractors. However, this type of arrangement is unlikely to offer much flexibility of supply arrangements or significant room for late product or service customisation, since all terms are pre-established.

On the other hand, the attraction of administrative convenience and flexibility of the supply arrangements offered by frameworks might be accompanied by an erroneous perception that 'administrative convenience' also involves less preparation and planning effort before initiating the exercise for the award of a framework agreement. Where this happens, both 'value' (ie, better terms from expected aggregated demand) as well as administrative convenience at the call-off stage could be negatively affected. If the requirement could have been determined in a sufficient measure as to allow for the establishment of all terms at the first stage, as well as to establish the required number of suppliers, then better terms might have resulted from the framework 'exercise'. Moreover, the simplest and most efficient ordering at the call-off stage is likely to result from frameworks that establish all terms at the first stage.

However, in the absence of adequate conditions (or preferences, or guidance), a superficial assessment and planning of the requirement and approach before initiating the award procedure for a framework may result in an inappropriate type of framework being used for the estimated procurement need in question – for example, a framework agreement with a larger number of suppliers and involving reopening of competition. Such an arrangement offers increased flexibility at the call-off stage since some terms could be established or refined at that stage. But it is important to ascertain at the planning stage whether that flexibility is in fact needed and not just a result of insufficient needs and market analysis, and planning. This certainly does not mean that frameworks involving second-stage

---

[67] ie, simpler ordering procedures or shorter delivery (lead) times.
[68] ie, late product or service customisation, low inventories, no commitment above actual needs.

competition should be avoided – quite to the contrary, they are needed and appropriate in some cases, which could include volatile or dynamic market conditions, a necessity or policy to maintain low inventories, delayed product or service adaptation or customisation, or simply an *objective* impossibility or undesirability to establish all terms at the first stage.

In principle, when planning a framework, one should attempt to ascertain whether establishing all terms is feasible. If it is feasible, it should then be considered whether this is also desirable.[69] Where both conditions are met, it then probably makes sense to consider awarding a (closed) framework agreement that does not involve reopening of competition at the call-off stage. This, in conjunction with establishing the smallest number of framework contractors capable, however, of filling the anticipated need (properly and completely), could result in a framework that offers both good value and administrative efficiency at the call-off stage. This 'scenario' assumes, though, a fairly stable relevant market for the duration of the arrangement in question, permitting terms/price adjustment formulas to be included in the framework from the outset to keep framework terms 'competitive' in comparison to those available on the open market.

However, an analysis of the procurement need may also reveal that, while establishing all terms is feasible, it is not desirable. Reasons for this could include an expectation that, for certain larger call-offs, contractors might be prepared to offer even better terms than those submitted in order to get access onto the framework, or an uncertainty over whether market conditions could arise during the framework period, possibly not capable of being dealt with through terms or price adjustment formulae alone. Thus, there could be two sub-options: either to organise a framework agreement involving reopening of competition[70] in respect of the terms whose establishment at the first stage is undesirable (and/or deserving refinement at call of stage), or to award a framework agreement establishing all terms/conditions and providing both for direct awards based on those terms/conditions without reopening of competition as well as for the possibility to reopen competition at the call-off stage under certain conditions.[71] It goes without saying that both configurations involve multiple-supplier frameworks.

The latter sub-option is explicitly provided for under the 2014 EU Public Sector Directive.[72] An element which could make this configuration of arrangement attractive is also the possibility to render it effectively committing for the supplier(s), where this is desired. Since all terms are established at the first stage, it follows that a condition could be included in the framework (from the outset) to

---

[69] In light of eg evolving needs and/or potential market evolutions.

[70] Amongst the framework contractors.

[71] In light of an expectation of competition reopening, some suppliers might not be prepared to offer their best terms at the first stage (so they can offer improved terms at call-off competitions).

[72] Art 33(4)(b)PSD. France does not provide explicitly for this option. Also, a similar option is not provided for explicitly in the 2011 UNCITRAL Model Law, or in the 2009 EU Defence Directive. However, it can probably be accommodated subject to appropriate transparency requirements and/or through the organisation of different lots.

the effect that, where there is no attendance in a call-off reopening of competition, the purchaser may award the order to the framework contractor whose terms, as offered at the first stage, provide best value for that order, and that the contractor selected in this way is bound to supply.[73] The same could apply in the case of a framework that does not establish all terms with precision. However, it might be less straight-forward (and possibly ineffectual) to ensure that a multiple-supplier framework in which some terms are not established *at all* at the first stage[74] be committing for the supply side, because setting the terms not established at the first stage requires a basis for setting them at the call-off stage, and in most cases it makes sense for this to involve reopening of competition.[75] In turn, this assumes attendance at competition reopening. While this might, in principle, be made compulsory under the framework conditions, for example subject to financial penalties or exclusion from the framework, the obligation to attend call-off competitions might be 'eluded' by framework suppliers by offering completely 'uninteresting' terms.

Finally, where there is an objective impossibility to establish all terms at the first stage, the framework should involve reopening of competition at the call-off stage, as a basis for setting those outstanding terms *and* for selecting the contractor for the call-off in question.

It can be noticed that frameworks that are committing for the supply side fit better with closed arrangements in which all terms are established at the first stage. While committing frameworks for the supply side are not entirely excluded for frameworks in which some terms are not established at all (or are only set within very loose limits), the suppliers could elude their commitments, as explained above. Where such configuration is linked with a purchaser's commitment to buy exclusively under that framework, collusion risks may be exacerbated, placing the purchaser in a weak position, as discussed in the context of Romania.[76]

In principle, a purchaser's commitment to buy under a closed arrangement is likely to result in better terms being offered to access the framework, since the suppliers' expectation of aggregated demand is higher. On the other hand, attention needs to be paid to the fact that the purchaser is likely to remain stuck with those suppliers and with the terms established for the duration of the framework. Appropriate controls are thus particularly needed in this type of framework. Also, unless specific circumstances apply, a balanced approach is advisable: it usually makes sense for a framework that is committing for the purchaser to be committing for the supplier(s) too. Conversely, as discussed in Chapter three, the World Bank regulations require frameworks to be non-committing on both

---

[73] A more elaborate condition might permit purchasers to award an order based on terms submitted by framework contractors at the first stage, even where there is (some) attendance in call-off reopening of competition, but it does not result in better terms for that order than those offered at the first stage. Certainly, strict transparency controls are needed to prevent abuses.

[74] Or are established within very loose parameters.

[75] Subject to limited exceptions.

[76] Chapter 5, section 5.3.2.2.1 of thus book.

the supply and demand sides. It should also be borne in mind that a framework that is committing for the demand side but not committing for the purchaser may offer additional flexibility but it is likely to come at an additional cost. Two aspects have an impact here: first, retaining availability usually involves an effort and has a price-tag and, second, expected aggregation of demand is lower. Conversely, a framework that is committing for the purchaser but not committing for the supply side seems to make sense only in very exceptional circumstances, such as severe shortages in the relevant market segment.

Returning briefly to closed frameworks that do not establish all terms, their usefulness is beyond doubt in some circumstances. These include mainly cases where there is an objective need for late product or service customisation, or the subject-matter of the arrangement or some terms cannot be pre-determined sufficiently at the first stage because the requirement is dynamic, or there is a plurality of users envisaged with varying needs concerning the subject-matter. It should, however, be considered that additional flexibility may come together with less efficiency or security of supply, compared with frameworks establishing all terms.

The variety of approaches on commitment – or lack of commitment – in frameworks throughout the systems/instruments investigated in this book (as to which see section 6.3.4) suggests that the subject requires continuing attention. Sources of inspiration could again be found in the UNCITRAL Guide to Enactment and in the older (2001/2004) versions of the French Public Procurement Code (CMP). As regards the latter, the subtle design of (closed) frameworks involved not only a gradual departure from 'traditional' purchasing but went beyond this. Thus, frameworks involving reopening of competition did not envisage establishing a minimum or maximum aggregated volume of purchases under the arrangement in terms of quantity or value[77] (unlike frameworks without second-stage competition). Indeed, in frameworks involving reopening of competition, the overall requirement is unlikely to be pre-determined in strict detail, and this could include, in many cases, that a minimum or maximum cannot be pre-established as well. Further, it seems that the requirement for a purchaser not to purchase the subject-matter of the framework outside the framework in question only applied to single-supplier arrangements and to multiple-supplier arrangements that did not involve reopening of competition.[78] At the same time, the 2004CMP did not appear to require frameworks involving reopening of competition to be committing on the demand side. Again, it could have been useful if such provisions had been turned into guidance (and adjusted as appropriate).

Finally, when planning/preparing for emergencies, it is likely that a multiple-supplier framework that is committing for the framework suppliers and that does

---

[77] Art 71(IV) and (V) of 2004CMP.
[78] Art 71(I)(4) in relation to art 71(III) of 2004CMP.

not involve reopening of competition would provide optimum security/availability of supply and second-stage administrative convenience, ie speed. Whilst this configuration involves setting all (key) terms in advance, which could be rather inflexible given the unpredictable features of crises, it would nevertheless seem an appropriate starting point for preparation analysis: if not feasible given the potential needs and market features and evolution, then other configurations could be investigated in the relevant circumstances.

6.4.2.2.3. Closed or Open Framework?

In this section 'open framework' refers to genuinely open arrangements (on the supply side) in which suppliers can apply for admission at any time throughout their duration, and not to arrangements that are only reopened at predetermined times, such as those in the UK post-Brexit Procurement Bill and some of those envisaged by the World Bank regulations. As shown, the latter arrangements substantively appear as a series of subsequent *closed* frameworks for the same subject-matter and within similar parameters; and also, at the time of writing this book, the arrangements reopened at predetermined times (in the UK bill and WB regulations) seem insufficiently articulated in their relevant regulatory frameworks.

Arrangements such as open framework agreements under the UNCITRAL Model Law, or some potential configurations of dynamic purchasing system in the EU (and Member States') public and utility sectors,[79] are multiple-supplier arrangements that involve reopening of competition at the call-off stage. Thus, to answer the question whether an open framework is an appropriate way to address a procurement need, a purchaser should have identified first that: (i) PUIR is preferable over 'traditional' purchasing; and (ii) a single-supplier framework is not appropriate; and (iii) a multiple-supplier framework without reopening of competition is also not appropriate. Once the purchaser determines that a multiple-supplier arrangement involving second-stage competition is desirable, it should then consider whether this should be closed or open.

In the EU directives there is a condition applying to dynamic purchasing systems and this concerns the subject-matter of the envisaged arrangement, which must be 'off-the-shelf' or 'commonly used' items,[80] such as, say, printing paper, or stationary. A similar recommendation can be found in the UNCITRAL Guide to Enactment for open frameworks. However, such items can also be procured by using a closed framework arrangement in both systems. The requirement for the process to be (completely) electronic is also not a differentiator, since closed framework agreements may also be conducted electronically.

---

[79] Configurations based on electronic catalogues that are then used by the purchaser at call-off stage to 'develop' a 'basis' for further competition.

[80] The language of the directives is more convoluted: Chapter 5, section 5.3.3.2 of this book.

Under the circumstances, one of the aspects that should be assessed is whether the relevant market segment is competitive enough to secure sufficient interest and participation in call-offs. If there is only a limited number of relevant suppliers, the purchaser may consider having some competition at first stage, which would mean a closed framework. On the other hand, price volatility or very dynamic markets make it necessary for terms to be set very close to the moment when a need materialises. It thus makes sense to have most (or all) competition at the call-off stage. Where the requirement is particularly heterogeneous, as could be the case in multiple-user frameworks, resulting in varying terms being needed for the various orders[81] which cannot be anticipated when the framework is designed, again, an open framework might actually offer the best chances of meeting such requirements.

On the other hand, and particularly where fairly stable market conditions prevail in the relevant segment, it should also be considered whether the benefits of likely wider competition at each call-off in case of an open framework arrangement outweigh the potential for better terms being offered in light of expected aggregation of demand in case of a closed framework involving call-off competition. In open frameworks, the fact that newcomers may come into play at any time is likely to hamper potential collusion among framework contractors. Terms offered at the call-off stage are more likely to reflect those generally available on the market, and the risk of the purchaser remaining stuck with obsolete (ie, unfavourable) terms appears thus much lower in open frameworks. However, the administrative cost of preparing and evaluating (complete) tenders for each call-off should also be factored in.

6.4.2.3. Circumstances when 'Supplier Lists' May Be Appropriate

Deriving from my definition of a 'supplier list', such an arrangement is likely to be appropriate when it is possible to assess the 'suitability' of suppliers potentially interested in some procurements (before needs materialise), but where it is not possible, or not desirable to establish any terms at that stage. This could be the case where future procurement needs are too vague at the time of planning/preparing a supply arrangement or where market conditions could change in a way that is favourable to the purchaser. Still, time and effort can be saved when needs materialise, in particular where these are recurrent in some way, since identification of interest and/or 'suitability' will have already been performed (once, for a number of subsequent purchases). Mandatory lists, as to which see eg, section 6.3.5 above, may be notably useful in case of complex critical items for which the assessment of supplier 'suitability' can be a lengthy process (potentially involving testing, homologation, etc) that would significantly affect timeliness

---

[81] Such as delivery to different locations, within different time-limits, different warranty conditions, etc.

of procurement if that process would only start once needs materialise, for instance in case of critical railway safety equipment. In such cases, being able to conduct the procurement only with suppliers whose suitability has already been established can be essential.

Whilst supplier lists provide for less convenience and less efficiency at the call-off stage in comparison to frameworks, lists could be useful in many situations in which framework arrangements cannot objectively be employed, for instance where specifications are not available in advance, or where, although some regular needs are identified in advance in general terms, they are not homogenous enough to permit any sort of framework arrangements, including by lots. However, it is relevant to bear in mind that certain configurations of list may, to some degree, overlap with certain configurations of open frameworks (there being nuances as well). For example, dynamic purchasing systems under the 2014 EU Public Sector and Utilities Directives, in their 'standard' configurations only provide for an assessment of 'selection criteria' at the first stage, whereas the configuration involving electronic catalogues might establish some terms at the first stage though not through competitive comparison of submissions. It will certainly be for the purchaser to establish, on a case-by-case basis, which configuration is appropriate in specific circumstances.

A wider interpretation of 'regular purchases' could actually support a more strategic plan and implementation of an organisation's purchases. From this perspective, it can be noticed that 'genuine' one-off purchases (requirements), which due to their very particular features, specifications or complexity, require an entirely dedicated full-cycle purchasing process – separate from, and independent of, any other purchases – may actually not be very numerous. At the other side of the range there may be recurrent (regular) requirements of a sufficiently homogenous nature and that can be specified to a sufficient degree in advance to be approached by using framework arrangements. But between completely standalone purchases (one-off) and those that can be consistently grouped together (in frameworks), organisations or projects usually face quite numerous procurement requirements that do not necessarily fall into any other of these categories, but that could be linked in some respects, in order to streamline their acquisition to the extent possible (through supplier lists).

6.4.2.4. *Choosing among Pre-Existing Arrangements*

It is possible that a purchaser may have access to a number of pre-existing arrangements for the same (or very similar) items. For example, in the UK, 'generic' multiple-supplier framework agreements have been extensively used.[82] These are frameworks usually established by centralised purchasing bodies that can

---

[82] Chapter 5, section 5.3.2.3.3 of this book.

be used by various purchasers in the covered sectors. However, users might not have been consulted or involved in the preparation of those frameworks by the bodies establishing them. In such cases, a user might not even be aware of the framework(s) that he is entitled to use, and in this connection a central register of all available arrangements appears particularly useful, as envisaged in the UK post-Brexit reform.[83] Where more than one already existing framework is available for a purchaser, the question arises as to which one should be chosen.

Regulatory instruments in the EU, the reviewed Member States, or the UK, do not address specifically these matters. However, in light of increasing use of 'Centralised purchasing techniques',[84] particularly in states where a plurality of centralised purchasing bodies operate, such rules or recommendations could be beneficial.

In order to ensure that purchasers are aware of the frameworks that they are entitled to use (as a prerequisite of comparing them), an obligation could be introduced for purchasers (ie, potential users) to ascertain the frameworks that they are entitled to use. For this purpose, consulting the central register envisaged in the UK post-Brexit procurement reform would be a very easy method. Where no such register is available, enquiring with the central purchasing bodies or any alternative means ought to be used. Also, in the absence of such a register, an obligation could be introduced requiring framework 'organisers' to inform all envisaged users of their access to procure under the framework in question. Certainly, as discussed in Chapter five, it would be preferable if the 'organiser' actually consulted and involved users both in the preparatory and in the execution phases, to take account of the estimated needs and monitor the execution of the envisaged purchases (and this does not affect the benefits of a central register).

In the literature it has been pointed out that

> Based on the transparency principle ... an obligation is arguably implied for the purchaser to show objective commercial grounds for choosing one particular framework, to ensure that the discretion to choose between frameworks is not abused for illegitimate reasons, such as to favour national providers.[85]

Value for money should also probably require objective commercial judgement when choosing among the frameworks.[86] It is just common sense for a purchaser to compare its options and choose the one that best satisfies its procurement needs and offers the best terms. Under the UK post-Brexit Procurement Bill, a similar obligation can likely be implied from section 11PB, generally requiring purchasers to 'have regard to' procurement objectives that include value for money, public benefit and integrity.

---

[83] Chapter 5, section 5.4.2 of this book.

[84] Recital 69 of EU 2014PSD.

[85] S Arrowsmith, *The Law of Public and Utilities Procurement*, 1st edn (London, Sweet & Maxwell, 2005) 692.

[86] A 'parallel' with placing an order under the GSA Schedules in the US federal system is possible on this point, though they are a significantly different type of arrangement.

In some cases, the 'assessment' of the frameworks that could be used may end up without a comparison per se being needed, for example where only one of the pre-existing frameworks meets the user's needs. Where the frameworks to which a user might have access were all of the type that had already established all terms, a comparison among the terms they offer would seem straight-forward. However, where both a framework establishing all terms and a framework involving reopening of competition at the call-off stage appear capable of meeting the user's envisaged need, *firm* terms (under the former type of framework) would need to be weighed against (some) *likely* terms[87] to be offered during second-stage mini-competition (under the latter type). It could happen that the terms already established at the first stage under both types of frameworks provide, on their own, a sufficient and meaningful basis for comparison. But in many cases this is improbable, since very relevant terms, such as the price, may be subject to the reopening of competition. On the other hand, in some cases, the more efficient/convenient ordering 'procedure' (including reduced time and administrative costs) involved by a framework which establishes all terms might, in itself, offer a sufficient reason to opt for it. Where two (or more) frameworks involving reopening of competition are 'assessed', a comparison between *likely* terms may need to be conducted. The matters might benefit from further investigation in relation to future regulations or guidance. In the EU, comparing frameworks placed by central purchasing bodies in different Member States may become relevant.[88]

Options between a pre-existing framework arrangement and a pre-existing 'supplier list' type of arrangement, in systems where these coexist,[89] are likely to be straight-forward, in light of the nature of the two types of arrangement. If a framework arrangement can satisfy the purchaser's envisaged need, it is probable that the convenience of simply placing an order under the framework will be convincing. But if none of the available frameworks meets the user's needs, he might consider using an already existing 'list' arrangement, since at least some part of a full purchasing exercise (ie, 'suitability') has already been carried out at the time the purchaser initiates its exercise.

Another hypothesis that might arise in the context of 'generic' frameworks concerns the type of needs that users could satisfy by making a 'call-off' under a framework established by a centralised purchasing body – namely, whether an order should only address a 'one-off' type of need, or whether a call-off placed by a user could in fact consist of a (secondary) framework arrangement meeting a recurrent or indefinite need of the user in question.[90] In the US, under the GSA Schedules system, there is explicit provision for 'blanket purchasing agreements' that can be concluded by agencies with schedule contractors to address an agency's recurrent needs. Across the Atlantic, in France there is explicit provision that a

---

[87] ie, those not established, or not precisely established, at the first stage.
[88] eg, art 39PSD.
[89] eg, in the EU (and Member States) utilities sector.
[90] Or, possibly, such needs of a group of purchasers among users of primary framework.

call-off under a framework agreement involving reopening of competition could consist of a '*marché à bons de commande*' (framework agreement establishing all terms).[91] The EU directives do not address the matter explicitly, and a number of interpretations are possible.[92] It also seems that 'secondary frameworks' may be permitted under the post-Brexit Procurement Bill.[93] These matters go beyond the strict subject of 'generic frameworks' and are dealt with at section 6.6.3 below. It is worth mentioning here the complexities that might arise if a user intended to award a call-off consisting of a (secondary) framework arrangement and had available a number of (primary) frameworks to choose from. Such occurrence might not be entirely excluded and the policy on it is at the moment unclear.

6.4.3. Approaches at Regulatory Level for Guiding Purchasers[94]

Purchasers' decisions on whether or not to use a PUIR arrangement, including the selection among various types of PUIR arrangements, can be influenced or driven at regulatory level mainly by two aspects. The first aspect refers to imposing an obligation on purchasers to justify their decisions to employ PUIR and to record that decision and the reasons justifying it. This requirement could be subject to internal review (or approval),[95] to 'external' approval,[96] to judicial review,[97] or a combination of the above. These reflect many nuances of how thoroughly the requirement for an analysis of the envisaged need and relevant market conditions, as well as for justifying PUIR decisions, is to be implemented through regulation. The second aspect refers to providing actual conditions for use of PUIR, or various types thereof. These are circumstances to which a regulatory instrument relates permission (or denial of permission) to organise PUIR. Such circumstances may concern the characteristics of the estimated procurement need, or features of the relevant market. The two aspects may be used together or separately.

Four positions appear thus possible. First, an instrument could provide both for a requirement for decision justification and recording, and for conditions. This is the case, for example, in the US federal system regarding (some) decisions concerning single- or multiple-supplier indefinite-delivery contracts, or in the UNCITRAL Model Law regarding whether or not a framework agreement can be used, rather than 'traditional' purchasing. A variant of this position could involve the provision of preferences in the legal instrument, accompanied by the

---

[91] Chapter 5, section 5.3.2.4.2 of this book.
[92] ibid.
[93] s 44(1)PB in relation to s 2PB.
[94] This section does not refer to options concerning the use of any pre-existing arrangements.
[95] See the US system (Chapter 4 of this book).
[96] As in WB-financed projects.
[97] As in the UNCITRAL Model Law.

possibility for purchasers to proceed differently than the preferred option in the instrument, provided that there is substantive justification for this (an example of this approach in a legal instrument is the provision on multiple-award preference in the FAR). Such approach could in fact be useful on a larger scale in regulating PUIR in a balanced and flexible way, beyond decisions between 'traditional' procurement and PUIR or between various types of PUIR.

Second, the requirement to document and justify a decision may not be accompanied by conditions provided for in the instrument. For example, this is the case of the UNCITRAL Model Law in as far as decisions among various types of framework agreements are concerned.[98] Here the circumstances supporting the option selected are to be identified by the purchaser and their appropriateness is to be confirmed, or denied, through judicial review (if challenged). Enacting states using the Model Law can, however, include conditions in their laws, from the circumstances recommended in the Guide to Enactment.

A third position might be to have no requirement for decision justification, but to provide for conditions. In such cases it would still be advisable for entities to keep records of decisions (even though not required), since this will help them deal with enforcement mechanisms (such as supplier review).

The fourth position is where the legal instrument (hard law) provides neither for a requirement for decision justification, nor for conditions. This has been the case, example, for previous and current EU directives, and for implementing instruments in the Member States reviewed. As shown, the approach seems appropriate for the directives, in light of their role for the EU's internal market, but it might be questionable in Member States, particularly where it is not supplemented by meaningful guidance on the subject. The 2014PSD appears to preclude Member States from including in their domestic instruments conditions for use of the various types of framework agreements it provides for. In contrast, the 2004PSD allowed for such measures to be included at national level, but the Member States reviewed had not made use of this margin of discretion.

Each procurement system can choose, from the means discussed above, a combination that suits its balance of objectives in its relevant context. Such means should be regarded (together with other appropriate requirements) as methods to facilitate and promote beneficially the use of PUIR in confidence, rather than unnecessarily inhibiting the use of certain types or configurations.

For instance, while potentially very effective in 'driving' PUIR decisions, the combination 'requirement to justify decision plus conditions provided for in the instrument' could result in rather inflexible mechanisms, as it might be argued that the older legislation in France under the 2001 and 2004CMP was in certain respects concerning frameworks. As shown, a more flexible option could involve the provision of preferred options in the legal instrument, permitting, however, purchasers to proceed differently than the preferred option in the instrument if

---

[98] This decision is distinct from a general decision to embark on a framework agreement.

there are substantive good reasons for this. On the other hand, providing for the possibility of subjecting PUIR decisions (and justifications) to judicial review by potential bidders[99] seems an adequate approach in most cases[100] and particularly where such review mechanism involves a reasonably low level of disruption to the procurement process.[101] This would require that the decision and justification are publicly available from the initiation of the award procedure for the PUIR arrangement, and that a short time-limit for challenging (and for settling the challenge) is provided for. Certainly, in the case of procurement initiated during or in the aftermath of an emergency/crisis and needed to deal with the consequences of such disaster, or of other situations involving properly defined (major) public interest, challenges should not result in stopping or suspending the procurement.

6.5. Controls: Duration and Various Facets of Stage Consistency

Controls could be regarded as legal requirements aimed at securing an appropriate and beneficial operation of PUIR, other than procedural requirements per se, or review mechanisms. Whilst 'conditions' discussed in the preceding section drive decisions to embark on PUIR, controls prevail *after* the establishment of PUIR. Controls seek to secure that the 'parameters' initially established for an arrangement are not substantially altered during the period of arrangement, and that certain features of an arrangement do not affect equal/fair treatment or competition.

Some of the controls are straight-forward, for example the requirement for the duration of a closed framework arrangement to be limited, and not to exceed a maximum period as provided for in an applicable regulatory instrument. The purpose of this limitation is to prevent 'market closure' as regards purchases under the framework for an indefinite or excessively long period, which would affect competition. Certainly, a purchaser should determine in each case a reasonable and appropriate duration of a closed framework, by taking into account the anticipated requirements and market features, and not 'automatically' use the maximum permitted duration. In some systems – such as under the EU directives – it is

---

[99] As under the UNCITRAL Model Law.

[100] I have already suggested that consideration could be given *de lege ferenda* to requiring justification of decisions to embark on 'traditional' purchasing as well (ie, as opposed to PUIR). Such decision might also benefit (in some cases/contexts) from being subject to judicial review; see also n 101.

[101] Certainly, standing/competence should be limited to reviewing 'abusive motives or … error' (and/or whether legal conditions for use are met, where applicable) and should not include 'commercial merits of the choice' as per C Nicholas and S Arrowsmith, 'The Challenges of Constructing a Supplier Review Mechanism for Urgent Procurement: An Analysis in the Context of the UNCITRAL Framework' in S Arrowsmith et al (eds), *Public Procurement in (a) Crisis: Global Lessons from the Covid-19 Pandemic* (Oxford, Hart Publishing, 2021) 156, 159.

permitted to use a longer period than the maximum period recommended by an instrument, where there is justification for this. However, other systems are stricter on this matter. The WB current regulations, for instance, provide for a maximum of three years, with a possible extension of a further two years, but no possibility for longer duration beyond this is envisaged. In general, a maximum period of three to five years is considered to offer a reasonable balance, though in some sectors longer maximum recommended periods are provided, for example in the EU defence sector (seven years), and EU utilities sector (eight years).

For a genuinely open arrangement, its duration is far less relevant, since suppliers can join the arrangement at any time and the market is not closed and competition is thus unlikely to be affected. Also rather straight-forward are prohibitions of making (substantial) amendments to closed frameworks.

However, other controls that could be very relevant are more difficult to 'pin down', as they might be implicit rather than explicit in the instruments, or arise from general principles in a particular system. 'Stage-consistency' controls fall into this category. An example is consistency between the criteria used in a closed framework arrangement at the two stages. While some differences between the two sets of criteria may be inherent in some cases, radical discrepancies may detract from achieving the objectives of the framework. It is important that both sets of criteria 'converge' towards the particular features of the subject-matter of call-offs and take account of relevant market features. For instance, selecting framework contractors for consultancy projects based on lowest price (only), followed by awarding orders under that framework using the criterion of the most economically advantageous tender (ie, focusing on quality of proposals), may easily result in selection of framework contractors who are not particularly relevant for the actual call-offs. This is unlikely to make sense commercially. But also, where the use of inconsistent criteria means that contractors that might have been better placed to meet call-offs were not admitted on the framework arrangement, equal treatment might be breached as well.

Similar consequences can also be generated by issuing excessive orders, such as what is referred to as 'down-selection' within the US federal system: the placement of an order that reduces 'the group of potential vendors', for example by narrowing 'the field of eligible vendors for future orders under a multiple award ID/IQ contract to a single vendor'.[102] This is one of the reasons for which a task or delivery order could be subject to a protest before the Government Accountability Office (GAO). Indeed, down-selections call into question the number of suppliers allowed by the purchaser to become a party to the arrangement in the first place. Thus, it could be regarded as a stage-consistency issue, and it likely involves misuse or an abusive operation of a closed framework arrangement. In the EU

---

[102] NB Bleicher, WI Dunn, DI Gordon and JL Kang, 'Accountability in Indefinite-Delivery/ Indefinite-Quantity Contracting: The Multifaced Work of the U.S. Government Accountability Office' (2008) 37(3) *PCLJ* 375, 390.

context, a similar obligation appears to apply under the requirement for framework agreements 'not to be used improperly or in such a way as to prevent, restrict or distort competition'.[103] On the other hand, an order of a particularly long duration, large quantity, or high value issued toward the end of the duration of a closed arrangement that is out of proportion by comparison to usual call-offs under that arrangement, could also be an excessive call-off. It de facto extends the closed framework when, instead, reopening the competition to the market for those requirements should have occurred.

Another aspect of stage consistency relates to ensuring that terms offered by framework suppliers at the call-off stage are in direct relation to those offered to access a closed framework. From this perspective, objective price/terms adjustment mechanisms may need to be included from the outset. It should be noted that an adjustment mechanism appears more straight-forward to devise and implement where all terms are established during first stage of a framework or some terms are subject to refining at the call-off stage. The matter could be more challenging, though, when some terms were not established at all during the first stage, since there would be no reference point for call-offs. In such cases, it might have been preferable to opt for an open framework arrangement in the first place.

Stage consistency involves many facets, as discussed in previous chapters. Devising appropriate means to achieve it could be challenging in light of the inherent flexibility envisaged for PUIR, but much needed if such arrangements, and in particular closed frameworks, are to achieve their intended objectives. Some inspiration could be found, mutatis mutandis, in the provisions of the 2011 UNCITRAL Model Law on Public Procurement and the attending Guide to Enactment. In any event, stage consistency appears to need increased attention in regulation, policy and/or guidance.

6.6. Procedures

6.6.1. First-Stage Procedures: Setting Up the Arrangement

First-stage procedures are determined by the type of arrangement. By the very nature of a PUIR arrangement, involving incomplete transactions at the first stage,[104] the procedures for setting up such arrangements, inevitably, also tend to be incomplete in some respects compared to 'traditional' purchasing. As shown, some types and/or configurations of PUIR arrangements lean actually very close

---

[103] Recital 61 of EU 2014 Public Sector Directive, art 51(2)3 of EU 2014 Utilities Directive, and art 29(2)6 of 2009 Defence Directive.
[104] As discussed at section 6.1 above.

to traditional purchasing. For example, for the award of a single-supplier (closed) framework arrangement that establishes all core/key terms, very few procedural 'adjustments' are likely to be needed, compared to 'traditional' purchasing. However, the further away a PUIR arrangement departs from that position, the more different first-stage procedures are likely to be.

In the reviewed systems, generally, there is convergence that 'traditional' award procedures are used for awarding all (recognised) types of closed framework arrangements. The process usually involves some level of competition at the first stage, against a common time-limit for submission of bids, followed by a competitive assessment of bids and reduction of the number of contractors to be admitted onto the arrangement, on this competitive basis. Some additional aspects certainly need to be addressed, such as informing the market that a framework is envisaged, its characteristics, estimated quantities, second-stage rules, terms that may be refined then, etc. Also, care needs to be exercised in handling the envisaged number of suppliers, including aspects of potential abuse, such as permitting a higher number than envisaged simply to favour a particular supplier, or only allowing a lower number in order to prevent a certain supplier from joining. Thus, in case of multiple-supplier frameworks, once the tender evaluation and the ranking of bids submitted as per the award criteria are complete, the award goes to the appropriate number of suppliers, in the order of evaluation ranking. For instance, where a certain maximum number of suppliers is envisaged, all bidders from the one ranked first to that maximum number are to be admitted to the framework, whereas those ranked lower than the maximum would not be admitted.

Apart from such adjustments, procedurally, there are no significant differences from 'traditional' purchasing. The systems reviewed provide for the possibility to use the entire range of 'traditional' award procedures when establishing a closed framework arrangement. Certainly, in case of award procedures only permitted in certain conditions – such as procedures involving less open competition or less 'transparency' – both conditions for using (a certain type of) closed framework (where applicable) and conditions for the award procedure would have to be met. The closer a framework arrangement is to a 'traditional' purchase, such as a single-supplier framework or an arrangement establishing all terms, the more amenable it is likely to be to a variety of first-stage procedures, possibly including, where justified, those not providing for full and open competition.[105] A case-by-case analysis of the procurement need and circumstances surrounding it will indicate what first-stage procedure for a closed framework arrangement is likely to be appropriate. As with 'traditional' purchases, in most cases the use of procedures providing for the widest transparency and competition are likely to be beneficial for frameworks as well. Such analysis could start from those procedures, and consider the 'special' ones only where needed.

---

[105] An aspect addressed in the context of 2011 UNCITRAL Model Law on Public Procurement, by C Nicolas in 'A critical evaluation of the revised UNCITRAL Model Law provisions on regulating framework agreements' (2012) 21 *PPLR* 19, 39–40. It is relevant also to other systems.

The further away a PUIR arrangement departs from traditional purchasing, the more significant adjustments to first-stage procedures are needed. This is particularly the case of genuinely open arrangements on the supply side. Certainly, providing for the possibility of suppliers joining an arrangement at any time during its duration is incongruent with having a common deadline for submission of bids by all interested suppliers and evaluating them competitively.[106] Some characteristics of first-stage procedures for genuinely open arrangements derive from this. First, to ensure that the arrangement remains open, it is vital for the market to be made aware and kept aware of this feature throughout the arrangement duration. Thus, permanent publication of the solicitation is required for dynamic purchasing systems in the EU, and repeat publication at least annually for open framework agreements under the UNCITRAL Model Law. Second, since no competition takes place at the first stage, genuinely open arrangements can either provide just for 'suitability' assessment of interested suppliers, or for this together with establishing some terms but not in a competitive fashion.[107] In effect, in genuinely open arrangements, applications for admission (ie, submissions) can only be assessed by reference to the requirements stated by the purchaser in the solicitation. Third, it is important for admission applications to be assessed within a reasonably short period of time, such as is provided for EU dynamic purchasing systems, but not for EU qualification systems (in the utilities sector), as was discussed in Chapter five, section 5.3.4. Certainly, admission criteria must be equal for all interested applicants.

Establishing terms during the first stage of a genuinely open arrangement (such as open framework agreements under the UNCITRAL Model Law or dynamic purchasing systems under the EU system) can be more nuanced. Some terms in these arrangements may be included by the purchaser in the solicitation, as 'requirements' or 'conditions' for admission, in a similar way to 'qualification' or 'selection' criteria. For example, specific minimum warranty or maintenance conditions, as specified by the purchaser, could be required for any future purchases (in addition to technical specifications). Interested bidders must confirm/accept observing these requirements in their applications to join the arrangement. Such terms are initially established by the purchaser (as limits, or even firmly, where applicable) and then 'ratified' by suppliers upon applying for admission.

It is relevant to note that the so-called 'indicative submissions'[108] in UNCITRAL open framework agreements should be regarded, in fact, just as partly indicative,

---

[106] As mentioned, the 'open' frameworks in the UK post-Brexit Procurement Bill (and some configurations under the IBRD regulations) appear in fact as a series of subsequent closed frameworks on similar terms; they thus only permit newcomer suppliers to apply for admission at predetermined points during the duration of the arrangement and *not* anytime; given this hybrid nature, open frameworks in the UK Bill refer to two configurations: one with a limited number of suppliers and one without such limit (though the latter appears to defeat the concept of a competitive first stage).

[107] In the UK Post-Brexit Procurement Bill, for the open framework configuration without limit on the number of suppliers, the method for establishing terms at the first stage appears unclear (see also preceding note).

[108] Art 60 of the UNCITRAL Model Law.

since terms confirmed by bidders at the first stage can only be improved at the call-off stage (as they have been conditions for admission). Where terms presented by applicants in first-stage submissions exceed (rather than just confirm) the purchaser's requirements, two approaches appear possible. Certainly, any course of action would need to be clearly stated in the procurement documents for the arrangement. First, those terms can be deemed committing for the bidder but only at the level required by the purchaser, as a condition for being admitted onto the arrangement. If, for example, the purchaser requires that any supplies delivered under any call-offs have a warranty period of at least one year, a bidder may offer in its application a warranty period of two years. The purchaser determines that the two-year warranty period meets its one-year requirement, and considers that the bidder commits to a one-year warranty period (as its minimum offer for call-offs competitions). Within a second approach, where terms offered by applicants for admission onto a (genuinely) open framework arrangement exceed those required by the purchaser, those terms could be deemed committing at the level offered by that bidder. Taking the same warranty period example as above, the purchaser determines that the two-year warranty period meets its one-year requirement, but considers that the bidder may be, or will be, required to commit to two-year warranty period in call-offs. This approach appears to be envisaged for dynamic purchasing systems in the 2014 EU Public Sector and Utilities Directives, in the option involving submission of electronic catalogues by purchasers at the first stage and the purchaser then using those electronic catalogues at the call-off stage to 'constitute tenders' adapted to a particular call-off.[109] In fact, the purchaser does not 'constitute tenders', which would defeat the very idea of competition, but prepares the basis of competition using the electronic catalogues received with a view to having them 'completed' by suppliers for the purposes of the call-off in question. When implementing this technique in practice, purchasers need to exercise great care for securing equal treatment.

In the US federal procurement system an alternative 'method' of establishing terms at the first stage, without a competitive exercise per se, can be found in the GSA Schedules. Here, as shown, the submission from a supplier applying for admission is assessed against, and must at least equal, the 'most privileged price' offered by that supplier to any other client of his (in addition to an assessment of the supplier's 'responsibility', including eligibility and qualifications). The arrangement is suitable for a plurality of purchasers without the need of detailed estimates from each purchaser, since the terms offered at the first stage are 'geared' to the high *potential* of sales that a purchasing vehicle available to all US federal Government agencies presents. The arrangement provides for flexibility, potentially without affecting the terms offered, though it seems difficult to assess whether a committing arrangement of large scale (and involving competition at the first stage) could result in better terms. The 'success' of GSA Schedules is 'enabled' by the sheer

---

[109] Art 36(6)2 of 2014PSD and art 54(6)2 of 2014UD.

volume of the US federal Government purchasing, capable of attracting suppliers to offer their 'most privileged price' in light of potential sales, without guarantee of sales. This could explain why a similar arrangement is not present in any of the other procurement systems reviewed in this book.

As regards 'supplier list' arrangements, first-stage procedures simply tend to be 'incomplete' procedures by reference to a 'traditional' award procedure. It is only the 'suitability' of applicants for supplying/providing certain items that is being assessed against the requirements (possibly including specifications) stated by purchaser. No terms are being established. All applicants meeting the requirements are admitted, though a further reduction of the number of 'suitable' candidates could take place. Examples in the systems reviewed include 'qualifications systems' in the EU (and Member States) utilities sector, the EU dynamic purchasing systems in their 'standard' configuration of the 2014 EU Public Sector and Utilities Directives, and dynamic markets envisaged in the post-Brexit Procurement Bill.

6.6.2. Second-Stage Procedures: Call-Offs or Nearly Full Award Procedures

6.6.2.1. Call-Off Procedures under Single-Supplier Framework Arrangements

For PUIR arrangements leaning closer to the 'traditional purchasing' end of the spectrum, call-off procedures tend to be straight-forward. Thus, in a single-contractor framework arrangement[110] call-offs are generated/awarded by the purchasers, with or without consultations with the supplier,[111] and in any case, according to the terms and within the 'margins' set when the arrangement was established.

6.6.2.2. Call-Off Procedures under Multiple-Supplier Framework Arrangements that Establish All Terms

Moving now a little further away from traditional purchases, to multiple-supplier frameworks that establish all terms (with precision) at the first stage, it can be noticed that awarding call-offs based on those terms without reopening of competition has received limited attention. This applies to both regulatory instruments and guidance. In this type of framework, awarding call-offs does not involve the establishment or refinement of terms, but only allocation of work among

---

[110] Such as a framework agreement of this type under the UNCITRAL Model Law, or in the EU (including Member States), or a requirements contract in the US federal system.

[111] The possibility of consultations is explicitly provided for under the EU Public Sector and Defence Directives (and implied in the Utilities Directive).

framework contractors. The terms applicable to an actual purchase will be those set at the first stage.

The relationship between objectivity and equal treatment has been discussed in the EU chapter. It is useful to revisit here the implications this is likely to have for the call-off stage of frameworks establishing all terms. It is submitted that, unless compelling reasons dictate otherwise, the typical position should be for call-offs to be allocated to the supplier who ranks first (offers best value) *for the call-off in question* based on its initial tender and on pre-determined evaluation criteria for call-offs. If the first ranked framework supplier for the call-off in question is unable (or simply not available, if the framework is not committing for the suppliers) to perform it then the call-off should be offered to the second ranked supplier, and so on (the 'cascading' method).[112] Where call-offs have similar 'structure' to the overall estimation of needs (and award criteria for call-offs are the same as, or very similar to, the award criteria for the framework itself) it is possible that the best ranked supplier at the first stage also ranks best for the call-offs. If this happened throughout the duration of the framework for all call-offs, the plurality of suppliers could be called into question, since better planning at the outset might have pointed towards a single-supplier framework.

However, some parameters may 'vary' from one call-off to another during the life of a framework. For example, only some items from the overall schedule of items covered by the framework may be required in a call-off. It could be that for those specific items the original tender submitted by tenderer A at the first stage provides better prices than those offered by tenderer B, even though the total price offered by tenderer B was the best of all tenders for the overall schedule of items and estimated quantities (throughout the framework), which had been used for the purposes of evaluation at first stage.[113]

Unless specific quantities are established, or minimum quantities are guaranteed, *for each* of the framework contractors *individually* when the framework is set (namely, total overall quantities under the framework for each framework contractor), 'aleatory' methods for allocating call-offs among frameworks contractors – such as by rotation or in alphabetical order – should be avoided.[114] The same applies to frameworks establishing a guaranteed (or minimum guaranteed) quantity under the framework, for all framework suppliers jointly, but without breaking that quantity down into specific quantities guaranteed for each framework supplier. These methods, in those circumstances (ie, lacking guaranteed quantities *for each individual supplier*) could affect value and equal treatment, as well as fail the required 'objectivity' test. They could also be easily abused, for example by manipulating quantities and issuing larger call-offs to a preferred supplier and much smaller ones to the others. Even manipulation excluded, it could easily happen that using,

---

[112] See for further details Albano and Nicholas (n 1) 60–66.

[113] For simplicity, this example uses the price as the only award criterion but similar situations may arise in practice where both price and non-price criteria are used.

[114] See discussion in Albano and Nicholas (n 1) 66–69.

say, the alphabetical order method would not 'direct' the call-off to the supplier whose initial offer provides best value for the specific call-off in question.

It would be superficial to regard 'aleatory' methods as 'objective' simply because they are publicised in advance and, in theory, they are not subject to interference in that they operate 'mechanically' in accordance with a pre-established order. Where overall quantities to be procured under the framework are not guaranteed individually for each framework contractor, 'aleatory' methods for allocation of call-offs among them are likely to present the 'objectivity' of a lottery for the purchaser and contractors alike.

Conversely, those methods may be valid where overall quantities for each framework supplier have been established when the arrangement is set in order to fulfil the (minimum) guaranteed requirements. In such cases quantities guaranteed to each supplier provide controls as to the overall allocation of work, and the actual distribution of call-offs is neutral from both value and fair treatment viewpoints. A 'mechanical' method for distributing call-offs – such as rotation or alphabetical order – does not affect the overall quantities for each supplier, or the overall value for the purchaser under the framework (though manipulation of the timing and quantities of individual orders to various suppliers might be an issue in some cases).

This type of arrangement could be useful for security of supply. The purchaser could allocate overall quantities under the framework for each of the successful tenderers based on the terms in their tenders at the first stage. For example, it could pre-determine in the framework procurement documents that the first ranking bidder gets 50 per cent of the overall guaranteed quantity, the second ranked gets 30 per cent and the third gets 20 per cent. However, where the requirement on demand is scarce, an alternative approach could be pursued. A purchaser may ask tenderers to state in their tenders (at first stage) the overall quantity they commit to supply under the framework. When evaluating offers, the purchaser admits onto the framework the number of suppliers needed to cover the intended overall quantities and in the order of their ranking.

A call-off allocation method based on ranking of tenderers during the first stage (and cascading, as necessary) could also be used to secure minimum or guaranteed quantities to each framework supplier, if allocations on this basis to each of them are limited to those guaranteed quantities. Specific attention needs to be given to the situation where an arrangement provides for *minimum* overall quantities for each framework supplier and the purchaser is entitled to make orders above those minima, once the minima for all framework suppliers have been met. Irrespective of the method used for making call-offs up to fulfilling individually defined minima, any additional order should be awarded to the contractor whose initial tender to enter the framework offers best terms (ie, ranks first) as applied to a specific call-off.[115] This is because any maximum for each individual supplier

---

[115] Using criteria for the call-off stage. Cascading should apply as well.

will not be guaranteed, meaning that above the minimum guaranteed, using 'aleatory' methods could result in inadequate value or could be abused, for example by favouring certain suppliers with higher orders. An alternative method for awarding orders above the minimum guaranteed for each framework supplier could be by reopening competition among them. The possibility of having a framework agreement establishing all terms under which some call-offs are awarded directly on those terms and other call-offs are awarded through reopening of competition is explicitly recognised in the 2014 Public Sector Directive, subject to certain conditions.

Other situations when 'aleatory' methods for awarding call-offs could be contemplated by a legislator or practitioner might include the need to avoid excessive/exclusive specialisation of a single source (which could affect further competition), or pursuing set-asides for SMEs or other objectives of 'horizontal' policies, as legally permitted, subject to required transparency, and taking care not to foster discretionary approaches or favouritism. However, given their potential for affecting value and for being abused, 'aleatory' methods should – as a matter of good practice – always be regarded as exceptional, and their use should require a thorough justification.

From this perspective, the silence of the 2011 UNCITRAL Model Law on Public Procurement in respect of call-offs without reopening competition seems particularly surprising, bearing in mind its rigorous approach to multiple-supplier frameworks involving reopening of competition. While it can be argued that the approach towards call-off allocation methods without reopening of competition in frameworks establishing all terms (with precision) is implied in the objectives of the Model Law,[116] the relevant consequences may not be immediately visible. In my view, the matter requires increased attention and explicit addressing in legal instruments.

From this perspective, an interesting possibility for frameworks that are non-committing for the purchaser is provided, as shown in Chapter 3, section 3.2.2.2, in World Bank SPDs. These link allocation amongst framework suppliers at the call-off stage (where mini-competition is not involved) to ranking of suppliers at the first stage and to an overall pre-determined and pre-disclosed total/upper value or quantity of aggregated call-offs to be awarded to each framework supplier. There, the supplier with the best ranking is first awarded call-offs up to the upper aggregated value/quantity; then the second lowest (or second-best ranking) receives call-offs to the aggregated limit, etc, thereby limiting the risk of manipulating orders, and providing some control as regards overall value for money under the arrangement (where there is consistency between orders and the overall schedule of items for the framework).

Still, as shown, I submit that, *de lege ferenda* and where regulations are silent, unless compelling reasons dictate otherwise, the typical position should be for

---

[116] Similar approach could relate to such call-offs under the EU directives.

each call-off (in frameworks that do not involve reopening of competition) to be allocated to the supplier who ranks first (offers best value) *for the call-off in question* based on its initial tender at the first stage and on pre-determined evaluation criteria for call-offs.

6.6.2.3. Call-Off Procedures Involving a 'Competitive' Exercise, Limitations and Exceptions Thereto, and Transparency Issues

As regards multiple-supplier frameworks that do not establish all terms (with precision) at the first stage, these usually involve reopening of competition at the call-off stage. That 'mini-competition' has a dual purpose: to complete the transaction in the sense of setting specific terms for the call-off that were not established (precisely) at the first stage in the framework arrangement; and to select the supplier to whom the call-off is awarded, with the aid of terms set or refined in the 'mini-competition'. In many cases, the choice of framework supplier to whom a call-off is awarded will be determined exclusively by the terms that are subject to reopening of competition and the offers submitted by framework suppliers in this regard. For example, without limitation, where the call-off award criterion is the price alone, clearly all other terms established at the first stage with the framework suppliers are acceptable to the purchaser *and* irrelevant at the call-off competition stage. In effect those terms will not affect the call-off competition or its outcome.

However, in cases where call-off award criteria involve a combination of price and non-price factors, two different situations may arise. First, the terms subject to reopening of competition at the call-off stage are exhaustive of the terms considered in award criteria for the call-off. All other terms established at the first stage with the framework contractor are acceptable to the purchaser and irrelevant at the call-off competition stage. A second, more complex, situation entails that some terms established at the first stage (with each framework contractor) but not subject to reopening of competition at the call-off stage might still be considered, together with the terms that are subject to reopening of competition, in the overall call-off stage evaluation. Thus, some of the terms proposed by a framework supplier at the first stage to get admission onto the framework may also have some weighting in the award criteria for call-offs, even though those terms may not be subject to revision at the call-off stage. The latter option might be suggested by the 2014 EU Public Sector Directive and Utilities Directive for dynamic purchasing systems in the configuration involving use of electronic catalogues from which the purchaser collects information upon call-off competitions. However, the situations when this method could prove useful in practice appear limited, and it may affect (real) competition at the call-off stage.

Beyond the issue above, second-stage competitions are generally straightforward from a procedural point of view. Basically, they involve inviting all (relevant) framework suppliers to attend call-off competitions, providing for a reasonable time-limit that is common to all framework suppliers for making call-off submissions, and awarding the call-off based on pre-determined award criteria. The explicit procedural safeguards provided by the UNCITRAL Model Law regarding call-off competitions should be viewed as a source of inspiration including for procurement systems not using the Model Law and when implementing frameworks in such systems (to the extent not repudiated in those systems). Additional procedural safeguards could also be considered in some cases, such as a public opening of submissions, which is likely to increase trust among framework contractors that call-off awards are made correctly and transparently.

Particular attention needs to be given to transparency requirements at the call-off stage. Here again the UNCITRAL Model Law offers 'state-of-the-art' explicit provisions. First, it is important to ensure that all framework suppliers are aware of any call-off competitions, and not just some of them. The 'capability' of any framework supplier for any call-off under a framework should have been pre-assessed at the first stage, as a condition for their admittance onto the arrangement. A 'reassessment' of capability at the call-off stage would thus be an unnecessary and redundant exercise, defeating the 'philosophy' of PUIR, which is to carry out certain procedural steps just once for all (or at least a number of) purchases under the arrangement. Such 'reassessment' at call-off stage could also be easily abused, resulting in discretionary exclusions from call-off competitions.

Nevertheless, there may be situations when a framework supplier (or some framework suppliers) is/are not capable to carry out a particular call-off despite their 'general' capacity for the framework. For example, a call-off might be larger than the volumes estimated at the first stage and this could exceed the capability of a particular framework supplier. For such cases, as a procedural safeguard, it is important to ensure that the suppliers in those situations are at least informed of the intended call-off even if not invited.[117] That information needs to be issued at the same time as any invitations for the call-off so that suppliers not invited can defend their right to attend where appropriate.

Allowing a purchaser to exclude certain framework suppliers from call-off competitions without any transparency presents a high risk of misuse or abuse. It thus seems surprising that none of the EU Member States reviewed in this book have contemplated a requirement to inform all framework contractors about intended call-off competitions. Further, since erroneous or abusive exclusions from call-off competitions could affect not just best value[118] but equal treatment as well, including potential discrimination on a nationality basis, it is equally surprising that the said requirement is not provided for under the EU directives.

It should also be noted that even the US federal regulations – which provide for increased discretion for procurement officers in devising ID/IQ ordering

---

[117] Art 62(4)(a) of 2011 UNCITRAL Model Law on Public Procurement.
[118] Arguably, a concern mainly for Member States, and less so for regulation at EU law level.

procedures – require, where orders (above certain thresholds) are placed on a competitive basis, that a notice concerning that order must be made 'to all contractors offering the required supplies or services'[119] or 'to all awardees',[120] though specific exceptions apply.[121] However, for lower value orders[122] the contracting officer need not contact each of the multiple awardees under the ID/IQ contract before selecting an order awardee if the contracting officer has information available to ensure that each awardee (under the ID/IQ contract) is provided a fair opportunity to be considered for each order.[123]

In exceptional circumstances only one of the framework suppliers may have the 'capacity' to perform a certain call-off. This could be where technical reasons dictate that a single-source order is adequate (eg, the highly specialised nature of requirements) or where the call-off is a follow-on of a previous one and interoperability with the items purchased requires the use of the same supplier as for that previous order.[124] In such cases competition would be pointless and the establishment of (outstanding) terms will inevitably have to be through negotiation. Given the 'uniqueness' of the possibility to purchase the requirement under the existing arrangement, the purchaser's position to negotiate could be rather weak. This could be exacerbated where a framework is committing (or exclusive) for the purchaser, or non-committing for the supply side.

Situations like these, arising under *framework agreements*, are not dealt with specifically under the EU directives but they can arguably justify a call-off award to the 'capable' framework supplier without reopening of competition.[125] Nonetheless, under dynamic purchasing systems, no such limitation of call-off competition is permitted since 'Contracting authorities shall invite all admitted participants to submit a tender for each specific procurement'.[126] The silence of the EU directives in regard to the applicability (or otherwise) of circumstances allowing the use of the negotiated procedure without prior publication to call-offs (in frameworks envisaging second-stage competition) has generally been cascaded in the legal systems of the Member States reviewed. The notable exception is an explicit permission to award a call-off under a framework agreement that does not establish all terms without reopening competition for 'technical reasons' under the 2019 French Public Procurement Code (*Code de la commande publique* (CCP)).[127]

Looking across the Atlantic, as shown, it can be seen that FAR provides for circumstances similar to the 'technical reasons' exclusion referred to above, as

---

[119] FAR16.505(b)(1)(iii)(B)*(1)*.
[120] FAR16.505(b)(1)(iv).
[121] As to which see below.
[122] Under simplified acquisition threshold.
[123] FAR16.505(b)(1)(ii).
[124] FAR16.505(b)(2).
[125] Art 33(5)(a) of 2014PSD.
[126] Art 34(6)1 of 2014PSD; art 52(6)1 of 2014UD.
[127] Art R2162-10 of the 2019CCP.

justification for making awards to a specific ID/IQ contractor without consult-ing the others. Such circumstances include where 'Only one awardee is capable of providing the supplies or services required at the level of quality required because the supplies or services ordered are unique or highly specialized'[128] or 'The order must be issued on a sole-source basis ... because it is a logical follow-on to an order already issued under the contract, provided that all awardees were given a fair opportunity to be considered for the original order'.[129] Other similar situa-tions are listed in the FAR, including a need that 'is so urgent that providing a fair opportunity would result in unacceptable delays'[130] and where 'It is necessary to place an order to satisfy a minimum guarantee'.[131]

At the same time, it is certainly important to ensure that exceptions from order-stage competitions are not misused or abused. Under the FAR this is done by requiring justification for such course of action, as well as the approval thereof.[132] However, the circumstances allowing for awards to a specific contractor, with-out considering the others, are regarded as 'exceptions to the fair opportunity process'.[133] It means that a notice to all awardees concerning an intended order is not generally required where an exception to the competitive exercise is to be applied to that order. But FAR *does* require the publication of a notice concerning the award of an order for most cases when exception to the fair opportunity is pursued.[134]

From this perspective, the fact that the 2014 EU directives offer the option not to publish any award notice for any contracts awarded under framework agreements presents significant risks.[135] Since there is no requirement to inform framework contractors about an intended call-off under a limitation of, or excep-tion to, reopening of competition, as well as no requirement to publish a contract award notice, such awards may be completely 'below the radar' of any supplier review.

Under the UNCITRAL Model Law particular situations potentially lead-ing to limitations of, or exceptions from, second-stage competition under closed framework agreements that do not establish all terms *and* under open frame-work agreements are not addressed explicitly. However, limitations or exceptions attributable to 'capacity' can be dealt with by using the 'transparency' option that

---

[128] FAR16.505(b)(2)(i)(B).
[129] FAR16.505(b)(2)(i)(C).
[130] FAR16.505(b)(2)(i)(A).
[131] FAR16.505(b)(2)(i)(D).
[132] FAR16.505(b)(2)(ii).
[133] FAR16.505(b)(2). Providing 'each awardee a fair opportunity to be considered for each order exceeding the micro-purchase threshold' is the general rule for making orders under multiple-supplier ID/IQ contracts: FAR16.505(b)(1). The micro-purchase threshold is usually US$10,000 under FAR2.101. 'Fair opportunity' consists of different transparency and 'competition' requirements.
[134] FAR16.505(b)(2)(ii)(D).
[135] Some EU Member States have adopted this possibility, eg France.

provides for issuing invitations for intended call-offs to the framework suppliers *'then capable* of meeting the needs ... *provided that at the same time notice of the second-stage competition is given to all parties* ... so that they have the opportunity to participate in the second-stage competition' (emphasis added).[136]

To conclude, none of the systems/instruments reviewed seems to address the matter of potential limitations of, or exceptions from, call-off competitions comprehensively. However, the UNCITRAL instruments and the US federal procurement system do provide for fairly coherent approaches. In contrast, the EU and the reviewed Member States seem to leave these matters much to the interpretation of practitioners. The subject might benefit from further attention in future reforms of all systems investigated. In light of such future adjustments a few suggestions are made below.

It is thus submitted that, first, the requirement to inform all framework suppliers of any intended call-offs should be introduced. This should apply both to limitations of and exceptions to competition. It needs emphasising that the requirement for a notice of any intended call-off cannot be regarded as an excessive burden: in closed framework arrangements the number of framework suppliers tends to be limited, whereas open frameworks (under both the EU directives and UNCITRAL Model Law) are conducted through electronic means. However, in case of extreme urgency, consideration could be given to publishing a call-off award notice only (upon or after the award of the call-off).

Second, for legal certainty it is preferable to state in legal instruments the circumstances in which limitations to and/or exceptions from competition at the call-off stage are permitted. Similarly, where a legislator takes a rigid approach and does not envisage any limitations or exceptions to call-off competitions, this should also be clearly stated.

Third, a requirement for justification of any limitation or exception to call-off competition should be included in the relevant legal instruments, together with any necessary details, such as an approval process for it. Consideration could also be given to providing that justification in the notification to framework suppliers not invited to the call-off in question. A clear explanation, at an early stage, of the objective reasons why a certain framework supplier is not invited to participate, could in many cases avoid supplier challenges. On the other hand, corrective measures can be taken quickly where necessary, including by the purchaser.

6.6.2.4. Further Transparency Matters Related to Framework Call-Off Procedures

Transparency at the call-off stage goes beyond the matter of informing *all* framework suppliers about intended call-offs under frameworks that involve competition

---

[136] Art 62(4)(a)(ii) of 2011 UNCITRAL Model Law on Public Procurement.

at the order stage. In this respect the UNCITRAL Model Law achieves a high level of 'diligence'. Additionally to the information requirement above, for this type of framework, the Model Law requires the purchaser, pursuant to evaluation of call-off submissions, to 'promptly notify each supplier and contractor that presented submissions of its decision to accept the successful submission at the end of the standstill period'.[137] It follows that contract awards under second-stage competitions within framework agreements are subject to a proper debriefing of unsuccessful contractors, allowing for meaningful challenges to awards to be lodged by the latter where appropriate.[138]

However, neither debriefing nor a standstill period applies to awards of procurement contracts within frameworks 'without second-stage competition'.[139] This approach is probably based on the idea that in case of these awards there is no other supplier/contractor to have presented submissions at second stage.[140] Nevertheless, *all* contracts under framework agreements (with or without second-stage competition)[141] are subject to a 'public notice of the award of a procurement contract'.[142] Contracts whose price is less than the threshold must be included in 'a cumulative notice of such awards' to be published at least yearly.[143] Thus, any contract under a framework agreement, including those under frameworks without second-stage competition, or those of low value, are subject to some 'visibility', at least post-award. Information requirements under the UNCITRAL Model Law provide for a significant degree of 'contestability' regarding call-offs within frameworks with second-stage competition, and some degree of 'contestability' concerning call-offs within frameworks without second-stage competition.

In contrast, the provisions of the EU directives suggest some limited consistency. On the one hand, rightly, the general policy is towards including call-offs within framework agreements and dynamic purchasing systems under the scope of the rules concerning review procedures, as provided for by the 'Remedies' directives. This is appropriate since call-offs are in fact the actual procurement contracts, whereas the framework agreement per se represents, rather, the outcome of a procedural stage and in any event an 'incomplete' transaction. Further, it is the call-off stage that allocates work among framework suppliers. It thus makes sense for call-offs to be subject to scrutiny, separately from and additionally to, that afforded to the framework arrangement itself.

Nevertheless, the 'transparency' requirements for framework agreements (as provided for in the directives) might not always support this objective thoroughly.

---

[137] Art 22(2). The requirement does not apply to awards of contracts whose 'price is less than the thresholds' or 'Where the procuring entity determines that urgent public interest considerations require the procurement to proceed without a standstill period' (art 22(3)(b) and (c)).
[138] Both the debriefing and standstill period do not apply to lower value awards.
[139] Art 22(3)(a) of the Model Law.
[140] Which could be questionable from a 'contestability' point of view.
[141] Just as any procurement contract, or indeed, framework agreement.
[142] Art 23(1) of the Model Law.
[143] Art 23(2) of the Model Law.

As shown at section 6.6.2.3 above, there is no (explicit) requirement for frameworks involving reopening of competition at the call-off stage to inform all framework suppliers of any intended call-off (competition), including those not invited to attend because they are not considered 'capable' for the call-off by the purchaser. Further, the 2014 EU Public Sector and Utilities Directives offer an option not to publish any sort of contract award notice for call-offs under framework agreements. Where that option is pursued, call-offs under frameworks establishing all terms and call-offs awarded under an exception to reopening of competition, will not be subject to any transparency measure, and thus completely 'below the radar' for any 'supplier-driven' review procedures. In these cases, the other framework contractors will not be aware that a call-off has been intended and/or awarded. This seems a peculiar approach for the directives, given that such call-offs could be of significant value, and the complete lack of transparency is likely to increase risks of discrimination, including on the basis of nationality.

It is also unclear why there is a difference in regulating contract award notices in the directives between call-offs under framework agreements and those under dynamic purchasing systems. In the latter case, such notices are required either for each individual call-off or grouped quarterly.[144] Thus, transparency through contract award notices is stronger under dynamic purchasing systems although call-offs are less vulnerable than those under framework agreements (since in dynamic purchasing systems all call-offs are subject to competition through inviting tenders from all suppliers admitted to the system).[145]

In the US federal system orders under ID/IQ contracting are generally exempt from 'transparency' requirements. Some categories of orders remain uncovered by any means of transparency. Nevertheless, the FAR does afford some publicity to certain orders placed under exceptions to fair opportunity (above the simplified acquisition threshold). This is something that the EU directives may fail to do in relation to call-offs awarded under limitations or exceptions to second-stage reopening of competition under framework agreements.

Also, a useful transparency feature of the US federal procurement system is a database available online and dedicated to PUIR 'intended for use by multiple agencies'.[146] Thus, when considering how to approach a particular procurement requirement, an agency has the opportunity to check, in a single place, whether any pre-existing procurement vehicle could be used to place an order to fill that need. It plays the role of a centralised 'repository' for all types of multiple-agency procurement vehicles.[147]

---

[144] eg art 50(3) of 2014PSD.

[145] eg art 34(6) of 2014PSD.

[146] FAR5.601. The website is www.contractdirectory.gov/contractdirectory/.

[147] A similar medium is envisaged in the post-Brexit UK procurement reform (see Chapter 5, section 5.4.2 of this book).

Concluding this section, it is suggested that, unless compelling reasons dictate otherwise, procurement officers should, as a matter of good practice, afford maximum possible transparency at the call-off stage of a framework arrangement. This might exceed the requirements of applicable legal instruments, which, as shown, may sometimes be incomplete or inconsistent. At policy level, legislators or policymakers may like to look at how other systems have addressed certain matters, as a source of inspiration. In many ways, the UNCITRAL Model Law and the attending guidance could play that role, but each system can provide 'ideas' for other systems, as shown.

6.6.2.5. *Mixed Call-Off Procedures and 'Limited' Competitive Exercise Call-Off Procedures*

Some systems provide for a certain type of call-off award procedure that is determined *only* by the type of framework arrangement, and that must be applied for any call-off within that framework. For example, the UNCITRAL Model Law provides that call-offs under closed framework arrangements not establishing all terms are awarded by reopening competition among (in principle) all framework suppliers, whereas call-offs under closed frameworks establishing all terms are awarded based on those terms and the rules provided for in the framework agreement, without reopening competition.[148]

Other configurations of framework, however, permit different types of call-off under the same arrangement. Thus, the EU's 2014 PSD explicitly allows, under a framework agreement that sets all terms, for some call-offs to be awarded *without* reopening competition and others *with* reopening of competition.[149] This configuration allows purchasers, for example, to award smaller orders (up to a certain threshold) without reopening competition, which provides maximum efficiency and convenience at the call-off stage; and to reopen competition for larger orders with a view to obtaining better terms for bulk sales.

Similarly, this 'mixed call-off procedure' configuration could be usefully implemented in frameworks that provide for a minimum quantity or value of purchases determined for each framework contractor individually (overall for the entire duration of the framework). Up to filling those minimum guarantees any method of allocation of call-offs could be used, including 'aleatory' ones.[150] For any call-offs above the minimum guarantees, a purchaser may consider reopening competition among framework contractors, or it may continue to award call-offs without reopening competition but not by using 'aleatory' allocation methods.

---

[148] Art 2(e)(iv) and (v) of Model Law. Somewhat similar provision can be found in the EU defence directive (DD) (art 29 (4)). However, as shown, under these instruments it is still probably possible to accommodate both types of call-off procedures under a single framework that establishes all terms.

[149] Art 33(4)(b).

[150] See section 6.6.2.2 above.

A distinct situation could arise in frameworks that do not establish all terms. In section 6.6.2.3 we looked at potential exceptions to call-off competitions. An addition to the circumstances which might justify such exception could be for call-offs of very low value. It could be more efficient for such call-offs to be awarded without reopening competition, for example by conducting a 'brief' consultation (negotiation) with the supplier whose terms as offered to access the arrangement (at the first stage) appear to be the best terms for the call-off.

In the past such an exception had been provided for in the French Public Procurement Code (CMP) for a specific type of 'framework' arrangement that normally involved reopening of competition at the call-off stage.[151] A maximum value for each individual call-off under the exception had been provided, as well as a maximum permitted annual aggregated value of such call-offs. Neither the EU directives nor the UNCITRAL Model Law currently provide for exceptions for small value call-offs.

However, such provision does exist in the US federal procurement system for orders below the 'micro-purchase threshold',[152] for which contracting officers are not bound to 'provide each awardee a fair opportunity to be considered'.[153] For orders above this threshold, the FAR provides for several ranges of order size depending on which increasing degrees of transparency, competition and contestability requirements apply to the ordering procedures. Contracting officers in the US federal system enjoy quite some discretion in designing ordering procedures, particularly regarding smaller orders, while 'full' competition among awardees under comprehensive procedural and transparency safeguards is provided for very large orders exceeding US$6 million.[154] Order protests, other than for reasons of 'down-selections'[155] or of exceeding 'the scope, period or maximum value of the contract', are only permitted for orders exceeding US$10 million.[156] While providing increased flexibility, which could be appropriate for the US federal system, this approach leaves outside effective scrutiny many multiple-award contract orders.

On balance, and in light of a potential 'starting point' for future reforms as regards framework arrangement call-off procedures, structuring these procedures by whether the framework establishes all terms of future purchases, or otherwise, subject to certain adjustments, seems preferable to a system of various degrees of 'competitive' and transparency requirements applicable to ranges of order sizes. Thus, for frameworks establishing all terms it probably makes sense

---

[151] Art 72(I)(4)(d)7 of 2001CMP; art 71(V)(3)(a) of 2004CMP. The exception and the specific type of framework were not carried forward into the (domestic) regulatory instruments that followed.

[152] Usually US$10,000 under FAR2.101.

[153] FAR16.505(b)(1).

[154] FAR16.505(b)(1)(iv).

[155] See section 6.5 above and Chapter 4, section 4.2.4 of this book.

[156] FAR16.505(a)(10)(i)(B). After 30 September 2016 the authority to protest such orders is maintained only for some agencies (Department of Defense, NASA and the Coast Guard), under FAR16.505(a)(10)(ii).

for call-offs to be awarded on the basis of those terms and conditions provided in the framework or, in *some* circumstances, through reopening of competition. Where the framework does not establish all terms, it usually makes sense to reopen competition among all framework suppliers, subject to full procedural and transparency safeguards, to establish (or refine) those outstanding terms needed for each specific call-off. Some exceptions from call-off competitions could be provided though, such as for technical reasons, extreme urgency or very low value orders.

6.6.2.6. *Second-Stage Procedures in 'Supplier List' Arrangements*

In 'supplier list' arrangements the second stage of the arrangement involves nearly-full 'standard' award procedures, except for the 'suitability' assessment having been conducted during the 'first stage'. That assessment could relate to all relevant aspects of 'qualification' (capability, experience, resources, including financial ones, etc), just some of these, and/or it could include specifications of items whose purchase is contemplated. The 'second stage' of the arrangement then completes that assessment as needed, with suppliers on the list who express interest in a specific contract and/or are selected in further qualification stages, and who have submitted (complete) tenders for the specific contract. Those procedures will be conducted only with suppliers that are on the 'list', in case of 'mandatory lists', such as qualification systems in the EU utilities sector. The intrinsic nature of such lists means that second-stage procedures are incongruent with open tendering procedures, since the latter must permit any interested supplier to submit a tender, and not just those whose 'suitability' has already been assessed. But 'restricted' procedures, 'negotiated' procedures or those involving dialogue with suppliers seem to fit a 'mandatory supplier list' arrangement. The actual choice of procedures is determined by the specific procurement system allowing for a mandatory list.

In case of optional lists though (as discussed, for example, in the context of EU official lists)[157] any 'second-stage' award procedure seems possible, including 'open tendering', since registration on that list is not compulsory as a condition for participation in certain award procedures. Thus, if a supplier not on an optional list submits a tender, the purchaser will just have to conduct both 'first stage' and 'second stage' together (for that tenderer and any other supplier who chooses this course of action).

Second-stage procedures for awarding individual contracts are usually not 'defined' at the first stage of a supplier list arrangement, but when an individual second-stage procurement process is actually initiated. Certainly, nothing prevents a purchaser from determining from the outset (when the list is initially established) the award procedure(s) that he intends to use at the second stage.

---

[157] Chapter 5, section 5.3.5 of this book.

Procedures 237

However, this is unlikely to bring any benefit for any of the parties and, instead, it affects the flexibility offered by the arrangement. Exceptionally, one of the arrangements reviewed establishes from the outset the procedure that is to be followed for the award of any contracts under it, ie dynamic purchasing system in the EU 2014 Public Sector and Utilities Directives.[158]

6.6.3. Intermediary Stage

Some configurations of PUIR may involve an intermediary stage. Examples in this connection are provided by the conclusion of a blanket purchase agreement (BPA) under US GSA Schedules, or the use of a qualification system in the EU utilities sector for awarding a framework agreement. These configurations involve three successive stages towards completing individual transactions, in parallel with narrowing down and specifying certain parts of the originally estimated requirement.

As regards the second example above, a qualification system might define some classes or types of items, and establish a 'list' of suppliers interested and assessed as generally 'qualified' ('suitable') to supply. The framework agreement exercise within the qualification system would then specify in more detail the requirement and establish some terms.[159] At the same time the framework exercise could limit the number of possible suppliers in light of the purchases contemplated under the framework, and how well the interested suppliers respond to the estimated requirement for the framework. Complete transactions arise only when individual contracts are placed under the framework.

Another possible scenario for arrangements involving an intermediary stage is what we call 'frameworks in frameworks': a configuration where a call-off under a framework arrangement is also a (secondary) framework arrangement, rather than a 'one-off order'. Certainly, such secondary framework must be consistent with the (primary) framework and subject to controls, for example awarding secondary frameworks only by using appropriate procedures (ie, properly adapted from those that would be applicable to 'one-off' orders under the primary framework), precluding secondary frameworks that could affect, limit or distort competition,[160] as well as using appropriate procedures for awarding orders under the secondary 'framework'. The procedure conducted under a 'primary' framework for awarding a call-off consisting of a 'secondary' framework would 'act' as an 'intermediary' stage towards complete purchase transactions (ie, orders under the secondary framework).

---

[158] The configuration that does not establish (at the first stage) terms for future purchases.
[159] Or establish all terms, but without commitment to buy, and/or sell.
[160] Or have an effect similar to a 'down-selection' (ie an excessive award that affects the reasonable chances and expectations of the other framework suppliers to get work under a framework).

As the US 'GSA Schedules' arrangement indicates, 'frameworks in frameworks' could be appropriate under large centralised schemes. Under this US federal arrangement, there is explicit recognition and regulation of such 'secondary frameworks' aimed at filling 'repetitive needs',[161] referred to as 'blanket purchase agreements' (BPAs). The relatively recent development of regulations concerning (specific) procedures for orders under BPAs seems to reflect both the use of BPAs *and* the need to control such use. BPAs can be single- or multiple-supplier arrangements, with a preference being stated in the FAR for 'multiple-award BPAs',[162] as well as single- or multiple-agency arrangements, subject to certain conditions.[163] Where a BPA is placed, procedures for awarding it represent an 'intermediary' stage of a purchase 'process' under GSA Schedules 'architecture'. The 'first stage' consists of assessing applications submitted by interested suppliers to become schedule awardees. The final stage consists of award procedures for individual orders under the BPA.

Another explicit recognition of possible 'framework in framework' configuration is provided by the French procurement system. Under the French Public Procurement Code, a call-off under a framework agreement not establishing all terms could be a (secondary) framework agreement that *does* set all terms.[164] This configuration could be very useful both for single- and multiple-purchaser frameworks, whether it involves a single- or multiple-supplier 'secondary framework'. Where specific (recurrent) requirements can be sufficiently defined when a call-off is initiated, such 'secondary framework' presents the significant advantage of eliminating the need for repeated competition for those recurrent needs (under the primary framework).

As discussed in the EU chapter, while the directives are silent regarding possibilities for intermediary stages (consequently, for 'frameworks in frameworks'), such call-offs are not explicitly ruled out either. It is possible to interpret the rules in the directives as permitting 'secondary frameworks' under framework agreements, which might apply to primary frameworks both of the type establishing all terms and of the type not establishing all terms (and it could also apply to dynamic purchasing systems). Similarly, regarding 'secondary' frameworks these too might be of the type establishing all terms and/or of the type not establishing all terms. However, the combination of a 'secondary' framework not establishing all terms under a 'primary' framework establishing all terms would be illogical.

Where the interpretation referred to in the preceding paragraph is contemplated, I emphasise the importance of appropriate conditions, controls and transparency requirements at each level of such arrangements. These need to be enhanced significantly since the consequences of misusing or abusing call-offs

---

[161] FAR8.405-3(a)(1).
[162] FAR8.405-3(a)(3)(i).
[163] FAR8.405-3(a)(6).
[164] Art R2162-8 of 2019CCP.

consisting of 'frameworks' could be (much) harder than those concerning 'one-off' orders. Some 'framework in framework' configurations could make more sense in case of multiple-purchaser 'primary' arrangements, and less so under single-purchaser ones. Also, leaving call-offs (consisting of 'secondary' frameworks) under 'primary' frameworks establishing all terms, outside any 'transparency' measure, in the same way that some 'one-off' orders inadvertently are under the current directives, could present a high risk of misuse or abuse. Potential negative consequences may be wider since a 'framework' call-off is likely to be longer term and higher value than a 'one-off' order. The same would apply for a 'framework' call-off awarded under a limitation or exception to reopening competition under a 'primary' framework not establishing all terms.

Appropriate decision-making processes – possibly 'driven' by conditions included in the applicable legal instruments – as to designing and establishing a 'primary' arrangement that could cater for 'secondary frameworks' are also very important. For example, policy might provide that such arrangements are only permitted to centralised purchasing bodies. But proper decisions are also needed at all levels (including the intermediary stage) of an arrangement like this. An unregulated 'inflation' of 'generic' framework arrangements (particularly those closed on the supply side), also permitting the award of secondary 'frameworks' under them, could have undesired effects on the procurement market.[165] From this perspective, whilst the fact that the UK post-Brexit Procurement Bill can easily be interpreted to permit the award of 'frameworks under frameworks' is very welcome, it remains to be seen whether additional requirements or guidance will be provided to promote their appropriate and balanced use.

The aspects above are just some examples of issues that should be considered when contemplating an explicit recognition of an intermediary stage under frameworks. It will be interesting to follow developments of the phenomenon of 'frameworks within frameworks' in the future, including (or even in particular) in 'non-US (federal)' environments.

6.7. Legal Review and Oversight

6.7.1. First Stage

As regards potential review avenues during the first stage of a PUIR arrangement, a distinction is necessary between closed and (genuinely) open arrangements on the supply side. Generally, in the procurement systems/instruments analysed in this book, procedures for the award of closed framework arrangements are subject

---

[165] See eg the discussion concerning 'generic' framework agreements in the UK (Chapter 5, section 5.3.2.3.3 of this book).

to review processes that are similar to those applicable to awards of 'traditional' procurement contracts.[166] This is usually straightforward and appropriate, though some issues may arise.

A theoretical exception from subjecting the first stage of a framework arrangement not establishing all terms (and involving reopening of competition) to review procedures could have been derived in France, under the 2006CMP, emerging from the classification of such frameworks as 'contracts', whereas the French and EC remedies provisions did not expressly refer to that type of framework.[167] But such an approach was, rightly, denied by the French administrative judiciary (including the Conseil d'État) that considered challenges against procedures for award of such framework arrangements.[168]

It is interesting (and quite worrying) that, after the passage of some time, some arguments in a couple of decisions of the CJEU might also be interpreted to call into question the scope of application of the Remedies Directive to the first stage of certain PUIR arrangements under the EU procurement directives.[169] However, it would be unreasonable to extrapolate in this way since the first stage of PUIR arrangements sets prerequisites for awards of procurement contracts, and it is an integral part of the two-stage PUIR procurement process. In the EU context it could also affect the principle of non-discrimination including based on nationality.

Beyond these aspects, in some systems, as shown in this book, certain specificities of frameworks may not be expressly addressed, or may be insufficiently or ambiguously addressed in substantive rules concerning the design and award of frameworks. This may also lead potentially to such aspects being improperly specified in procurement documents for a framework from the outset. Legal review of such issues could thus prove more complex and/or less effective. In these cases, the main cause of such undesirable outcomes rests with the substantive rules concerning frameworks, rather than with the actual review mechanisms, since those substantive rules may not provide appropriate arguments for a review exercise. Examples could include improperly specified criteria for awarding call-offs; the silence of legal instruments concerning allocation of work among framework contractors in frameworks establishing all terms at the first stage; some aspects of 'stage consistency'; whether a certain type of 'framework in framework' is permitted and under which conditions, etc. Another example may refer, in some legal instruments, to the lack of specified conditions upon which use of a framework is permitted,[170] and/or absence of a requirement to justify the choice of using a

---

[166] eg the EU remedies directives, or the UNCITRAL Model Law.

[167] L Folliot-Lalliot, 'The French Approach to Regulating Frameworks under the New EC Directives' in S Arrowsmith (ed), *Reform of the UNCITRAL Model Law on Procurement: Procurement Regulation for the 21st Century* (Thomson Reuters/West, 2009) 194, 211–12.

[168] eg, cases CE No.316601 (20 May 2009), and CE No.368448 (5 July 2013) of the Conseil d'État, settling appeals.

[169] See Chapter 5, section 5.3.2.5 (fn 224) and section 5.3.3.4 (fn 305) in this book.

[170] eg the EU directives.

framework arrangement (and/or its type).[171] Conversely, as shown, even though the UNCITRAL Model Law affords significant attention to conditions for embarking on a framework arrangement and justifying the options pursued, enforcing these measures efficiently and effectively through challenge proceedings could be affected by an inappropriate transparency requirement (which appears to be an error in the Model Law and implementing states could choose to rectify it in their national instruments).[172]

As regards the first stage of genuinely open arrangements on the supply side (frameworks or lists), two features of such arrangements have an impact on supplier review. First, there is no competitive exercise at this stage and, in effect, no competitive reduction of the number of suppliers. Second, there is no common time-limit for interested suppliers to make submissions, since they can apply at any time during the life of such arrangements. These two features combined mean that a supplier, or interested supplier, may have less information about other suppliers or interested suppliers, than in a closed (or 'traditional') procurement exercise. In turn, this could to some extent affect the efficiency of supplier review. The usual challenge rights and avenues would normally apply to the application for admission of *each* interested supplier in its relationship with the purchaser. Thus, supplier review could offer an appropriate protection against erroneous or abusive rejection of an application for admission, but might be less effective as a means to control erroneous or abusive *admissions* onto the arrangement. In light of this and because no standstill period applies to establishing an open arrangement, or at the admission of an applicant after the arrangement has been established,[173] first-stage procedures under open arrangements would generally benefit from increased ex-ante or ex-post controls from procurement control bodies.

6.7.2. Second Stage

Addressing supplier review at the second stage of PUIR needs a distinction to be made between: closed framework arrangements, open framework arrangements, and 'supplier lists'. As regards supplier review at the call-off stage under closed framework arrangements, very different, quite opposite approaches could be identified among systems reviewed. Striking a reasonable balance between procurement efficiency at the call-off stage and the need for monitoring and oversight (in order to avoid misuse or abuse) affects the 'remedial' action available.

---

[171] ibid.
[172] Chapter 2, sections 2.2.1.2 and 2.2.1.3.2 of this book.
[173] Conversely, a 'suspension' of operation of an open arrangement as a result of a challenge by an applicant whose admission was rejected, should also be denied in general. Procurement efficiency and effectiveness under the arrangement will probably take priority over the harm that the claimant suffers from not being able to attend some call-offs if its challenge is successful and its admission is thus delayed (see UNCITRAL Guide to Enactment to the 2011 Model Law on Public Procurement, point 16, pp 286–87, re art 60(8) of the Model Law).

It should be stressed here that the call-off stage within closed framework arrangements has tended to be less 'monitored' and therefore more vulnerable from a 'contestability' viewpoint. Possible causes include a sharp focus on efficiency at the call-off stage,[174] the view that some types of closed framework arrangement could be regarded as a procurement contract[175] and thus the contestability attached to its award suffices, or an insufficient adaptation of supplier review avenues applicable for 'traditional' purchasing to the specific features of the framework call-off stage.

On the other hand, actual allocation of work to a supplier under most frameworks occurs when an order is placed. That is, the actual obligations to buy and sell respectively only materialise, with regard to a fully specified requirement, at the call-off stage. It thus makes sense for the call-off stage to be subject to appropriate monitoring mechanisms, of which supplier review forms a significant part.

Contestability is generally needed and justified as regards the call-off stage, irrespective of whether call-off stage involves reopening of competition or otherwise. Where the award of an order affects competition conditions at the first stage, consideration should be given *de lege ferenda* to providing for some (limited) challenge avenues for tenderers whose submissions were rejected at that stage regarding such order awards.

Many hindrances to appropriate supplier review under closed frameworks arise from inadequate provision for transparency measures or other substantive procedural requirements,[176] rather than from the provision for 'challenge procedures' per se. Another aspect that needs contemplating relates to the delivery disruption that some supplier review mechanisms may cause to the intended convenience and efficiency of ordering under (closed) frameworks. Consideration could thus be given to excluding small orders from supplier review procedures. If this course of action is pursued, awards of such orders might benefit from being supplemented with increased ex-post (hierarchical or, preferably, third-party) monitoring. Also, an aggregated limit in terms of the value of small orders could be imposed, above which even small orders could become subject to supplier review procedures.

Alternatively (or additionally), orders up to a certain (individual) value could only be subject to certain remedial measures that cause less disruption to the purchasing process, such as penalties applicable to the purchaser, damages or shortening of the duration of an awarded contract. However, a wider or full range of remedial (or interim) measures – including standstill periods, suspension of the call-off procedure, or setting aside a concluded call-off – is likely to be appropriate for larger orders comparable in size with 'traditional' procurement contracts to which such review measures would apply.

---

[174] See US federal ID/IQ contracting.

[175] eg *marchés à bons de commande* (in older French instruments).

[176] Such as, under EU and UNCITRAL systems, the absence of an explicit provision as to the 'method' for allocating orders among framework suppliers under frameworks establishing all terms.

It certainly is no easy job to balance all the elements above and gear them to the features and objectives of a particular procurement system, or to specific circumstances, such as emergency procurement in dealing with crises or catastrophes.

As regards the current stage of supplier review at the call-off stage under closed framework arrangements, it can be seen that the 2011 UNCITRAL Model Law on Public Procurement provides for a wide and thorough coverage of supplier review mechanisms related to call-offs under framework agreements. There the approach is for call-offs to be regarded as procurement contracts and thus, in principle, the entire range of supplier review avenues is made available for the call-off stage. This is generally well supported by transparency requirements.

However, consideration could still be given to strengthening a few aspects under multiple-supplier frameworks. Thus, in relation to framework agreement procedures without second-stage competition (namely frameworks that establish all terms), the award of call-offs is not subject to a requirement that notification of a decision to award a call-off (including relevant elements that led to the award) be sent to all framework contractors. Also, such awards are not subject to a standstill period. This basically leaves call-offs of any value, under frameworks establishing all terms, outside challenge mechanisms until publication of a notice of the contract award. Since such publication occurs after conclusion of the call-off contract, remedial actions available are inevitably limited to those applicable after entry into force of a procurement contract, and corrective measures before the conclusion of the contract (in breach of an applicable law) appear excluded. The mere fact that the call-off stage does not involve competition in this type of framework does not appear a sufficient reason to deny 'pre-award' challenges for such call-offs, since a multiple-supplier framework does not predetermine precisely the allocation of specific call-off requirements among framework contractors.[177] Such allocation thus takes place at the call-off stage and could, quite easily in my view, involve breaches of an applicable law.

Similarly, call-off awards under an exception to reopening competition within frameworks not establishing all terms, also seem to be outside the remit of legally required notifications concerning call-off award decisions and of the standstill period. With the notable exception of an award for objective and exceptional urgency, this approach seems unjustified, and might benefit from strengthening in the future.

Another 'transparency' aspect concerns frameworks that do not establish all terms and, therefore, involve reopening of competition at the call-off stage. In this case, the requirement for a notification of the intention to accept a call-off-stage

---

[177] An exception to this could be provided by frameworks establishing all terms *as well as* guaranteed (fixed) quantities for each framework supplier *individually*. However, such arrangement could be regarded as a set of interlinked traditional contracts rather than PUIR (to the extent that no call-offs above guaranteed quantities are made).

competition submission (at the end of the applicable standstill period) only applies to the other suppliers in such competition presenting submissions for the call-off.[178] It does not apply to suppliers who, although invited to make call-off submissions, did not attend the exercise, or who were not invited to make submissions since they were not among those deemed 'then capable of meeting the needs' associated with that call-off.[179] This is recognised in the Guide to Enactment as a 'vulnerable' point.[180]

Indeed, consideration could be given in further reforms to requiring provision of 'standstill notice' to *all* framework suppliers, and not just those who presented submissions for the call-off competition. Even framework suppliers not invited to participate in a specific call-off competition, or who did not attend (although invited), are likely to have an active – and in many cases justified – interest in challenging illegal awards under the framework they are a party to. However, a distinction may be made in regard to the challenge rights provided to different 'categories' of framework suppliers (ie, 'recipients' of standstill notifications). Thus, the challenge rights of framework suppliers not invited could be limited – at that stage – to situations when the actual call-off award differs from the conditions that led to the determination that certain suppliers were not 'capable' to meet the needs and therefore were not invited to make submissions for the call-off.[181] Similarly, all framework contractors, including those not invited, or not attending a call-off, could have an interest in challenging call-offs that exceed the scope of the framework agreement.

A related, but distinct, matter concerns applicability of the standstill period to the award of any call-off involving reopening of competition and exceeding a certain threshold, to be established in the procurement regulations of enacting states (except in case of urgent public interest).[182] It might have been preferable to provide an option for enacting states, or even for purchasers, to choose between: *observing a standstill period* before conclusion of a call-off, and thereby avoiding challenges after the award of the call-off; and *contracting without observing a standstill* period subject to supplier challenge avenues permitting the 'overturn' (ie, annulment, cancellation or termination) of the awarded call-off.[183]

In contrast, overall, the EU supplier review mechanisms at the call-off stage of framework agreements (ie closed framework arrangements) seem more vulnerable and their coverage less thorough. However, this is not determined by the supplier review 'concept' per se. The 'remedies directives' do extend, in principle,

---

[178] Arts 62(3), 62(4)(d) and 22(2) of the Model Law.

[179] Under art 62(4)(a) of the Model Law the purchaser is required to notify framework suppliers about any call-off competition that the latter are not invited to attend. These notifications must be issued simultaneously with any invitations sent to suppliers deemed 'then capable'.

[180] Guide to Enactment (n 173 above) at 290 (explanation to art 62, at point 7).

[181] This is certainly distinct from the right to challenge the actual grounds invoked by the purchaser when deciding not to invite certain framework suppliers, where those grounds are unjustified.

[182] Art 62(4)(d) in conjunction with art 22(2) and 22(3)(b) (interpreted *a contrario*) of the Model Law.

[183] Similarly to the provision under the EU directives.

the challenge avenues and corrective action applicable for 'traditional' procurement contracts to call-offs under framework agreements. But this is not adequately supported by transparency requirements concerning implementation of a framework agreement, as already discussed. Nonetheless, the EU system provides flexibility as regards the application of a standstill period to call-offs awarded by reopening competition under framework agreements.[184] Thus, Member States may provide under the Public Sector Remedies Directive for derogation from the application of standstill periods to call-offs under framework agreements.[185] Where the derogation is not provided for, standstill periods must apply to all call-offs (above the EU thresholds). The derogation has been provided for in national legislation by all EU Member States reviewed in this book and, thus, the option is cascaded to purchasers in those Member States.[186] Where standstill is not observed by a purchaser, the awarded call-off is subject to ineffectiveness if above EU thresholds (and if awarded in breach of rules concerning the reopening of competition at the call-off stage).[187] Nonetheless, the purchaser can avoid the risk of ineffectiveness of a call-off by voluntarily observing a standstill period (and relevant notice to participants in the call-off competition) for the award of the call-off in question.[188]

It is relevant to point out in this context that the UK post-Brexit Procurement Bill maintains and expands the option between standstill and ineffectiveness for call-offs under frameworks, apparently irrespective of how a certain call-off is awarded (with or without second-stage competition).[189]

In sharp contrast with both the UNCITRAL and EU (or Member States) and indeed with the UK post-Brexit Procurement Bill, in the US federal procurement system supplier review provision at the call-off stage of closed framework arrangements provides for an *explicit ban* on protesting orders under ID/IQ contracting.[190] Exceptionally, such protests are permitted under FAR 'on the grounds that the order increases the scope, period, or maximum value of the contract', or for orders 'valued in excess of $10 million'.[191] Additionally, the Government Accountability Office has also retained competence to review protests concerning orders that could be regarded as 'down-selections'.[192] While this approach may be considered

---

[184] S Arrowsmith, 'Methods for Purchasing On-Going Requirements: The System of Framework Agreements and Dynamic Purchasing Systems under the EC Directives and UK Procurement Regulations' in S Arrowsmith (ed), *Reform of the UNCITRAL Model Law on Public Procurement: Procurement Regulation for the 21st Century* (Thomson Reuters/West, 2009) 141, 177–81.

[185] Art 2b(c) of Directive 89/665/EEC (as amended).

[186] However, the transposition of potential ineffectiveness of call-offs when standstill is not applied on their award does not appear clear (express) in Romanian instruments.

[187] n 185.

[188] Art 2d(5) of Directive 89/665/EEC.

[189] ss 44(1)PB, 48(1)PB, 49(3)(c) and (4)PB, 94(1)(d) and (2)PB. The same applies for contracts awarded under dynamic markets (s 49(3)(d)PB).

[190] FAR16.505(a)(10)(i). See Chapter 4 of this book.

[191] FAR16.505(a)(10)(i)(A) and (B).

[192] See Chapter 4, section 4.2.4, and section 6.5 above.

to meet the level of ID/IQ call-off efficiency desired (and/or needed) for US federal agencies, as well as being consistent with the level of trust and capacity of US federal procurement workforce, it is not trouble free. The explicit ban on ID/IQ order protests leaves many awards outside any supplier review mechanism, and the US$10 million value threshold above which any order can be challenged seems particularly high. However, the ban on order protests does not apply to orders or BPAs under the US GSA Schedules.[193]

As regards genuinely open arrangements, EU dynamic purchasing systems benefit from a more thorough supplier review approach at the call-off stage (than framework agreements), stemming from stronger transparency requirements, as was discussed. Also, the option between standstill and ineffectiveness applies to call-offs under this arrangement. The UNCITRAL Model Law treats second-stage competitions in the same way for closed and open framework agreements,[194] and this includes supplier review mechanisms as well as the requisite transparency requirements (but, as in closed frameworks, standstill is compulsory for all call-offs above the threshold, except in case of urgent public interest).[195] Similarly, from a supplier review perspective, the UK post-Brexit Procurement Bill treats awards by reference to dynamic markets in the same way as awards under frameworks (and the option between standstill and ineffectiveness does apply).

The second stage of 'supplier list' arrangements does not generally present particular issues as regards supplier review mechanisms. 'Call-off' procedures are nearly 'full' traditional award procedures, among suppliers admitted onto the arrangement, except for 'suitability' (or some elements of 'suitability') that had been assessed at the first stage, as requirements for admission. To the extent that access onto the list (at the first stage) is open and fair on equal terms, supplier review at the call-off stage under supplier list arrangements should be straight-forward and similar to that which applies to 'traditional' purchasing methods. However, caution should be exercised in mandatory-type lists where not all suppliers admitted to the list are then invited to the procedure for a particular contract. This is likely to require additional transparency over such (further) selection of suppliers to avoid misuse or abuse and to facilitate potential challenge where appropriate. Similarly, in optional lists, caution should be exercised to ensure that there is no discrimination or favouritism against/among suppliers registered and/or those not registered on the list, and that equal/fair treatment fully applies concerning their potential access to specific procurements which the list relates to (to the extent that non-registered suppliers prove their 'suitability' in relation to such specific procurement; see also Chapter 5, section 5.3.5).

It can be concluded that second-stage supplier review mechanisms deserve particular attention.

---

[193] FAR8.404(e).

[194] Second-stage procedures are dealt with jointly under the same provisions (in art 62 of the Model Law).

[195] See arts 22–23 and 64–68 of the Model Law.

6.7.3. Overlaps and Relationship between Stages

The relationship or overlap between stages of a PUIR arrangement could present, in certain circumstances, supplier review complexities. The first category of such matters concerns closed framework arrangements and recognising the interest that unsuccessful suppliers having tendered at the first stage (and having been denied entry onto the framework) could have in challenging certain types of call-offs, in particular those that exceed the scope of the framework, or otherwise affect the conditions of competition at the first stage. We have already shown in the context of EU public sector frameworks without second-stage competition that notifying the other framework suppliers of a call-off award decision should be considered.[196] Further, thought could also be given (more widely, not just in the EU context) to extending issuance of those notifications to unsuccessful tenderers at first stage. This would strengthen oversight concerning such call-offs, since framework contractors might not be wishing to challenge call-offs exceeding the framework scope (even if they become aware of them)[197] in the hope that they too could benefit from it in a future call-off; whereas clearly none of the framework contractors will be interested to challenge a call-off affecting conditions of competition at the first stage, when suppliers were selected.

Second, an aspect of overlap between stages could arise in genuinely open arrangements that may require specific attention from a supplier review perspective. It refers to situations when a call-off procedure under the arrangement is launched before a pending application for admittance onto the arrangement from a 'newcomer' is considered. In effect, this means that the 'newcomer' may be unable to attend that call-off, for example if the assessment of the application is finalised and a decision concerning admittance, or otherwise, is taken after the time-limit for making submissions for the call-off. However, this matter could be better addressed by the substantive rules on time-limits for assessing applications, or, as in the UK post-Brexit Procurement Bill in respect of dynamic markets, the configuration requiring consideration of applications for admission onto the market 'from suppliers that have submitted a tender as part of the competitive tendering procedure'.[198]

Third, the reverse situation where suppliers which are already a 'party' to a genuinely open arrangement wish to challenge an abusive (or erroneous) decision to admit a 'newcomer', seems less problematic in terms of immediate consequences. If there are (legal) impediments preventing a supplier already admitted from challenging such a decision,[199] nothing should prevent challenging the award

---

[196] See Arrowsmith, 'Methods for Purchasing On-Going Requirements' (n 184) 181.

[197] Under the current instruments they may only learn of them from a contract award notice, if applicable.

[198] s 34(4)PB.

[199] Or where a challenge has been lodged but it is pending resolution; such challenge should not suspend the admission decision, since this could 'facilitate' abusive challenges from suppliers already on the arrangement who will want to limit competition at the call-off stage in this way.

of a call-off to the 'newcomer' (on that basis). Certainly, this implies that suppliers already admitted should be provided with relevant information concerning admittance decisions of any 'newcomer'; in the absence of such information, they are unlikely to be aware whether there is any basis for challenging.

The fourth aspect worth noting here relates to the consequences of a declaration of ineffectiveness of a framework agreement under the UK (pre-Brexit based) procurement regulations on contracts awarded under that framework *before* declaration of ineffectiveness.[200] Consistent with the UK approach to recognise only prospective ineffectiveness,[201] and not retrospective ineffectiveness,[202] call-offs awarded based on a framework agreement in respect of which a declaration of ineffectiveness has been made, but prior to that declaration, are not to be considered ineffective merely because of that declaration. Instead, a separate application is required for each such call-off that will be considered individually in light of its particular circumstances. A similar approach appears to be maintained under the post-Brexit UK Procurement Bill.[203]

Finally, where the call-off stage of a PUIR arrangement includes an intermediary stage,[204] considerations concerning review and remedial action should in principle apply mutatis mutandis, as appropriate to any intermediary stage.

[200] See Chapter 5, section 5.3.2.5.1 of this book.
[201] ie effects of ineffectiveness only concern the future, and not the past.
[202] ie where ineffectiveness affects both the past and the future.
[203] s 93(7)PB.
[204] See section 6.6.3 above.

7

Conclusions: Articulating a Discipline for Purchasing Uncertain or Indefinite Requirements in Public Procurement

As shown in Chapter one, this book examined PUIR arrangements as regulated in selected procurement systems or instruments and why they are regulated as they are, and assessed considerations that tend to promote or detract from fulfilment of certain objectives of the regulation of PUIR. A common structure related to the 'core' elements of the underlying commercial process of such 'transactions' was used both for the examination of individual arrangements in each system or instrument *and* for wider transversal perspectives amongst them.

Whilst all systems/instruments examined provide for arrangements that fall under my definition of PUIR arrangements, each case study, and each type of arrangement therein, offers a partial and varied picture of the 'spectrum'. The approaches of individual systems or instruments are determined by their own overall objectives, but challenges are faced by all systems in 'calibrating' regulation of PUIR arrangements to their intended objectives *and* to the inherent uncertainties or indefinite aspects of such arrangements.

Certainly, regulations alone cannot solve all problems of procurement and in particular of PUIR, where a vital part is played by market awareness (which includes market uncertainties) and a strategic approach towards market evolutions in relation to estimated needs for the subject-matter of the envisaged procurements. However, regulations may require, encourage, limit or prohibit certain practices. From this perspective, refining the 'tuning' of PUIR regulations may be desirable from many viewpoints, including by reference to a system's own objectives, as has been pointed out throughout the previous chapters.

A comprehensive classification (taxonomy) of potential arrangements was developed (in Chapter six, section 6.3) from over 20 types of arrangement across the examined procurement systems and instruments. Its purpose is not only to 'contain' the possible configurations of PUIR arrangements, but, more importantly, to highlight the interaction (and conditioning) between various features of an arrangement. These aspects may not be immediately evident from an existing legal instrument, in particular where it covers multiple configurations under the 'same roof'.[1] However, the interactions and conditioning referred above are particularly relevant in choosing and implementing an appropriate configuration of PUIR arrangement in practice, as well as in designing policy and regulation concerning PUIR arrangements.

On this basis, a general framework for analysis of whether the use of a PUIR arrangement would be appropriate, and for choosing a desirable type or configuration of PUIR arrangement, depending on the circumstances of the envisaged requirements and of the relevant market, has been suggested in Chapter six, section 6.4. This is an area that can cause particular difficulty in the use of PUIR arrangements and has tended to be neglected in (many) current systems. Additionally, in section 6.4.3 a conceptual framework was outlined concerning approaches that regulatory instruments could take to encourage an adequate decision-making process at purchaser level regarding the use (or otherwise) of a PUIR arrangement and the choice of a suitable type of arrangement for specific requirements.

The book also analysed (in Chapter six, section 6.6) the problems that might arise from inadequate call-off procedures, which might 'invalidate' the outcome of the first stage of PUIR arrangements. We saw that in frameworks that do not establish all terms for future purchases, reopening competition at the call-off stage amongst all framework suppliers is usually appropriate for establishing the outstanding terms and choosing the supplier to carry out the call-off in question. Whether that competition involves tendering and/or negotiations, and whether or not express substantive rules for that competition are provided for in a legal instrument, are matters for each procurement system to consider in light of its relevant procurement context. Express provision is likely to offer legal certainty and promote value and integrity, whilst tendering is likely to offer (needed) simplicity at the call-off stage, but there could be (probably rather limited) situations when competitive negotiations with all relevant framework suppliers might be useful. However, irrespective of what call-off competitions involve under a particular system or instrument (ie, tendering or negotiations), where limitations or exceptions to call-off competition may be appropriate (such as 'technical reasons', extreme urgency, occupied capacity, small orders up to a certain aggregated value, etc), the permitted limitations or exceptions ought to be expressly specified in the relevant legal instrument, as well as subject to appropriate transparency and potential legal review.

Conversely, where all terms concerning future purchases are established at the first stage of a framework, reopening competition is not usually needed, though it could be useful in some circumstances. It is, however, important to ensure that the allocation of work amongst framework contractors based on those terms is subject to objective (and pre-disclosed) rules/criteria. Many of the systems/instruments

---

[1] eg framework agreements in the EU.

reviewed are almost silent on what the actual method of allocation should involve. In this connection we saw that in most cases it is appropriate to allocate work to the framework supplier that offers best value for the specific call-off based on the offer originally submitted by that supplier at the first stage in order to be admitted onto the arrangement, and on pre-disclosed award criteria stated for call-offs. At the same time, 'aleatory' allocation methods (such as rotation of suppliers) should be used only exceptionally in very specific circumstances, since they can affect both value for money and equal/fair treatment.

Inadequate transparency requirements at the call-off stage could also render a framework arrangement vulnerable to misuse or abuse, and most of the systems/ instruments examined in this book appear to have afforded limited attention to this aspect. The notable exception is provided by the UNCITRAL Model Law, which should be regarded as a standard. However, even this instrument makes a distinction concerning transparency requirements at the call-off stage between frameworks involving reopening of competition and those not involving such competition, that in the current author's view is unjustified. It is relevant to point out that UK post-Brexit Procurement Bill does not appear to make such a distinction in terms of transparency requirements, which is very welcome, but it also does not seem (at the time of writing) to include express transparency safeguards (amongst framework contractors) when initiating call-off competitions.

In relation to the above, it has been also analysed (at Chapter six, section 6.7) the balance between efficiency at call-off stage and 'contestability'. We saw that, in general, oversight and review mechanisms are needed, though some adjustments (in comparison to the mechanisms usually available for 'traditional' purchases) might be desirable in relation to certain call-offs under frameworks. The experience of the US federal procurement system indicates that very limited 'contestability' could support procurement efficiency at the call-off stage (in closed frameworks) but it presents risks to fair treatment and value. On the other hand, under the UNCITRAL Model Law, the mandatory application of standstill periods to all call-offs involving reopening of competition (above the relevant threshold) could affect efficiency in some cases, and an option between observing the standstill period and ineffectiveness of the contract, as provided for in the EU remedies directive,[2] appears preferable (to the extent that a solid and nuanced post-award remedies system is available).[3] The apparent expansion of this approach, in the post-Brexit UK Procurement Bill, to cover call-offs awarded with, and those awarded without, second-stage competition is, again, very welcome.

We have also identified and discussed (mainly at Chapter six, section 6.6.3) potential new configurations of arrangement such as certain types of 'frameworks in frameworks'. Whilst such arrangements could prove very useful devices for

---

[2] For the public sector.

[3] Uncertainty over this aspect (in some potential enacting states) is likely to have led to the position of the UNCITRAL Model Law on mandatory standstill in respect of call-offs involving reopening of competition.

centralised purchasing, the risks they pose are elevated, and would thus require significant strengthening of certain requirements concerning their operation.

In light of the complexity and volume of the subject-matter of this book, the summary of findings provided above (in this chapter) is inevitably partial, presenting an inherent risk of 'over-simplification' and removal of some issues from the context generating them. They have thus been presented here subject to this reservation. A reference is made to Chapter six for overall findings and proposals, and to the system chapters (Chapters two, three, four and five) for discussions and findings pertaining to individual systems/instruments. A summary of the main (recent) developments concerning the PUIR phenomenon, as emerging from the systems examined, is presented below.

With the notable exception of the (currently ongoing) UK post-Brexit procurement overhaul, recent reforms of other major public procurement systems have generally manifested a continued preference for framework arrangements over the supplier list type arrangements. The 2011 UNCITRAL Model Law on Public Procurement missed the opportunity to recognise 'lists'. In the 2014 EU Public Sector Directive, dynamic purchasing systems partially migrated towards a 'mandatory list' type of arrangement but, as shown, they can be regarded as a rather restricted configuration (as regards the subject-matter of procurements, and procedures applicable to the second stage of the arrangement). But the 2014 EU Public Sector Directive did not 'import' a more generalist type of list, somewhat similar to qualification systems from the EU utilities sector procurement, or along the lines of the provisions on multi-use lists in the WTO Government Procurement Agreement. In effect, EU Member States too are prevented from employing such arrangements (for the public sector). Further, the new 2016 World Bank regulations do not appear to envisage any longer 'pre-qualification' for a number of contracts to be awarded in time.

Subject to the observations in Chapter five, section 5.4.1, the emergence of the 'dynamic markets' concept in the post-Brexit Procurement Bill, as a 'generalist' type of 'supplier list' arrangement, contemplated to be available for the public sector as well, seems a very positive development, though it is currently a 'work in progress'. As discussed, reservations towards open supplier lists do not appear justified if proper regulation of such arrangements is in place. This involves, without limitation, permanent advertising and other appropriate transparency, objective criteria and rules for admission applied equally to all interested suppliers, appropriate (fair) second-stage procedures that are transparent for all suppliers admitted onto the list, and appropriate review mechanisms for both stages.[4] Too much caution has been exercised so far in legal instruments with regard to recognising open supplier lists (in particular those of a 'generalist' nature) and this deprives purchasers of valuable vehicles for efficient grouping and organising of

---

[4] Closed 'lists' (and in particular mandatory ones) should not be permitted though, since they can easily affect the benefits of real and substantive competition, and foster favouritism.

a wide range of indefinite but predicted purchasing needs. A notable exception to such caution is provided by the EU Utilities Directive (as regards qualification systems). It remains to be seen whether, when the legislative passage of the UK post-Brexit Procurement Bill is complete, and the law is enacted, the 'dynamic markets' concept meets its promise and alleviates reservations towards this type of arrangement more widely by adequately addressing the elements pointed out above. If it does, then there is likely a high chance that 'dynamic markets' may inspire further reforms in other procurement systems.

In this connection, it can be argued that the 2014 EU Public Sector Directive offers a particularly dichotomist approach, if not a double standard as regards 'caution' in addressing PUIR arrangements. In parallel with barring mandatory open lists (other than dynamic purchasing systems), this directive may also prevent Member States from limiting – through domestic legislation – the use of frameworks to certain types or purchasers, or from providing for additional conditions and controls to their operation. At the same time, continuing limited attention has been given in the directive to a number of aspects concerning framework agreements, which could quite easily offer gaps fostering improper or abusive use of such arrangements.[5]

From the case studies of this book, it can be seen that many types (or configurations) of arrangement are missing from one system or another. It is not suggested that all systems should permit the same types or configurations of PUIR arrangements, or, even less so that they should be regulated in exactly the same way. Even with the increased harmonisation brought about by international trade agreements, much will continue to depend on the objectives of individual systems, institutional and human resource capacity, legal or administrative culture. Nevertheless, wide ranges of possible PUIR arrangements are repudiated from the current systems, whereas some aspects of the recognised arrangements may benefit from increased attention in the regulation. This seems a common feature of current systems, to varying degrees.

The legal instrument currently providing for the widest range of PUIR arrangements is the EU utilities procurement directive. From this perspective a somewhat comparable approach concerning PUIR seems to characterise the UK post-Brexit Procurement Bill; note also that in this case the approach is also likely to extend to the public sector. A comprehensive and balanced approach to 'framework'-type arrangements is offered by the 2011 UNCITRAL Model Law and the accompanying guidance for implementation.[6] The US continues to offer the only centralised arrangement for regular purchases establishing terms at the first stage without a comparison *amongst* offers received, and using the supplier's most privileged prices charged in its business with its other clients (the GSA Schedules Program).[7]

[5] See Chapter 5, section 5.3.2 of the book.
[6] Which I recommend that it should be considered mutatis mutandis, as sensible, even in systems which are not necessarily based on the UNCITRAL system (such as EU Member States, and the UK).
[7] Chapter 4, section 4.2.5 of this book.

More generally,[8] procurement needs with some degree of regularity as well as some degree of uncertainty are a usual and frequent occurrence for many purchasers. The sheer volume of purchases under framework agreements in the EU or, for example, GSA Schedules in the US is proof of this. Some (rather few) types of PUIR arrangements in the spectrum are quite similar to 'traditional procurement'. But the majority of the possible PUIR arrangements present very specific features stemming from the plurality of the uncertain or indefinite aspects involved (terms, commitment, specification), as well as from the plurality of suppliers and/or purchasers involved in the same arrangement (which can be definite or indefinite[9]).

In my view the regulation of all these complexities requires a direct and comprehensive approach, rather than a fragmented approach based on 'traditional', 'one-off', single-agency single-contractor procurement, that is 'patched' in various ways so as to cater for PUIR. This seems pretty much the case of the current regimes, which deal with PUIR arrangements 'by way of exception', in an indirect or accessory fashion. For example, 'wrapping' dynamic purchasing systems in the EU directives with a restricted procedure 'cover' appears somewhat of a fiction. The regulation of PUIR appears, in some cases, both convoluted and insufficient (in different ways in the various public procurement systems or regimes). The limits of adapting 'traditional' procurement to 'indefinite' purchasing have already been discussed. They range from getting stuck in inadequate concepts, such as requiring the outcome of the first stage of a framework arrangement to be a contract,[10] or even regarding it as a procurement contract, to difficulties in regulation arising from trying to regulate too large a range of arrangements under the same 'roof',[11] to precluding certain types or configurations of arrangement which may be useful in some circumstances,[12] or to providing too tight or excessive conditions and controls unjustifiably limiting uses, or on the other hand, providing insufficient conditions or procedural controls to facilitate the adequate use of certain arrangements or configurations.

This book sets a basis for articulating a discipline for and a new approach towards PUIR regulation and policy, by streamlining concepts and experiences, as well as by drawing an organised network of integrated focus points and potential solutions across various procurement systems. Structuring procurement regulation in two main areas appears thus sensible: one dealing with definite or 'one-off' (traditional) purchases, and the other dealing with indefinite or uncertain or regular (non-traditional) purchasing arrangements.[13] This would allow much needed

---

[8] ie not in relation to any specific procurement system.

[9] See Chapter 6, section 6.3.3 of this book.

[10] See approaches in France, or US ID/IQ contracts.

[11] EU framework agreements.

[12] Amongst others, mandatory lists under the UNCITRAL Model Law on Public Procurement, or under the EU Public Sector Directive (save for dynamic purchasing systems).

[13] There would certainly be interconnections between the two.

room to focus properly on PUIR, facilitating adequate consideration and development of all relevant aspects, and in particular those that may not be immediately visible from a 'traditional' purchasing perspective (some of which, as we saw throughout the book can be quite complex). Examples include, to name just few, in the case of open arrangements, the potential consequences of overlaps between stages in terms of procedures or in terms of judicial review; or the possibility of what we called 'frameworks within frameworks'.[14]

Substantive rebalancing of approaches to PUIR regulation and policy appears desirable if PUIR is to discharge its full potential for efficiency and effectiveness in public procurement. Rebalancing would involve consideration of an expansion of the range of PUIR arrangements permitted by regulation, as well as of their coverage and scope, connected with enhanced and proportioned conditions, controls, procedures, and oversight mechanisms promoting a beneficial use of those arrangements.[15] Certainly, the extent of desirable reforms and their detailed approach will differ from one procurement system to the other, depending on their balance of objectives and their prevailing procurement context, such as capacity, legal traditions, or administrative environment. The current post-Brexit procurement reform *could* be an excellent opportunity for a first major step in that direction that might then provide some inspiration on this concept of PUIR reform to other procurement systems internationally. At the time of writing though, as shown, with the UK post-Brexit procurement legislation still in the drafting process there is insufficient information available to draw conclusions.

The last two decades have brought significant progress in the area of PUIR arrangements. Milestones clearly include the recognition of framework agreements in the EU 2004 Public Sector Directive, the recognition of both closed and open framework agreements in the 2011 UNCITRAL Model Law on Public Procurement, the 2011 development of provisions concerning BPAs and ordering under them within US GSA Schedules, and the review of the dynamic purchasing systems in the 2014 EU directives. Still, as suggested above, I anticipate that major reforms in the field of purchasing uncertain or indefinite requirements are yet to come.

---

[14] See Chapter 6, section 6.6.3 of this book.
[15] This would also permit more strategic procurement planning and approaches at purchaser level, supporting efficiency and effectiveness at that level.

BIBLIOGRAPHY

Albano, GL, 'Homo Homini Lupus: On the Consequences of Buyers' Miscoordination in Emergency Procurement for the COVID-19 Crisis in Italy' (2020) 29 *PPLR* 213, 219.

Albano, GL and Nicholas, C, *The Law and Economics of Framework Agreements: Designing Flexible Solutions for Public Procurement* (Cambridge, CUP, 2016).

Andhov, M and Vornicu, R, 'A Comparative View of the Use of Procurement Techniques and Electronic Instruments by Central Purchasing Bodies' in C Risvig Hamer and M Comba (eds), *Centralising Public Procurement: The Approach of EU Member States* (Cheltenham, Edward Elgar Publishing, 2021) 36.

Andrecka, M, 'Framework Agreements, EU Procurement Law and the Practice' [2015] (2) *Upphandlingsrättslig Tidskrift* 127.

Arden, P, 'Legal Regulation of Multi-Provider Framework Agreements and the Potential for Bid Rigging: A Perspective from the UK Local Government Construction Sector' (2013) 22 *PPLR* 165.

Arrowsmith, S, 'Dynamic Purchasing Systems under the New EC Procurement Directives: A Not So Dynamic Concept?' (2006) 15 *PPLR* 16.

—— 'Framework Agreements in the EC and UK' in S Arrowsmith (ed), *Reform of the UNCITRAL Model Law on Public Procurement: Procurement Regulation for the 21st Century* (Danvers MA, Thomson Reuters/West, 2009) 141.

—— 'Framework Purchasing and Qualification Lists under the European Procurement Directives: Part I' (1999) 8 *PPLR* 115.

—— 'Framework Purchasing and Qualification Lists under the European Procurement Directives: Part II' (1999) 8 *PPLR* 161.

—— 'Implementation of the New EC Procurement Directives and the Alcatel Ruling in England, Wales and Northern Ireland: A Review of the New Legislation and Guidance' (2006) 15 *PPLR* 95.

—— 'Methods for Purchasing On-Going Requirements: the System of Framework Agreements and Dynamic Purchasing Systems under the EC Directives and UK Procurement Regulations' in S Arrowsmith (ed), *Reform of the UNCITRAL Model Law on Public Procurement: Procurement Regulation for the 21st Century* (Danvers MA, Thomson Reuters/West, 2009) 131.

—— 'Modernising the EU's Public Procurement Regime: A Blueprint for Real Simplicity and Flexibility' (2012) 21 *PPLR* 71.

—— 'Public Procurement: an Appraisal of the UNCITRAL Model Law as a Global Standard' (2004) 53 *ICLQ* 17.

—— 'Recommendations for Urgent Procurement in the EU Directive and GPA: COVID-19 and Beyond' in S Arrowsmith et al (eds), *Public Procurement in (a) Crisis: Global Lessons from the Covid-19 Pandemic* (Oxford, Hart Publishing, 2021) 63.

—— 'The Approach to Emergency Procurement in the UNCITRAL Model Law: A Critical Appraisal in Light of the COVID-19 Pandemic' in S Arrowsmith et al (eds), *Public Procurement in (a) Crisis: Global Lessons from the Covid-19 Pandemic* (Oxford, Hart Publishing, 2021) 21.

—— *The Law of Public and Utilities Procurement*, 2nd edn (London, Sweet & Maxwell, 2005).

—— *The Law of Public and Utilities Procurement: Regulation in the EU and UK*, 3rd edn (vol I) (London, Sweet & Maxwell, 2014).

—— 'The Purpose of the EU Procurement Directives: Ends, Means and the Implications for National Regulatory Space for Commercial and Horizontal Procurement Policies' (2012) 14 *Cambridge Yearbook of European Studies* 1.

—— (ed), *Reform of the UNCITRAL Model Law on Procurement: Regulation for the 21st Century* (Danvers MA, Thomson Reuters/West, 2009).

Arrowsmith, S and Nicholas, C, 'Regulating Framework Agreements under the UNCITRAL Model Law on Procurement' in S Arrowsmith (ed), *Reform of the UNCITRAL Model Law on Procurement: Procurement Regulation for the 21st Century* (Danvers MA, Thomson Reuters/West, 2009) 95.

—— 'The UNCITRAL Model Law on Procurement: Past, Present, and Future' in S Arrowsmith (ed), *Reform of the UNCITRAL Model Law on Procurement: Procurement Regulation for the 21st Century* (Danvers MA, Thomson Reuters/West, 2009) 1.

Arrowsmith, S and Treumer, S, 'Competitive Dialogue in EU Law: A Critical Review' in S Arrowsmith and S Treumer (eds), *Competitive Dialogue in EU Procurement* (Cambridge, CUP, 2012) 3.

Arrowsmith, S, Linarelli J and Wallace, D Jr, *Regulating Public Procurement: National and International Perspectives* (Kluwer Law International, 2000).

Arrowsmith, S et al (eds), *Public Procurement in (a) Crisis: Global Lessons from the Covid-19 Pandemic* (Oxford, Hart Publishing, 2021).

Bleicher, NB, Dunn, WI, Gordon DI and Kang, JL, 'Accountability in Indefinite-Delivery/Indefinite-Quantity Contracting: The Multifaced Work of the U.S. Government Accountability Office' (2008) 37 *PCLJ* 375.

Bovis, C, *The Law of EU Public Procurement*, 2nd edn (Oxford, OUP, 2015).

Bowsher, M QC and John, LE, 'The Use (and Abuse?) of Framework Agreements in the United Kingdom' in HR Garcia (ed), *International Public Procurement: A Guide to Best Practice* (London, Globe Business Publishing Ltd, 2009) 349.

Cibinic, J Jr , Nash, RC Jr and Yukins, CR, *Formation of Government Contracts*, 4th edn (Washington DC, The George Washington University) (Wolters Kluwer, 2011).

Constantinesco, L-J, *Tratat de Drept Comparat (Comparative Law Treatise)* vol 1 (Bucharest, Editura ALL, 1997).

Ebert, GM, 'Protests of Orders: a Drizzle or a Downpour: Examining the Results of Government Accountability Office's Exclusive Protest Jurisdiction Following the 2008 NDAA Amendments to FASA' (2016) 45 *PCLJ* 613.

Eyo, A, 'Evidence on Use of Dynamic Purchasing Systems in the United Kingdom' (2017) 26 *PPLR* 237.

Falle, J and Dwyer, C, 'United Kingdom' in J Davey and J Falle (eds), *The Government Procurement Review* (London, Law Business Research, 2013) 230.

Filipon, Ş, 'The Winding Road from Policy Objectives and Procedural Rules to Practical Reality: An Overview of Framework Agreements and Electronic Procurement under the New UNCITRAL Model Law' (Paper prepared for the PPGR VI Conference, June 2013, Nottingham, UK).

—— *A Review of European Union's Public Procurement Procedures in External Environments*, MSc Dissertation, University of Strathclyde, UK, 2006.

Folliot-Lalliot, L, 'The French Approach to Regulating Frameworks under the New EC Directives' in S Arrowsmith (ed), *Reform of the UNCITRAL Model Law on Procurement: Procurement Regulation for the 21st Century* (Danvers MA, Thomson Reuters/West, 2009) 193.

Frilet, M and Lager, F, 'France' in R Hernández García (ed), *International Public Procurement: A Guide to Best Practice* (London, Globe Business Publishing, 2009) 217.

Gatenby, A, Gillian, B and Dobson, L, 'United Kingdom' in J Davey and A Gatenby (eds), *The Government Procurement Review* (London, Law Business Research, 2017) 240.

Geddes, A, *Public and Utility Procurement: A Practical Guide to the UK Regulations and Associated Community Rules*, 2nd edn (London, Sweet & Maxwell, 1997).

Georgopoulos, A, Hoekman, B and Mavroidis, PC (eds), *The Internationalization of Government Procurement Regulation* (Oxford, OUP, 2017).

Gordon, DI, 'Bid Protests: the Costs are Real, But the Benefits Outweigh Them' (2013) 42 *PCLJ* 489.

Gordon, DI and Kang, JL, 'Task-Order Contracting in the U.S. Federal System: The Current System and Its Historical Context' in S Arrowsmith (ed), *Reform of the UNCITRAL Model Law on Procurement: Procurement Regulation for the 21st Century* (Danvers MA, Thomson Reuters/West, 2009) 215.

Gordon, DI and Racca, GM, 'Integrity Challenges in the EU and U.S. Procurement Systems' in GM Racca and CR Yukins (eds), *Integrity and Efficiency in Sustainable Public Contracts: Balancing Corruption Concerns in Public Procurement Internationally* (Brussels, Bruylant, 2014) 117.

Górski, J, 'The World Bank's New Procurement Regulations' (2016) 11 *EPPPL* 301.

Gourley, AWH and Cliffe, A, 'United States' in H-J Prieß (ed), *Getting the Deal Through Public Procurement: An Overview of Regulation in 37 Jurisdictions* (Global Competition Review, 2013) 242.

Hendrix, L, 'Lessons from Disaster: Improving Emergency Response through Greater Coordination of Federal, State, and Local Response Efforts' (2021) 51 *PCLJ* 69.

Hutchinson, RR, 'Oversight of GSA Federal Supply Schedule Contracts: From Internal Compliance Programs to Civil False Claims Actions' (2008) 37 *PCLJ* 569.

Jin, J and McLaughlin, M, 'Procurement and Distribution of Critical COVID-19 Supplies: The Experience of USAID' in S Arrowsmith et al (eds), *Public Procurement in (a) Crisis: Global Lessons from the Covid-19 Pandemic* (Oxford, Hart Publishing, 2021) 291.

Kelman, S, *Procurement and Public Management: The Fear of Discretion and the Quality of Government Performance* (Washington DC, AEI Press, 1990).

Kipa, MW, Szeliga, KR and Aronie, JS, 'Conquering Uncertainty in an Indefinite World: a Survey of Disputes Arising under IDIQ Contracts' (2008) 37 *PCLJ* 415.

Kotsonis, T, 'The 2014 Utilities Directive of the EU: Codification, Flexibilisation and Other Misdemeanours' (2014) 23 *PPLR* 169.

Kucharski, J, 'Modernising IT Procurement: One Small Step Towards Progress, One Giant Leap for Federal Contracting' (2022) 51 *PCLJ* 299.

La Chimia, A and Trepte P (eds), Public Procurement and Aid Effectiveness: A Roadmap under Construction (Oxford, Hart Publishing, 2019).

Lalonde, PM, Yukins, C, Wallace, D Jr and Matechak, J, 'ABA SIL International Procurement Committee Year in Review 2007' (2008) 42 *The International Lawyer* 479.

Larsen, MK, 'The New EU Public Procurement Directives' in R Nielsen and S Treumer (eds), *The New EU Public Procurement Directives* (Copenhagen, Djøf Publishing, 2005) 10.

Lichère, F, 'Award of Contracts Covered by the EU Public Procurement Rules in France' in ME Comba and S Treumer (eds), *Awards of Contracts in EU Procurements* (Copenhagen, Djøf Publishing, 2013) 69.

Lichère, F, Caranta, R and Treumer, S (eds), *Modernising Public Procurement: The New Directive* (Copenhagen, Djøf Publishing, 2014).

Lichère, F and Richetto, S, 'Framework Agreements, Dynamic Purchasing Systems and Public E-procurement' in F Lichère, R Caranta and S Treumer (eds), *Modernising Public Procurement: The New Directive* (Copenhagen, Djøf Publishing, 2014) 185.

Lohnes, MJ, 'Attempting to Spur Competition of Orders Placed under Multiple Award Task Order and MAS Contracts: The Journey to the Unworkable Section 803' (2003-2004) 33 *PCLJ* 599.

Manzini, A, Butler, L and Trybus, M, 'Central Purchasing Bodies in the United Kingdom' in C Risvig Hamer and M Comba (eds), *Centralising Public Procurement: The Approach of EU Member States, European Procurement Law Series* (Cheltenham, Edward Elgar Publishing, 2021) 316.

Moss, S, 'Procurement and Distribution of Critical COVID-19 Supplies by International Organizations: The World Bank' in S Arrowsmith et al (eds), *Public Procurement in (a) Crisis: Global Lessons from the Covid-19 Pandemic* (Oxford, Hart Publishing, 2021) 271.

Nagle, JF, *History of Government Contracting*, 2nd edn (Washington DC, The George Washington University, 1999).

Nash, RC Jr, O'Brien-Debakey, KR and Schooner, SL, *Government Contracts Reference Book: A Comprehensive Guide to the Language of Procurement*, 4th edn (Wolters Kluwer Law & Business/ CCH Incorporated, 2013).

Nicholas, C, 'A Critical Evaluation of the Revised UNCITRAL Model Law Provisions on Regulating Framework Agreements' (2012) 21 *PPLR* 19.

—— 'The 2011 UNCIRAL Model Law on Public Procurement' (2012) 21 *PPLR* NA111.

—— 'UNCITRAL and the Internationalization of Government Procurement Regulation' in AC Georgopulos, B Hoekman and PC Mavroidis (eds), *The Internationalization of Government Procurement Regulation* (Oxford, OUP, 2017).

Nicholas, C and Arrowsmith, S, 'The Challenges of Contructing a Supplier Review Mechanism for Urgent Procurement: An Analysis in the Context of the UNCITRAL Framework' in S Arrowsmith et al (eds), *Public Procurement in (a) Crisis: Global Lessons from the Covid-19 Pandemic* (Oxford, Hart Publishing, 2021) 156.

Popa, N, *Teoria generala a dreptului (General Theory of Law)* (Bucharest, ALL Beck, 2002).

Risvig Hamer, C, 'Regular Purchases and Aggregated Procurement: the Changes in the New Public Procurement Directive regarding Framework Agreements, Dynamic Purchasing Systems and Central Purchasing Bodies' (2014) 23 *PPLR* 201.

Risvig Hamer, C and Comba, M (eds), *Centralising Public Procurement: The Approach of EU Member States, European Procurement Law Series* (Cheltenham, Edward Elgar Publishing, 2021).

Sánchez-Graells, A, '"If It Ain't Broke, Don't Fix It"? EU Requirements of Administrative Oversight and Judicial Protection for Public Contracts' in S Torricelli and F Folliot-Lalliot (eds), *Contrôle et Contentieux des Contrats Publics – Oversight and Challenges of Public Contracts* (Brussels, Bruylant, 2018) 495.

—— 'Prevention and Deterrence of Bid Rigging: A Look from the New EU Directive on Public Procurement' in GM Racca and CR Yukins (eds), *Integrity and Efficiency in Sustainable Public Contract: Balancing Corruption Concerns in Public Procurement Internationally* (Brussels, Bruylant, 2014) 171.

—— *Public Procurement and the EU Competition Rules*, 2nd edn (Oxford, Hart Publishing, 2015).

—— 'The UK's Green Paper on Post-Brexit Public Procurement Reform: Transformation or Overcomplication?' (2021) 16 *EPPPL* 4.

Sarfaty, GA, *Values in Translation: Human Rights and the Culture of the World Bank* (Stanford University Press, 2012).

Schooner, SL, 'Desiderata: Objectives for a System of Government Contract Law' (2002) 11 *PPLR* 103.

Schwartz, JI, 'Katrina's Lessons for Ongoing US Procurement Reform Efforts' (2006) 15 *PPLR* 362.

Sherry, RJ, Koehl, GM and Armstrong, SA, 'Competition Requirements is General Services Administration Schedule Contracts' (2008) 37 *PCLJ* 475.

Sims Curry, W, 'Contracting during Emergencies' in W Sims Curry, *Government Contracting: Promises and Perils* (New York, Routledge, 2010) 209.

Telles, P, 'Awarding of Public Contracts in the United Kingdom' in ME Comba and S Treumer (eds), *Award of Contracts in EU Procurements* (Copenhagen, Djøf Publishing, 2013) 251.

Torricelli, S, 'Utilities Procurement' in M Trybus, R Caranta, and G Edelstam (eds), *EU Public Contract Law: Public Procurement and Beyond* (Brussels, Bruylant, 2014) 223.

Trepte, P, 'All Change at the World Bank? The New Procurement Framework' (2016) 25 *PPLR* 121.

—— *Public Procurement in the EU: A Practitioner's Guide*, 2nd edn (Oxford, OUP, 2007).

—— *Regulating Public Procurement: Understanding the Ends and Means of Public Procurement Legislation* (Oxford, OUP, 2004).

Treumer, S, 'Contract Changes and the Duty to Retender under the New EU Public Procurement Directive' (2014) 23 *PPLR* 148.

Trybus, M, *Buying Defence and Security in Europe: The EU Defence and Security Procurement Directive in Context* (Cambridge, CUP, 2014).

Vacketta, CL and Curley, S, 'An Effective Compliance Program: A Necessity for Government Contractors under IDIQ Contracts and Beyond' (2008) 37 *PPLR* 593.

Vornicu, R and Dragos, D, 'Central Purchasing Bodies in Romania' in C Risvig Hamer and M Comba (eds), *Centralising Public Procurement: The Approach of EU Member States* (Cheltenham, Edward Elgar Publishing, 2021) 266.

Wang, P, 'China's Accession to WTO's Government Procurement Agreement: Domestic Challenges and Prospects in Negotiation' (The University of Nottingham, China Policy Institute, Briefing Series, Issue 48, March 2009) 8.

Williams-Elegbe, S, *Public Procurement and Multilateral Development Banks: Law, Practice and Problems* (Oxford, Hart Publishing, 2017).

Woodward, AE, 'The Perverse Effect of the Multiple Award Schedules' Price Reductions Clause' (2012) 41 *PCLJ* 527.

Yukins, CR, 'Are IDIQs Inefficient? Sharing Lessons with European Framework Contracting' (2008) 37 *PCLJ* 545.

—— 'Emergency Procurement and Responses to COVID-19: The Case of the US' in S Arrowsmith et al (eds), *Public Procurement in (a) Crisis: Global Lessons from the Covid-19 Pandemic* (Oxford, Hart Publishing, 2021) 393.

—— 'GSA's Commercial Marketplace Initiative: Opening Amazon and Other Private Marketplaces to Direct Purchases by Government Users', George Washington University Law School, *GW Legal Studies Research Paper No 2021–04.*

Yukins, CR and Williams-Elegbe, S, 'The World Bank's Procurement Framework: An Assessment of Aid Effectiveness' in A La Chimia and P Trepte (eds), *Public Procurement and Aid Effectiveness: A Roadmap under Construction* (Oxford, Hart Publishing, 2019) 277.